D0593337

THE COMPLETE BOOK OF *fly fishing*

THE COMPLETE BOOK OF

DISTRIBUTED BY A. S. BARNES AND COMPANY

fly fishing

by JOE BROOKS

PUBLISHED BY OUTDOOR LIFE

Published by Book Division,
Times Mirror Magazines, Inc.

Manufactured in the United States of America

Library of Congress Catalog Card No. 68-30939

Ninth Printing, 1976

Designed by EMIL SILVESTRI

To Mary

CONTENTS

PREFACE *1*

1 FLY FISHING TACKLE *5*

2 PRACTICAL CASTS *39*

3 CLASSIFICATION OF FLY PATTERNS *77*

4 DRY FLY FISHING FOR TROUT *87*

5 WET FLY AND NYMPH FISHING FOR TROUT *122*

6 TERRESTRIALS *144*

7 STREAMERS AND BUCKTAILS FOR TROUT *158*

8 LANDING BASS ON THE FLY *179*

9 INSHORE SALTWATER FLY FISHING *217*

10 CHUMMING AND OFFSHORE FLY FISHING 285

11 FLY FISHING FOR ATLANTIC SALMON 296

12 THE LANDLOCKED SALMON 317

13 TROUT THAT GO TO SEA 325

14 FLY FISHING FOR PANFISH 344

15 STREAM MANNERS AND SAFETY 350

16 CLOTHING 365

17 KNOTS 373

FLIES AND FLY TYING MATERIALS 382

INDEX 388

THE COMPLETE BOOK OF *fly fishing*

PREFACE

THROUGHOUT HISTORY, FLY FISHING HAS REMAINED THE peak of the angler's art. Other weapons of attack on dwellers of lake and stream and ocean may come and go, but when a man has tried every one, if he is a philosopher at all, he will come back to the fly rod. For the light wand offers other inducement than merely winning the physical fight with wily trout or rambunctious bass or some hard hitting denizen of the seas. The greatest enjoyment derived from the use of the fly rod is not necessarily the fish caught—though it is my contention that, given reasonably good fly fishing conditions, the fly rod will outfish any other rod—the greatest satisfaction lies, rather, in the performance of the cast, the dexterous use of the entire equipment, rod, line, leader and fly.

No other method of fishing gives the angler the same pleasure from a well delivered cast, or from watching the leader turn over out there at the end of the forward throw, dropping the fly gently upon the dish-calm surface of a pool. Or the thrill of laying out a long line into a stiff breeze. Or of seeing line and leader follow the direction of the rod and curve around to right or left, as the case may be, the better to light in just the pinpoint spot necessary to get a strike.

There is great challenge to floating a fly over a trout that is rising in a difficult place. To get a hit from such a fish, the fly must go over his position at the right speed, neither faster nor slower than the naturals drifting beside it, nor shifting sideways, but right down the groove, looking smart and unsuspect and very much like some real-life food he might expect to see floating over him. The satisfaction an angler derives from fooling a distrustful trout is one of the things that make fly fishing. As is the lift he gets when a smallmouth black bass whops his popping bug, thoroughly convinced that it is a real, live frog; or just plain mad enough to want to knock that annoying thing for a loop. And the solid thump of a fish hitting a streamer, be it in lake or stream or salt, telling the angler that the lure has gone through the water as he intended, looking just like something that fish wants to eat.

In no other branch of fishing is there this same direct, blow-to-blow contact with the fish, a personal contact that is maintained throughout the fight. For though the long, light rod, dipping and bobbing with every twist and turn of the fish will tire that lunker quicker than either plug rod or spinning rod, nevertheless the fly fisherman makes or breaks his own game by the way he handles the line coming from the reel, and by the amount of pressure he puts on the slender leader tippet, which is, of course, the weakest part of fly fishing equipment.

Unfortunately there has been a tendency among writers to make fly fishing sound difficult and thus many a would-be fly man has been diverted from this most satisfactory sport. The purpose of this book is to show that with a little practice, fly fishing is, not easy, but quickly learned, and that once learned it pays dividends such as no other type of fishing can offer. If I stray sometimes from the old rule of thumb methods it is because I believe that like everything else, fly fishing changes. The day is past when young ladies learned to walk with a book balanced on their heads and fishermen learned to fly cast with one tucked under their arm. Today's fly man is free of arm and free of hand. His free-arm casts are efficient and he takes his light fly rod where an old-timer never dared.

Fly fishing was originally limited almost entirely to trout and salmon waters and most of the lore of fly fishing originates in these two species, but today the lover of the light wand carries it into all types of water. The sunnies and the basses were long since added to the trouts and salmons, and more recently fly rod enthusiasts have moved into the salt. Although to a degree it had been practiced by a few hardy adventurers for a long time, saltwater fly fishing has come into its own only in the past fifteen years. But in that time the tide has risen steadily until now fly fishermen the world over are throwing flies in many oceans and along countless beaches, bays and lagoons.

The saltwater fish definitely have it all over their sweet-water cousins when it comes to putting up a fight, and there are innumerable species on which the angler may test his skill.

We used to consider fish of 100 pounds to be beyond the limits of the fly fisherman's gear; but modern tackle has been adapted to the pursuit of big gamesters, and today the fly man goes after anything he can coax to his fly. With improved tackle, new, stronger knots, new types of flies and new techniques, the fly rod in the salt has accounted in recent years for tarpon to 151 pounds, striped marlin to 148 pounds, sailfish to 136 pounds. And even as this is being written, some adventurous modern saltwater fly fisherman, somewhere, is out chasing more big game to add to the lists. It takes first-class physical condition to battle such monsters on light gear, and the odds are greater for losing the fish than for landing him, but the battle is worth it—thunderous, tumultuous and awe-inspiring.

Other chargers of the seven seas have one or another attribute to make the heart jump, either great speed, phenomenal leaping ability, or tremendous power. The bonefish and permit, those flashing streaks of silver, lead the shallow-water speedsters by a city block, while the high-jumping ladyfish and dolphin will be remembered for their contortions for a long time. Found along both the east and west coasts of the United States is another game fish that might have been especially designed for the fly man's pleasure—the striped bass. A great surface hitter to a popping bug, the big "bull" striper provides thrills no end when he swirls under and finally socks the angler's offering, and the ensuing fight will strain the fly tackle to the utmost.

But saltwater fly fishermen have proven that the fine tackle can take it and anglers who used to look askance at anything over 10 pounds as being too heavy for their way of angling will tackle the biggest fish they can coax into a strike. It doesn't mean that they expect to land one of those giants (though secretly they always hope to do so) but it does mean that they want to be in on the soul-shocking hit, see the acrobatic antics of a high-jumping powerhouse, and watch the line melt from the reel as a silver rocket flashes across a shallow flat, headed pell-mell for the deep.

Throughout this book I have attempted to give the dope on those species of fish most commonly sought by fly fishermen—when, where and how to fish for them, what to use and how to use it, and to supply any other special knowledge I have picked up during forty years of fly fishing. Most of all, through this book I hope to pass on to the reader some of the thrills and pleasure I have derived from fly fishing and to impart to him some of my own enthusiasm. Wherever you live, somewhere close to you may be found one or more of the great gamesters of which I write. Have a go at them. Good luck, and tight lines!

Joe Brooks

CHAPTER/1

FLY FISHING TACKLE

BEFORE EVEN PICKING UP A ROD, THE POTENTIAL FLY caster should understand the basic difference between fly casting and other forms of casting. In other forms, a heavy lure is thrown, pulling a light line after it, while in fly fishing, a heavy line is thrown, pulling the light lure behind it. Once this point is clearly understood, the importance of matched equipment becomes clear, and matched equipment starts with the rod.

RODS

Originally fly rods were made of wood, preferably bamboo, and the purpose of the rod was to deliver an artificial fly lightly upon the surface of a stream in such a manner that it would float freely and deceive a trout into taking it for the real thing. Today's fly rod may be made of glass, bamboo or graphite and its purpose is to deliver any one of a variety of concoctions designed to look like anything any fish might conceivably want to eat.

Fly rods are built according to specifications which will give suitable action for the job they are designed to do, and just as in golf a player picks up a different club for each special shot, so in fly fishing, the lie of the fish, or the nature of the fish, or the type of water being fished, determines the rod the angler chooses. There are fast-action rods with the action extending only a few inches from the tip and there are medium-action sticks where the action comes down to the middle of the rod. There are slow-action rods where the entire stick works all the way down and into the grip. Each of these rods has a definite job to do. For instance, in general, small-stream fishing calls for a 7½-foot rod weighing from 3 to 3¼ ounces, and a DT-4-F line with a 10-foot leader tapered down to 4X, 5X or 6X tippet. For larger streams an 8-foot rod with a DT-5-F line and a leader of 12 to 14 feet, tapered down to a 4X or 5X tippet should do the job for you. (For explanations of DT-5-F, etc. (*see* LINES, page 17).

Many dry-fly rods have fast-tip action; and it is true that the beginner may do better at first with the fast tip as it does not call for the fine timing required with a slower rod. Stiff action means that the butt section is stiff, so that the action is limited almost entirely to the tip, reaching down only a few inches or at most to the middle of the rod. To look for the action, the angler should hold the rod grip firmly in both hands, extending the rod in front of him, parallel to the ground, and impart a sideways motion to the stick. He can then readily see where the action is and how far it comes down the rod.

Gradually, over the years, for all types of fly fishing, I have gone to the slow-action rod. Once you master the timing you have greater ease in casting, greater delicacy of presentation, and it is easier to handle line and fly in the water. The only exception I make is when I go for 100-pound tarpon, sailfish, tuna or marlin. Then I use a very stiff rod in order to be able to lift these behemoths up towards the surface, or pull them through the water, neither of which is possible with a soft rod. But for everything else, from trout to bonefish to sunnies, to Atlantic salmon, I like the slow-action rod with the action coming well down into the butt.

If I had to choose one stick for all kinds of trout fishing I

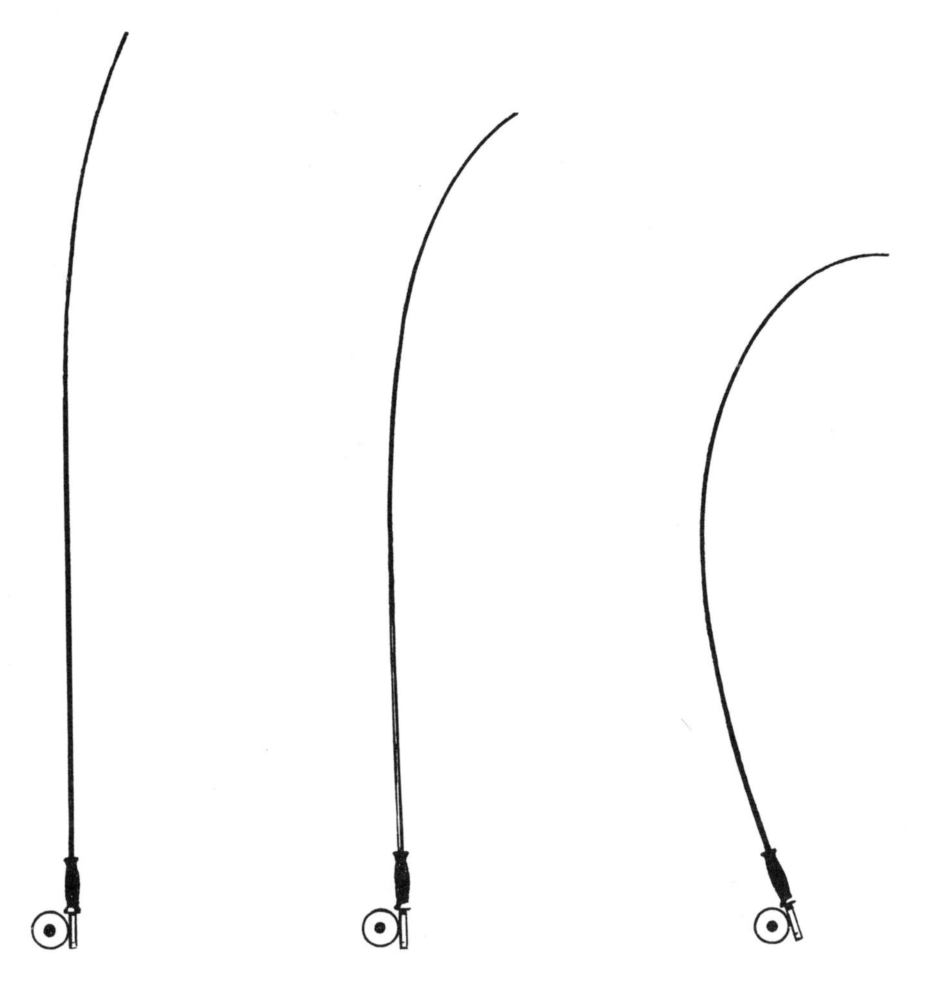

Just the last few inches of the tip work in the fast-action rod (left). The medium action (center) begins to bend at about the middle. The slow-action rod (right) gives action throughout entire length, even down into the handle.

would select the slow-action, 8-foot rod weighing 4 to 4¼ ounces. Equipped with a DT-5-F line this rod can be used for either wet or dry flies, small streamers and bucktails, nymphs and weighted nymphs. When casting a dry fly with the slow rod, however, the angler must remember to wait for his back-cast, giving the fluffy, light dry fly plenty of time to make its journey back, loop over and straighten out before he makes the forward thrust, or he will produce a flat forward cast that will tangle leader and fly in the line.

Any time your fly, wet or dry, catches on or hits the line as it goes forward, you can be sure that timing is at fault. The forward cast has been started while the line is still going backward, and as a result the line comes through flat, with a very tight bow, and catches on itself. You get the same result if you use a heavy fly on a very light rod and leader. It will throw your timing off and result in a jerky, sloppy cast.

In smaller rivers and ponds, bass fishermen often use an 8½-foot, slow-action fly rod and WF-6-F or WF-7-F line to cast some of the smaller poppers and streamers. But the slow 9- or 9½-foot stick is made to order for either smallmouth or largemouth black bass, in most places where you find them. With these rods you want either a WF-7-F or WF-8-F line, a forward taper with the weight out front to help push out the wind-resistant streamers, bucktails and popping bugs.

For smallmouth in both rivers and lakes, the 8½-foot, slow-action stick with a WF-7-F line does the trick; but when fishing for largemouth much larger bugs and flies are usually used, calling for a 9- or 9½-foot, slow-action rod with a WF-8-F line. Especially in the brackish water, or large lakes that largemouth frequent, the bigger outfit makes for much easier casting and allows the angler to get the lure out with only one, or at most, two false casts. With a stiff-action rod and these big, wind-resistant lures, it would be difficult to get distance without a great deal of false casting and the angler's arm would be worn out at the end of the day.

The 9- and 9½-footers are also commonly used in saltwater fly fishing. When you are fishing the salt there is usually some wind and to meet this contingency alone the slow, 9- or 9½-foot rod is far ahead of either a shorter or a faster stick, both of which would call for repeated false casts to get line out in the wind, especially with the large, wind-resistant flies used in the salt.

The long, slow rod also allows you to make long casts and, because of the height of the rod, to drop your fly in water five inches deep and, by holding the rod high as you retrieve, to then swim that fly nicely through this thin water. The slow action is also of prime importance because saltwater fish are continually on the move, not on a feeding station, as are trout,

A demonstration of how a 9-foot fly rod can take it. Note the fine taper of this bamboo rod with action going down into the grip. Author has hooked an 8-pound gray snapper on the Bermuda reefs.

and the angler must flip the fly out fast to an oncomer before it sees him and flushes. In many cases saltwater fly fishing calls for split-second action. The faster the fly is delivered, the more likely it will get a hit. A slow-action rod will get the line out with a single false cast, while a shorter, stiffer stick would require several.

In my opinion the 9½-foot stick has it over the 9-footer for saltwater casting because it can do everything the shorter one can, and can do a couple of them better. It enables the caster to keep his backcast high, and lets him impart better action to the fly, which is important in the salt; and it also enables him to keep the fly high in the water when fishing the shallows, so that it will not sink and catch on underwater growth. However, a 9-foot rod with slow action will also handle the WF-8-F line which is best suited to ocean fishing.

There are some 10-foot rods which have suitable slow action for saltwater fly fishing, but in general the manufacturers have made them too heavy and too stiff, under the mistaken impression that this is what is needed for bonefish and other denizens of the salt shallows.

The only place I have seen really big rods give creditable performance is on some Atlantic salmon rivers, and even for this fish the trend has been more and more toward the smaller rod classifications until today on most North American rivers anglers are using 8½- and 9-foot rods and enjoying their fishing just that much more. However, in some of the big waters of the Norwegian rivers, which produce the largest Atlantic salmon in the world, there is definitely a place for the big, two-handed rods.

I arrived at the Aaroy River in northern Norway equipped with a 9-foot rod and was startled when my host, André de Ganay, produced a 16-footer. But when we reached the river I saw why that greater length was needed.

In the first place, when fishing for Atlantic salmon it is necessary to put the fly over their position in the stream in just the right way, so that they see the fly right, or they will not take. This particular river was only a mile long, dropping with great speed to the fiord below. There was more fast water in it than in any salmon river I had previously fished. I soon discovered

André de Ganay of Paris needed this two-handed, 16-foot rod to catch his 32-pound Atlantic salmon in the plunging Aaroy River in Norway.

that with the extra length of his rod, especially when standing on the casting platforms with which the river was lined, André could cast and hold his line up clear of the near fast water, while mine, even though I mended it carefully, would nearly always be swept quickly down and away, so that the fly never got near the salmon, which were lying just beyond the near current.

With the long rod it was possible to manipulate the line and hold it high while the fly floated very nicely over the fish. And of course, with the long rod it was possible to cast much farther with the very heavy flies also required by that heavy water.

The very long rod also helps in landing a salmon in places where upjutting rocks form a hazard. You can steer the tired fish through such stick-ups and so land him that much more easily.

So there is no doubt as to the efficiency of the extra-big rods in such specialized cases. But on smooth stretches of salmon water, the 8½- to 9½-foot rods undoubtedly allow for more delicate casting and have plenty of backbone to fight any Atlantic salmon you are likely to encounter. The 8½-footer equipped with a DT-7-F or WF-7-F line and a 14-foot leader serves for dry-fly work and the 9- or 9½-footer equipped with a WF-8-F, for streamers and wet flies.

At the other end of the rod gamut are what I call "trick rods" or "stunt rods," sticks that are less than 7 feet in length, which are amusing in the hands of an expert but are not practical tools for the average fly man. The 7½-foot rod, even, is very limited. Expertly handled, it works well on very small water, in tight places where dense underbrush and trees make trouble for the caster. But it must be lined accordingly, with a DT-4-F line, to bring out the action of the rod (*see* LINES).

But fly fishing is for pleasure and underpowered fly rods just do not fit into the picture. It's tough enough to get out far even with an 8-foot, 4-ounce rod and a DT-5-F line, so why make it more difficult by trying to do the same thing with a fancy stick?

No matter what he may read about 1½- and 2-ounce rods, when the beginning angler goes out to try to fish with one,—and indeed, many an angler who has fished for years will feel the same way—he will soon discover that the casting is really rough. You just cannot cover big water with this outfit, and when there is any wind you are out of luck entirely. You are confined to small flies, which is all right, but the average angler wants to fish all manner of flies, and he needs all the rod and line help he can get in order to reach out where the fish are. So it's better for the beginner to leave the short rod to those experts and others who enjoy this type of fishing.

While bamboo is the traditional material of fly rods and to my mind still produces the only satisfactory true dry-fly stick, nevertheless glass is taking over the market. There is still considerable variance in the construction of glass rods, to the extent that one 8-foot stick may need a WF-8-F line to bring out its action while another of the same make would call for a DT-5-F. But manufacturers of glass rods are coming fast with improvements, especially in the longer sticks, so that in the 8½- and 9-foot rods the feel of the action is very close to that of bamboo. And it is reasonably safe to say that if you bought an 8½-foot glass rod in any tackle store in the country, you could match it properly with a DT-7-F line, while with the 9-footer, a WF-8-F would bring out the proper action. Most of the shorter sticks, however, still leave much to be desired. Generally they are too powerful and therefore require a too-heavy line for small stream or otherwise delicate fly work. And until this factor is conquered, bamboo will continue to be the choice of those who want a good dry-fly action or otherwise small rod.

While there are many excellent three-piece rods on the market, the two-piece stick has certain advantages which count enough in the long run that experienced fishermen are turning ever more to the two-piecer.

The three-piece rod utilizes more ferrules than the two-piece rod, which makes it heavier, and that is a point where weight is measured in ounces. And each ferrule contributes just a little toward a jerkier action than that which is obtained by the uninterrupted length of cane or glass, as the case may be. To carry this theory to its ultimate, a one-piece rod would be best —and it would—but even the small rod, say a 7-footer, would

Experienced fishermen are turning ever more to the two-piece fly rod because of its lightness and control. *Courtesy of The Orvis Co.*

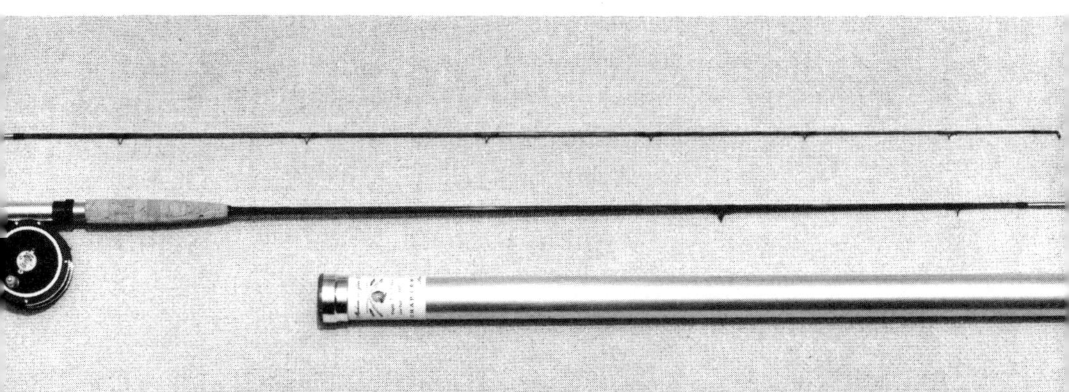

require such a long carrying case as to make it unwieldy for traveling. Therefore the two-piece rod that offers as many of the advantages of a single-piece stick as possible, and breaks down into convenient length for packing, is the ideal solution.

Aside from a good strong case to protect them in transit or when stored in cupboards, fly rods, whether bamboo or glass, require very little care. It is best to wash them off with fresh water after use in the salt and it always pays to dry them before storing after use. The guides should be cleaned out after fishing, too, as grease adheres to them from the line, gathers dirt and then moves back onto the line, making it heavy and causing it to sink. Guides should also be checked regularly for wear as they become damaged from the line shooting through, and a worn guide can ruin the finish on a line in a hurry.

REELS

Most standard trout reels are large enough to hold only the fly line, with no room for backing. These small reels are good enough for most trout fishing, but where the angler may tie into a long-running fish or a heavy fish in heavy water, he can be a very busy man chasing the trout along the stream to prevent it taking all his line and snapping it at the reel core or straightening the hook of the fly. For this reason, if the prospective buyer expects to find such fish, he will be well advised to purchase a slightly larger reel—of which there are many on the market—with capacity for 150 feet of 12-pound-test nylon squidding line backing, as well as the fly line. This is for trout fishing only, as this small amount of backing and also the light breaking strength should not be used for bigger fish, either fresh or salt.

Thus, the automatic reels are suitable for average trout and for all the bass and panfish, but they do not have sufficient capacity for use on long runners. And in the salt there would also be the danger of the mechanism rusting and freezing.

For salmon and steelhead, both long-running fish, and for the saltwater species, where again the fish are long-distance racers, the reel should be large enough to take the big fly lines

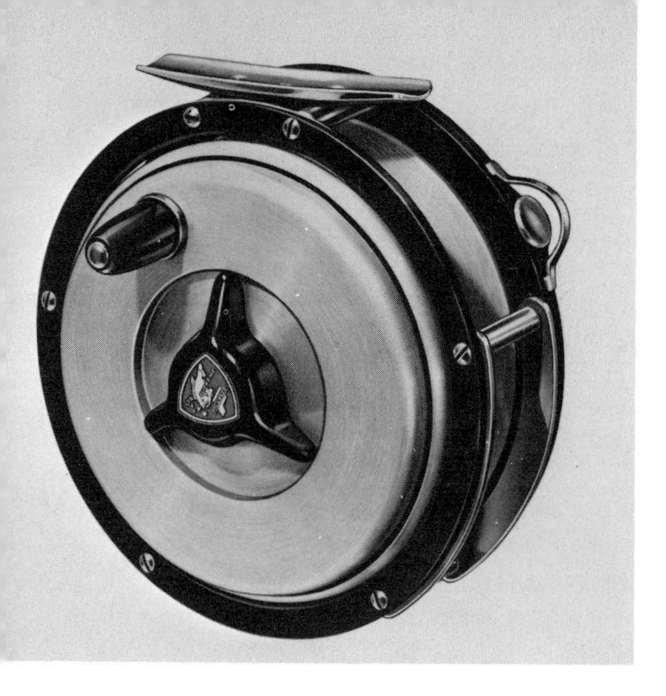

The Pflueger Supreme, a large reel with room for fly line and more than 200 yards of 18-pound-test nylon squidding line backing. Suitable for salt water or big fish in fresh water.

Fin-Nor fly reels feature extra smooth, easily manipulated drag. The small #1 reel is for small trout. The #2 will handle most big fish, even those that make runs of 600 feet. The #3 is designed for 150-pound tarpon, sailfish, marlin and tuna, having enough capacity for the fly line plus 250 yards of 30-pound-test dacron backing. The #4 has an extra-wide spool and can be used for many offshore fish.

such as the WF-8-F and WF-9-F, plus 200 yards or more of 18-pound-test nylon squidding line backing. These reels range in price from $20.00 to $135.00, and if price is not the main object, then by all means the angler should buy the most expensive reel of those suitable for the fishing he plans to do, just as he would purchase the best of any engineered product.

In this regard, there are a few multiple-action reels on the market of high quality and in the high price brackets. The multiple action brings the line in faster, but most fishing contests stipulate "single-action reel" and it is well to keep this in mind when purchasing a new reel. However, there are fine fly reels that have an antireverse mechanism that allows you to hold the reel handle in one position while the line peels off the reel spool.

Whatever the choice, a good, dependable drag is important, even with fish that do not run, because sooner or later every fisherman yanks line from the reel, for one reason or another —and the spool overspins and he winds up with a tangle that tests his temper.

The Princess, one of the fine trout reels made by Hardy of England.

Like rods, reels require very minor care to keep them in good order. If used in saltwater, the reel should be wiped with a cloth which has been dampened in fresh water, and occasionally every reel should be taken apart and the inner parts checked and greased or oiled as necessary.

Aside from a little protection against bumps and falls while being carried, this is all the care necessary for most fly reels.

FLY LINES

Great care should be taken to be sure that the rod is properly lined. It is a moot point whether the underlined or the overlined rod is harder on the caster. Overloading will result in sloppy casts, poor presentation and lack of accuracy, and it is difficult to manipulate the fly with a too-heavy line on a too-light rod. Underlining the rod will cause just as much trouble. There will not be sufficient weight to carry the line back on the backcast, allow it to turn over, then follow the forward cast and shoot the line with authority. The angler will have to resort to false cast after false cast, inching the line out that way and finally ending up with shattered nerves and a sore arm.

A fly line is named according to the way it is tapered—that is, the way it varies from thick to thin diameters. Generally speaking, the lighter the line, the harder it is to cast, though that doesn't mean that the heaviest line is necessarily the best for all kinds of casting. Each line is tapered to fill certain requirements. All fly casting is dependent on weight of line. You cast the line. Leader and fly follow after. Before World War II, fly lines were made of silk with what was called an "oil" finish to make them water resistant. Every line bore a letter indicating its diameter, ranging from H, which indicated a diameter of .025 inch, to A, at .060. The popular HCH double-tapered fly line had a middle section measuring .050 (C), tapering at each end to .025 (H). All line manufacturers adhered to this system, because only silk was used. After World War II, while some lines were still made of silk, there were newcomers to the scene: nylon, which is lighter than silk, and dacron, which is heavier. Various finishes were applied in place of the oil. For the first time fly lines were available which were lighter than water so they would float indefinitely without dressing. Similarly, there appeared heavier lines which would sink faster than undressed silk lines.

Modern fly lines are basically made by shaping a synthetic coating over a straight, braided core, to produce what are known as torpedo, rocket or bug tapers. They are also designated as either floating lines or sinking lines. In the interests of clarity, the American Fishing Tackle Manufacturers Association has adopted a universal identification code, in each case explanatory of the line it describes. These are DT for double taper, WF for weight forward, F for floating line, and S for sinking line. With these they combine a number which designates the weight of the first 30 feet of the line—the part that is generally used in casting. Thus a DT-6-F is a double-tapered line whose basic weight is 160 grains; while a WF-7-S is a weight-forward sinking line whose basic weight is 185 grains. The table below gives the comparative weights of the different numbers available.

AFTMA STANDARD FLY LINE WEIGHTS

#	WEIGHT	#	WEIGHT
1	60	7	185
2	80	8	210
3	100	9	240
4	120	10	280
5	140	11	330
6	152	12	380

However, it should be remembered that these vary considerably from one manufacturer to another. In the following pages, the line designations are those used by Scientific Anglers, Inc., of Midland, Michigan.

Most extremely light fly rods require a No. 4 or 5 line; medium-action, all-round trout rods usually take a No. 7 or 8, and the majority of bass-bug, steelhead and saltwater fly rods are properly balanced by a No. 10 or 11 line.

Cross sections of fly lines showing tapers. Top to bottom: level line, double taper, standard-weight forward taper, bug taper or saltwater taper, shooting head. *Courtesy of Scientific Anglers, Inc.*

To select a fly line, the fly-rodder must first decide whether he wants a double-tapered or a weight-forward fly line, a floater or a sinker, and then choose the weight.

For instance, a DT-5-F fly line, which fits the average 8-foot, 4-ounce fly rod, is so tapered as to give: 1) sufficient weight in the belly for casting in the atmosphere of the average trout stream; 2) sufficient light taper on the forward section to fall lightly on the water and so not scare fish; 3) sufficient light taper back of the belly section to allow for easy shooting of the line. For bigger rods such as those used in saltwater fly fishing or for throwing big, wind-resistant bass bugs or large streamers, a forward taper is needed. These lines, also frequently called torpedo-taper, bug-taper or weight-forward lines, are listed from lightest to heaviest as WF-5-F, up to WF-10-F, or in the sinkers, WF-5-S to WF-11-S. The sinking lines also come in a Hi-Density classification, which means that the line sinks more rapidly than the above.

A line which sinks in its entirety has its place in fishing, especially in deep lakes, but when you are fishing a river the current is inclined to push the line along out of the current and deposit it in the dead water at the angler's feet. There is no way to manipulate or mend these lines because of the fact that the entire line goes down. Much more satisfactory in rivers is the Wet Head, of which the first 30 feet is designed to sink while the balance of the line floats. Because the angler can fairly easily mend and manipulate the floating part of the line, he can keep the high density head out in the current where the fish are, and as a result he will up his take considerably. These lines are designated as WF-7-F/S—that is, Weight Forward-7-Floater/Sinker, and so on through the weights.

In many cases nowadays anglers use this line instead of the former shooting head. The shooting head is a length of heavier line, usually 30 feet, which is attached to a lighter running or shooting line. The purpose is to enable the angler to make long casts; but with the two features incorporated in the one, it is easier to use this line than one which requires splicing.

Tierra del Fuego is probably the windiest place I've ever fished. On my first trip down there I found my friends Bebe Anchorena and Jorge Donovan both using 10-foot, slow action rods equipped with light DT-6-F lines. They would get the wind in back of them and then roll cast their flies out, and could really get them out, too, long casts into the Rio Grande, some as much as 90 feet.

But they were limited to one direction—downwind. They were casting almost directly downstream and not reaching the deep run across from them, about 60 feet away.

"Why don't you cast straight across?" I asked. "Hit that run and work your streamers across it."

"We can't reach it," said Bebe. "The wind blows our lines back and down from it."

They were two of the best roll casters I have ever seen, and I knew that if they had the right equipment, even the howling gale on the Rio Grande wouldn't faze them. My outfit was ready by that time, a 9-foot rod weighing 6 ounces and equipped with a WF-8-F line, and a 12-foot leader with a 30-pound-test butt section next to the line, tapered to a 6-pound-test tippet (*see* LEADERS).

"Try this," I said, shoving it into Jorge's hands. "And see what a difference this heavier line makes."

Jorge made his cast, using the double haul to get speed and bringing the rod tip down hard, almost to the water, on the forward cast. The line shot out there like an arrow, across current in spite of the wind, and when it hit, a nice trout took the fly.

Not only in such unusual circumstances, but in all cases the matching of line and rod is all important. Not long ago I was fishing a trout stream and had just delivered a cast when another angler who had come quietly up to watch, spoke out.

"How did you do that?" he asked. "You hardly seemed to try and look where it went. I almost break my wrist trying, and I get 30 feet."

I looked at his outfit. He had a 9½-foot rod that must have weighed at least 6¾ ounces, and on his reel he had a level 4 fly line.

"No wonder you can't cast," I said. "That rod needs a WF-8-F line. It would even handle a big WF-9-F. You're using a rod powerful enough to throw big bugs in a heavy wind and the line belongs on a rod weighing not more than 3 to 3½ ounces. Try mine," I invited.

He put out 40 feet after a couple of attempts. Then, getting the feel of it, he cast the fly a good 55 feet.

"Boy! I could really cast if I had an outfit like that," he grinned. "I bet it cost plenty of dough."

"No," I said. "It's just an average outfit in the middle price range. But it's matched up right. That's a DT-5-F line on an 8-foot, 4-ounce rod. The whole thing—rod, line and leader—cost about $35.00."

I let him use my outfit for a while. His casting became better, smoother, and pretty soon he caught a fish. First thing he did when he went home, I bet, was to get himself a matched outfit.

Mismatched outfits are the chief reason that many potential fly fishermen get discouraged. For maximum casting efficiency, my recommendations are:

7½-FOOT ROD	DT-4-F
8-FOOT ROD	DT-5-F
8½-FOOT ROD	DT-6-F, WF-6-F, OR IN WIND, WF-7-F
9-FOOT ROD	WF-8-F OR WF-9-F
9½-FOOT ROD	WF-8-F OR WF-9-F

I should add that a glass rod will often handle a heavier line than a bamboo rod of the same length. And in either glass or bamboo, a stiff-action rod needs a heavy line to bring out the action.

A short, stout rod, say 7 feet in length, will often require a No. 8 line; and such a line will allow the caster to throw a long line but does not permit him to achieve the delicacy that is possible with the more flexible rod and its matching lighter line.

In the case of forward tapers, it should be noted that for trade reasons some manufacturers leave from 6 to 8 feet of level line on the end of the forward taper and this level section must be cut off to the point where the taper narrows down to the level line—else the level line will fold up at the end of the forward cast. It just won't have enough punch to turn over the end of the line and leader.

I purposely do not recommend level lines because most level lines do not shoot well and because with the same diameter right to the end, usually they fall too heavily on the surface of a small or still pool. The same casts can be made better all around with a forward-tapered line which will shoot better for long-distance casts, handle big flies better, cast better in the wind, and allow greater delicacy on small streams and slick water. The tapered line will cost twice as much, or more, but it's worth the price.

A good line, properly cared for, should last a fly fisherman two or three years, depending on how much it is used. The life of a fly line used in the salt is much less, especially if used in boats where grease, oil and gasoline get on the line, as do sand and dirt from the bottom of the skiff. Between these hazards and such accidents as hanging up on protruding nails, getting between cracks in the floor boards, and being stepped on, fly lines in general have a very rough and exceedingly short life in the salt.

So the saltwater fly fisherman is well advised to keep his skiff clean and to clear away all debris and obstructions before he starts to cast. Besides keeping his line clean for better casting, it will save him money.

Now let's take the above line specifications, one by one, and see the whyfor.

A 7½-foot rod is obviously for use in small streams, for delicate dry-fly work, for wet flies or for nymph fishing. In these situations the fly should drop on small pools gently and accurately. To do that, a small diameter line is needed. So the lightest commonly manufactured taper is recommended—the tapered front or forward part of the line for delicate presentation of leader and fly, the 4 section heavy enough to provide casting weight on that light rod, and the same light taper at the back of the 4 section for easy shooting behind the comparatively light belly.

Incidentally, the DT-4-F, like all double tapers, has the added advantage of giving double service, in that when the forward end begins to wear, the line can simply be reversed.

It is in this field of handling light lines that the glass rod has not yet approached the bamboo. Most 7½-foot glass rods are so powerful that they call for a DT-6-F line, and some for a WF-7-F or WF-8-F, and an angler who drops a big-bellied line of either of those classifications on a small, still surface will scare the spots off any nearby trout. Aside from that, he will find it extremely difficult to make an accurate, lightly delivered cast.

An 8-foot rod will be used for trout fishing with dry fly, wet fly or nymph or small streamer. Such a rod will weigh 4 to 4½ ounces, and calls for DT-5-F, again the economical double taper. The 5 section is big enough to make casts plenty far enough to take fish and a heavier line such as a DT-6-F is too big for the delicate work needed in quite pools. Anything lighter than an DT-5-F, on the other hand, would be difficult to throw and would entail hard work on the part of the caster.

An 8½-foot rod will be used for bass bugging, or for throwing big streamers or weighted nymphs, in which case the WF-7-F line is ideal, the light forward section drops the line lightly on the surface, the No. 7 belly furnishes the weight to get it out. If the 8½-footer is being used for dry-fly fishing for Atlantic salmon, or for dry-fly fishing for smallmouth bass or landlocked salmon, or for big trout, then the lighter-tipped double-tapered DT-7-F is recommended in order to deliver the fly more lightly on the surface of pools. However, if the angler is limited to one line, then the WF-7-F will do the all around job.

A 9-foot rod will be used for fishing in wind, on salt water where long casts are needed, and in big rivers and lakes. A WF-8-F line will bring out the action best, providing plenty of power for long casts and for pulling the shooting line out after it.

A 9½-foot rod will also be used in salt water or on big lakes and rivers and will take either a WF-8-F or a WF-9-F, according to the action of the rod. In most cases, a 9½-foot bamboo rod works well with the WF-8-F, while a glass rod of the same length requires the heavier shooting section of the WF-9-F.

Manufacturers build lines of various belly lengths such as the short bug taper, the short saltwater taper, and the regular weight-forward taper. Each of these lines has its place.

Remember that it is the heavy belly section that is being

thrown, and also remember that most tapers are developed by tournament casters who stand up on a platform with no obstructions behind or around them, and an assistant to feed the shooting line through the guides for them. There is no hurry—plenty of time and plenty of room. So the tournament caster uses a long belly line to get the extra weight for an extra-long throw.

But the situation is entirely different on a tree-lined river or stream. The room for the backcast is limited and the angler must depend entirely on himself to get line out. With the shorter belly he can make a short backcast and then shoot the whole of the short belly, which in turn will pull the lighter back taper out for a good cast. With a longer belly it would be necessary to make several false casts to get enough line out to make the cast, and where is all that line going to go on the backcast? Up in a tree, of course, with the result that there is no forward cast. The line is not heavy enough at the front to make that short backcast and then shoot out all its additional heavy length.

Equally important is the fact that with the short belly it is possible to get off a quick cast to an oncoming fish, by making one backcast and then shooting the line.

Occasionally it will be necessary to make two false casts to get out enough belly in order to make an extra-long cast, but usually, if he is in a boat, the caster has the shooting line coiled in the bottom, and with rod ready and, say, 15 feet of line, plus leader from rod tip to hand, he can cast that much into the air, shoot a bit more of the line lying on the bottom, come back again, and then let the works go.

That operation takes only a few seconds and the fly is in front of that oncoming fish. And there are many fish, especially saltwater species, where a split second makes the difference in getting hits.

The same technique applies when wading. The line can be held in coils in the left hand, or even allowed to trail in the water behind the fisherman as he wades along.

In some kinds of fishing, as for instance, steelheading, where extra-long casts are often required, anglers use a shooting basket. The basket is strapped around the waist, so that line can be stripped into it, where it coils neatly, out of the wind or the pull of the water, and therefore shoots out easily when you make the next cast.

There is a place in fishing, of course, for the long belly. It can be used when fishing from a boat where there is plenty of room around the caster, or from the shores of lakes and rivers where there are few obstructions and plenty of room for the backcast. Or when it is all a case of casting blind, with loads of time, rather than spotting moving fish. In such circumstances the longer belly certainly allows the angler to get off some long throws. A good caster, for instance, can consistently reach 85 to 90 feet, and a very good one as much as 100 feet. But with a WF-8-F with a 12- or 18-foot belly it is also easy to get off casts plenty far enough to take fish. And, as a matter of fact, casts over 80 feet in length are seldom good fishing because at that distance it is difficult to see the fly or to tell the reactions of the fish to it. And when a fish does hit at that distance, the strike impulse is so slow traveling the length of all that line, that the angler often misses. By the time he feels the fish, strikes, and the strike impulse gets way out there where the fish is, the fish has often spit the fly out, or is in the act of so doing, and therefore is not well hooked.

So, while many anglers like to talk about what a long line they can throw, more importance should be attached to such things as careful approach, casting from the right position, and having complete control of line and fly, rather than to making a long and beautiful throw and as a consequence missing the strike, scaring the fish and winding up with only the memory of a fancy cast.

The essence of efficient, easy fly casting is a floating line. A dry, high-floating line makes casting easier, while a heavy, sinking one is difficult to lift or to manipulate and often means missed strikes and badly disturbed pools. So lines should be greased before each use—even those lines which the manufacturer states do not need to be greased. And the grease should be applied just before fishing, or it will sink into the line and lose its effect. To grease a line the night before the next day's fishing is wasted effort.

So important is a well-greased, dry line that I carry two

Charles Radziwill of Buenos Aires stretches his fly line between trees and rubs line dressing in with his fingers to assure a good float.

extra reels with me if I expect to be out all day. When one line becomes heavy and starts to sink, I take that reel off and substitute one of the spares.

Many a beginner has asked me why I grease the line, then apparently wipe the grease all off again.

"I put the dressing, or grease, on to make the line float," I tell them. "Then I rub it off so the line won't sink."

Confusing? No, it's literally true. The right amount of grease will make the line float, but an excess gets from line to rod guides, becomes dirty, works back onto the line, the dirt picks up water thus making the line heavy, and the line sinks. To avoid this vicious circle, the line should be greased by dipping the first two fingers lightly into the dressing, then working the line between fingers and thumb to spread the dressing on the line. The line can be pulled through the fingers in strips about two feet at a time, and it is wise to grease as much of the line as is likely to be in the water during casts. When this length has been greased, then take a clean cloth and run the line through it, as it is reeled in. This removes all superfluous grease.

Many manufacturers claim that their lines don't need dressing and some supply a cleaning paste to wipe the line with, claiming that all the fisherman need do is keep the line clean and it will float for a long time. But I grease them all and get a better job from the line for doing so.

I used to fish only the floating line and try to get down when I needed to do so by using a long leader and extra-heavy fly. The new sinking lines which have appeared in the last few years have caused me to change my tactics somewhat. The new lines are designed to fit each need. As described earlier in this chapter, you can have one that goes down completely, or one that sinks only in the forward part, thus allowing you to manipulate the balance just as you would a floating line.

I am also one of those who believe that color in a fly line is more important to the fisherman than to the fish. Trout, bass or bonefish, to name a few, will hit flies served up on the end of the line whether it is amber, green, camouflaged, or what have you, as long as the leader is long and has a fine tippet. But a light color does help the angler in that he can spot the end of his line in the water and know where the end of the line lies, which helps in finding and handling the fly, particularly allowing him to know just when to pick up neatly and cleanly and quietly so as not to disturb nearby fish. A fly line of a solid color down to within a few feet of the end, and then the balance in amber color, or any other light shade readily picked up by the eye, would be of great help to flymen.

Little care is required to preserve a fly line and keep it in good condition, but since fly lines are fairly expensive, it's well worth while to follow a few simple rules.

The line should be kept clean of grit or other dirt which may be picked up when fishing along beaches, in rivers, or from the bottom of a skiff. After use, a fly line should always be thoroughly dried by stripping it off the reel and dropping it loosely, coil by coil, on a couch or large chair, never on a floor where it would pick up dust or where someone might step on it and crack the finish. Allow it to dry overnight, then reel it up and put it away in a clean place until the next use.

New lines, or lines which have been stored on the reel for a long time, should be stretched to take out the kinks before being used for casting. Have a friend hold the end of the line and stand still, while you walk away, unreeling the line until the entire length is out. Then pull back on it until all the stretch is out. Pull back several times, then rewind the line on the reel.

If the line is being stored for a whole winter, or such a long period, it is advisable to take it off the reel and coil it loosely, in loops at least a foot in circumference, then tie it—again loosely—with several pieces of cord and lay it flat in a drawer.

LEADERS

Leaders are used in fly fishing so the fish will see the fly but not the line to which it is attached and will grab the fly without suspicion. One of the major reasons novice fishermen don't catch fish is that almost invariably they start out with the misconception that it is difficult to cast a long, thin leader. So they tie on a heavy, straight piece of leader material that bounces to right or to left at the end of every cast and drops on the water far too hard to fool any suspicious trout. Or it "folds," not having the power to turn over and drop the fly on the surface.

Yet a long leader is one of the greatest strike getters in fishing and a tapered leader is one of the greatest aids to good casting. If the butt section, next to the line, is heavy enough, a long leader is easy to cast and enables the angler to put the fly down accurately and quietly.

It is this heavy butt section that makes the leader lay out, and from it the leader is gradually tapered down to the tippet required for the fish being sought.

For bonefish I taper the leader down to a 6-pound-test tippet, or occasionally, if there is a lot of tough grass on the flats, I use an 8-pound-test tippet. When fishing the ocean flats where there are sea fans, coral and sponges, I sometimes go to a 10-pound-test tippet. For brown trout in clear, shallow streams, I go to a 4-, 5- or 6X tippet, while for the same fish in big, rough rivers, and using streamers, I tie on a 4- to 6-pound-test tippet. But in all these leaders, regardless of the heavy or delicate tippet, I start with the same 30-pound-test butt section and graduate down to the desired size.

In each case, the butt section and the tippet section should be longer than the other graduations. For instance on a 14-foot leader tapered down to a 6-pound-test tippet, the ideal arrangement of lengths is 3 feet of 30-pound-test butt section, 2 feet of 25, 2 feet of 20, 18 inches of 15, 1 foot of 12, 1 foot of 10, 18 inches of 8-pound test and 2 feet of 6-pound test. With such a heavy butt section the leader will have what it takes to turn the fly over, while the long, light tippet will make for a minimum of water disturbance, will be less likely to be seen by the fish, and will allow the angler to work the fly better.

By using heavy diameters in the butt section it is possible to cast a leader 25 feet in length, and I know one man who always uses a 30-foot leader. He catches a lot of fish, too, and while that is going to the opposite extreme, nevertheless there is no doubt about the efficiency of a long leader. Just to try it out one time, I tied a 45-foot leader, graduated from 45-pound-test nylon leader material at the butt down to a 6-pound-test point. With that leader and a DT-5-F line on an 8-foot rod, I cast 70 feet.

And while such leaders are an unnecessary extreme, and would be no good for short casts, the illustration at least points up the fact that a properly tapered leader is but an extension of the fly line. And any fly fisherman who switches from a short, untapered leader to a properly graduated one, 10 to 14 feet long, will soon find his hits increasing.

In the taking of trout, especially, there is no doubt in my mind that it is the thin tippet that pays off. Once in Maryland I was fishing Beaver Creek, a small limestone stream. As I worked upstream I came to a long, narrow pool, not more than 20 feet wide. I paused to look things over, and immediately saw a fish break. That trout really looked big and without thinking I cut off the light tapered end of my leader and tied on a 1X tippet. I crawled on my hands and knees into position and while still kneeling began to cast. The fly floated perfectly over the brownie's feeding station. Every once in a while he would rise and pick a natural off the surface. Each time he did that I got gooseflesh, and felt like putting a 10-pound-test leader on. But my offering floated forlornly along, untouched.

Then, heart in mouth, I went back to my 4X tippet. The third float he took, and I had him for half an hour before the hook pulled out. I departed, having learned a lesson. Back I came a week later. Once again I saw and heard his break and once again it was too much for me. This time I started with a 2X tippet but once again I went down to the 4X before he hit. Then I was so tense that I struck too hard and left the fly in his mouth.

The third time I started with a 4X tippet and he took the first float. I had him on for about three seconds before the hook pulled out. But the fourth time did it. Having really learned my lesson, I started with the 4X tippet and again he took on the first float. After a half hour of battling to keep him from tangling in some roots on the far side of the pool, I beached him. He looked about 7 pounds, a beautiful fish. I took the hook out and returned him to the water. Later I went back to try for him again and he wasn't there. Then, via the grapevine I heard that someone had taken a 6-pound, 12-ounce brownie from that pool by using an illegal bush-bob.

That experience alone made me realize that to consistently take brownies, the finer the leader the better—and the same applies in most types of fly fishing. It also taught me what a licking a 4X gut tippet will take. Such a thin strand is capable of landing a really big fish as long as the angler doesn't try to horse him in.

Where the water is deep and heavy, however, it is safe to use a heavier tippet. For instance, on the Taylor River in Colorado, early in the season I often use a 2X tippet, changing to 3X in the quieter parts of the pools. In fast, rushing water the fish do not notice the heavier leader and it is needed to bring a fish upstream after he has hit and plunged downstream into the swift water, where any quick jerk of the fight might break a fine leader. The same holds true in any similar water like the Gunnison and East Rivers in Colorado, or the big Montana rivers during the early part of the season—rivers such as the Yellowstone, Madison, Big Hole and Big Blackfoot—and in parts of the Deschutes in Oregon, as well as during the early fishing in the big Eastern streams. But when the river drops and grows crystal clear, tie on the 4X tippet in a hurry for regular strikes.

You will get even more hits on a 5X. Don't be afraid to go light, especially if there is lots of water and not many impediments. A 5X tippet has a breaking point of 3.3 pounds, and if you cushion the fight of the fish with upheld rod you can land some really big fish on such a tippet.

For many years dry-fly men used gut for their tippets, but in recent times nylon leader material has taken over completely. Gut has faded from the picture, to take its place alongside the horsehair leaders of early angling history. A few anglers still cling to it, but most of us are too lazy to go through the trouble, first, of finding gut, and then of keeping it damp, which is necessary so it will not break easily. There is no doubt that gut will lay out better than nylon, with fewer curls and twists. But leader kinks can be taken out of the nylon by stretching the leader between the hands, or pulling the line between two folds of inner tube. A commercial device for this purpose has been designed by the well-known fly caster Don DuBois, and is marketed under the name "Whirl-a-Way."

The fly caster must also watch his nylon tippets in cold weather as they will sometimes snap in the air as he false casts. This is not because of any casting fault. If it is cold enough it can happen to anyone.

The leader tippet is one of the most important parts of the fly man's equipment. The thinner it is, the more strikes he will have. At the same time, the thinner the tippet the more chance that the fly will land in a heap of tippet, a sort of bird's nest on the surface. This happens when the tippet does not straighten out, turn over and drop the fly lightly on the water. It can happen because you are casting into the wind, even a slight breeze, but it may also occur because the leader is too long, or not properly tapered. The butt section may be too light, the middle too long or too light, or the tippet too long. It can also come from pressing, holding the rod grip too hard, tightening up the muscles of the forearm, and trying with mighty swipes to send the fly out. Loosen up, take it easy—and check your leader.

Even a long and finely tapered leader floating along the surface may sometimes look very large indeed and may cause a fish to refuse your offerings. As far as I have been able to discover there has never been a really successful concoction on the market to make leaders sink. All the several kinds which are available last only for one cast, then, a false cast or two and there is the tippet, riding high and unhandsome again. So now, when I think a sinking tippet is needed for a certain fish, I rub the leader-sink on and gamble all on one cast because I know that if that one cast does not produce, I'll never go to all that trouble again.

Most leader-sink has a soap base and many anglers make their own. Or they use that which is readily available along most river beds—mud. Rub a little of that on and the leader will sink for a cast. Better still is fish slime. If you have a fish in your creel, just wet your fingers and rub them along the side of the fish, then on the leader, and it will sink. But in spite of the fact that I occasionally resort to some of this procedure, there will always remain in my mind some doubt as to whether or not a sinking leader is any better than a floating one. For although the sight of the tippet on the water disturbs me considerably, and I feel it must disturb the fish, too, yet 99 per cent of the times I take fish I do so with the whole leader floating on the surface.

Similarly, I am inclined to believe that color in leaders is of no great consequence, so long as the leader is fine enough.

In this day of ready-packaged deals, knotless leaders have appeared on the market and there is certainly nothing against them as a starting point. However, in practical use there is really no such thing as a knotless leader. Once he has changed flies on the stream, the angler has taken the first step toward removing the carefully prepared taper. He may untie the clinch knot where the fly is attached to the leader by pulling on it with his finger nail, but it will come away curled up and probably will have to be clipped before another fly can be tied on. After a couple such fly changes, the length of the light diameter required at the end of the leader has been so shortened that it is necessary to tie on another tippet to maintain the proper leader length and fineness—and there is the knot. Or the angler may lose part of the leader by hanging up on an overhanging branch—and again, there is the knot.

Certainly fish see knots because sometimes small fish will strike at a leader knot, but I don't believe a well tied small blood knot used for joining the various sections of a leader together scares them enough to make the angler lose strikes. And any slight disadvantage is offset, to me, by the fact that the knots add a little weight, which makes casting easier, and I, for one, will gladly accept any help I can get in improving my casting.

Knots in leaders occasionally pick up moss and floating grass, and you have to spend some time cleaning them before making another cast. In this circumstance the knotless leader is an advantage; but this does not happen often enough to be much of a problem.

So, while I am not belittling ready-tapered, knotless leaders, they are not by any means essential to good fly fishing, and even if the fly fisherman has his tackle kit crammed full of them, he will still have to know how to tie a blood knot. In other words, it's more important to know how to tie a blood knot than to know where to buy a knotless leader.

Dan Bailey, of Livingston, Montana, makes leaders which do a fine job. The top, heavy section is made of hard nylon, for better casting. The bottom half is of soft nylon, for better presentation, and so the trout will not be able to see it as easily.

All too many anglers put on a tippet of one weight, maybe hitting what they consider a happy medium in breaking strength, and never vary from that. Yet for really efficient fishing, every species and every situation may call for a different leader, and the knowledge of what leader to use, or the lack of that knowledge may easily make or break a man's fishing throughout the season.

For instance, in heavy water, wet-fly fishermen often use very heavy tippets and get away with it. The heavy tippet has the advantage there, of absorbing a sudden, hard strike, when the angler might ordinarily break off his fish. On the other hand, in clear water and still pools, he must go down to 2X, 3X or even 4X tippets to consistently take trout. But in this case he is using a light delivery, casting carefully, and hiding from the fish. He can watch his line for evidence of a hit or can spot the telltale flash as the fish takes, so he is ready and can set the hook with only a slight lift of the rod tip, thus avoiding snapping his leader.

Even the difference between 3X and 4X diameter often will be the difference between taking or not taking trout, especially browns.

When fishing for smallmouth or largemouth black bass, on the other hand, a heavier leader tippet than that used for trout is in order. A very light leader might snap under the force of the strike the angler uses with these species. For smallmouth bass a 4- to 6-pound-test nylon leader tippet is small enough not to scare the fish and strong enough to stand the heavy hit combined with the angler's instinctive reaction. For largemouth, an 8- to 10-pound test is the choice. Largemouth don't seem to spot a large leader as readily as do smallmouth, and the bugs and flies being fished are usually larger. Then too, largemouth are heavier, and often lie around old docks, weeds and other obstacles upon which a light leader tippet might readily come to grief.

With the advent of some of the new nylon leaders it is possible to go very fine and still have considerable strength in the tippet. In salt water I am continually amazed at how much a nylon leader will stand. It is almost impossible to break a 12-pound-test tippet. I have tangled with tarpon weighing up to a hundred pounds, fighting them with a 12-pound-test leader for as long as three hours. Eventually the tarpon always frayed through the leader with their gill covers but the nylon never broke under the pressure.

However, many a leader has broken from lack of care, and nearly always such a break comes at a time when the angler is particularly anxious to land a big one. The longer I fish the more I realize that you don't get too many shots at really big fish and that when you do, everything must be just right. And because the leader is the weakest part of fly fishing equipment, special care should be taken to be sure that delicate strand is in good repair.

The ones we lose are the ones we remember—and who wants to remember a record fish, lost just because of faulty equipment? I'll never forget one terrific fish that paid me a brief visit. I was down at the Isle of Pines, Cuba, fishing with Vic Barothy. I had just landed a bonefish that ran up and down along the length of the skiff as I tried to bring him in close enough to land. Finally I got him in, took the hook out and released him. As I straightened, Vic spoke.

"Look what's coming!" he said. "Looks like a permit!"

Down the flat a good 300 feet away a fish was pushing up a wave in front of him as he traveled slowly our way.

Without thinking to check my leader I hurriedly made ready to cast. When he was about 70 feet away I shot that inch-long white bucktail out. It dropped two feet in front of and a foot our side of him.

The wave turned without hesitation and rushed the fly. I had a hit and started to raise the rod tip to strike. And then the whole thing collapsed. The line fell in the water, everything went slack, and the fish got out of there a mile a minute.

"He was 30 pounds," said Vic. "You broke him off."

"I didn't break him off," I said. "The hook must have pulled out. I didn't even have time to strike."

I brought the line in and looked at the leader. It was cut through up in the butt section, the 30-pound-test section. The bonefish had put a nick in it when he ran up and down along the skiff.

Had I checked that leader I would have had time—just—to change to another. Here was the one time when everything was in my favor to take a big fish. There were no obstructions around, nothing but open water for half a mile, no big sea fans, no upjutting coral heads, just a wonderful chance to let that fish run and fight. Maybe I would have landed him, maybe not, but I'd surely have liked to have a good leader to try it.

So, especially when fishing in the salt for such rough-mouthed, scaled-finned fighters as the tarpon, ladyfish, snook and others, it always pays to run the fingers the length of the leader each time, after playing and landing a fish. And after a long fight with a fish, it is a good precaution to cut the bug or fly off, and retie it, just in case the knot has weakened.

The more careful the fisherman is with his equipment, the better are his chances of landing those big hulks, and the lesser ones, too.

Nylon leader material now on the market varies in designation according to the manufacturer. Some material which is very thin has a high breaking point; and the X classifications vary slightly, too, from one manufacturer to another. But in general they will be approximately as follows:

X CLASSIFICATION	DIAMETER	BREAKING POINT
0X	.0110	9.0 pounds
1X	.0098	7.2
2X	.0090	6.3
3X	.0080	5.2
4X	.0071	4.3
5X	.0061	3.3
6X	.0047	1.2

RECOMMENDED TIPPET STRENGTH FOR VARIOUS SPECIES

FRESH WATER		
BREAM, SUNNIES, OTHER SMALL FISH		3-POUND TEST
SMALLMOUTH BLACK BASS		4- TO 6-POUND TEST
LARGEMOUTH BLACK BASS		6- TO 8-POUND TEST
BROWN TROUT		3-POUND TEST
BROWN TROUT	USING STREAMERS	5-POUND TEST
SEA RUN BROWN TROUT		10-POUND TEST
BROOK TROUT		3-POUND TEST
BROOK TROUT	USING STREAMERS	5-POUND TEST
SEA RUN BROOK TROUT		6-POUND TEST
CUTTHROAT TROUT		3-POUND TEST
SEA RUN CUTTHROAT, CALLED BLUEBACKS, HARVEST TROUT		4-POUND TEST
GRAYLING		3-POUND TEST
RAINBOW TROUT		4-POUND TEST
STEELHEAD (SEA RUN RAINBOW TROUT)		10-POUND TEST
WINTER STEELHEAD		12-POUND TEST

SALT WATER

MANGROVE OR GRAY SNAPPER	8-POUND TEST
BONEFISH	6-OR 8-POUND TEST
TARPON, BABY (UNDER 20 POUNDS)	8-POUND TEST
TARPON, BIG (OVER 20 POUNDS)	12-POUND TEST
CHANNEL BASS (REDFISH)	10-POUND TEST
STRIPED BASS (TO 10 POUNDS)	8-POUND TEST
STRIPED BASS (OVER 10 POUNDS)	12-POUND TEST
JACK CREVALLE	10-POUND TEST
HORSE-EYE JACK	10-POUND TEST
LADYFISH	8-POUND TEST
SNOOK	12-POUND TEST
SPOTTED SEATROUT	10-POUND TEST
BARRACUDA	12-POUND TEST

SALT WATER FISH IN DEEP WATER, BY CHUMMING OR SIGHTING

DOLPHIN	10-POUND TEST
MACKEREL	10-POUND TEST
FALSE ALBACORE	10-POUND TEST
BONITO	10-POUND TEST
GROUPER	10-POUND TEST
YELLOWTAIL	10-POUND TEST
BERMUDA CHUB	10-POUND TEST

SPECIAL LEADERS FOR FISH THAT MIGHT BITE OR FRAY THROUGH LEADER TIPPET

BLUEFISH 10-POUND TEST WITH 12 INCHES #4 WIRE LEADER ADDED

SAILFISH 12-POUND TEST WITH 12 INCHES 80-POUND-TEST NYLON ADDED

MARLIN 12-POUND TEST WITH 12 INCHES 100-POUND-TEST NYLON ADDED

TARPON 12-POUND TEST WITH 12 INCHES 100-POUND-TEST NYLON ADDED

TUNA 12-POUND TEST WITH 12 INCHES 100-POUND-TEST NYLON ADDED

BARRACUDA 12-POUND TEST WITH 12 INCHES #5 WIRE LEADER ADDED

SHARKS 12-POUND TEST WITH 12 INCHES #5 OR #7 HEAVIER WIRE LEADER ADDED

CHAPTER/2

PRACTICAL CASTS

It was on a beautiful day forty years ago that I first realized what a lousy fly caster I was. I had fished trout streams in New York and Maryland and Pennsylvania since I was a kid. I knew most of the bass waters of those states, too, and I'd taken a fair share of fish. So, like any twenty-year-old, I thought I was plenty good.

Then I went bass fishing with Tom Loving of Baltimore. Tom was the first man to tie a fly for shad, he was one of the first to take striped bass on flies, and he was a pioneer in fly fishing for brackish-water largemouths. Those last were what we were after on this particular day. We were on Frog Mortar, a tributary of Chesapeake Bay.

"Big bass lie under those duck blind frameworks," Tom said. "You have to drop the popper right beside the blind, and then work it slow and easy."

He took his turn first, while I manned the oars. Following his instructions, I held the skiff out about 70 feet from the blind, so I thought he must be going to cast to some other spot first. But after a couple of false casts he heaved that big, wind-resistant bug out 70 feet and dropped it right against the blind. My eyes rolled back in my head but I finally got them focused and saw Tom give the bug a pop, then let it sit still a few seconds—and water flew a foot high as a 5-pound black bass socked that cork-bodied fooler.

"Nice, eh?" said Tom as he put the fish on a stringer.

"Nice is right," I said. "Gee, what a cast!"

Tom took a lunker bass from each of the next three blinds. Then it was my turn.

"We're too far out," I protested, as he held the boat 60 feet away from my target.

"They'll see us if we go any closer," he said. "Try it from here."

I never got the big bug close, and in the end Tom had to row me in to 35 feet. I finished up with a couple of puny 10-inchers—and resolved to learn to cast a fly the way Tom could.

I soon found that you have to work at it, as in any other sport. But you don't have to wait until you are over water to practice. You can practice in a gymnasium, or on a lawn, or even on the street. Practice may not make perfect but it goes a long way toward perfection and the enjoyment of a well-executed delivery, plus the undoubted dividend of more and bigger fish when you do get on the water, will well repay the time spent on it.

Probably the best practice outfit is an 8-foot rod and an DT-5-F fly line. This rod and line will be light enough for lots of practice and will have the fineness necessary for making good casts. Once proficient with such an outfit, an angler should be able to cast with any fly rod and matching line. And that outfit will almost certainly prove useful in later fishing for practically any trout or pan fish likely to be encountered, up to and including those the angler may go for with light bucktails and streamers.

Once the prospective fly caster has his outfit, the next step is to pick up the rod. As in golf, there are devotees of various plain and fancy grips and most beginners have been made so nervous by all the talk that when they first pick up a rod they try to squeeze the cork right off the grip. Naturally, you can't get a smooth delivery with your muscles bunched into knots.

The rod should be grasped lightly, with the fingers held comfortably around it, the thumb placed either on top of the

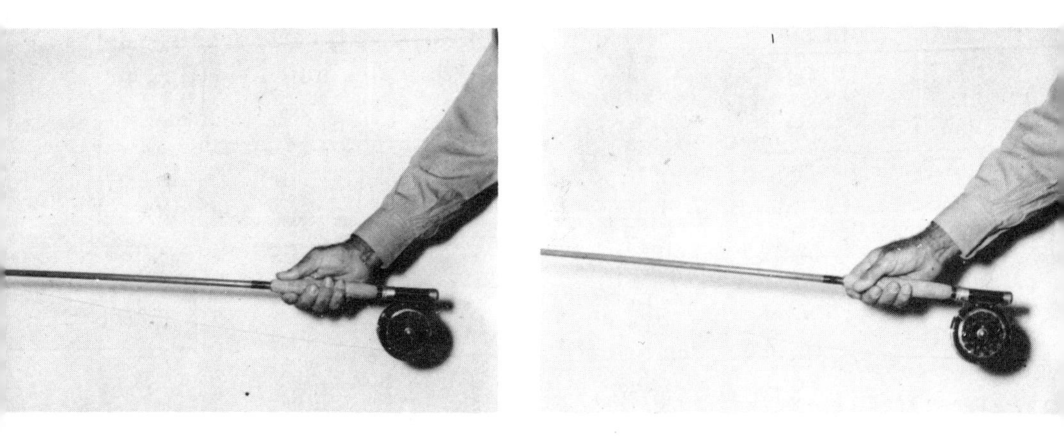

Hold the rod naturally, lightly, with thumb on top (left) or with thumb turned down a bit (right).

rod or down a bit on the side of the grip—whichever seems more natural. Either hold is satisfactory and many casters use both, at one time or another. Some casters recommend putting the index finger along the top of the rod handle. Many fine casters use this position but I, personally, do not find it comfortable. For many years I cast with my thumb down on the side of the grip; but now I use the position shown in the above left photograph, as it seems to give me the best control of the rod and allows me to get more power into the cast. We live and learn, and change to what we think is an improved method—the important thing is that the beginner should use the grip which feels the most comfortable.

The fastest way to good casting is to perfect the basic straightaway forward throw. Every other cast stems from this, and I know plenty of fly fishermen who have never gone beyond it, yet take their share of fish.

There are three parts to the forward cast—pickup, backcast, and forward throw—and each depends on the other. A good pickup means a good backcast and a good backcast means a good forward cast.

"But how can I get out enough line to make a cast?" asked one young lad I was teaching. He pointed to the flimsy leader and 2 feet of line hanging from his rod tip. He'd been false casting that back and forth for several minutes, getting nowhere.

So I explained: when starting from scratch, like that, pull a couple of feet of line off the reel with the left hand, start working the rod back and forth, false casting. The moving rod will pick up the line and pull it through the guides. Then, still false casting, pull several more feet from the reel and work that out, and soon you'll have enough line in the air to make the forward cast.

Another way to get initial line out is to strip line from the reel and let it drop on the water or the ground, or on the bottom of the skiff, as the case may be, and then start false casting. On each false cast, then, shoot several feet of line out, until you have enough to cast.

For the pickup, bring the end of the line in on the water to about 35 feet from the rod tip, so the line will not be too long to control and the weight of it won't overload the rod tip. Now extend the arm out toward the fly, then raise the rod to a 40-degree angle. This will lift most of the line from the water, and as you keep it coming slowly toward you, lift the rod tip slowly until only a foot or two of leader and the fly remain to be raised.

From this point a backward and upward flip of the wrist will lift the fly with scarcely any water disturbance. The line will shoot smartly back, high up, the leader and fly following it, and then roll over and straighten out. Stop the wrist and rod at about the 2 o'clock position and—while the line is still rolling over—drop the arm about 5 inches, keeping the elbow bent, then start the forward throw.

To do this, bring the wrist forward (not downward) with a slow snap, as if you would hammer a nail on the wall in front of you and at about the level of the top of your head. Aim the cast slightly above the parallel to the water, not down at it. Follow through with the rod and stop the rod when it is in front of you at about 45 degrees above the horizontal. The line will keep shooting on out until the leader and fly at its end will roll over, straighten out, and drop lightly to the water.

When I was telling this to Edwin Nelson one time on the

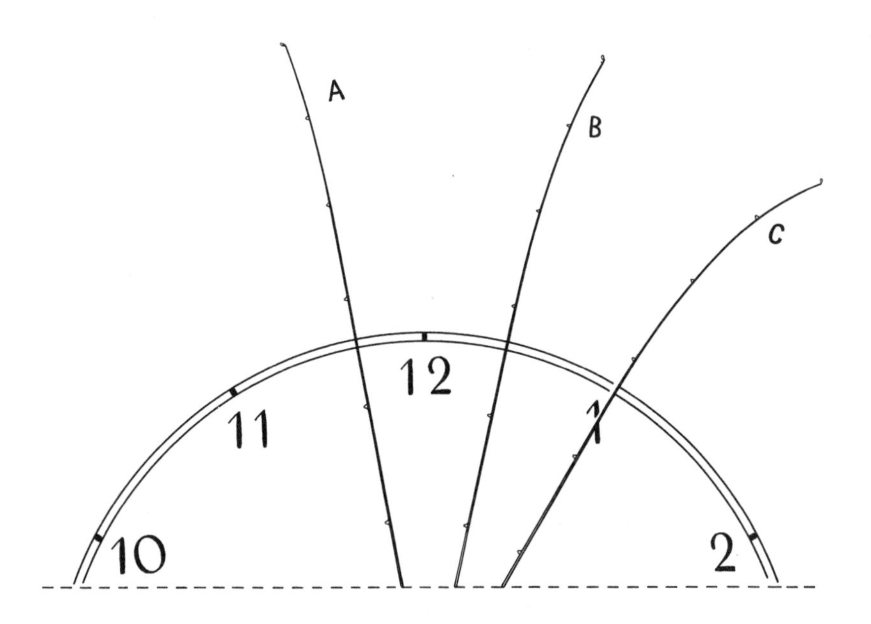

Don't begin cast at A, or even B, since only the last several inches of the rod will get into the cast and the line will slam down on the water. Start at C and let the entire rod work for you. You can even take the rod back to the 2 o'clock position, especially when you want to make a long throw and use the double haul.

Yellowstone River in Montana, he pointed out that most fly casters say that the backcast should be stopped at 1 o'clock.

"How come you say 2 o'clock?" he asked.

"They may *say* '1'," I replied. "But they *do* '2.' Or more."

Even so, I went on to explain, most casters don't start their forward throw from back there. They bring their arm forward, then snap the wrist and make their cast at the 12 o'clock position, or even forward of that, thus getting only the tip of the rod into it. When you start the forward cast from back at 2 o'clock, you get the whole rod into the cast.

"Watch me," said Edwin. "Tell me what's wrong."

He threw his line into the water, hard, about 40 feet out. Line and leader were a mixed-up bird's nest.

"Just what I've been saying," I told him. "You stopped your backcast at 1 o'clock, but you didn't cast from there. You let your arm and rod drift forward to 11 o'clock and then snapped your wrist. There was no place for your line to go but right down into the water. If you start the cast farther back and aim

In the pickup—first step in making a good forward cast—bring end of line in on the water to about 35 feet from rod tip. *Photos by Bill Browning.*

The end of the forward cast. Right at this instant the line in the left hand will be released and will shoot out through the guides. Rod will be held in same position until fly leader and line fall to the surface of the water.

Watch your backcast until you know what rod, line and leader are doing, and soon your timing will be automatic.

for a point slightly above the parallel to the water, the line will have plenty of time to go out, and turn over and drop, instead of banging the surface."

He did better the next time but he didn't let his forward cast go until his rod was at 12 o'clock. Again the line hit with a bang.

Like many others, Edwin was having trouble knowing just what the rod and line were doing in back of him. They believe they've stopped at 1 or 2 o'clock, when actually they have drifted forward. They imagine the line is high up in the air, when actually it is almost slapping the water behind them.

"Watch your backcast," I suggested to Edwin. "Turn your head and look back each time, to see what the line is doing. And just as you see the leader begin to drop, back there, start the forward cast. Keep doing this and before you know it your timing will become automatic, so that you know exactly what's going on behind you without having to look."

Hurrying the backcast is one reason so many anglers snap flies off. While the line and leader are still turning over near the end of the backcast, everything has slowed down. If the wrist is snapped at this point, as you would crack a whip, then the end of the leader flips around with a jerk and pops the fly off. Start the forward cast slowly and smoothly, and roll the wrist—don't snap it.

The best way to get the feel of all this is to put line in the air and keep it there. Put out 35 or 40 feet and begin false casting and keep it going back and forth, back and forth, without letting the line drop fore or aft. Do this for five minutes, rest, and then do it again. Nothing will improve timing more quickly.

The next time I saw Edwin he was ready with another question.

"Which should hit the water first?" he asked. "The line or the fly?"

Now that may not seem too important when you are using a long, thin leader because the line will fall too far back to be seen or heard by the fish you're working. But in a small, smooth-surfaced pool a line that slaps down hard is dynamite.

"How do you make the fly hit first?" was the next thing that

Edwin wanted to know, so I explained that, too, pretty much as follows:

With the rod held straight up, or at most at only a very slight angle out from the perpendicular, make the usual forward cast but make it harder than necessary for the distance and aim about 5 feet above the surface. When the line gets out where you want the fly to drop, stop the rod tip up high, at 11 o'clock. The line shooting out will come up hard against the reel core and the force of it will hold the line straight out, momentarily, while leader and fly snap down to the surface, just like a drop in baseball. Then the line comes softly down after it.

Len Kinkie was with us that day, and he spoke up. "You're always talking about shooting the line," he said. "What do you mean?"

To shoot a line, I told him, means getting extra distance without having to do a lot of false casting. Most beginners, and many experienced anglers, too, false cast far too much. You wonder if they're ever going to let the line go, and by the time they do, their timing has begun to fall off and they end with a sloppy cast. Two or three false casts should be sufficient to handle

SHOOTING LINE FOR DISTANCE. To reach way out without false casting, strip in line from previous cast, loop by loop, holding in left hand (left). As forward cast is made, raise left hand and release loose coils of line (center). Power of rod shoots line forward, pulling coils of line after it (right).

almost any cast from 15 to 100 feet. And the fewer the false casts, the less chance of frightening fish.

I showed Len how to make his retrieve from the previous cast, in strips 2 or 3 feet long, looping each one in his left hand as he did so.

"Now," I said, "as you make the forward cast, release the looped line, raising your left hand a little. The forward impulse of the cast line will pull the looped, or shooting, line out after it. You can pick up 35 feet of line, make your cast, and get 25 feet more on the shoot."

"Makes a 60-foot cast easy, eh?" said Len with a grin that meant he didn't believe it. But within ten minutes he was shooting that extra 25 feet for some very nice 60-foot throws.

A modification of shooting the line will get an angler into some tricky spots under bushes and rocks, which he could never hope to reach in any other way. Ordinarily, a cast to such a spot falls short, or the line, in making the usual wide loop at the finish, hooks up on a branch or on the bank. This can be overcome by shooting the line as described above, but this time holding the rod "side arm," at an angle of about 45 degrees above the water. Simply make the forward cast in this position, and shoot the line, then bring the rod tip down hard in a follow through, down to only a foot from the surface. The line will go into the opening "flat" rather than in the usual wide loop, and the fly will light neatly in the pocket.

Much the same technique is used to cast into the wind. Make the backcast, going well back with the rod, so the line is about parallel to the water, then make the forward throw and shoot the line. Follow through and bring the rod tip down hard, to within a foot of the surface. This really gets you out into the wind.

A slight modification of this cast can be used to put out a short throw, perhaps only 35 feet, in difficult conditions: for instance, if you are fishing a small pool and don't have room for a long cast, and you are kneeling to hide from the fish. Make an extra hard, regular throw, then as you come through with the forward cast put extra strength into a roll-over of the wrist, a sort of slow motion snap, and bring the rod tip down to within a foot of the surface as you follow through.

More advanced, but easy enough to learn once the forward shoot has been mastered, is the shooting of the backcast. To do this, merely release some of the shooting line that is held in the left hand, as the backcast is made. The line will shoot out through the guides, back of you, until you stop it by clamping down with the fingers of the left hand. In this way it is possible to shoot 10 to 15 feet in back, and still maintain good control, and then shoot the rest of the looped line on the forward cast, without any false casting at all. This is much the fastest way to reach an oncoming fish.

Many difficult-looking casts are merely variations of the basic forward throw. I remember fishing a pool on Fishing Creek in Maryland, one time, and meeting a friend as I left the stream.

"I wish I could cast both right- and left-handed," he said in an envious tone. "It sure helped you in that pool."

"What do you mean?" I asked.

Then it dawned on me. From where he had been watching, at the top of the pool, standing well back so as not to spoil it for me, he had seen only my cast as I proceeded up the right side of the pool—the same side he was on. He had been able to see the rod working, but not to see me.

"I was fishing backhanded, not left-handed," I laughed. "I was pressed close in against the bushes because it was too deep for wading farther out. And the fish were rising right against my bank. I had to fish backhanded to them."

To make the backhand cast, simply grip the rod as usual, then extend the right arm across in front of you, elbow slightly bent, so that wrist and hand are at shoulder height and the rod slants upward at an angle of about 40 degrees. Then turn the wrist so that the back of the hand is to the left side of the face. From such a position it is easy to proceed with false cast, then cast, just as in the basic throw.

Another important variation on the basic forward throw, which looks difficult, but is really quite easy, is that old favorite of dry-fly men, the S-cast, or serpentine cast. The angler strips extra line from the reel—say 4 or 5 feet more than is needed for the distance to be cast. He makes his throw, and at the end of the forward cast he stops the rod high and even pulls back with it. The line will "hit" the reel as it shoots out and will jump back and fall to the surface in a serpentine manner. Before these curves of line straighten out in the current, the fly will get at least a couple of feet of free float. The beginner should make a big effort to perfect the S or serpentine cast, as he will find need for this throw in almost all freshwater river fishing. There is no other cast as important in showing a drag-free floating fly to the fish.

Once these casts have been mastered it is easy to move on to the more difficult throws which not only add fun and satisfaction to fly fishing, but many times put a fish in the creel which otherwise would not have been there.

The change of direction cast is a big-league throw. It goes out and gets fish which ordinarily could not be reached. And although it looks difficult it is really a fairly simple throw as long as the angler will take his time and let the rod and line do the work. First, line is stripped off the reel and several false casts are made, keeping the line going just fast enough to prevent it

CHANGE OF DIRECTION CAST. Begin false casts back and forth as in the forward cast, then pivot from waist and turn wrist slowly to point where you want line and fly to go.

from dropping, fore or aft. Then the caster allows the backcast to drift out behind him and pivots from the waist to the right. As he does so, he turns his wrist to the right and powers the line forward with a slow but positive snap of the wrist. The slow-moving line will go straight out to the right and fall on the water in the desired spot.

The same thing can be done done to the left, in the same way: false casts are made up and down, then, when the line is behind him, the caster pivots from the waist to the left, brings the wrist around to the left, and delivers the forward throw, producing a straight-line cast to the left.

Once when I was demonstrating the cast in a gymnasium in Richmond, Virginia, a number of men came out of the crowd to ask questions after the session was over.

"Those trick casts look pretty," said one man. "And they're fine for exhibitions. But when would I ever use them?"

"These aren't trick casts," I said. "They're practical ways of catching fish."

"How would that change of direction cast to the right ever pay off?" he asked, unconvinced.

"Suppose you're fishing slow water where drag is not a problem," I said. "You're in the midst of false casting when you see a riser or a cruising fish out to your right. A fish you want to get to fast. So you use the change of direction cast and you're there."

"You say that's for slow water," he said. "What about fast rivers, then?"

"Use a variation of the change of direction," I answered. "Just add a curve to it. I'll give you an example. I remember one time on the Laramie River in Colorado, I was facing upstream, close against the brushy shore on my left, while directly across the current a good fish was coming up. I couldn't face him and backcast because of the trees. Deep water ruled out wading to another position. A roll cast wouldn't have a chance for a free float because of the speed of the current. I needed to toss a curve of line upstream and across, one that would bend around to land the fly and leader a few feet downstream from the line. That would give me a couple of feet of drag-free float before the current grabbed the line and began to drag the fly. And I could mend the line to get a little more, too.

"So I turned my back to the shore, held the rod horizontally in front of me, and started to false cast up and down the river, parallel to the shore. I kept the line going back and forth slowly, just fast enough so it wouldn't hit the water. When I had enough line out, I let the backcast roll slowly downstream behind me and started the forward cast. As I brought the line forward, I turned my wrist slowly to the right, until the rod pointed 4 feet above where I'd seen the fish. The line turned to the right and the end of the line and leader turned over and dropped the fly right on the spot. It floated down, without drag, to the fish, and he took it hard."

"What about the change of direction to the left?" asked another fellow. "Do you use it very often?"

"Sure I do," I said. "And it really pays off. Once on the Yellowstone River near Livingston, it saved the day for me.

"It was early October. The big browns were moving and I was after a lunker. I put on a No. 4 muddler and started casting straight across the stream, working the fly back through the fast current in foot-long strips. As I moved downstream I came to a bank on my right, so near and so high that I couldn't get a backcast above it. And with a horizontal backhand cast I couldn't get out to the fish. On top of all that, it was almost impossible to get that big fly out with a roll cast.

"So I thought of the change of direction cast to the left. Facing downstream and standing at the edge of the water, I started to false cast downstream and up, down and up, parallel with the shore. Then I started a downstream forward throw, but turned left from the waist and rolled my wrist slowly to the left. The line followed wrist and rod, curving across the current to land 40 feet out, far enough to get hits from fish."

Like those men from Richmond, many anglers think these unusual casts are merely for exhibition. But they're part and parcel of a good fly caster's craft. They'll take fish he would never get otherwise. And besides that, there is considerable fun and satisfaction in being able to toss a curve, an aerial roll, or any of the more intricate casts.

The main thing to remember is that the cast must never be rushed. Timing is of the essence, and it's surprising what you can do with a fly line once you get it into the air. That famous fly caster, Herb Welsh of Mooselookmeguntic, Maine, could actually spell out his name in the air above him (but not the name of his home town!), without ever stopping his line or letting it touch the ground. Welsh did this to please show crowds, but many a good fly caster can put his line in the air and, with a circular motion of the rod tip and a well-timed roll of the wrist, make the line perform a complete circle overhead. And from any part of that circle he can deliver a fairly accurate and lengthy cast. And that is merely the ultimate in the change of direction cast.

In all casts special attention must be paid to timing. Slow and easy does it. Too abrupt a change of direction at any time in the process of a cast from pick-up right on through, can end with the angler tied in knots in his own line.

Timing is also the essence of the curve casts—the curve to the left and the curve to the right. The curve to the left comes in handy time and again and is the easiest to learn. It is done by holding the rod so that it points to the caster's right, a bit above the horizontal position. The false cast is made and then the line is shot harder than necessary for the distance to be reached. When the speeding line has run all the way out, the angler pulls back on the rod tip. The jerk of the stop kicks the end of the line and leader around to the left.

With one important difference this is exactly the same technique used to cause the fly to light on the surface ahead of the line. The difference is in rod position. In order to have the fly hit the water ahead of the line, the rod is held at a very slight angle from the perpendicular; while for the curve to the left, in order to land the fly downstream from the line, the closer to the horizontal that the rod is held, the wider will be the curve. And for most purposes, the wider the curve, the better.

Not long ago an angler asked me what I considered to be the most useful of the curve casts.

"The curve to the right," I answered without hesitation. "Aside from the straightaway cast it is the one most often needed."

The curve to the right is probably used more than any of the other advanced casts because most right-handed casters like to fish with the near bank on their left in order to have the casting arm as free from brush interference as possible. The curve to the right is used to drop the fly so that it will float down the current ahead of line and leader, and will be free of drag. Thus the fish will take the fake for a natural and grab it without hesitation. There are also many times when an angler wants to get around some natural obstacle or into a hole under brush where only a curve shot could take him.

The easiest curve to the right is a modification of the change of direction cast. The usual up and downstream false cast is made and then, as the forward cast is begun, the wrist is turned to the right. When wrist and rod are turned, the line will follow, gradually curving around, and leader and fly will fall on the water in an arc to the right.

I remember watching a friend take a fish from a tough spot with this cast while fishing on Rattlesnake Creek in Pennsylvania. A branch stuck out 3 feet beyond the other tree limbs on the right bank, to which he was casting. About 4 feet upstream from that branch and only a foot out from the shore, a nice fish was rising.

My friend studied the situation carefully, then swung into action. He false cast up and down the river a couple of times, shot the line out a foot from the end of the branch—and turned his wrist slightly to the right. The line went straight out past the branch but gradually the end of the line and leader curved in, and when the leader turned over it dropped the fly 7 feet beyond the branch and 3 feet beyond the fish. The lunker slurped it in as it came over him, and the fight was on.

When my friend finally landed that fish, he turned and looked at me. His grin was wider than the curve he had thrown.

"I've been practicing that cast for a week," he said. "This was the first chance I've had to try it. It sure takes them out of the tough spots."

Where water is racing out of the tail of a pool, a loose, sloppy curve to the right is a useful variation. This curve is done from the left-hand side of the drop off, and is executed by throwing a short line, aiming 10 or 12 feet above where the fly is supposed to hit, and powering the throw only with the middle section of the rod. No tip is put into it at all. The line will go out sloppily, with no force, and will fall in a curve to the right. The extra 10 feet of line cast in this casual way allows enough slack

THE ROLL CAST. At the start of this cast the end of the line lies on the water in front of you. As you bring the rod back, the line rolls back to you; then, as you bring the rod forward, the line leaves the water and shoots out. The photograph of the line (opposite page) shows its movement in the roll cast. The front section rolls outward from the angler, pulling the fly after it.

for a good float before drag sets in. In such a spot it is just about the only cast that will consistently take fish. An upstream S-cast would fall over the fish and scare him. A straight line would be whisked out of there by the fast current. And if the fisherman were to creep upstream and make a straight-across cast, the fish would see him.

Yes, curves get the fish—not only a leery trout in thin water but a buster of a bass lurking under a dock, or a flashy bonefish tailing on the far side of a mangrove shoot in salt water. It's surprising how many times a curve cast is needed in the course of a day of fly fishing.

One of the prettiest casts of all is the roll cast, and it has as much practicality as beauty. This cast is invaluable when brush or trees close behind the caster prevents a backcast. To execute the roll cast, 25 or 30 feet of line and leader are allowed to rest on the surface. Then the rod is raised to the 1 o'clock position so the line forms an arc from the rod tip to the water. Then, when the rod is brought forward with the same slow wrist action used in the regular forward cast, the line will follow the rod, come in beside you, and roll on up and out, whereupon the fly will flip over and land gently on the surface.

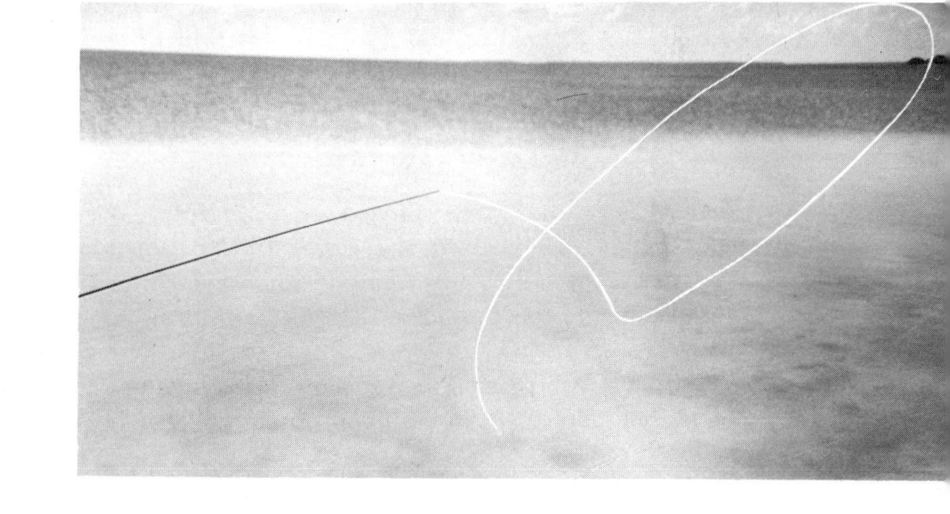

A roll cast made with a backhand snap of the rod often gets into a difficult spot on the fisherman's own side of the river. And on certain angles of retrieve you can use it for a backhand pick-up, returning to the regular wrist position on the false cast.

A version of the roll cast can be utilized to great advantage when the angler is casting with a strong wind behind him. The wind, in such circumstances, will usually knock the backcast down and as the fly comes forward low, it will sock him on the back of the neck or dig into his ear. But he can make the wind work for him if he uses a roll cast. That way, the line never goes in back of him to blow forward and snag him, and he can still get pretty good distance and accuracy, sometimes with a mere flip of the wrist. This was brought home to me very plainly during a pack trip to the Hillgard country with Jim Goodrich of the 320 Ranch at Gallatin Gateway, Montana. Jim and I were fishing Gnome Lake when an extremely hard wind started to blow. It came roaring down over the bank behind us so it was impossible to throw a line back into that gale. The roll cast looked like the deal, but when I started to bring the line slowly back along the surface of the lake, preparatory to making the roll, the wind hit the line and held it 30 feet in the air—so, with only 10 feet of line and the 12-foot leader on the surface, I made a quick forward flip with my wrist and the line in the air went on out, pulled the rest of it from the water and placed it gently down 50 feet away from me.

It is even possible to shoot a roll cast and I have seen good fly men roll out a line a distance of 80 to 90 feet to take fish they never would have reached with a regulation cast, while such a gale was howling at their shoulders. When shooting a roll cast, especially with a heavy, forward-tapered line, there should not be more than 25 feet of line resting on the water when the cast is made. If a lot of line, say 40 to 60 feet, of such weight as a WF-7-F or WF-8-F is left lying on the water it will be almost impossible to do a roll because of that heavy weight so far out.

The roll cast is especially good for a pickup in fast water. Every time I think of this pickup, I recall the day I was fishing the Upper Potomac River near Shepherdstown, West Virginia, with my young nephew, Paul Levering. At noon I came up river and saw Paul standing knee deep in a riffle. He made an upstream cast and then as line and leader swept back toward him in the heavy current, he tried to pick them off the water. The line was moving so fast that when he lifted his arm, hoping to get line into the air, it rode in against him, wrapping around his legs, some of it tangling around his wrist and the fly rod, until he looked like a pretzel maker's nightmare. He turned to me in despair.

"What am I doing wrong?" he wanted to know. "What causes all this?"

"In water like this," I said, "the line is moving so fast that when you try to pick it up, your arm goes way back and you are just pulling the fly in closer all the time. Half the time it never even gets into the air."

"What can I do?" he asked.

"When the line and fly are riding down on you like that," I said, "and when you raise the rod to pick up line—right then, you are in a perfect position for a roll cast. The line is out on the water in front of you, your rod is high, so it's no trouble to bring it back to the one o'clock position. From there, all you have to do is make the forward part of the roll cast."

Paul tried it and made a perfect roll cast. The line came in close to him, then rolled up and over as he made the forward cast. Line, leader and fly flipped over and the fly hit nicely about 25 feet out.

"That's easy enough," said Paul. "But I want to cast 40 feet."

"Do the same thing," I said. "But this time, when the roll has been completed, and the fly gets out there all the way, make a back cast just as the fly starts to drop, and there you are. You can continue to false cast till you're ready to make the throw."

Paul tried that, and again did fine.

"All right," he agreed. "It works. But what if I'm bringing the fly in for a roll cast pickup and a fish hits just when I'm about to pick up? I'll have slack line and won't be able to strike him."

"Not by pulling back on the rod the way you usually strike," I agreed. "But you can rush the roll cast and get the same effect. It will jerk the line toward you and hook the fish."

Carried still further, the basic roll cast becomes the aerial roll

For backhand roll cast, the author tips rod to left across body. Still slanting rod left, he starts wrist snap. Line circles up off water to shoot fly ahead.

cast, a maneuver that will get a trout fisherman out of many a jam when both he and the fish are surrounded by brush. I recall a perfect illustration. On Fishing Creek in Maryland I was trying to get to a fish that lay in a small run at the head of a pool that was hemmed in with bushes. I was hemmed in, too, and the only way to cast was from a 20-foot opening in front of me directly across to the head of the pool where the trout was slowly working his fins, waiting for a natural.

I stripped off 15 feet of line and gripped the fly by the bend of the hook so it wouldn't catch my fingers. Then I flipped the fly and leader into the air ahead of me and started to feed line through the guides. Then, line in air, I made a forward cast, picked the line up in the air, and made a back cast. Still false casting, I gradually got the line going in a neat vertical circle, like a wheel rolling, a bit to my right and a little in front of me. When I had 15 feet of line out, I made a forward cast and dropped the fly right on that trout's nose. He took.

If I had put that fly down on the surface in such a confined space, even once, for a regular retrieve and pickup, the fish would have busted out of the county. Such a cast is seldom needed, but on occasion it's the only one that can pay off.

The roll cast is also a great help in freeing a fly snagged on a log or other obstacle. The harder you pull toward you, the deeper the hook sinks. But nine times out of ten, if you slack up on the line and do a roll cast to throw line out beyond the fly, it will pull the hook out of the obstacle, away from you.

All these casts will be used many times in a season of fly fishing and they help to make fly casting great sport. But the cast that provides the fireworks is the double haul, a cast originally worked out by tournament casters. We owe them many, many thanks.

Plenty of anglers who know the double haul never think of applying it beyond bass-bug fishing or saltwater fly fishing, where they're using heavy-duty tackle. Yet the power supplied by the double haul is needed even more when the outfit is small because then even the slightest wind will cause plenty of trouble.

On the Big Hole River in Montana, Walt Weber and I were fishing a beautiful stretch of water where we knew there were

THE TIGHT BOW. Ideal when a headwind is blowing at you, this cast puts your line close to the surface and under the wind. Pick up the line and make your usual backcast, but as the line travels back, drop your elbow about 6 inches. Give forward cast extra power, bringing rod tip down

some good fish. We were using 8-foot rods and DT-5-F lines, with 12-foot leaders tapered down to 4X tippets. Walt's fly was a No. 10 Whitcomb and the wind was trying to blow it right back every time he cast.

"You need more power to get out into the wind with that big fly," I said. "Why don't you use the double haul?"

"Never thought of it with this small outfit," he answered.

"You need it now, more than any other time," I told him. "Because you're casting a long, thin leader, and it needs that extra push."

"Won't it slap down too hard on the water?"

"No," I said. "First of all, you're casting it several feet above the surface. The great force of the cast is dissipated in the long leader as it rolls out and over. The fly acts as a buffer. It slows up and drops quietly."

The double haul takes all the work out of casting and saves the angler's arm a lot during a whole day of fishing. It lets those who get a kick out of casting a long line—and who doesn't?—really go to town. It calls for perfect timing, but is otherwise easy. As you start the pickup, take hold of the line immediately below the butt guide with the left hand, and pull

smartly almost to water. Your line will shoot out on a level plane, the final turnover of the leader and fly being held down flat. This cast also gets your fly under overhanging brush.

down. At the same instant you start this pull, snap the right wrist back and upward. This pull, coupled with the lift of the rod, will give great speed to the backcast. While the line is speeding back, let the left hand, still holding the line, drift up to below the butt guide. As the line and leader straighten out behind you, start the forward cast with a snap of the wrist and at the same time pull down on the line with the left hand again. False casting this way gives the line such terrific speed that you can shoot out slack line held in the left hand for amazingly long casts.

I explained to Walt, that day, that it acts something like a bow and arrow, with the rod tip taking the part of the bow, firing the line forward.

"Did you see that?" he interrupted. "Looks like a good fish about 60 feet out there."

"Quite a rise," I agreed. "But in this wind you haven't been getting 60 feet."

"All right," he grinned. "You win. I'll use the double haul."

He got line up, false cast some line out, using the double haul, then let it go. It bored out into that wind right to the spot 60 feet away. He couldn't have walked over there and placed it more accurately. I saw the fish when it took. It was plenty big. When Walt set the hook, it tore down our way.

"How'd you like that double haul?" Walt asked me.

"How do *you* like that fish?" I countered. "You wouldn't have got to him without the double haul."

"He's only fair," said Walt.

Then that brownie jumped. I shot a glance at Walt. His eyes were out on crutches. He couldn't talk.

"He's only fair," I said for him, but he was too busy to even give me a dirty look.

Finally he beached that fish. It was a 4½-pound brownie and put Walt on the Wall of Fame in Dan Bailey's fly shop in Livingston, Montana, with those anglers who've been fortunate enough to take trout over 4 pounds on a fly.

When the wind is really howling, it's still possible to get a fly out by a combination of double haul and bringing the rod tip down hard at the end of the forward cast. I remember one day in early October when I was fishing the Yellowstone with Len Kinkie.

"I can't get out in this wind," he said at last. "It's just too tough."

"What you need to do is cast a tight bow," I said. "Bring your rod down hard on your forward cast. Then shoot your line."

The tight bow is good for getting under overhanging branches, too, or under banks, but most of all it saves the day when it's windy.

"How do you do it?" asked Len.

"Make the usual high backcast, but as the line travels back, drop your elbow about 6 inches," I said. "When the forward cast has started, give it extra power, bring the rod tip down

DOWNWIND CAST (below, left to right). Sometimes a tailwind gives you trouble by batting down your backcast. Then make a short backcast, letting your line and fly fall almost to the water 10 feet behind you. Now begin your forward cast, which should send the line up at a 45-degree angle to the water. Stop the rod at about the 1 o'clock position and shoot your line. It will go into the air (above), straighten out until it's about level with your rod tip, then settle to the surface.

smartly, almost to the water. The line will shoot out on a level plane, the final turnover of the leader and fly being held down flat. Watch what happens in this wind with an ordinary cast."

I made a cast, trying for a spot about 30 feet away, where a trout should be rising. I stopped the rod high. The wind caught the line and leader and blew them back in my face.

"Now look," I said.

I made another cast and this time brought the rod tip down to the surface. The line shot out under the wind but not quite to where I wanted it to go. It needed more of a trick than that.

I stripped more line from the reel, false cast the entire 40 feet into the air, and using the added weight of that extra line, made the forward cast again, brought the rod tip down hard, and threw the fly out the 30 feet I needed.

"That's something to know," said Len. "I believe I'll start fishing again."

The next time I saw Len he had two nice rainbows, taken in the teeth of that wind.

A strong wind blowing from behind the caster can be just as troublesome as a head-on blow, but there are several ways, besides the downwind roll cast already described, by which an angler can outwit the wayward wind. It is often possible to cast horizontally, with the rod parallel to the water instead of overhead, and thus get the fly out without losing an ear. And another way is to shorten the backcast, let the line and fly fall almost to the water behind you, then make the forward cast upward, at a 45-degree angle, stop the rod at about 11 o'clock position, shoot the line, and let the wind take it on out. The fly and line will clear your head with room to spare and at the end of the forward shoot the line will fall to the surface. Never having found this cast described, I have named it simply "the downwind cast."

Poor handling of the retrieve in windy weather will cost the caster fish, too, because it will prevent him getting all the strikes he should. If the rod is held too high the wind will catch the line and blow it along, causing drag to the fly. Or it will blow the line in such a way as to give slack line when it is least wanted; and sometimes a heavy wind will lift the whole shebang, line, leader and fly, right off the water. But if the rod tip is held down almost to the water, within an inch or two of the surface, the wind doesn't catch the line at all and retrieve can be made without either drag or slack.

The handling of the retrieve is important with all casts because the way the line is retrieved affects the pickup, and hence the following cast. Some anglers, particularly trout fishermen, work the line around their fingers, or make a figure 8 with it in the palm of the left hand. But for general mobility, quickness and line control, the strip method of retrieve is best.

To execute this retrieve, the rod is held with the thumb and middle finger sticking out from the grip, the thumb over the top and the middle finger coming around underneath. Hold the line between the extended thumb and finger and strip it in below that with the free left hand. At the conclusion of each strip, transfer control of the line to the waiting thumb and finger and hold it taut until the left hand brings in another strip. You can drop the line as it comes in, either in the bottom of a boat or on the surface of the water. It may also be held in coils in the left hand. With the strip method of retrieve the line can be brought in fast or slowly, as the angler wishes, and he always will have a tight line, ready for a strike or for the pickup for the next cast.

The strip method is especially good in fast water. When fishing a riffle, or rapids or a fast glide, I usually make a 25- to 35-foot cast upstream—a short line is always best in fast water—then give a couple of fast, arm-length strips as the line charges down. I raise the rod tip then and do a roll cast pickup. Or, when the line is 15 feet above me, I toss it up and backward, and then deliver the forward throw. The result is the same.

Show me a man who can fish a small stream successfully and I'll bet he'll do all right on bigger ones. But the reverse is not always true. The little stream separates the lucky from the

Author uses strip method for retrieves, thumb and middle finger of the hand on rod grip controlling the line while the other hand pulls it in length by length. *Courtesy of Miami News Bureau.*

skillful. In a couple of weeks on a small stream an angler learns more about trout and the way they operate than he does in three months on bigger water. First of all, he sees practically every fish he casts to. He watches how they feed, on minnows or digging in the gravel for nymphs, and how they take flies. He soon discovers that in shallow water trout are extremely wary—as are all fish, for that matter—and on the alert all the time, and that therefore they are hard to take.

I remember one novice fisherman who asked me to take him out and give him a few tips. I took him to just such a low, clear stream as I have been describing. He just looked at it, then at me, and headed home.

"What's the idea?" he shouted back at me as he went. "I'm just a beginner."

"That's why we're here," I answered. "You'll find out more about trout in one day on a stream like this than you would in a week on bigger water. It's like going to a movie. You can see everything that goes on."

He came back and we started out together. He didn't wet a line that day, just waded along beside me, taking it all in.

He soon learned that the basic principle of fly fishing is that feeding trout face upstream, waiting for food to come to them with the flow of water. They use one position so consistently that "feeding station" is a common term among fly men; and they take that position at a spot where they can see an approaching tidbit in plenty of time to rise up and snatch it, and then return to their feeding station without ever having moved more than a few feet from that one spot. So that, in order to reach all the fish in a pool, and to reach them without first being seen by the fish, an angler must start at the bottom and work up. Old advice, to be sure, but it pays off in trout fishing. The tail of the pool should be fished first because there are generally some fish hanging out there, facing upstream. If the caster enters the pool above them, he is sure to be spotted in a hurry. Rushing into a pool will kill it, quick. Waves pushing up, gravel grinding under waders, line slapping down hard or ripping off the surface as it is picked up for the next cast—all these things keep creels empty. So move slowly and quietly into casting position. If you chase the trout ahead of you, wait a while before starting to cast. Give them time to forget, which, fortunately they do rather quickly. Once you have established yourself as part of the scenery of the pool they will return to their feeding stations and immediately become fly conscious again.

The best way to put them down so you won't catch any, is to fish downstream, for they'll see you a mile away and though they may not flush, they know you are there. You must come in behind them and crouch, creep and crawl into casting position. Then, working upstream, you can hit every spot where a trout might be, especially with a dry fly. If the situation is such that it is necessary to fish with a wet fly, then the wet fly should, in most cases, be handled as much like a dry as possible—cast up or up and across stream, rather than below your position.

Before the first cast is made, the angler should scan the pool very carefully, and figure where trout should be lying, and where is the best spot from which to cast, and how much float he can get over a riser he has seen, or over a point where he thinks there may be a fish. It takes a great deal of patience and care of approach and presentation. But the reward, when he takes a nice fish from small waters, is worth all he has put into it. This is fishing when fishing is an art.

Many a fisherman has felt mighty foolish when caught in some of the peculiar attitudes necessary when stalking a trout in a small stream. But if occasionally he gets the last laugh plus the tricky trout, he is indeed well paid for his foolish look. One time I was kneeling at the edge of the water halfway up the left side of the Pumphouse Pool on Big Hunting Creek in Maryland. I had crept in on hands and knees and eased into position in about the only spot among the trees and bushes that a cast could possibly be made.

I was ready to swing into action when another angler came ploughing through the bushes behind me. He hesitated and stared.

"Just what are you doing?" he asked. "Praying?"

"That's just about it," I said. "Praying that I can get my backcast under those tree limbs so I can put a fly out there about 30 feet where I saw a fish come up."

"You sure look foolish," he said, and then, as the trout rose again, took a natural, and sank back down, he cheerfully added, "You'll never get a fly over that fish, anyway. It's impossible. If you keep your backcast low enough so you don't catch the trees, you'll only hook the ground."

There was a space of only 4 feet between the tree limbs and the ground and only 20 feet between where I was kneeling and the bushes through which the fisherman had come. It looked tough, all right.

"That's why I'm kneeling," I said. "With a horizontal cast I may be able to do it. If I get the line going back and forth fast, it'll stay on a level plane. Then I can get 20 feet distance back of me and shoot the other 10 feet of this line I've stripped off. Takes wrist action," I went on. "And terrific line speed."

"You'll never get a fly over him," said the scoffer.

I made my backcast on a level plane. It just missed the trees behind me and when I shot 10 feet of line the fly dropped neatly right above the riser. It floated down. He took.

Before releasing that trout I silently held it up for that joker to see. He didn't say a word, just walked away. But I'll bet he now uses his knees for something besides praying.

Lots of times, because of brush and other natural hazards, it is hard to make a long cast on a small stream, so you have to settle for a short one. But the average fly caster has plenty of trouble making short casts because there is so little weight to

In "impossible" spot, kneel for horizontal cast.

In close quarters, bend the rod for bow-and-arrow cast.

throw. This is the time to limit the casting action almost entirely to the wrist, keeping the arm out of it, just snapping the wrist hard as the forward cast is made. Then follow through, coming down hard with the rod tip, almost to the water.

The same technique applies when casting into the wind. That means almost always because there is usually at least a breath of air stirring and with the light terminal tackle used on small streams, even the slightest puff will blow fly and leader back in your face. So concentrate on the snap of the wrist and the follow through.

Another aid to short-line casting is to build up the butt section of the leader where it is attached to the line, using a heavy section there, 3 feet of 30-pound-test nylon leader material and tapered down from there gradually to the desired point, 3X, 4X or 5X. With such a taper it is surprising how much more easily short casts can be made.

While trick casts, as previously mentioned, are strictly for the show performer, the bow-and-arrow cast is a good one to learn if the fisherman plans to fish small streams. It's a big pay-off deal when you have to get a fly out in really close quarters. The fish it helps you land from tough spots will long be remembered.

Years ago I was standing beside a pool on the Cheat River in West Virginia. The pool was 25 feet long and 15 feet wide. I saw a 9-inch trout swim into view, grab a minnow. He held it sideways in his mouth for a second, turned it, and then swallowed it headfirst. Then he swam slowly upstream for 15 feet and stopped. I was pressed so tight against the bushes that I knew he hadn't seen me, but I didn't dare false cast or he would spot me. My arm waving out over that narrow water was bound to scare him. So I grabbed the fly by the bend of the hook, bent the rod back until it made a bow, and with a hard snap of my wrist shot the fly out like an arrow, so that it hit a foot above the trout. He came right up and took. And many times since then I've found that this is one so-called "stunt cast" which is often practical on a small, brushy stream.

While the roll cast is also very helpful on small water, it should be limited to short line use only. The commotion made by lifting a lot of line and leader from the surface of a little pool is likely to scare the fish and put them down. When conditions appear to call for a roll cast and yet more line is needed than can safely be lifted from the surface, a glance at surrounding treetops may show you a way out. High up, maybe there's an opening where you can put the backcast for an ordinary throw. Sometimes there's a space among the treetops or over a bush, with just room enough for a backcast.

To get into that hole, the angler turns and faces that way and uses a regular forward cast to get the fly up into the opening. Then, while the line is rolling over, he turns in a slow pivot and makes the forward cast, dropping the fly this time on the water. When first trying this cast, the tendency is to rush the cast, with fatal results. Once you get the cast up there, you have plenty of time to turn slowly and make the forward throw.

The same effect can be achieved by using a backhand cast to put the fly up into that hole, and then make the regular forward cast. That is, the angler does not turn bodily. But he must watch his backcast.

There isn't any easy way of taking trout from a still pool, but a light and well matched outfit will help. The lighter the fly line, the better. And the longer and finer the leader, the more strikes will come to the fly. This is the place for a fast-action dry-fly rod 7½ feet long and weighing from 3 to 3½ ounces, equipped with a double tapered DT-4-F nylon fly line and a leader from 10 to 12 feet in length and tapered down to at least 4X and sometimes 5X or 6X.

That leader sounds long and light and tough to cast? It isn't easy. But such an outfit is not as difficult to handle as many anglers believe. I've often heard fishermen say they couldn't possibly cast such a long, light leader, and when I've handed it over and they tried it they were usually surprised at how well they did. Their mistake was in not trying. And if you don't use a long, fine leader you are going to miss catching lots of trout and having lots of fun. The novice should start with a 10-foot leader and when he has become used to that, lengthen it a foot or two, always keeping the tippet down to at least 4X. In shallow, clear water, trout are just not going to bust up and hit a fly tied on anything heavier. In glassy pools you either use a 4X tippet or finer, or you don't catch the first trout.

Back to stream, deliberately cast to treetop hole.

One summer I fished slick water with one of the country's top fly casters, Paul Stroud of Chicago. Trout fishing is an exact science with Paul, and his knowledge of tackle and stream technique help him take more than his share of fish. The stream we fished came out of a huge spring, ran through a meadow for a mile or so, and emptied into a bigger river. Here and there in the middle, long strands of grass waved slowly to and fro in the current. Innumerable channels cut through the grass, and the scoured river bed showed clean and gravelly.

We walked upstream along the bank looking for rising fish, rods in hand, ready. It was going to be a job to take canny old brown trout from that mirror smooth water. The stream had the reputation of being so tough that many people claimed the fish in there were just not catchable.

We soon spotted a trout rising in a little run against our bank. Paul did a crouching approach and finally crawled the last 10 feet, until he was only 25 feet below the fish. He false cast with his rod horizontal to the water in order to prevent the trout from seeing it, and then threw a curve to the left which landed the fly 3 feet above the active fish. When the fly came over him, he took.

Looks easy, I thought. But right there, simple as it seemed, is the summation of years of experience plus a nice efficiency with the tools of the fly caster's profession.

A little later I saw Paul pull another neat trick out of his bag of experience. He made a cast to a riser and the fly fell a couple of inches beyond the slow-moving current and sat there, stationary. Paul lifted the rod tip, slowly, and gave the fly a slight boost that moved it into the current where it started serenely along, as if it belonged there, looking exactly like a downed insect floating along with the push of the water.

A beginner would never know just what that little boost meant—that it avoided the possibility of downing nearby fish by lifting line and leader for another more accurately executed cast. Many anglers, anxious to rectify a bad cast, will rip the line off the surface and slam it back again, causing all kinds of water commotion and as often as not getting no nearer their objective with the second try. When trout fishing in almost any kind of water, it pays to take things slow and easy; and when fishing low, clear pools, the more careful you are, the more fish you will catch. You must even watch your shadow in such a pool, so it doesn't run ahead of you to the spot you want to fish.

Even in the largest rivers it is necessary to exercise considerable care both in wading and casting to avoid frightening fish. Many a time I've seen a fisherman plunge into the pool in what he thinks is a safe spot, only to find he has chased half a dozen trout off their feeding stations, or from their resting spots.

One of the most common mistakes beginners make is that they shy away from the difficult looking shots. It's surprising how seldom a fly does get hung up on obstructions, and if it does so occasionally, what does it matter? Those are the spots where the trout usually hang out, resting and feeding.

Once I was fishing with Ray Red on the Tomichi, a slow-moving meadow stream just on the edge of the town of Gunnison, Colorado. We saw a nice fish rising only a foot out from the bank. But just below him, between his position and ours, a dead stick was lodged. It jutted 4 feet out from the bank and was about a foot above water. This was a puzzler. We couldn't go above him or even opposite him on the pool without being seen. A curve to the right wouldn't reach him, and it was impossible to throw a fly under that low-hanging stick and get a float over him.

"Guess we'll have to pass him up," whispered Ray.

"There's one chance," I said. "Cast as if that stick weren't there. Throw some slack and the line will fall loosely across the stick. When you strike, the line will leap up from the stick and come tight between the rod tip and the fish."

"Suppose he doesn't take?" Ray argued. "In that case the fly will be sure to catch on the stick."

"Not necessarily," I said. "As line and leader pull over the stick and you see the fly come off the water, give the rod a quick pull. That will jerk the leader against the limb, and the light little fly will maybe be flipped over it. It's worth a try."

"Yeh," said Ray. "Maybe. And if he does take he'll probably slam back this way and break me off. But here goes."

He cast just right. And sure enough, the trout passed up that first try. But Ray flipped the fly over the stick all right, so he got a second chance. That time the trout took. He darted upstream and Ray was able to lead him across the pool, away from that pesky stick, and into his net, as if he had a nose ring on him. He got a nice 14-incher that he nearly missed for not trying.

Confidence in your own ability and in your knowledge of what a fish will do when hooked goes a long way in fly fishing, too. Last summer Frank Rose and Bill Boyd of Twin Bridges, Montana, took me to the Ruby River at a point near Laurin. The Ruby is small as Montana rivers go, with pools 50 feet long and from 15 to 25 feet wide. Dead tree limbs hang down into the water everywhere you look. There are so many hazards you might think it impossible to get even a short float. It's strictly a dry-fly stream because a nymph, wet fly or streamer is almost sure to snag on all that bric-a-brac.

The first trout we saw was feeding an inch in front of some bare limbs that hung well down into the water.

"A 2-pounder," I said as we watched him rise.

"Yes," said Frank. "But if he hits he'll break you off on those limbs and if he doesn't hit, you'll get tangled in them."

I knew that nine out of ten fish in such a situation will hit and take off upstream, away from the feeding spot which has suddenly produced that barbed fly. So I said nothing but dropped the fly 3 feet above the trout. We saw him rise slowly, open his mouth and take. And when I set the hook he slammed upstream like a shot and came out in a beautiful jump right in the middle of the pool. I kept the pressure on and held him out there, away from the bushes. I finally landed him, a nice 15-incher.

The next one we spotted was in a similar location. It was Frank's turn.

"You were lucky," he said. "Your fish took the first cast. What if mine doesn't? I'll be hooked for sure on that dead limb."

"If he doesn't take," I said, "skid the fly out of there in a hurry, before it catches. As long as you do it with an even pull and don't yank the fly off the water, its disappearance won't scare him. Then you can throw to him again."

On the first four casts Frank had to pull his fly away from that overhanging branch, but he always managed to get it out smoothly, and in time. And on the fifth float a good pound fish hit the light Cahill as if he hadn't eaten for a month. And like my fish, this one dashed to the middle of the pool and came out in a nice jump.

At the next pool we saw a riser out in the middle and another right in front of a branch that dipped into the water. It was Bill's turn.

Author false casting preparatory to shooting the line. Note loops of the line held in left hand, to be released in final cast. *Photo by Bill Browning.*

"You'd better try the one in front of the branch," I suggested.

"Why?" asked Bill. "The one out in the pool will be easier to get to."

"Sure," I said. "But he'll break you off."

"I'll try him anyway," said Bill. "He looks bigger."

The trout took his fly on the first cast. He charged right in to the bank and wrapped the 4X tippet around a submerged tree limb. He broke Bill off, but fast.

Bill turned to me. "You meant," he said, "that if I cast to the one that's in by the bank, he'd run out into the pool, while this one, already being out there, would head for the bushes."

"Sure," I said. "Think back. Every trout we've caught from those difficult lies busted right out into the pool, away from the jumble of stuff he could have cut us off on. But hook a good trout in the open, on a small stream and he'll invariably dash for cover—a cut bank, a log jam, brush of any kind."

"I never thought of it before," said Bill. "But that's the way they act, all right."

"Yes," said Frank. "When they're in a tight spot, feeding, and they feel the hook go home, they think the trouble must come from all that stuff around them. So they want to get out of there. And the ones feeding in the open figure the opposite —that safety lies in heading for cover."

CHAPTER/3

CLASSIFICATION OF FLY PATTERNS

FLY FISHING CAME LATE TO AMERICA BUT IN THIS VAST country where every man regards the woods and waters as his own, it quickly grew into a flourishing sport. Early anglers copied the fly patterns long in use abroad and at first they found that, as is still the case in remote places, the native American fish were not too choosy about what they hit. But as more fly men fished, our Eastern streams began to be overworked, trout became harder to catch, and especially after the suspicious brown trout was introduced to remedy the situation of declining native species, anglers discovered that to consistently take fish meant more than just tossing any old fly to a rising trout. They found it took the right fly, and as a result they began to study stream life, gathering a smattering of entomology in order to be able to match through their various stages the natural insects upon which trout prey.

Today there are more anglers in America who know the history, technique and tradition of tying artificial flies than will be found in any other country. Every area in the United States has its share of tyers producing standard patterns that are good not only in their own bailiwick, but wherever trout are found. And these same men also come up with variations of the standard ties, new flies that are uniquely suited to their own area and do a special job on a special fish, or under special circumstances.

All artificial flies are not necessarily tied to represent natural flies. Many are made to imitate minnows, mice, frogs, beetles and other types of aquatic or streamside life, both insect and animal, and the flow of inventions designed by resourceful fishermen is never ending. For instance, in Pennsylvania I bumped smack into a whole new line of flies tied by Vince Marinaro and Charlie Fox, which they developed as a result of their study and analysis of the insect life along the limestone streams of their home state.

This pair of anglers has come up with what they label "terrestrials," that is, flies that are designed from naturals which are born of the earth rather than the water. Of particular interest to me were the Japanese beetles and the jassids, as I had encountered times when bass in the Susquehanna River would take nothing but a Japanese beetle; and again and again I have fished streams that fairly cried for a jassid. So I tucked a few in my pocket before heading west, and sure enough, found that they produced wonderfully on Montana's many spring creeks.

I think that in these terrestrials our Pennsylvania friends have come up with a set of flies which, while not a substitute for the hatch of the moment, or for the stream food of major importance in any one place, will still be universal fish takers.

Terrestrials cover a wide range of land insects that either fall, crawl or are blown into the water. Almost all of them are fished dry but some are also good when played under the water. They imitate the green worm, leaf hoppers, many different types of beetles, various kinds of ants of different colors —red, brown, black, white, and black with red tail—and jassids. One of the very best trout-attracting terrestrials is the big daddy long legs. This is a deadly number that they'll hit every time it comes down the stream, but it is a tough one to tie and is so fragile that each hit just about ruins it so that the trouter who intends to fish a daddy long legs needs a good supply in his box.

Many of the flies tied by neophytes are merely hopeful concoctions of the tyer's fancy, signifying nothing in the world and more often than not looking like something that a mother trout might use to scare her young, rather than a real gone lifelike natural. But in time these adventurers discover that in order to be consistent takers of fish, their inventions must subscribe to certain rules as to appearance and the way they may be fished. In the main, flies fall readily into certain classifications according to their construction and the way they are handled in the water. These are:

DRY FLIES
WET FLIES, INCLUDING NYMPHS
STREAMERS AND BUCKTAILS
TERRESTRIALS

Added to these feather and tinsel creations are the fly-rod lures, not too often used but still a part of the fly man's equipment, small spoons and wobblers; and a whole new selection of flies tied for saltwater gamefish which have recently been adding so much to the fly-rodder's sport; and the sliders and popping bugs used in all fields of fly fishing—trout, bass and the salt. With these I include the big popping bugs and streamers used since 1961 for such great gamesters as tarpon, sailfish and striped marlin. These I have classed, for description in this book, as:

FLY AND SPINNER COMBINATIONS
HAIR BUG AND POPPING BUGS
SALTWATER FLIES

In some cases there must be overlapping, as for instance with ants. In addition to the ant fished under the surface like a wet fly or nymph, the black flying ant has long been a favorite dry fly on Eastern streams and, particularly when swarming, these aerial performers seem to tickle the taste buds of trout. I re-

Three favorite dry flies (left to right): gray Wulff, size 10, black gnat, size 16, and the tiny gray midge, size 20.

Wet flies, showing typical slant of wings toward shank of hook (left to right): March brown, size 6, and royal coachman, size 6, both favorites for trout; and Jock Scott, size 2, for Atlantic salmon.

member fishing a lake one day when the place literally came alive with flying ants. They fell on the surface by the thousands and just as suddenly as the ants had appeared, the trout started to rise all over the lake, sucking in the downed insects. I got into the act, too, with a size 20 flying ant, dry. Business was good right off, and stayed good for a half hour. And many other times the flying ant has produced when there was no obvious supply of naturals. For this reason it has long been one of my favorite dry flies.

Flies that are good in one part of the country are nearly always good in others, too, so that I seldom denote flies as "Eastern" or "Western" flies any more. Most of the Eastern flies were tied to match hatches on Eastern streams but have proven out elsewhere, too. And flies tied for a small stream in one part of the country will usually prove just as effective on small streams elsewhere.

But East or West, when a hatch calls for a certain fly, then the angler must have it. There is no more exasperating experience than to be in on a hatch where flies are all over you, swarming across the surface, and trout are hitting into them with what looks like reckless abandon—till they come to your offering. You may take the odd fish, but to really cash in on the situation you need the right fly and the right size fly, be it in the dry, wet or nymphal stage.

One of the average trouter's greatest fears seems to be that he will have to use a small fly.

"Size 20!" he says with obvious dread.

First, he is afraid he can't see the fly, and second he is sure that the fish can't see it and third, he doesn't think that the bend of the hook in a small fly is wide enough to hold a big fish.

Yet flies tied on hooks in sizes 18, 20 and 22 consistently bring in big trout, fish of three and four pounds. Perhaps the fact that the bend in the hook is so small as to not allow any play explains it. The hook sinks in to the hilt and there is no room for the hook to straighten out, as might happen with a longer shanked hook with a wider bend.

A hook that straightens out usually does so on the strike, when the point of the hook jabs into a hard part of the fish's

Two types of streamers—the black ghost (left), size 6, with long white feather wing; and the white marabou with light plumage feathers which wave gently in the water, appearing to breathe.

mouth. Or when the fish is lipped or, as some anglers say, "when you pull his nose." Then a small fly will often come back with the bend opened up. Bending the hook back into shape does not seem to weaken it to any great extent, however, and I've often bent a hook back and continued to use it and land many more fish with it. However, all flies should be examined regularly, especially after missing a couple of strikes, to be sure that the hook has not been straightened out to some degree, and also to be sure the point has not been knocked off on a rock.

For special occasions, some of the very small flies are tied on bigger hooks. Such a fly is the popular snow fly used on the Yellowstone River, which is open for fly fishing all winter. These tiny numbers were first tied to use in winter and spring when big hatches of the tiny naturals showed. Tied on 5X short hooks, they are dressed to fit a size 18 or 20 hook, but the 5X is heavier, and has a much wider bend and will do a real job of holding and fighting a big fish. The only difficulty is to maintain a good float, as the heavier hook tends to pull the lightly dressed fly under the surface. But if kept loaded with fly buoy, it will usually stay up there to get plenty of hits.

Bucktails are flies tied with hairwings. These two lunker getters are the Mickey Finn, size 8 (left), and the dark Edson, size 10.

Two well-known fly experts in the Montana area use these snow flies regularly. Merton Parks of Gardner, at the north entrance to Yellowstone Park, believes that the snow fly is a winter fly that lays its eggs in water but pupates in ice and snow. He ties a black snow fly to ape this little natural, on a 5X short hook and although the real fly is almost too small to match accurately even with that, still his concoction gets plenty of hits. It can be fished either wet or dry but Parks likes to fish it dry.

"But sometimes you see an eddy that has foam in it," he says. "The fish will be rising and taking things from the foam. Then I use the snow fly wet, tossing it to the far edge of the foam and bringing it back in a slow, even retrieve. They sock it hard."

"Sometimes you are casting over ice," he went on. "But it's worth it."

"When is the best time?" I asked. I'd like to try it sometime."

"It's good all winter," he said. "But March and April are the best months, and the first few days of May are very good. One day last May I went out for an hour and a half, and in that time, using the black snow fly, I took three 3-pounders, and five 2-pounders, besides several that went a pound."

Dan Bailey of Livingston ties a similar fly, really a midge, and finds that its use is not confined to the winter months. Last

A fly and spinner combination, the coachman "Pilot," for bass.

October I saw him put it to great service on the famous Spring Creek at Lewistown, Montana. Dan noticed that the prevalent hatch was so small that he could hardly match it with a size 22 hook. He tied a gray snow fly on a 5X short hook and floated it over a riser. That fish took then, and came right out, a really big rainbow with more than his share of aerial ability. That fish turned it on and it took Dan fifteen minutes to bring him to net, a fine 4-pounder that gave it all he had, and he had plenty. Dan showed me the 5X short hook, afterwards. It was still in its original shape, not showing the slightest sign of opening. A size 18, 20 or 22 hook might have taken that rough treatment, or it might have opened up, but the odds were at least slightly in the favor of the 5X short.

"It was good to know I had my fly tied on that hook," said Dan as if reading my mind. "I could fight him harder than if I had been using a smaller lighter wired one, like an ordinary 20. And nothing but the small size would have turned the trick here."

So it pays to cover every possibility and to have enough flies along so a trip will not be spoiled by shortage of either size or pattern. Of course, the fisherman who ties his own flies can take his fly tying material along and, after seeing the hatch,

Popping bugs and hair bugs are widely used. At left is a frog-type popping bug; above is Phillips fly-rod popper, weedless. Hair bug at lower right is Jack's Bass-Houn.

he can tie the fly he thinks will match it, and so be away ahead of the fellow who depends on buying his flies. But one way or the other, it pays to be ready with a good supply.

In this book I do not propose to go into the intricacies of the actual tying of flies. That is a field in itself, while I am concerned herein with the practical business of casting a fly so it will take fish. However, over a long period of time, fishing as often as I do, searching for fun and material, I have used just about all the standard flies and have come upon almost as many more new and strange creations, tied both here and in other countries. And because I think it is important for a beginner to have a basic knowledge of what flies work fairly consistently almost anywhere, I am listing in the text of each of the following chapters the patterns and the fly-rod lures that I have found did a good job for me. Properly fished, these standard flies have produced and will continue to produce over the years.

CHAPTER/4

DRY FLY FISHING FOR TROUT

THE DRY FLY

THE DRY FLY IS DESIGNED TO MATCH A NATURAL AQUATIC fly or a terrestrial that has fallen and is floating on the surface of the water. The artificial must look as nearly like the natural as possible, for the trout, and in fact most fish, have eyes that would put the human 20 / 20 vision to shame. Trout take natural freshwater shrimp, and daphnia, or water fleas, that are not much larger than a pin point and a size 12 fly probably looks as big as a dinner plate to them, so that a faulty tie is quickly perceived and passed up.

Therefore the dry fly must be fashioned with much thought to size, color, slant of wings and set of hackle. It should be well balanced so that it will alight and sit perkily on the surface of the water, not being pulled this way or that by the weight of the hook so that it rests unevenly on the water. A good fly does not sit on its tail, nor yet lean on its chin. The nearer the parallel to the water, the better, even though many natural flies come down the current resting on their sides, with only one wing sticking upward.

There are many variations of the dry fly. The most common

A good collection of standard dry flies. *Courtesy of The Orvis Co.*

is the standard upright wing tie patterned after one or another of the common natural flies found on a stream. Many of these same patterns are tied in a "spentwing" variation, with wings outstretched, like a downed natural. It seems to me that spent-wing flies would make a better match to the real thing if they were tied to float awash instead of with a full hackle which places the flat wings above the surface. Then there are other dries that are designed to ride the big waters where the current pours in at the head of a pool, large creations that the angler can readily spot in that heavy water, or in white riffles elsewhere on the river. These big-winged ties have been produced by many different people and are called by many different names, but the end result is the same—they are the answer

Rough, heavy waters need big-winged ties such as the Wulff patterns of hairwing flies or the Trude patterns. This is the sure strike special, a Denver tie, a fine example of the Trude fly.

Spider, left, and variant, right, are both great producers for trout throughout the country. *Courtesy of The Orvis Co.*

to a great need for a fly that will tempt those lunkers that are up there in the rough water waiting for something substantial to come their way. The Wulff patterns of hairwing flies are proven fish takers in this group, and the Trude pattern, and the sofa pillow, mostly tied with a goodly degree of white to make them easy to see in the fast water. Right up there floating along with them are a couple of big flies that can be fished both above and below the water—the Bailey's bi-fly, the Joe's hopper, and the great muddler minnow which made its reputation as a bucktail fly but is now mopping up on Western streams when used as a dry fly.

Also constructed with an eye to the angler's vision are the bivisible flies. These are tied in various patterns but always with white hackles at the front so the angler as well as the trout can see the fly. This is a fly that enters almost every trout fisherman's fly box shortly after he reaches forty years of age. Because, size of hatch regardless, it is important in dry-fly fishing to see the fly.

To start with, every trouter should stock his fly box with a few basic flies which are consistent fish getters everywhere.

One friend once asked me: "If you could have only ten dry flies to fish, country-wide, what would they be?"

This was my choice:

LIGHT CAHILL, SIZE 16
GRAY MIDGE HACKLE FLY, SIZE 20
BLACK FLYING ANT, SIZE 20
RED VARIANT, SIZE 14
BLACK GNAT, SIZE 12
GRAY WULFF, SIZE 10
BLUE DUN, SIZE 16
ADAMS, SIZE 12
QUILL GORDON, SIZE 14
JASSID, SIZE 20

This is only the barest necessity, each fly guaranteed to be useful sometime, anywhere. To really meet the vagaries of a trout's appetite, and to give the angler the most from his fishing, a well-equipped fly box also should be stocked with the flies listed below, in many different sizes and patterns.

STANDARD DRY FLIES, *hook sizes 6 to 20*

ADAMS
BLACK FLYING ANT
BLACK GNAT
BLACK QUILL
BLUE DUN
BLUE QUILL
BROWN HACKLE, PEACOCK
BROWN HACKLE, YELLOW
DARK CAHILL
LIGHT CAHILL
CAHILL QUILL
COACHMAN
ROYAL COACHMAN
GINGER QUILL
GRAY HACKLE, PEACOCK
GRAY HACKLE, RED
GRAY HACKLE, YELLOW
HENDRICKSON
LIGHT HENDRICKSON
IRON BLUE DUN
PALE EVENING DUN
LIGHT CAHILL QUILL
MOSQUITO
MCGINTY
OLIVE DUN DARK
PINK LADY
QUEEN OF WATERS
QUILL GORDON
RED ANT
RENEGADE
RIO GRANDE KING
RED FOX
ROBERTS
TUP'S INDISPENSABLE
WILLOW
WHITE MILLER
WHITCOMB

BIVISIBLES, *hook sizes 6 to 10*

BROWN BADGER	BADGER
GRAY GINGER	GINGER
GRIZZLY	BLACK

WULFF HAIRWING DRY FLIES, *hook sizes 6 to 12*

GRAY WULFF	WHITE WULFF
GRIZZLY WULFF	BLOND WULFF
BLACK WULFF	ROYAL WULFF

SPECIAL TIES (DRY OR WET), *hook sizes 6, 8, 10, 12, long shank hook*

BAILEY'S BI-FLIES	JOE'S HOPPER*
BI-FLY YELLOW	GOOFUS BUG**
BI-FLY ORANGE	DAN'S HOPPER

TRUDE FLIES, *hook sizes 8, 10 and 12*

SURE STRIKE SPECIAL	PROFESSOR
COACHMAN	TEAGLE BEE
ROYAL COACHMAN	BLACK PRINCE
GRIZZLY KING	GRAY TRUDE
RED TRUDE	

VARIANTS, *hook sizes 10 to 16*

DONNELLY'S LIGHT VARIANT	MULTI-COLORED VARIANT
RED VARIANT	GINGER VARIANT
BLUE VARIANT	BADGER VARIANT

* Also called Dan's hopper, Michigan hopper (8 and 10 long shank).
** A hair wing fly with divided wings, body and tail formed by pulling deer hair back over the body and tying it at the bend of the hook. This floats fly better, gives buggy appearance.

SPIDERS, *hook sizes 14 and 16*

BROWN SPIDER	GINGER SPIDER
GRAY SPIDER	BADGER SPIDER
BLACK SPIDER	FURNACE SPIDER

SKATING SPIDERS, *hook sizes 8, 10, 12, 14 and 16*

ADAMS SKATING SPIDER	HONEY SKATER
BLACK SKATING SPIDER	BADGER HACKLE
NEVERSINK SKATER	SLATE

SPENTWINGS, *hook sizes 12 to 16*

BLUE DUN SPENTWING	ADAMS SPENTWING
LIGHT CAHILL SPENTWING	GINGER QUILL SPENTWING

DRY FLIES FOR ATLANTIC SALMON, *hook sizes 6 to 10*

BROWN BIVISIBLE	GRAY WULFF
ROYAL COACHMAN WULFF	BLACK WULFF
BLACK BIVISIBLE	GRIZZLY WULFF

LANDLOCKED SALMON DRY FLIES, *hook sizes 10 to 16*

GREEN DRAKE	GINGER QUILL
BROWN BIVISIBLE	BLACK GNAT
BLACK BIVISIBLE	ROYAL COACHMAN
GRAY WULFF	ADAMS
LIGHT CAHILL	RED VARIANT

FISHING THE DRY FLY

While most anglers class dry fly as the most demanding way of fishing, it is nevertheless the best way for a beginner to start. With a wet fly or a streamer, you are usually fishing the stream by your knowledge of where the fish *may* lie. But with a dry you are in on all the sights and sounds of the river, going by every signal a fish can flash to you as he eats or swims. The dry fly is also easier to cast than the wet, and the angler can see drag when it occurs and sees the fish strike and is therefore able to set the hook more quickly.

The whole principle upon which dry-fly fishing is based is that the fly should come down the stream exactly like a downed natural. Yet there are many anglers who fish for years without discovering that their fly is practically never floating free! It may seem to be moving with the current—but look carefully—is it traveling faster than the bubbles and bits of flotsam on the surface? Is it going more slowly? If either of these things is true, you have drag and the chances of a strike are slim. Is the fly floating downstream opposite you in a straight line or is the fly line bellied out ahead of it, dragging the fly crosswise, even the least bit, across the current toward you, telling the trout that there is something peculiar about that insect? Sometimes the amount of drag can be so small as to fool even a veteran, but never a trout.

Without that natural float, strikes are going to be as few as icebergs in Florida, even when trout are popping so fast in the middle of a hatch that you would think that all you would have to do is throw a fly on the surface and wait for the hit. It seems as if a fly would never run the gauntlet of all those feeding fish. But when a trout comes up and gobbles a natural exactly an inch from your lonely artificial, you begin to get the true story. They are turning up their mandibles at your fly because it isn't a right looking fly. It's either going too fast or too slow or it's going across current. In the meantime, those naturals are coming along as they should and therefore why worry about strange-acting, odd-looking affairs that seem to have a motive power of their own?

True, now and then a maverick trout will rush a fly that is skidding across the surface, and it's true, too, that you can take trout by dabbling, skittering, and various other ways. But these methods are usually productive only under certain specific con-

Holding line over fast water to prevent current from sweeping it and fly out of spot where trout lie on other side.

ditions which will be described later in this chapter. The angler who substitutes such methods for float is betting on chance against skill, and if it's meat he's after, he is going to wind up with plenty of air around the fish in his frying pan.

"What makes drag?" asked my nephew Paul Levering, when I was first teaching him to fly cast.

"Drag is caused when the fly is pulled by the leader and line at a rate slower or faster than the current, or across current," I answered, "instead of riding straight downstream like a natural fly that is at the mercy of the current."

Paul made a cast and dropped his fly on the smooth surface of the pool. It looked good, with wings cocked high, but it wasn't moving. It was resting in still water. Then the current caught the line and bellied it downstream, pulling the leader and fly after it.

"You have drag now," I told Paul.

"But the fly's riding high," he protested. "It looks all right."

"Just because the surface is smooth and the fly sits up doesn't mean you don't have drag," I said. "Look at the naturals beside it."

Paul's fly was moving quite a bit faster and in a different direction. Any trout down there below was going to know there was something different and wrong about that fly. And as if to prove it, even as we watched, a fish came up and took one of those naturals within inches of the strange-acting artificial.

Once more Paul cast and the fly floated through untouched.

"There are at least half a dozen fish rising out there," he said. "You'd think one of them would hit."

"Pick out a single fish," I said. "Then figure the water for a good float to him. Forget all the other fish. Concentrate on just that one."

Such a situation is like shooting into a covey of rising quail. If you don't bear down on one, you'll miss them all. Regardless of how hard trout are feeding, if you don't put the fly down the groove to a certain fish, you'll do remarkably little business.

"I'll try that one, then," said Paul, nodding towards a riser about 30 feet out and slightly above us.

"Take a gander at the speed of the current between you and the fish," I said. "It's moving fast, and that's the water that's going to hurt you. It's one of the toughest spots to get a free float—when there's a fast current between you and where you want the fly to float."

"Try the S-cast," I suggested. "This is a perfect place for it."

"What's the S-cast?" asked Paul.

I described it to him, as explained earlier in this book (*see chapter entitled* PRACTICAL CASTS).

"It will give you at least a couple of feet of free float, and that should be enough when the fish is hungry."

"Wish me luck," said Paul, getting his line in the air.

He false cast and when he had 35 feet out he cast hard and the line shot out, hit the reel as he stopped the rod, and the fly lit as lightly as a bird, 4 feet above the rising fish. It bobbed jauntily along right over him absolutely free of drag. That 14-incher grabbed it without fear and a few minutes later, his face one big grin, Paul was landing his first trout.

Like all rules, the free float edict has exceptions, and one spot where a dry fly does not need to be floating dead center in order to get hits is in the eddy back of a protruding rock. In such an eddy a natural does not float normally, but is pulled and whirled by the varying currents, and for this reason the monster trout that may well lurk there will not be too upset by a fly that isn't floating free. But in such a spot the line is usually grabbed by the current as soon as it lights, whisking the fly out of there before it has time to float at all and before the fish can even see it. In that case, the angler must wade in close and cast a very short line, 12 or 15 or at most 20 feet, then hold the rod as high as possible so that the line is kept clear of the water altogether and only leader and fly are on the surface. That way it is possible to get a foot or two of float, or at least for the fly to whirl lightly around in the eddy, and that is usually sufficient for a strike.

The same technique pays off at the head of a pool. Cast across the fast water and where the current is pouring in hard, hold the arms high, rod in one hand and line in the other. When the current is very heavy you can often obtain a decent float this way even where an S-cast or a mended line would be bellied out of there in a hurry. A line handled this way is free of the water and the dry fly will float naturally down the far side of the current.

A beginner should keep his eyes going the entire time he is on the stream. The quickest way of getting on to trout habits is to watch them feed. In a clear stream you can get a close-up view of how they take a fly. On their feeding stations they generally seem to see the fly as it comes down the current, about 4 feet above them. Then, as it comes nearer they rise a bit higher to meet it, and as it comes over them they drift back right under it and suck it in.

When trout are not on their feeding stations working on a hatch, but are after minnows, they cruise around, usually working the still, shallow water, and they spend a lot of time covering the tails of the pools where the water thins off.

The first time I fished the Big Hole River near Melrose, Montana, I was so anxious to get fishing that I forgot to figure the water. I slipped into the tail of a beautiful-looking pool that was 400 feet long and about 70 feet wide. I waded out to knee depth and after a warm-up cast or two to take the edge off my eagerness, I started to look around. I should have known better. Where I was standing, and as far as I could see, the bottom was smooth and pebbly, with no break anywhere, no grasses, no rocks. This wasn't holding water, this was cruising water, and it wasn't cruising time. That would come later, about dusk. What was I doing here now?

I scrambled out and moved on upstream along the bank and went into the head of the pool about 75 feet from the top. I waded carefully out and at once saw trout rising in the fast current near the head of the pool. From then on I had fun. And just before dark I walked downstream again and in the tail of the pool saw trout cruising, snatching naturals from the surface. This was the time to be in that water. So I went well down below the working fish, waded in and crept up to within casting distance.

Cruising fish call for special treatment. A fly slipping along on the current as usual doesn't always pay off. They will slam it hard if it happens to come across their path, but those fish have left their feeding stations, they are on the make, out looking. You can see the V they cut as they swim just under the surface, and watch the water bulge as they grab a nymph just before it reaches the top. They take an erratic course across the pool, so that you must figure which way your fish is going, then quickly drop the fly about four feet in front of him. Generally he will spot the fly and take it on the go. Sometimes it helps to impart a jiggling motion to the fly with the rod tip, making the fly shiver and shake on the surface, then let it sit quietly, give it another twitch, then bring it slowly along the top to pick it up for the next cast—tease them good! Trout may hit a fly during any of the above maneuvers, and they often hit when you are bringing the fly along the surface because they think it is a freshly hatched fly taxiing across, trying for elevation.

All of these tricks take a little time, a little practice, a great deal of patience. But the amount of work a fisherman puts into them will be more than repaid in the increase in his take. There's nothing quite like the pleasure of looking at a stream at the end of the day and knowing that you've fished it well and taken from it as much as any angler is entitled to take—enough fish for the pan, and a world of enjoyment.

Most trouters fish far too rapidly. A few casts in one pool and then they are off to the next. Small pools, say 50 feet long and 40 feet across, don't take long to cover, but some of the larger ones, 100 to 200 feet long, call for a couple of hours of fishing to work them properly. Many times, especially when fish are rising, I take two hours to fish a pool 200 feet long and 100 feet across. And I have action the whole time.

The approach to a pool is more important than many fishermen think. Before even starting to fish, the dry-fly man should study the pool or run carefully. Trout always lie facing upstream as they feed and therefore the logical approach in order not to be seen, is from the tail of the pool. But somehow the beginner naturally gravitates to the head of the pool. Once there, he either stands on the highest rock, where all the trout in the pool can see him, or he wades noisily out into the center and casts hither and yon as he walks down the middle, flushing trout helter-skelter from their feeding places with every clumsy step.

If you start at the head of the pool, crouch as low as possible and wield the rod horizontally and try to fish from the bank. If there are bushes, stand in front of them so that your movements will not be flashed against a clear sky. Walk softly so that vibrations will not be sent out to be picked up by the fish. It all sounds extremely on the cautious side but if you would take more fish and take them consistently, these things do make the difference.

Even at the bottom of a pool it is always wise to move in with caution. In some pools the water hesitates before dropping over the lip and trout like to lie there, taking their food the easy way, where the water slows and they can rise up to their prey with a minimum of effort. In front of rocks the water also backs up and slows and usually there is a fish there, ready for whatever tidbit the current offers. The fast current on either side of a rock is another natural feeding place for trout, as is the eddy behind a rock. Fishing such an eddy means only a foot or two of float before the fly drags and it is necessary to get close, drop the fly lightly and hold the rod high as you can to prevent the line from catching in the swift current between you and the eddy and thus hastening the drag. But fish hit fast in eddys and usually a float of only a foot will bring a strike from a fish that is there and is hungry.

Fish out the bottom of the pool and work your way slowly up along it, fishing the different currents as you go. Once an angler is in the pool and working quietly along, the fish will usually become accustomed to him and often begin to break all around him, some of them practically leaping into his pockets. It is always startling when a trout rises right up in front of you, and usually it happens just when you are tossing your fly to some spot 60 feet away. It makes you realize—too late—that short, well-placed casts will usually do the trick.

As an example, one day while I was fishing the Taylor River, trout started to rise all around me. I took one fish 10 feet directly upstream from me and after things quieted down and the risers appeared again, I had a hit from a splasher not 15 feet below me. He had made a wave when he broke for a natural and he seemed like a good fish. I sent a downstream cast to him, throwing harder than I needed to for the distance and stopping the rod upright so as to land the line on the surface in serpentine fashion and allow the fly to float naturally over the riser before drag commenced. It didn't go over the riser, however, as he came up to meet it with determination and accuracy. The fight was on and he came out in a sidelong leap that showed me that I had been right about his size. He looked close to 3 pounds—but—another jump and my line flew high in the air as he shook the hook.

Usually at the head of a pool the fast water pours in tumultuously and then a big fly is by far the best. Rainbows are fast-water fish, but you'll find plenty of brownies up there with them, too. In a big, even-flowing pool it usually is best to work the pool from left to right or vice versa, depending on which side the angler is fishing.

I like to cast up and across stream and start with the first cast straight up for about 40 feet, make a couple of casts, then put the next throw 2 feet over to the right, and continue the procedure until I have covered all the water which I can reach comfortably and with accuracy. As the direction of the cast moves across the pool, I shorten the line to avoid drag and wind up that series when the cast is directly across stream from me. Then I move upstream and start the next series of casts at a point just below where the previous series had ended. It's very much like the wet-fly method of "drops" used in Atlantic salmon fishing, only the reverse. That is, the fisherman drops upstream.

There are many small things which, either done or left undone, may mean the difference in a day's take when fly fishing. Most dry-fly men don't get close enough to the fish. They try for long casts and end up with a long line that puts the fly beyond true control. Rather than try for a longer line to reach a fish, the dry-fly man should try for better wading. And though trout are easily frightened, they also forget quickly. Many times when an angler chases a fish off its feeding station, if he will only stand still for a while and wait, the fish will return and start feeding again, and then he will take. So careful wading is an important part of dry-fly fishing. Get close to the fish, and keep the cast as short as possible.

When casting to a trout which has been seen in the water or has been spotted rising, it is best to drop the fly several feet in front of him. Give the fish plenty of time to get set to take, allow him to see the fly coming down the current for some distance up the pool. Now and then a trout will take a fly as soon as it lands, but on the whole you do better by letting the feeder see the fly coming from at least 4 feet away.

Try not to make the false casts over the spot where he is lying. Rather, the false casts should be made to the side, and then with a quick change of direction, the fly can be steered to the spot above him where you want it to land. In places where the fish can be seen and the angler is very close to him, a horizontal cast will do the trick, as sometimes in such close quarters the fish may see the rod in the air as it waves back and forth with the vertical cast. Scientists say the trout's area

When making a short cast to an oncoming fish, the rod is stopped at 2 o'clock, the line still going back. The forward cast will then be made with a very strong and hard snap of the wrist. *Photo by Charles C. Ebbets.*

of vision widens like an inverted cone, so it helps fool them when you keep the rod low.

Another error common to many anglers is that they lift the fly too soon after it has gone over a trout that did not take. Ripping the line off the surface right in back of him will fix him for fair, and the angler might as well go on to the next pool and find a new fish to work on. The fly should be allowed to float well below the fish, 6 feet at least, then be retrieved carefully well in toward the fisherman before being lifted for the next cast. Then, with the fly still coming his way, a lift of the arm will pull the line quietly off the surface, and a snap of the wrist will shoot both line and fly and leader noiselessly up into the air.

If the fish has risen to the fly and missed, rather than just not showing interest, then the angler should wait a while before putting the fly back over him again. Give him time to get back on his feeding station and to forget that what he just hit had a most peculiar look. Then the chances are much better for a repeat than they would be if the fly were slammed right back at him.

Fishing a fly in such a place calls for short line work with rod held high throughout cast, retrieve and pickup. If fish hits, rod is held up at arm's length to better skid fish across water and into protruding watercress at angler's feet. *Photo by Bill Browning.*

While fishing the Gunnison River one day I had a most unusual experience. I had made my cast and the fly had scarcely lit when I saw a trout come up for a natural 2 feet behind and directly in line with my fly. The trout missed and the natural fluttered downstream. He followed and hit at it twice more and missed both times. Then my fly came along and the trout had a go at it. He missed, or perhaps I missed, and then the trout further pursued and finally took the natural. All this fast and exciting action occurred within a 15-foot distance. Completely unnerved, I brought my fly in, hooked it in one of the guides of the rod, got out a cigarette, lighted it, and smoked that entire fag before allowing myself to cast over the spot where that trout had first showed. I thought I saw a flash down below the fly as it went over his former position but nothing happened. I waited at least a minute more before casting again. This time he took hard and my patience was rewarded when I landed a 16-incher.

The dry fly is the ideal way to fish a grassy stream where water cress grows along the banks and matted grass floats in patches on the surface. One day I came upon young Dick DePuy as I was fishing such a spring stream. Three feet out from the far bank a nice trout was rising.

"Take him," I said to Dick.

"I'll catch on the grass," said Dick. "This wet fly sinks fast."

"Try a dry," I suggested.

"How about that grass?"

He pointed to the 3-foot island of it.

"Drop the fly a couple of feet above the fish, let the line fall on the floating grass, and you should get over the fish O.K.," I said. "Then strike and keep your rod high and you can probably skid him across the surface and in to you."

It worked that way. The 10-inch brownie took on the first float and when Dick struck, the line jumped up from the grass, and holding the rod high, Dick pulled the struggling trout along the top to his net.

"Now you try one," said Dick. "There's another one rising just above where I took this one."

I walked into the water, dropped the dry fly in buoy solution to make it float high and dry. Then I made a couple of false casts and dropped the fly on the surface a couple of times just a few feet away from me and well away from where the fish was rising.

"Why are you doing that?" asked Dick.

"When the fly first hits the water," I explained, "the fly buoy puts a fine film of solution on the surface, and in such clear, still water as this, the fish might notice it and shy off. It's small things like that that may mean the difference in taking or not taking a fish out of a tough spot."

Many anglers fish a difficult stream as if they were afraid of it, stacking the cards against themselves before they even start. They snatch the line and fly out of every danger spot, oblivious to the fact that the biggest trout of them all may well have chosen that very spot as a safety area. For instance, when fishing the water along a log jam, you may think that the fly is about to float down and catch on the logs or brush. But look closer—you will see the water cushioning outwards from the logs and it takes the fly with it, safely along the edge. And it's right along the edge that the lunkers lurk. The angler who fearfully whips the fly out of there misses the chance of a strike from a big one, and probably scares the spots off all the trout around.

It seems as if the dry-fly man's greatest delight is trying to take fish under difficult conditions. He can have a lot of fun thinking and figuring and scheming ways to make them hit. He gets a kick out of taking advantage of the weather, the time of day, the way the light falls.

One day just at dusk Len Kinkie came up to me where I was fishing near Twin Bridges, Montana.

"Can't see a thing any more," he said. "Guess we may as well quit, though I hate to when they're hitting so well."

I looked over my shoulder at the western sky where there was still a faint glow.

"There's still a little light," I insisted.

I dug into my vest for my magnifying glasses, bought at the 5 & 10 cent store for 79 cents. Even with those on, it was hard to tie the fly, but by holding it up against the sky, I made it with a couple of jabs.

"You won't see the fly on the water anyway," said Len.

Rare closeup catches a 2-pound trout as he noses the author's royal coachman (top). Then the trout sucks it in (bottom) and the author strikes back. It all happens in a flash. *Photos: Bill Browning.*

"Let's cross over the bridge," I said. "To the other side. And then I'll show you. We can get in another half hour yet. We'll be casting against the light then."

We moved into another pool over there, and sure enough, when we cast, our flies showed up plainly, silhouetted against the fading light as long as there was a glow in the western sky. We each took a couple more fish before total darkness dropped the curtain.

When the dry-fly man finds that fish are not rising, he has many a trick to fall back on to tempt the wily, sleepy, or too well fed trout to hit. He can coax them up by guile, or he can waken them from their sleep, or he can make them mad enough to hit even though they are not hungry.

One time on the Yellow Breeches in Pennsylvania, my dry fly, a size 14 black gnat, came bouncing down a fast glide,

4 inches out from a jumble of logs. The trout that dashed up for it changed his mind at the last second and almost ripped a fin off getting back home again. He was so big he gave me the shakes. Instead of resting him I had to rest myself. But after a few long minutes I managed to put that fly out there again.

My gnat came high-riding down the current as chipper as a birch bark canoe. Four feet down under those logs that wily old buster stuck his beezer out, but he stayed at the foot of the stairs. I kept casting, changing flies a dozen times, but still no soap. Something was haywire.

I got the brain cells working.

The fly was floating entirely free of drag. The leader was long and fine, tapered to a 4X tippet. I was crouched low so that fish couldn't see me. Everything was as right as a teenager. Yet something was keeping him from hitting.

"First of all, there's no hatch on," I mumbled to myself. "So he isn't out in the open on a feeding station."

"That's it!" I almost shouted. "He's deep under cover, hungry to a certain degree, but not enough to come to the table and reach for a knife and fork."

So, I figured, there were a couple of things to do if I wanted to make him hit a dry fly. I could manufacture a hatch by casting time and again to the same spot, floating fly after fly past him, and in that way convince him that soup was on. Or I could put on a size 12 spider, a big powder puff of a fly. Oversize flies will often raise a trout just out of sheer curiosity, and even if he does not then grab the big fly, he is usually aroused enough to take a swipe at a smaller offering that looks bona fide. Similarly, when an angler knows there is a fish, especially a big one, in a heavy current, he can often coax him out by casting a big hairwing fly or a grasshopper type fly to the far edge of the current, then, holding the rod high, skip the fly back across the surface. Many a big buster has come roaring out of the rapids to such an offering, which might very well scare the daylights out of him in calm water but only seems to make him mad, there in the hurly-burly of the current.

Since this particular trout had already showed enough en-

Grasp trout lightly around the middle. They seldom struggle if handled this way. *Photo by Bill Browning.*

thusiasm to take a glance at the black gnat, I decided to manufacture a hatch with it. After eleven casts and floats he came out from under the logs. Another eight casts pulled him up within a couple of feet of the surface. He looked ready. He also looked as if he would weigh 4 pounds.

On the next cast he spotted the fly, moved up within an inch of the surface, let go his fin hold in the current, drifted back with it, opened his mouth and inhaled the fly. I raised the rod tip and set the hook, but I couldn't hold him and he slammed back under the logs and broke me off. But what matter? I had fun putting one over on that tough old cannibal. It was the satisfaction of the play, calling the pitch and showing him the right offering in the right way. That's the main course in dry-fly fishing and for dessert there is the moving water, the peaceful meadows, and doing what you like best of all. It's this challenge and satisfaction that make dry-fly men unequivocally name their sport the tops in angling.

FISHING THE DRY FLY ON LAKES

Although fishing a dry fly on lakes calls for a slightly different technique than fishing one on a stream, the "match the hatch" rule holds good on lakes, too. One August day, as I came upstream to the outlet of Widewater Lake, 9000 feet high on the Montana-Wyoming line, I saw a sight I'll never forget. Silhouetted in the last glow of the setting sun, trout of all sizes were showing on the glassy surface. There were at least a hundred of them up at one time, some leaping straight into the air, others just bulging and some sticking their noses out for a choice tidbit. They swirled right under my rod tip and farther away, and as far as I could see down the lake, fish were splashing.

I saw the object of their attentions, too. There was a double hatch on. Midges swarmed over the surface and at the same time a bigger fly was emerging, a fly that could be matched with a size 12 light Cahill.

Because it was getting dark and I like to be able to see my fly, I chose to match the Cahill and I got ready for a picnic. A big trout swirled only 30 feet out and I dropped the fly on his nose. He didn't notice it.

A small trout came up so close to that Cahill that he made it shake with the waves he put out. A foot away another one splashed at a natural. But my fly sat there, not getting the first nod. And all the time I knew that right under it was a fat 2-pounder.

I cast for ten minutes without getting a strike, trying all the tricks I knew to make that fly do business. I imparted a quivering motion through the rod tip to the fly by holding my right hand high and making like a quaking aspen, sending the impulses down the line so the fly shimmied like a dog shaking water off its fur. Then I brought the fly across the surface in short jerks, making it jump over the water in 6-inch leaps. It still went untouched. Then I made it come smoothly along, like a natural fly taxiing for a takeoff. But not a single trout out there in all the feeding multitude would have any part of it.

So I dug down into my fly box and found a size 20 midge, a tiny gray hackle. I knew it would completely disappear out there, but those fish were feeding on one of two things, and it wasn't the larger fly. I would have to strike at the splash, when a trout hit.

On the first cast I let the midge sit there for a second, then pulled back with my rod and gave it the slightest motion. That did the job. A foot-long trout fell all over it and we were off to a flying start. For the next twenty minutes, until dark drew the curtain, I had fishing that was out of this world, and every fish that hit did so only when I laid it on the line with that little size 20 dry fly.

You seldom hit such a bumper hatch as that on a lake, and many times you won't see any flies coming out at all. But it's a sure thing that in almost any lake where there are trout, sooner or later there will be a rise, and the angler will be able to do business with a dry fly. And during the good old summertime, the natural feeding periods of early morning and early dusk usually bring cruisers to the top looking for food.

Best of all, dries will often take trout in heavily fished lakes when other methods of angling draw a blank. In some of the clear and shallow lakes, and along the shorelines of deep lakes near large centers of population, the fish have been hammered down by constant fishing so that they flee at the sight of hardware. The heavy splash and the brilliancy of brass, silver and mother of pearl get to be warning signs rather than beckoning gestures. True enough, those lures will often make fish mad enough to charge them, but after a while they catch on and the weird assortment of odd shaped and brightly polished jingle bells will wend their way, without hits, through the lake waters.

But a delicately dropped dry fly, tied on the end of a long, fine leader, does not scare them away, and more and more "fished out" lakes are yielding fine catches to fly men who realize this.

To make a consistent catch with dries, you must know how to work the surface flies, and this technique is the same on any lake, anywhere from northern wilderness to city reservoir, and whether the fish being sought is brook, brown or rainbow trout, cutthroat, landlocked salmon, Atlantic salmon or grayling. The fly must be made to imitate all the actions of a downed natural.

The first time I fished at Georgetown Lake near Anaconda, Montana, my fishing partner, Lee Elliott, looked doubtful when I broke out my dry-fly outfit.

"There are a lot of big fish in here," he said. "I've taken plenty of them with spinning tackle. But I've never tried a dry fly."

"A dry will take them if they are hitting at all," I said.

Fisherman-like, we headed for the far side of the lake. In 6 feet of water we looked down at thick weed beds, with patches here and there rearing up to the surface. There was scarcely any breeze, so we let the boat drift.

"I'm going to watch you for a while," said Lee. "I've never seen a dry fly worked on a lake."

I tied a 2X tippet on the end of my leader and put a size 10 gray Wulff on that and threw it out in the direction of one of those weed patches. I let it sit perfectly still for a few seconds, like a natural resting on the surface. Then I made it shiver and shake, like a natural freeing its wings or drying them off. Then I let it rest a second and then gave it a pull so it jumped across the surface a couple of inches, like a downed insect buzzing around a bit. Once again I let it sit still, then made it jump 9 or 10 inches, like a fly deciding to take off and not quite making it. Then I rested it a second and then brought it back in a smooth, even pull across the surface, like a fly really on the way, gathering speed to become airborne.

As I squared away for the next cast, Lee stopped me.

"How did you make that fly come across the surface so smoothly?" he asked.

"By using the 'strip' method of retrieve," I answered. "Strip an arm length of line at a time with your left hand, then, holding the line between thumb and middle finger of the right hand in case of a strike, bring the rod tip upwards for a yard, smoothly, and that continues the evenness of the fly's movement. Then reach for the line again with your left hand and make another strip, and then the rod action again."

With a retrieve like that, the fly can be made to come a long way across the surface without any sign of pause or interruption. Just strip, raise the rod, strip, raise the rod, and so on, for as far as you want to bring the fly toward you.

Lee caught on in a hurry and before the day was out he had taken his share of fish on a dry fly, too. We didn't break any records but we caught enough 3- and 4-pound fish to make it a standout fishing trip. And by using dries we had a grandstand seat when those far-better-than-average fish came up and hit those tantalizing dry flies.

When fish are cruising just under the surface, darting here and there for fallen tidbits, rather than feeding on one spot, I shoot the fly out and drop it 4 or 5 feet in front of them. If the cruiser keeps on coming, I make the fly shiver out there, like a natural drying his wings, and that usually turns the trick in a hurry. If the fish should turn off while the fly is in the air, a good hard jerk as soon as it hits the water will often attract the trout's attention, and if he sees it, he'll rush it fast. If he doesn't see it, then the fly must be carefully retrieved before it is lifted, far from the fish, for the next cast. More trout are scared by an angler ripping 30 to 40 feet of line off the surface than have ever been caught.

All the time I am working the fly, over feeder or cruiser, I try to imagine a trout under it, looking up at it and wondering whether or not to take. By believing and thinking that a fish is under the fly, you can work real enthusiasm into the retrieve, and suddenly he's there.

For fishing the smaller, clear, glassy lakes, an 8-foot fast-action dry-fly rod is best, along with a matching DT-5-F fly line and a 12-foot leader tapered down to 4X. With that outfit a small fly can be cast a goodly distance and still drop like a feather. For bigger lakes where there is a lot of wind, and for casting some of the larger, fluffier, wind-resistant flies, the 8½-foot medium-action fly rod serves better, with a WF-7-F fly line and a 12-foot leader tapered down to a 2X tippet. But if limited to one rod, the smaller one is preferable, and with a heavier tippet it is still possible to throw a line far enough to take plenty of fish.

The 2X tippet is necessary when you are using a big, fluffy fly such as the size 10 or 8 dry, or a skating spider, because a lighter tippet will twist, the twist moving on up into the leader and even sometimes into the fly line. The twist in the leader causes the fly to move erratically on the surface as the twist tries to unwind; or it may result in the tippet covering the fly or bunching around it in such a way as to scare trout from it. Besides that, the twisted leader will become weak and may break when you get a hit.

In the still, clear water of a lake, the leader is doubly important, and the longer and finer it is, the more strikes will come to the fly. Contrary to general opinion, a long leader is not difficult to cast provided that it is properly tapered. Most leaders are too light at the butt section and too heavy at the tippet. The weight and diameter should be where the leader is tied to the line and then the leader should taper down to the fine section. This heavy-to-light taper gives it the guts to shoot out and turn over the fine tippet and the fly (*see* LEADERS).

Because of the way a dry fly is played on lakes, the angler will leave a lot of flies in fish if he sticks to the 4X or 5X tippet, and sometimes it is necessary to choose between more strikes on the lighter tippet and fewer strikes but more fish landed on the heavier one. Usually it is best to start with the light tippet in a lake where you expect the fish to be small, and move to the larger terminal point if necessary.

Probably the most important part of dry-fly fishing on lakes is to have a high-riding line. If the line is heavy and inclined to sink, it is hard to cast, slaps noisily down on the surface, pulls the fly under so that all efforts at imitating a natural are lost in the resultant dunking; and a sinking line delays the strike impulse when you do get a hit, and therefore may cost you a fish. The line should be well greased, as described in the LINES chapter of this book. That is, rub the line dressing on with the fingers, then run the line back through the fingers again to spread the dressing thoroughly and evenly, and then wipe it clean with a cloth.

Fly buoy is also an essential part of lake fishing with dries, or, lacking that, the fly can be greased with line dressing to help it ride high on the surface. A waterlogged dry fly is tough to handle, doesn't have the verve or dash needed to bring strikes, and is both difficult to pick up and to cast.

The best dry flies for lake fishing seem to be the big, high-riding ones, hairwings, hairbodied flies, variants and spiders. This may be more important from the angler's point of view, than from that of the fish, because it is easier to make them perform the way you want them to, and they float better and remain buoyant longer than the small ones. A big fly, properly worked, can be seen a long distance by a trout.

The hairwing flies—the gray, brown, and white Wulffs, are good floaters and have trout appeal, as do the black Wulff and grizzly Wulff. The red variant, the badger variant and the Donnelly's variant are good on lakes and so are Bailey's bi-fly, the Whitecraft and Carmichael's indispensable. The hair-bodied irresistible is also one of the best for lakes. For that matter, any of the flies tied with deerhair bodies float well and handle easily.

Any of the above flies, on hooks from 12 to 6, may fill the bill, but lake fishermen will also need smaller flies, particularly the midges on size 18 and 20 hooks, and flying ants on size 20. Sooner or later he will have to match a hatch of one or both of those tiny insects. And while color does not seem to be as important as size, except that trout in lakes perhaps show a slight preference for darker colors, I always carry just as great a variety as I do for river fishing, and then I am ready for whatever hatch may occur.

On one trip to Canyon Creek Ranch above Melrose, Montana, we were fishing Crescent Lake for rainbows and cutthroat trout. For half an hour we showed all the old reliables to trout that were rising along the shoreline, without a strike. At last I tied on the single hairbodied grasshopper I happened to have in my box. It took a fish on the first cast, and another, and another. Those trout were feeding on grasshoppers that day and they didn't want anything else. I would throw it out, let it sit still a moment, then give it a slight pull my way. They whacked it, and before we were through they had chewed the feathers right off the hook. But we had a nice mess of trout for dinner.

While it is usually possible to judge just what a lake will hold with a fair degree of accuracy, there are many that will pull a surprise on you. Once in Newfoundland I was fishing Serpentine Lake for sea-run brook trout. They had just come up the river and now were rising here and there around the shores of the lake, targets for a size 8 salmon fly, a fluffy-looking gray hackle that rides high on the surface.

I gave it a short jerk and struck as a fish took and I was busy with that 4-pounder for fifteen violent minutes. After that I took three more of the same size. They chewed all the feathers off that fly and I put on a royal Wulff next. I took another fish, and then, on my next cast I let the fly sit still for at least half a minute, then started it back in an even retrieve for 6 feet, then let it sit still again. Once more I started the fly my way and then the water erupted and I struck. A 15-pound Atlantic salmon came flying out like he was shot from a cannon, and that scared me so much that I struck again, with all my strength, and snapped the 3-pound-test leader like it had been a spider's web.

When I had time to get my nerves settled down, I realized that it was perfectly logical that there should be salmon in that lake. They had been in the rivers for a month, now, and more than likely a few would stop in the lake to rest before heading on through the river above.

Not long afterwards I saw another salmon leap clear of the water, a quarter of a mile down the shore. I headed for the spot and on my eleventh cast he took, and then when I set the hook he soared up high, a bright fish of 12 pounds. He fell back in and started for the middle of the lake. I stopped him after 200 feet and he came out again. Then he went off for 100 feet, on a sizzling run that left me shaky. But that effort tired him and I got him headed my way and finally landed him.

Even in such large lakes as Superior you can get some superlative dry-fly fishing if you hit them on a calm day and know where the fish are. The first time I fished Lake Superior, Don Gapen of Nipigon, Ontario, took me out to St. Ignace Island for coasters.

"Coasters are brook trout that have moved out of the rivers and live along the shores of the lake," he explained.

"How big?" I wanted to know.

"They average about 2 pounds," he said. "But it's not unusual to take a 6- or 7-pounder."

We started casting in toward the rocky shoreline. The water was so clear that out there, 60 feet from shore, you could look straight down through 45 feet of water and count the pebbles on the bottom. That first look was enough for me. Even though I knew a big old mossback might wallop my fly, I tied on a longer, finer leader for that clear water.

Don and I both started casting in toward the rocks, let the fly sit there, then gave it a 6-inch jerk, then brought it along the top, evenly. Between us we covered the shoreline pretty well, with never a strike. Then Don pointed.

"There's a rise," he said. "And that's right where the fish should be, over those big rocks."

Inshore we could see the big boulders on the bottom, an ideal place for fish to hang out. I put my fly in there, right at the corner of one of those boulders. A coaster fell on it with a thump and dashed off, making the reel sing. Ten minutes later I landed him, a deep and plump brookie that weighed 2¼ pounds. Before I could get my fly out there again, Don was into one. This baby knew how to fight. It took Don a long time to get him in. He went 3½ pounds, a swell brookie in any water.

For the next hour we had wonderful sport. We took a dozen between us, that 3½-pounder of Don's going top weight.

"Ten more minutes," said Don at 4 o'clock. "Then we'll have to head back to get to camp before dark."

I took a nice 2-pounder. Then I looked up in time to see the water boil, out where Don's fly had been. And right before my eyes, Don's rod jumped out of his hand and I saw him clutch harder at the fly line in his left hand and make a wild grab. He caught the rod before it hit the gunwale of the boat and began to strip in line a mile a minute. But there wasn't anything there. That coaster was probably a mile away, wondering what all the excitement was about.

Don sat down.

"How big?" I asked.

Don opened his mouth but he couldn't talk. He waved his arms wide.

"As big as Lake Superior," he croaked.

And that's the kind of fish you're always expecting, when you float a dry fly over the surface of a big lake.

SKATING SPIDERS

I believe the late Edward Hewitt was the first man to skate a spider for trout. In 1935 he wrote a piece on skating spiders for *Spur Magazine,* titling it "Butterfly Fishing" because he was convinced that trout take the skating spider for a butterfly. And this seems logical because you occasionally see a trout slap the artificial with his tail, as if trying to knock down a butterfly.

He called his big spiders Neversink Skaters, for the famous trout stream where he often fished. His original tie called for a wide hackle, 2 to 2½ inches long, tied on a light wire Number 16 hook, without tail or body. It was big and fluffy, yet delicate, so the angler could make it skip across the surface.

"If I needed to catch a fish to eat and the brownies were down," he once said, "I know the way to bring them up."

He meant the skated spider.

John Atherton, the famed artist, and an expert angler, claimed that if he had to limit himself to only one fly it would be a spider because it would take fish when used as an orthodox dry, or could be skipped when the occasion demanded.

To be completely buoyant and spritely, the skating spider should be tied from the very finest long-fibered throat hackles

To be completely buoyant a skating spider should be tied from prime hackles, usually 1½ to 2 inches in length.

of game chickens, but these are so scarce and expensive that many tyers use second-grade hackles and achieve a good fly that brings plenty of strikes.

Another expert with the spider, Norm Lightner, of Carlisle, Pennsylvania, ties skating spiders with saddle hackles, placing them in the middle of the shank of the hook and shellacking both sides to keep the hackles fast in their moorings and to make them skate better.

Hewitt claimed that any hook larger than size 16 was too heavy for effective skating, and there is no doubt that the 16 is best. But the small hook may straighten out on the hit or when the angler is forced to hold a fish out from running under a brush pile. On big Western rivers anglers use the 12 and 14, and they will skate lightly when properly handled.

A hook with a straight eye is best, or failing that, one with the eye up. A hook with a down eye will pull down as you work it, destroying the lightness.

Hewitt tied his first Neversink Skaters with red and brown hackle wrapped together. Atherton used a badger hackle spider, or a badger and furnace. Others which have been developed are the Adams hackle, all black, black and brown, two black and one brown tied together, all ginger hackle, all honey and all badger. Charlie Fox uses all black, all slate and the Adams hackle combination. He speaks of using skaters tied on size 8 and 10 hooks while fishing for Atlantic salmon. I have used these same large flies to get hits from Atlantic salmon, big brownies, and some good big landlocked salmon in the Traful River in Argentina. While the heavier hook makes these skaters drag a bit, they still get rousing strikes, and you can land the big fish on them.

A well-greased, floating line is the first essential when skating a spider, and both line and leader should be greased too. All this makes for lighter handling and line manipulation, and more buoyancy to the skating movements. Depending on the water you are fishing, when skating a spider you can use a fly rod 8, 8½, 9 or 9½ feet long. I like the longer rod because you can hold it high and give greater skating action to the fly.

For ease in casting the big, wind-resistant spiders, the weight-forward line is best. For the 8-foot rod this would be the WF-6-F; for the 8½-footer, a WF-7-F; for the 9- and 9½-footers, a WF-8-F.

I feel that a heavier line makes for clumsy retrieve and too much water disturbance regardless of how carefully you handle it. The 8-foot rod is a bit too small for bigger waters, and with the larger spiders even the WF-6-F line will not allow you to reach out quite far enough. If I had to stay with one rod, it would be the 8½-foot stick with matching WF-7-F line. With this outfit you can fish small streams as well as bigger rivers with wide pools, and even lakes. In all cases, the double haul is important. It takes all the line speed you can get to cast such wind-resistant flies.

The leader should be from 12 to 14 feet long. Because of the size of the spiders, a very light tippet will twist so badly that it is impossible to fish the fly. A 3X is just about the lightest tippet that can be handled without twist, and since the trout is not as cautious when he spots a big fly speeding across the surface as he is when he looks carefully over a fly, I generally use a 2X tippet.

The angler should throw a spider across and slightly upstream, and retrieve it at once. If the spider lights on its side, a pull of the line or rod tip will get it upright and then a longer pull makes it flit forward. You can occasionally take a fish on an upstream cast, but nowhere nearly as often as the up and across, straight across, or across and slightly downstream. When casting to a fish straight downstream you should throw off to one side and skate the spider across in front of him. When you try to retrieve a straight downstream cast, the fly moves heavily and leaves a trail on the surface.

Once a spider has become waterlogged it will not skate well, but continue to work it in. Often it will come to the top again, but, regardless, be sure to fish it out. A quick yank and pickup would scare any nearby trout.

Never try to respray a wet spider, even one that has dried somewhat. Keep half a dozen fresh ones on hand. You can dry all the used flies overnight, then spray the entire lot again just before your next fishing trip. There are many fly dressings on the market. A silicone which can be sprayed on is best for spiders, to be sure that each little filament is covered.

CHAPTER/5

WET FLY AND NYMPH FISHING FOR TROUT

WET FLIES WERE ORIGINALLY TIED TO REPRESENT CERTAIN dry flies which had been swept beneath the surface and were washing along underwater. They were usually more sparsely dressed, with a flat wing swept backward and lying along the shank of the hook, and with a soft hackle also tied to slant rearward, so that there would be nothing to impede the underwater float of the fly.

With passing time, many underwater flies have been added which do not even attempt to resemble a fly. They are minnows, caterpillars, grubs and so on, and to be perfectly literal, wet flies should therefore include streamers and nymphs. But the method of fishing them is so different that I have made an out-of-hand division, accepting as the average angler does, those classifications which have developed through practical use and common nomenclature.

This chapter, then, deals with those standard wet flies known to nearly every fly fisherman, old standards tied first many, many years ago and still great producers to the point that most wet-fly fishermen seldom bother with any others. These are the old-time flies such as the royal coachman, black gnat, gray hackle with yellow body, gray hackle with red body, brown

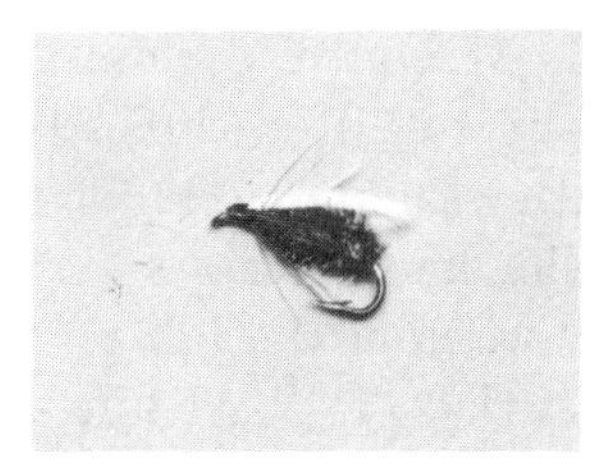

The author's favorite wet fly, the coachman, size 12 (above actual size, right enlarged). Trout find the combination of brown and white difficult to resist.

The wooly worm (left), size 6, is one of the most successful wet flies in use today, especially out West.

hackle, the quill Gordon, light Cahill, McGinty, cowdung, coachman, leadwing coachman, and the ginger quill, tied mostly on hooks ranging from 6 to 12. In recent years fly tyers have had calls for many of these ties on smaller hooks, sizes 14, 16 and occasionally size 18. It is hard to say whether the fish take wet flies in such small sizes for small terrestrials that have fallen into the stream, or for drowned dry flies, or for nymphs. Certainly many of them look more like nymphs, to the human eye at least, especially after they have been used a bit. And the more ragged they become, the more strikes they seem to attract.

Practically all the standard wet-fly patterns do a good workmanlike job. They catch fish and they catch them almost every time you use them. Most wet-fly anglers have a favorite fly which they are sure is deadly poison to the trout population, and with which they do take more fish than with others. There is a simple explanation—they fish that fly more often and they fish it with confidence, and hence they give it everything they have when they show it to a trout. Believing as they do that this is the fly trout have a yen for, they are more alert for the strike, more ready to take full advantage of every opportunity.

My favorite wet fly is a coachman, size 12. I can readily believe that a trout will see that white wing sooner than any other color, I believe that trout like a combination of brown and white, and I am sure that when I retrieve that fly in short jerks, it looks exactly like the small minnows so often found in trout waters.

There are some wet flies that are tied for a certain section of the United States and Canada, such as the wooly worm of the Rocky Mountain states, and the flies tied years ago especially to take wilderness trout, that is, native brook trout, called in various places speckled trout, red trout, brookies, and along the shores of the big lakes, coasters. Often referred to as Canadian flies, or Northern flies, these include the professor, royal coachman, scarlet ibis, Parmachene belle, brown hackle, gray hackle, Montreal, dark Montreal, March brown, dusty miller, Alexandria, and so on. It used to be that no angler headed for either Maine or Canada without a supply of these, plus that oddity the fontinalis fin, a tie representing the fin of a brook trout, which was often cut from a fish and used as bait.

Besides the standards and the Rocky Mountain and Canadian flies, there are quite a number of wet flies tied today with rubber bodies and hair hackles. These are used mostly in the West, where they are known as the "rubber-bodied hair-hackle flies," but they are beginning to come into use elsewhere, too. They are tied in many delicate colors with segmented bodies that look translucent, and are shaded from light color underneath to darker backs. I hate to use the word to a fly fisherman, but they have a very "wormy" look, and they surely are excellent trout getters.

The Mite flies, developed by F. B. Potts of Missoula, Montana, have hair hackles and hair or silk bodies with a bright-colored silk stripe laced into the bottom. They are easy to cast and look alive in the water. You can fish them like any other wet fly, but I like to cast them across current, mend my line, and let them float straight downstream on a slack line for several feet before imparting action to them, then bring them back in a series of short jerks. You will get hits throughout any part of this float and retrieve. A Western angler should never be without these fine flies.

Just as with dry flies, a wet fly that is good in one part of the country is usually effective in other parts, too, so that any division into Eastern and Western flies is impossible. However, there are a few ties entirely Western that are a bit too big for Eastern fishing. This group could really be called bi-flies because they can be fished either wet or dry. In fact many fishermen use them as a dry for the course of the downstream float then yank them beneath the surface and bring them back in short jerks, as a wet fly. Outstanding among these ties are the Joe's hopper, Bailey's bi-fly, the sofa pillow and that hot Colorado tie, the sure strike special.

Perhaps the all-time great Western wet fly is the wooly worm. Many Rocky Mountain anglers will tell you that the wooly worm is the one and only fly for that part of the country. It is tied in many sizes and colors and combinations of colors. The orange and black with a few sprigs of white mixed with the black at each end is probably the best of the lot, being a true imitation of the wooly bear, a caterpillar which appears in the fall. Weather prophets claim to be able to foretell the severity of the coming winter by the width of the orange band around the wooly bear's middle. Regardless of the width of the band, the trout bust it with vigor and it is one of the most successful wet flies in use today.

There are certain of the wets which should form the basis of the fisherman's fly book. These will give him a start, wherever he fishes, to be added to as he discovers the natural food of the fish in the stream and learns of the patterns which local fishermen are finding successful at the moment, or which have proved to be consistent fish takers over the years.

As with dries, I give the ten I would choose, could I have no others:

GRAY HACKLE, YELLOW BODY, SIZE 10
BROWN HACKLE, SIZE 10
COACHMAN, SIZE 12
ROYAL COACHMAN, SIZE 12
BLACK GNAT, SIZE 14
QUILL GORDON, SIZE 14
BLUE DUN, SIZE 16
LIGHT CAHILL, SIZE 16
MARCH BROWN, SIZE 12
GINGER QUILL, SIZE 16

And for further reference, I append a list of patterns and sizes with which a wet fly man could go anywhere and be reasonably sure of taking his share of fish.

STANDARD WET FLIES, *hook sizes 8 to 16*

ALDER	ROYAL COACHMAN
ALEXANDRIA	COWDUNG
BLACK GNAT	DENISON
BLACK PRINCE	MONTREAL
BLACK QUILL	WHITE MILLER

OLIVE QUILL	LORD BALTIMORE
GINGER QUILL	COLONEL FULLER
CAHILL	MCGINTY
LIGHT CAHILL	DUSTY MILLER
IRON BLUE QUILL	FLIGHT'S FANCY
BEAVERKILL	GRIZZLY KING
BLUE DUN	HARE'S EAR
BLUE BOTTLE	LARAMIE SPINNER
BROWN HACKLE, PEACOCK	MARCH BROWN
BROWN HACKLE, YELLOW	MOSQUITO
GRAY HACKLE, RED	MORMON GIRL
COACHMAN	PROFESSOR
LEADWING COACHMAN	YELLOW SALLY

RUBBER-BODIED HAIR HACKLE FLIES, *hook sizes 8 to 12*

GRIZZLY BEAR	GRIZZLY BEAR HONEY
HONEY BEAR	FUZZY BEAR ORANGE
BLACK BEAR	BADGER YELLOW
BLACK BEAR ORANGE	BROWN

SPECIAL WET FLIES

MIDGE SNOW FLIES, *hook sizes 14 and 16, 5X short shank hooks*

BLACK QUILL	OLIVE QUILL
BLUE QUILL	MOSQUITO
GINGER QUILL	

WOOLY WORMS,* *hook sizes 4 to 12*

BLACK	ORANGE
YELLOW	TRUE WOOLY BEAR (BLACK AND ORANGE)
GRAY	PEACOCK

* Can be tied with weighted bodies, also with turned down eye or with ringed eye for spinners.

HAIR HACKLE FLIES, THE MITES, *sizes 6 to 12*

SANDY MITE	BLACK FIBBER
LADY MITE	YELLOW FIBBER
MR. MITE	ROCK WORM
BUDDY MITE	FIZZLE

FISHING THE WET FLY

The wet fly is at once the hope of the beginner and the veteran. There are many old-timers who will use nothing else, for wet flies have paid off for them over the years with some mighty big fish that seldom rise to dries. And the novice, providing he can wade to within easy reach of a current where fish are likely to lie, and can heave the fly out there to drift in the current, can usually manage to hang a trout, even though his method may involve more dunking than finesse.

Nevertheless, to really fish a wet fly with the greatest success calls for a knowledge of fish lies, their feeding habits and the ability to cast the fly to the greatest advantage. With the exception of those times when a wet fly is played to imitate a moving bit of food, such as a minnow or shrimp or nymph, it seems to me that the one big thing with wets as with dries, to get consistent hits, is the free float, without any semblance of drag. Therefore, the up-and-across cast pays off best. With that presentation, the fly should float along naturally with the current and the trout will rise to it much as they do to a dry fly, thinking it is what it's meant to be, a downed fly, floating downstream.

On the up-and-across cast I allow the fly to float motionless for almost the complete length of its downward swim, until it begins to swing in below me in the current. Then I often manipulate the rod tip so that it will cause the fly to hop forward in a series of short jumps, a couple of inches at a time, and continue that technique until the fly is directly below me in the water, and then I bring it my way for 10 or 12 feet before lifting it as quietly as possible from the water.

This up-and-across-stream cast permits delivery without letting the fish see the angler. Since fish usually lie facing into the current, the angler is far enough below, or off to the side from them that they will not so readily spot him. It's true that a good wader can get into the stream and fish a wet fly on down and scarcely disturb the fish except for the ones he drives off their feeding stations as he wades. But the average angler is usually too noisy in his wading, waves his arms too much, and makes no effort to hide, so the fish can hardly avoid seeing him. Sometimes I wonder that many of them catch a fish at all, because they start at the head of the pool, standing on a rock or a bank high above the water, in plain view of any trout within 50 feet. And since the trout's eyes are aimed upward anyway, that wet-fly man is at a great disadvantage before he even starts to fish.

But in such a situation a wet fly cast straight upstream, from farther down, would have brought him hits from the very fish that thus spot him. In using the straight upstream cast in fast water, however, a very short line must be thrown in order to be able to retain any control and be ready to strike. A cast of 25 or 30 feet is plenty long enough, and then the line should be stripped at approximately the same speed at which the current is riding the fly down towards the angler—and as he raises the rod, he is then ready for the strike or for the pickup for the next cast.

Sometimes when trout seem to be lazy, they can be stirred into striking by throwing the wet fly across the current and then bringing it back at once in a series of foot-long jerks, much as a streamer fly is fished. This is one of the times when I am convinced the fish hits the fly as a minnow, not a fly.

When using the across-current cast, the line must be mended and the fly led down with the rod tip ahead of the line (*see* FLY FISHING FOR ATLANTIC SALMON). With that method the angler has good control of the line, avoiding a belly that would delay his strike to the fish; and the fly is presented broadside so the fish has a better view than if it were hurtling down head or tail first. Then, when the fly starts to swing in below, it can be given motion by imparting short jerks which should attract a trout's attention and cause him to go for it.

Another almost sure-fire method to get a hit on a wet fly is to let it float for several yards, then give it motion for a couple of feet, then stop the strip and let the fly float free in the current again. What the trout thinks of this one is any man's guess, but it may be that he mistakes the feathery fooler for a fly still struggling, or a wounded minnow, floating, fighting to regain his equilibrium, floating and fighting.

Whichever retrieve seems to be the payoff of the day, that is the one to stick to that day, as trout appear to follow a pattern in this. Once I have found out what they want I stay with it till they stop hitting, and then I try something else. And regardless of how the fly is played, it must be played with confidence. With a dry fly, the angler knows what the fly is doing, and if the fish are rising he knows they are there. With a wet fly he must *believe* that the fly is doing what it should be doing, and he must *believe* the fish are there. He must be convinced that they're down there just waiting to knock the hackles off his fly.

Most anglers fish far too fast, passing up chance after chance because they do not figure the water before they start. Every pool and run should be figured out and a pattern set for casting. This not only makes for more pleasant and leisurely fishing, it brings a better harvest from the water.

For instance, sometimes I spend more than an hour fishing a pool 100 feet long. But I cover all the water starting my first cast up and across current and not too far from me. I fish that cast through the length of the float and then make my next throw a couple of feet farther out. And so on, until I have fanned well out, 60 feet or more, and the fly has gone over practically any lie of a trout within that area. Then I move to a point just below that covered by my first series of floats, and repeat. This is the drop system of fishing a wet fly for Atlantic salmon and it is equally effective for trout. It pays off. It covers all the water and when you are through you are likely to find that you have picked up a couple of fish from spots you might ordinarily have overlooked.

To fish a wet fly properly calls for just as much, or even more, finesse than fishing a dry fly. A dry fly is easier to cast, the angler can see all the action, including the strike. But the wet fly is comparatively heavy and does not have the balance, the padding, so to speak, of the hackles of the dry, to set it down lightly and quietly. The hackles are tied facing backwards and are sparse, and therefore the fly comes down more heavily.

An up-and-across cast pays off. Fish has just struck and started away. Left hand helps play fish by stripping line. *Photo by Bill Browning.*

One thing that will help the beginning fly caster is a nicely tapered leader and one that is long enough to take up a lot of the shock of the heavy wet fly, allowing the lighter delivery that is a sure aid to getting strikes. Yet the majority of wet-fly fishermen seem to gravitate to unnecessarily heavy leaders and many a wet-fly addict I meet on the stream is all set up with a short, 6-foot leader running as high as 20-pound test. Even though in some circumstances, such as very heavy water, the fish might not spot this atrocity, the heavy leader hurts the action of the fly. A 9-foot, or preferably a 12-foot leader, would get many more strikes, especially when the water is clear. And for almost any trout, regardless of size, a 6-pound-test tippet should be more than adequate. For average fishing, the tippet can be almost as fine for wet-fly fishing as for dry. And certainly these calibrations are far less noticed by the fish.

Once on Slate Run in Pennsylvania, a good stream for small trout, I ran into a wet-fly fisherman coming down the creek. We stopped and talked awhile, and as we talked, a trout rose across from us.

"Why don't you show him that wet?" I asked.

"Oh, they won't hit a wet when they're rising," he said. "I've tried."

"As far as that goes," I said, "I've fished a dry over risers for many an hour and not caught them. Anyhow, throw it over there and give it a try."

As he got ready to cast I noticed that he was using a leader tippet that must have gone about 20-pound test. He didn't even get a flash in ten casts.

"See?" he said at last.

"Give me that fly," I said. When he took it off and handed it to me, I tied it on the end of my 4X tippet.

"Try this," I said, handing the rod to him.

He hemmed and hawed and said he couldn't cast such a leader as that 12-footer, and the whole thing was too light for him, and so on.

But his first cast went out there perfectly and dropped the size 12 black gnat he had been using just right. The trout took on that first float and came struggling out, a nice 12-incher.

That man looked at me as if he couldn't believe it.

When landing your trout, push rod well back to pull him in to you. *Photo by Bill Browning.*

"It's nothing but the leader," I said. "The fish can see the one you've been using."

It isn't often that you have such a chance to show how important the smaller leader can be. Or the trout may be selective and feeding on only one type of fly that happens to be emerging, but they will still take time out to sock a wet if it is presented to them right. Maybe it resembles the nymph of the fly they are taking, or maybe it just looks good, but either way, it's well worth while to cast your wet among the surface feeders.

The exception to the light leader rule comes when the fly is being retrieved in fast, foot-long jerks, in water where a heavy trout might hit in the middle of a strip and break the tippet. But the angler will have so many more strikes on light gear that even in such water it is more fun to keep the wet-fly leader down to a fine terminal point and take the chance of losing a fly or two.

Probably because they are fishing blind, rather than to specific fish, or rising fish, all too many wet-fly anglers fish in a hit or miss fashion.

Selection of the wet fly to be used is more a matter of chance than is the case with dry flies, where the angler sees the natural and the fish rising to take it right before his eyes. But many times a careful study of the stream will reveal flies floating down, or bugs or insects which can be matched with a certain wet fly, if not in exact conformation, then at least in color and size. And once a fish has been landed, it is easy to open him up and examine the contents of the stomach and quickly determine what is the main item on the menu that day.

FISHING NYMPHS FOR TROUT

The nymph is the underwater stage of an aquatic fly. Nymphs spend two to three years living under rocks on the bottom of the stream, encased in a sort of shell, then at various times they struggle to the surface, break their cases, and emerge as flies. Nymphs appear in many different forms, some flat-bodied, some round-bodied, and others appear to have built little houses around themselves, or put up nets to catch food.

Nymphs differ in the way they act prior to emerging as flies. Some crawl out on the rocks, while others go up the reeds alongshore and when the fly appears it lays its eggs there. When the eggs hatch, the little creature that is born crawls down the reed again to hide itself in the mud till it is time for the cycle to begin all over again. Still other nymphal forms are often seen floating downstream, riding along the surface as the fly works out of its shell and finally breaks free and flies away—if some hungry trout doesn't get it.

And so it goes, through a vast array of underwater forms of life which for fishing purposes we class together as nymphs. As a result of the great variety, it takes a close study of nymphs to match them with artificials and the tying of good nymphs is one of the most difficult phases of fly tying. Some of the products turned out are also the prettiest things in a fly man's book.

Since the nymph is usually underwater when the fish takes it, or barely to the surface, it should carry a little more weight than dries, and most commercially tied nymphs are weighted. In the case of some of the lighter, unweighted ones, however, anglers

A good collection of nymphs will include representations of many forms. Top row, left to right: brown bomber, black creeper, caddis larva, leadwing coachman, cream nymph, March brown, hellgramite, Zug bug. Second row: mosquito larva, green caddis, breadcrust, light Cahill, black midge, dark Hendrickson, Grande stone, dragon nymph. Bottom row: Gay's grub, Montana, golden quill, damsel. *Courtesy of The Orvis Co.*

frequently pinch on a split shot about a foot above the fly if it becomes necessary to get them down to reach a feeding fish.

While many private tyers turn out nymphs of their own design, commercial tyers in the eastern part of the country, where nymph fishing has a longer history than in the West, concentrate on the well-known light stone fly, yellow May fly, March brown, Tellico, ginger quill, brown drake, black and yellow, orange and black, black and the Ed Burke, all tied on sizes from 10 to 14. The smallest nymph I have ever been able to find was tied on a size 16 hook, but certainly there are naturals which would be matched with a size 18 or even 20, if these were available on the market.

On the other end of the line are such really big ones as the Western stone flies, called by various names—salmon, trout and willow fly—often so large that they are tied on number 6 long-shank hooks. Rocky Mountain tyers have done an imaginative job of imitating natural nymphs. Dan Bailey of Livingston, Montana, turns out a large stone fly nymph on a 2X long, number 8 hook, that is more natural looking than the natural. It is best in the early season while the big hatch is on, but will produce well all year. Some of the best Western nymphs in larger sizes are the Bailey's May fly nymph, caddis fly, the cross guinea, dark olive and cream May fly, all tied on 10 and 12 hooks. Tied on long-shank hooks in sizes 6 to 10, the light mossback with light olive and cream body is a good producer, and the dark mossback with body of dark olive and yellow is one of the best nymphs I've ever fished.

The first dark mossback I ever tried was handed to me by Dan Bailey, who invented this particular tie. He told me he thought it was one of the best early-season nymphs in the West. I started using it and kept taking fish. I tried it in August and September and up to mid-October and throughout all that time I had wonderful luck with it. About that time I went out one day with Dan and we tried the Yellowstone River about 20 miles upstream from Livingston. Dan started about halfway down a 200-yard-long pool and I moseyed on up to the top. I used the dark mossback and was into a good fish at once. I took four in a row and the last one went 3 pounds, a deep-bodied, high-jumping rainbow.

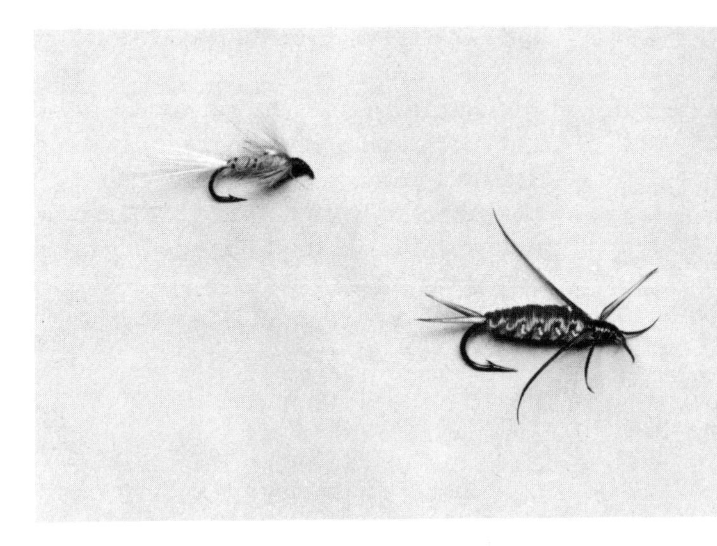

Two favorite nymphs—little May (left) and light mossback.

I noticed that Dan wasn't doing much, and then I saw him walking my way, well back from the river. Then he came out in back of me.

"What are they hitting?" he asked.

"The dark mossback," I said. "They've been hitting it all summer and fall, too. In fact, ever since you gave me that one last spring, I've been cleaning up with them."

Dan laughed. "That's typical. I tie the fly but I don't have the first one with me."

I gave him a couple from my box and he went back to his former position and took a fish on his first cast.

Potts of Missoula ties the Sandy Mite, Lady Mite, Mr. Mite and Buddy Mite, in sizes 6 to 12, to represent nymphs familiar in that area. These are hair hackle ties with either hair or silk bodies with bright colored silk strips laced into the bottom. The hackle hairs are shaped around the hook. And another Western favorite that has proven out elsewhere is the gray nymph in sizes 6 to 12, with a heavy, fuzzy body of muskrat fur, gray hackle and badger tail.

Nymphs which take fish both in the East and the West and which should always be in the angler's fly box are the caddis, the Hewitt nymphs, the flat-bodied nymphs in gray and black, and the nymph tied with gray fur body. The little black nymph tied on a number 12 hook is a good one, too. These should be carried in sizes from 8 to 18. And now and then the larger yellow and gray nymphs on size 6 hooks will also take plenty of fish in the bigger rivers.

Nymphs which should appear in the trout fisherman's box are:

NYMPHS (WEIGHTED AND UNWEIGHTED)

HOOK SIZES 8 TO 16

ALDER
BLACK AND ORANGE
BLACK AND YELLOW
CADDIS
MARCH BROWN
BROWN DRAKE
GINGER QUILL
TELLICO

HOOK SIZES 10, 12, 14 AND 16, 2X LONG-SHANK HOOK

YELLOW MAY
TAN MAY
BLACK MAY
OLIVE MAY
BROWN MAY
GRAY MAY

SPECIAL NYMPHS

HOOK SIZES 6 TO 12

GRAY NYMPH
FRESH WATER SHRIMP
TAN SHRIMP NYMPH, PINK STRIPE
OLIVE SHRIMP NYMPH, PINK STRIPE

DAN BAILEY'S NATURE NYMPHS—*Hook sizes 4 to 10, and 12 long-shank*

LIGHT MOSSBACK	LIGHT OLIVE AND CREAM
DARK MOSSBACK	DARK OLIVE AND YELLOW
BLACK MOSSBACK	BLACK AND DARK OLIVE

NYMPHS (WEIGHTED)

LARGE STONE FLY NYMPH	2X LONG-SHANK NO. 8
LARGE MAY FLY NYMPH	2X LONG-SHANK NO. 10
CADDIS FLY NYMPH	2X LONG-SHANK NO. 10
MARCH BROWN NYMPH	2X LONG-SHANK NO. 12
DARK OLIVE NYMPH	2X LONG-SHANK NO. 12
CROSS GUINEA NYMPH	2X LONG-SHANK NO. 10
ED BURKE NYMPH	2X LONG-SHANK NO. 12
MONTANA NYMPH	4 AND 6
TELLICO NYMPH	8 AND 10

Whenever anyone says to me, "There are lots of trout in there, but you can't catch them," I reach for my box of nymphs. That's what happened one day a couple of summers ago when I was standing with Randy Skelton looking over the slough back of his grandad's Rock Creek Lodge near Missoula, Montana.

"They're too hard to catch," Randy was explaining to me. "You can always see them feeding, but hardly anyone can catch them."

I soon saw why. It was a lovely stretch of stream with long grasses waving slowly in the quiet motion of the crystal clear water. Gravel beds showed wherever the current moved a little faster. It was the kind of water that calls for 12-foot leaders tapered down to 4X or maybe 5X or 6X. Trout were bulging all over the surface. But obviously this was no dry-fly deal. Those fish were nymphing.

Searching the water near the shore, I found several small gray nymphs. That's what I wanted to discover. Betting that they were the dish right now, I dug out a gray nymph, size 14, that was a good match for the naturals I had spotted. I added another 16-inch 4X tippet to my already 12-foot-long leader. Just before casting I greased the leader down to about 3 inches from the end, then applied leader sink to the last 3 inches. I wanted the entire line and leader to float, except for just enough of the tippet end to allow the nymph to swim an inch or so under the surface.

"Why will they take a nymph when they won't take a dry fly?" Randy wanted to know, as I explained to him what I was doing.

"The same old trout trick," I said. "Selective feeding. They're working on nymphs, taking them right *under* the surface, and they won't look at anything that's riding on top. That's why sometimes you can't catch trout with dry flies even though the air is thick with naturals. They're taking the nymphs before the flies emerge."

"Watch those fish out there," I went on. "Look hard and you'll see that they aren't slapping into flies riding on top, or breaking the surface the way they do when they suck in a fly. The water seems to bulge up, instead."

That meant they were grabbing those nymphs just before they reached the surface, and as they turned their bodies on the take, they put up a swirl that made the water move up, or bulge. Once an angler has seen that and recognized it for what it is, he can nearly always spot the difference between bulging fish and those that are taking surface flies.

Those trout were working about 40 feet out in the current where it ran over gravel smack alongside of a patch of water cress. I dropped the nymph a couple of feet above where I'd seen a rise, stripped in the slack, then held the rod tip slightly ahead of the floating line. With the last 3 inches under water, the line and leader drifted along, acting as a float, sort of bobber. I knew the nymph was right where I wanted it, 2 inches under water, moving a bit with the eddies, lifelike.

It floated along. No strike. It went on down, reached the end of the float and then swept across the current towards my bank. I raised the rod tip to a 40-degree angle and began to impart

The Navas brown nymph, tied in Argentina.

short jerks to the line by manipulating the tip. After a foot of that, I let the nymph float free again for a foot, then gave a few more jerks, to imitate the action of a natural nymph struggling to reach the surface, then picked it up and sent it back to the same place it had started from.

This time it didn't go far. I saw the leader jerk forward, raised the rod tip and was into a good fish. He tore downstream, back showing, then busted out in a long, splashy jump. What with his jumping and the hazards of grass beds in that slough, he gave me a rough ten minutes before I finally landed him. He turned out to be a beautiful 2-pound rainbow trout.

Many times when fish are feeding on nymphs, the operation is not quite as obvious as when they are bulging, as they were that day on the slough behind Rock Creek Lodge. Sometimes they are feeding deep, tails up, nosing out nymphs from the gravel, pushing them out from under rocks, then snatching them. If the water is fairly shallow, you can see the whole procedure, but if it is slightly deeper, then all the angler can spot is the flash of their sides as they work.

Trout are just as selective in their choice of nymphs as they are in feeding on dry flies and many times the angler must match the hatch or go hitless. Usually, however, by careful study of the water he can discover what nymph it is that the fish are taking. Or if he has landed a fish he can open it and soon determine what is the main diet of the day. Dump the contents of the stomach into clear water, stir with a knife or a pencil, and the nymphs upon which the fish has been feeding will float free and the angler can then try to match them with something from his fly box.

In one of his great books on fishing, Hewitt said that an expert nymph fisherman could clean out a trout stream. That statement is so true that probably the only saving feature is that there are not many good nymph fishermen. Most of them seem to think that nymphs can be presented to trout without stealth and that all that is necessary is to cast them out and let them ride down with the current. It's true that the occasional fish will be taken that way, but to be consistent and make the most of those situations that call for a nymph, the angler must use special tactics.

Sometimes fish will hit only nymphs floating free in the current, and other times they will only take an artificial that matches the struggles of the natural nymph swimming to the top to emerge as a fly. Therefore, sometimes the nymph should be allowed to float as a wet fly, and again it should be moved fast, in jerks, right under the surface. And other times it may be thrown upstream and allowed to float down much as a dry fly, only deeper. At such times strikes are very hard to see, and the angler must almost sense them, or strike every time the line seems to hesitate as if a fish had mouthed the fly. Now and then it will be bottom or gravel, but it pays to strike anyway.

While nymphs are usually fished just under the surface, there are many times when it is necessary to get down into deeper holes, and for this reason, many nymphs are weighted so that they sink slowly. Those who tie their own nymphs can soon discover how much weight to add for best results—usually the amount is very slight and therefore does not interfere with casting.

In deep pools, the nymph should be cast well upstream so it will sink as it comes down with the current. By the time it reaches the angler it will be deep enough to be spotted by the trout. Both leader and nymph always seem to float on top when you want them to go down, and sometimes a good stiff jerk on the line is needed to make the nymph sink, even though there is some danger of disturbing the pool by the commotion. A lot more trouble, but worth the effort, is the application of leader sink to the entire leader. If you are caught on the stream without a commercial leader sink, mud will do the trick, or if you have already landed a fish, then the slime from it will serve even better. And that old saying "Spit on the bait for luck" is no idle talk, either. Spittle on the nymph will also help to put it down.

Lots of times in deep water you never do see the fish working and then all you can do is float the nymph through the pool, deep, watching the line for signs of a strike. If you feel you are not getting down deep enough, a wrap-around lead or a pinch of split shot on the leader will get the nymph down. With that much extra weight, you will think you are getting hit after hit, when most of the time it is just the nymph catching on the bottom. But when trout are nosing into the bottom you can really cash in by letting a weighted nymph roll along and bounce off the rocks. You have to strike every time you feel anything on the line, and every time the line stops, but if it's a fish instead of a rock, you have him.

CHAPTER/6

TERRESTRIALS

TERRESTRIALS INCLUDE ANTS, BEETLES, DADDY LONG legs, houseflies, inch worms, Japanese beetles, grasshoppers and jassids—and many other insects that are born on the land and become trout food when they blow, fly, fall, crawl or jump into the water. They often come late in the season after the aquatic hatches have had their day, and they come on strong. There is something about a terrestrial that appeals mightily to a trout, be it the juicy crispness of the grasshopper, the tart taste of the ant, or the pepper speck on the tongue, the tiny jassid.

Grasshoppers are perhaps the oldest of the terrestrials used by fly fishermen. In some of our Western states the grasshopper, fished either wet or dry, is liked so much that very little else is used, other than the wooly worm. Even in this day of more sophisticated approach to trout, and better materials for tying, the old, beat-up 'hopper still takes its deadly toll. There are several different ties of this great fly, the Joe's Hopper, first tied by a Michigan barber, being the most popular.

I have always found grasshoppers particularly good on windy days. I'll never forget one time when I was fishing the Clark Fork of the Columbia River with Bruce Elliott of Rock Creek Lodge, near Clinton, Montana, and Russ Ward, Missoula tackle dealer. As we walked the grass banks looking for a good spot to cast, the wind began to blow up strong. Its sharp gusts swept a myriad of grasshoppers off the long grasses by the river and blasted them into the stream, where they drifted, struggling on the surface. Within half a minute trout were rising all along the bank, snatching at them. We put on Joe's Hoppers and what a couple of hours we had!

Ants run grasshoppers a close second, in the terrestrial line. I have used a size 20 flying black ant, dry, for many years and still call it my favorite on limestone streams, and indeed, on almost any type of stream. The smaller ants are used dry, especially those tied on small-sized hooks, such as 18, 20 and 22. The larger ants are generally fished wet, at varying levels beneath the surface. I always like to have in my box the follow-

Typical terrestrials the fly fisherman uses, top row, left to right: cinnamon ant, black jassid, brown jassid. Middle row: Letort cricket, Letort hopper. Bottom row: black fur ant, inch worm, beetle. *The Orvis Co.*

ing ants: wet, in hook sizes 8 to 20, black, red, black and red, and white; dry, in hook sizes 18, 20 and 22, black, brown, and cinnamon.

The size 12 black ant tied by the Phillips Fly and Tackle Company of Alexandria, Pennsylvania, is one of the best wet flies I have ever used.

Many times when weather, or muddy water, or feeding habits, were keeping fish down, ants have saved the day for me. One such day, Dan Bailey and I hit the Yellowstone when the water was still high and roily after a hard rain.

"It's clearing," said Dan. "But it's not ready for dry flies yet."

He moved on upstream, while I went right in where I was. I soon spotted a few ants drifting by. Some place up above, the flash storm had washed a colony of them into the river. They looked like a choice item for trout and I took the cue. I dug into my fly box and picked out a black ant, size 12. I was busy tying it on the end of a 3X tippet, attached to a 10-foot leader, when Dan called to me.

"Try an ant," he suggested, pointing to the river. He had spotted them, too.

We both got busy. Trout seemed to be everywhere and we caught them consistently. They all acted so hungry that I decided to see what else they would hit. I put on a yellow wooly worm, took one fish on it, and then didn't get another strike for twenty casts. I put on a royal coachman, size 12, wet. I made fifteen casts. No strikes. I tried a leadwing coachman. No soap. Here were three of the best-known wet flies on the Yellowstone River and trout didn't want them. I hastened to tie on the black ant again and in four casts I hung two trout, landed one, lost one. It was ants they wanted.

When fishing an ant, I usually use the same technique as in fishing a wet fly for Atlantic salmon. I start with a cast of about 12 feet, thrown across and slightly upstream, mend the line and as the ant reaches the end of the downstream float, I bring it back across the current in short jerks for about 3 feet, let it swim free for a couple of feet, then repeat the jerks. At the end of the swing through, when the ant is directly below me, I strip it my way for about 3 feet, again with jerks, then pick it up for the next cast. This time I lengthen the throw a foot,

The black ant (right actual size, below enlarged) can save the day at times, when fish turn down other artificials. They're especially productive in high-altitude lakes.

repeat the same procedure as before, and continue thus, lengthening each cast till all the near water has been covered. Then I move downstream to about the farthest point where the ant has worked and begin the series of casts all over again.

But if the fish are passing up such a presentation, there are other ways of getting to them. A short cast straight across current, then a retrieve in short jerks just under the surface, will often get a hit. And when fish are rising, sometimes they will not hit a drifting ant but a cast across and a couple of feet above a riser, brought back in 8- or 9-inch jerks, will get that baby nearly every time.

A few days after I had fished with Dan, I hit the Yellowstone again, this time with Edwin and Allen Nelson. It was clear and fish were rising, taking naturals. We fanned out and started to fish and soon I saw Edwin hook a nice cutthroat on a dry. A pair of rainbows fell in succession to my big number 10 hair-wing royal coachman as it danced along the waves of a fast ripple. They looked like brother and sister, both 14-inchers. It was a good start.

Then a fast-moving black cloud dropped its burden, putting the fish down and making us run for the willows. After the rain stopped, the wind came up. It scuffed the surface, making for very poor dry-fly fishing. We only landed one fish in the next hour. Finally we joined forces, compared notes.

"I like a wooly worm," said Allen, showing me the gray one he had just tied on. "They really catch fish."

"You're right," I agreed. "But have you ever tried this?" I showed him a black ant with a red tail, tied on a number 10 hook.

"There's something that really takes 'em," I said. "It's as hot as a Yellowstone geyser."

"I still like the wooly worm," he said. But he pocketed the ant just the same.

Ed and I went back to dropping our dry flies on the surface, while Allen moved upstream. Suddenly we heard him yell.

"Yippee!" he shouted. We saw a pound and a half rainbow flash in the air.

"Yippee!" he shouted again, as the crimson-streaked jumping jack reached upwards for a second time.

We watched him land the fish, then turned back to our dry-fly fishing again.

"Youie!" we heard him yell, ten minutes later, and we saw another rainbow trying for the moon.

I changed to a big dry fly, then a small one. Edwin was busy tying on different flies, too, but none of them got action. At last we gave in.

"Sure must be pay day for wooly worms," Edwin shouted to me. "I'm going to put one on."

"Me too," I yelled back.

But fifteen minutes later we were still hitless. Then Allen

really let out a yell. We jerked our heads around in time to see a huge trout thrashing on top. Allen's rod tip snapped back as we watched and Allen turned and started for shore.

"Where are you going?" shouted Ed.

"I'm getting out of here," said Allen. "They're eating me up. And besides that, that last fish took my fly."

As he splashed up to me, I pointed at the lamb's wool on his vest, where he had an assortment of flies showing.

"You've got another wooly worm there," I told him.

"Wooly worms?" he said. "I've been using that black ant you gave me. How about another?"

Edwin and I got ants on in a hurry. After that we had hits and we caught fish from then on out. The trout menu that day consisted of a single, all-in-one dish—black ants.

Ants are good medicine in high-altitude lakes, too, especially for cutthroat. On a pack trip to Charlie White Lake, near Emigrant Peak, Montana, Eleanore and Arnold Schueren and my wife Mary and I fished from the shore to trout that were swirling within easy casting distance. On dry flies we didn't do much, so I shifted to a black ant and those natives went to town. I had such fast and furious action that pretty soon everyone else wanted in. I dug into my fly box and produced what I had—three black, a couple with red tails, and two white ones. I divied up and we all went back to fishing.

We had decided to eat fish for dinner that night, so we were keeping some for that purpose and when there were enough, the women headed back to camp to start the fire. Arnold and I went on fishing, less carefully now, because we had all the fish we wanted—fishing just for the fun of fishing. We hooked into several pretty good ones that took us under the brush and around fallen logs with which the shoreline was littered. By the time we started for camp, we had lost all the ants.

Suddenly as we neared the tents, we heard yells. We rounded the curve in the path in time to see both women wielding frying pans at a totally unperturbed burro that was busily eating up our dinner fish. He was holding one fish headfirst in his mouth and every time he chewed the tail would flap up in the girl's faces. A couple more whacks with the frying pans finally drove Jack off to finish his dinner with the rest of the pack train, and then a quick count showed us the damage. We were short three fish for dinner. We had to go back to the lake, and this time, minus ants, it took us almost an hour to get those three fish.

I remember another time, too, when nothing but ants would take fish in one of those high-altitude lakes. We were 9000 feet up, at Lake of the Woods, in Wyoming. Mary and I were in one boat with Pete Redman of Dubois, while his son, Duane, had a couple of fellows from Texas in another boat.

Duane had told us that there were grayling in this lake.

"But sometimes they're awful hard to catch," he said. "Can't figure it out. They'll be rising all around, but they won't take anything."

I dug into my fly box and found five black ants. I gave him two.

"Try these," I said. "Sometimes they're good in these high-altitude lakes."

They were good that day, all right. Mary and I had great fun taking one grayling after the other. We whooped and hollered as we landed them, removed the ants from their mouths, and put the fish back.

Nothing but a great and gloomy silence came from the other boat. We could see the men casting and casting, but with never a strike. They moved closer to us.

"What are they hitting?" asked Duane.

"Ants," I replied. "Haven't you tried the ones I gave you?"

He shook his head.

"I left them in the jeep," he said. "Can you spare a couple more until we go in for lunch?"

"Sure," I said. "Come on over."

I handed him two more. They pushed off and soon their whoops and hollers were blending with ours. They were into fish, but good.

Similarly, although beetles are an occasional, rather than a regular food for trout, there are times when almost nothing else will do. During the height of the Japanese beetle migrations, I've opened trout whose belly linings were cut clear through with the bites of these insects before they perished.

A couple of years ago I was fishing the Laramie River in Wyoming, on the Lazy W Cross Ranch, near Glendivy. Strikes

The black beetle (left, actual size 18, right enlarged) that hit the jackpot for the author in Wyoming's Laramie River.

were few, and the fish seemed lethargic. Most of those that did show came up slowly and looked the floating fly over carefully, then just nudged it with their noses. I switched to nymphs and if anything, the going was slower. Then I spotted a couple of black beetles floating along. I tied an artificial beetle, black, size 12, on my leader tippet. No hits. Thinking that perhaps those drifting beetles had been dark brown, rather than black, I changed to that color. They scorned the brown beetle, and then a green one. In desperation I put on a size 18, black, and hit the jackpot. For the next half-hour I was busy taking trout. They hit that little beetle like they really wanted it. There wasn't any hesitation, there was no careful scrutiny. They just charged it and took.

Not content with that demonstration, I tied on a size 18 green beetle. They let that color go by. I put on a size 18 brown. They didn't even know it was there. They wanted a size 18 black, and nothing else would do.

Occasionally, when the usual underwater presentations fail to interest trout, I grease all of the leader and the bottom of the beetle with line dressing and let it float on top. At times I bring it back in a smooth, even retrieve that makes the beetle look like the real thing skimming across the surface. It works, too. In fact, the angler who isn't afraid to use a little ingenuity can find some mighty odd but successful ways to fish a beetle.

On one occasion when I was fishing a clear spring lake in Montana with Red Monical, we could see the fish cruising so close to the shore that it was like looking at them through a window pane.

We heard a familiar story. "No one can catch these trout," we were told. "The water is so clear that they see you every time, and won't hit."

One look convinced me that regardless of the fly, those fish would not take anything unless it were on the end of a very long fine leader. This place called for a 12-foot leader tapered to at least 4X. Even with that already set up, I added another 16-inch length of 4X tippet, then put on a size 12 black beetle.

Such slick-water beetle fishing also called for the same greased line and leader as nymph fishing, with the last 3 inches of the tippet treated with leader sink. Quietness, a lightly dropped fly and line, patience to wait before imparting even the slightest motion, careful timing of the retrieve, and a sharp lookout for the very slight leader movement that signifies a strike—these are all even more important in still, clear water than in riffles and ripples.

There was a barely perceptible current and I cast the beetle out and let it float there for at least a minute, then moved it my way, very slowly, in 6-inch jerks, for a couple of feet, then let it stay motionless again for another quarter minute. Then I repeated the jerks and picked it up for the next cast.

I worked the black beetle that way for a few minutes, then, when it didn't get a strike, changed to a green, size 14. Immediately I had a fish. After watching me land it, Red went down the shore a way, to try his luck. When I next saw him, he had a couple of nice fish taken on the same green beetle.

"I had to do some figuring," he said. "I missed several strikes because I couldn't see the line and leader moving when the trout hit. But I fixed those babies. I put on a number 10 hairwing royal coachman, then tied the beetle on an 18-inch length of 4X tippet as a dropper. The hairwing worked like a bobber, and boy, did it bob when those trout hit. I hooked them good, too."

Even if your fly box doesn't contain a single beetle, and the time comes when you suspect that a beetle is what is needed, there is a way to fake one. Once on a small Eastern stream in Maryland, I was using a size 20 dry fly and couldn't make those bulging trout take it. It was a limestone stream and this was my favorite fly, a black flying ant, and they should have liked it. But those nymph-feeding trout wouldn't take it, nor would they take a nymph when I finally gave in and tried several. They rocked the dries as they bulged right beside them, they pushed aside the floating nymphs to get at whatever they were eating. But they would have none of what I offered.

I sat down on a log and pulled out all of my fly boxes. I went through them carefully. Down in one corner of a dry-fly-laden section I spotted a small black beetle, size 18. I scattered flies in all directions as I grabbed that beetle and tied it on the 5X tippet.

And I was right! The first float brought a hard strike and I was so keyed up that I laid back on the rod like I was striking a 100-pound tarpon and left that one and only beetle in the trout's mouth.

Disgusted, I staggered back to my log and again fingered through the fly boxes. Not a beetle or a nymph that looked the least bit like a beetle!

Then I saw a black gnat, size 16. I grabbed that baby like it was peaches and cream, cut the wings off, snipped the tail off, and held it up. It looked almost like the beetle that had just brought such a rousing strike. The third time I floated that makeshift thing over a bulging trout, he took. I set the hook lightly, this time, and fought the fish boldly then, because I knew that I had at least half a dozen black gnats in my box that I could metamorphose into beetles. Nature is wonderful, but sometimes man can do a good job, too. To avoid getting caught as I did, you should always carry a few beetles in hook sizes 8 to 14, in black, brown, bronze and green.

Newest in the terrestrial field is the jassid developed on the Letort River in Pennsylvania and described by its innovator, Vince Marinaro, in his fine book, *A Modern Dry Fly Code*. With the help of Charlie Fox, on whose water on the Letort River the investigation and experimentation were done, Vince observed the jassids in the river and came up with matching artificials which were sensational fish takers.

It was in the natural course of events that the discovery of the jassid in particular, and the development of the use of the terrestrial in general, should have taken place in Pennsylvania; for although there are many such waters in Maryland, Virginia, West Virginia, Kentucky, Missouri and Ohio, the Quaker State is the traditional locale of these unique streams. Emerging out of faults in the limestone along the edge of the freestone, these rivers usually run through lush meadows, meandering quietly along with placid pools and long runs that cut channels through the dense stands of underwater weeds and grasses. The streams are seldom over 60 feet across and most of the pools are less than 80 feet long. However, there is usually a good flow of water, and the angler can pick up fish all along the way, from undercut banks, channels in the grasses, smack in the middle, or in eddies behind surface-matted grass, or the occasional tree root that extends out into the water. The best way, if the river has a good head of trout, is to loaf your way along, upstream, looking for the rings made by risers. This is the fun way, but if they are not rising, then you simply work the good holding water.

These streams are packed with beds of elodea, a dense weed that is the home of all manner of nymphs, cress bugs and other types of trout fodder; and there are many other grasses and weeds which harbor food. During the course of their exploratory work, Vince Marinaro and Charlie Fox became aware of a consistent rise of a particular nature. The fish that came up did not seem to break the surface, but appeared to be bulging, humping and cupping the water, but not breaking it. The rise made a V-shaped form on the surface that slipped down the current and dissolved. At first glance it would appear that they were nymphing, taking the nymphs as they neared the top to ride the surface, break their nymphal shucks and emerge, dry their wings and fly away. But at these times there was no hatch of aquatic flies. The first nymph did not make the surface. Nothing showed. And a steady bombardment of nymphs, cast and fished flawlessly, left those two veterans hitless. Yet the fish went on feeding; on what, the anglers could not see, but always with that characteristic and strange rise form.

The first day that Vince showed me this rise form I noticed that sometimes the V turned into a circle farther downstream.

"That's right," said Vince, when I mentioned this to him, "and if you are not sharp you might miss seeing the V, and cast to the circle, which wouldn't get you a hit because you would be throwing far behind the fish."

How many anglers must have suffered defeat before this same trout behavior on limestone streams, and finally, after throwing the fly box at the rising fish, have gone their way shaking their heads! How many must have searched the water in vain for the fly, or its nymph, on which those trout were feeding! How many have given up, saying "They just won't take anything."

Those rises were really hard to spot. When I was fishing with Vince he had to point them out to me, until I got onto it.

"That's the way it used to be with me," said Vince. "At first I didn't see that rise, or at best, I spotted only the circle drifting down. Then I began to notice the V-shaped rises, always the same, and it seemed to me that there must be something in the water that I couldn't see and that those trout were taking."

"There's one now," Vince said. "Try him."

My leader was 12 feet long and tapered down to a 6X tippet. I tied on a size 22 jassid that Vince handed me. Then I crawled toward the stream bank. Five feet from the water, and from a kneeling position, I made my cast and dropped the fly 5 feet above where the fish had shown. It was hard to follow but I glued my eyes on it, and knowing the line of drift, managed to see the tiny fly, watch it down to where the trout had been working, past that spot, on for 4 more feet. Then I saw movement, a foot below the surface, and suddenly I saw the fish rise right under the fly, and he took. I waited a bit, then raised the rod tip. I was into my first jassid-hooked brown. Working carefully I played him out, and in. Then I gently removed the hook from the corner of his mouth and put him back in the water.

"That's a dividend trout," I said. "There isn't the first show of aquatic insects. No spentwings, nothing that I can see but flat water. Except for those V-shaped rises now and then."

"That's it," said Vince. "Jassids fill the gap."

Early in his investigations, before he knew just what these small insects were, Vince opened trout and found them tightly packed with tiny terrestrials in many different colors. He collected a number and sent them to an entomologist.

"Formerly called jassidae," was the report, "but recently scientists have changed the name to cicadellidae."

Vince chose to use the earlier name, and condensed it to "jassid," and by that title these small insects and their matching flies have gone into angling records.

There are myriads of jassids in many colors, so many that there is no need to tie the artificial in any special hue. Almost any color of hackle will do the trick. Personally I like black best.

When Vince first tied flies to match the natural jassid he had poor results. They were realistic flies, but still those choosy trout passed them up.

It was not until he conceived the idea that with a fly as small as the jassid, perhaps the form was all-important, plus the way those little naturals floated awash. His next step was to tie the fly without a body. He used a flattened junglecock wing, "junglecock nail" fly tyers term it, which made the wings opaque. Now he had the silhouette only, and by clipping a small V on the underpart of the hackle, he produced a fly which would float in the water, rather than on it, awash like the naturals.

He soon found that this was, indeed, the way the trout wanted those jassids. And from then on, he and Charlie were catching fish from waters that seemed fishless to other anglers. It wasn't long before others in the area learned about the jassid, and soon the fly took its rightful place in American angling lore; and has become known wherever trout fishermen meet as one of the great flies of all time.

The jassid calls for special presentation, not so much a long and fine cast as a short and delicate one. From the first silent, creeping approach to the stream to the especially restrained strike, because of the lightness of the tippet, everything must be keyed to the tiny terrestrial. Only a very light tippet will allow the angler to drop such a fly lightly and loosely, will allow the tippet to float with a minimum of friction or water disturbance.

For those who aspire to tie the jassid, here is the pattern:

JASSID

BODY:	Tying silk, any color.
WINGS:	One medium to small junglecock nail, any color.
HACKLE:	Two or three, very small, turned as for a ribbing hackle. Any color, as short-fibred as possible.
HOOK:	20 short or 22 regular, model perfect.

The method of tying the jassid is very much the same as that used in tying any of the small beetles, except that the materials used are limited to tying silk, junglecock nail and hackle, all used sparingly. First tie in the hackle and wind the front, then spiral hackle front, turning the hackles one at a time in open turns, as for a ribbing hackle, and tie off at the neck. Next, clip the hackle, top and bottom, so that the fly has a low-riding appearance, as does the natural. This tie allows maximum support with the fewest possible fibers, 2½ turns being quite sufficient for a jassid to float beautifully.

Another good terrestrial is the daddy long legs. I remember using one of these with great luck in the Omme River in Denmark. When I first looked at that tule-lined, glassy water, I felt convinced that the smallest of flies would be what I needed. I tried them, pattern after pattern, without success. Then Sven Saaby, a well-known Danish artist, came along. He handed me a couple of daddy long legs.

"This is the best fly on the river," he said.

They were large, sparsely tied, on a size 12 hook.

I dropped my first cast into a run along the bank and watched it float serenely along. Then I saw the snout of the trout as he inhaled and I lifted my rod tip. Although I knew he was large when I saw his nose, I could hardly believe it when he came out and really showed me his size. He fought like the 3-pounder he was, but I finally pulled him over the landing net.

CHAPTER/7

FISHING STREAMERS AND BUCKTAILS FOR TROUT

A STREAMER IS A FLY TIED WITH LONG WINGS OF FEATHers and a bucktail is a similar fly tied with hair wings. The original streamers and bucktails were designed to look like minnows going through the water and many were tied to match the long time favorite patterns of wet flies, the royal coachman, the coachman, black gnat, grizzly king, yellow Sally, and so on down the list of conventional and proven patterns.

Most of the streamers and bucktails are tied on size 8 and 10 long-shank hooks, with sparsely dressed wing or wings. Some have bodies, but others show the bare shank of the hook. One of the most effective bucktails I have ever used was a size 10 white bucktail with only a wrapping of silver tinsel for a body, and a very sparse wing that extended just a bit below the bend of the hook. That fly can be dropped quietly in a very still pool and because of its thinness it doesn't seem to scare the fish.

Besides the wet-fly colors, streamers and bucktails are tied in all white and yellow, and all black—and more and more I, for one, am finding that the all black streamer or bucktail is a very fine taker of both trout and other varieties of gamefish.

Then modern fly tyers have come up with some new and

different designs, flies such as the optic bucktail, a great steelhead fly with bucktail wing and a built-up head with eyes painted on it; and the muddler minnow, a bucktail designed by Don Gapen, the well known tyer. The muddler minnow is now widely copied in many materials, but the original was made with a single genuine timber wolf hair wing plus a single feather wing. Although it was tied to imitate the darter minnow, when it is in the water the muddler can also look like the buggiest thing you have ever seen. Or it may look like a grasshopper, or another time, like a small mouse. How one bucktail can look like so many different things is a great puzzle, but whatever it happens to look like at the moment, it always seems to look good to the trout. It is as potent a trout fly as anything I have ever used.

That statement covers a lot of territory, especially when you consider marabou streamers. Marabous produce some monster fish. Because of the lightness of the feathers, every fiber seems to move, waving gently, appearing to breathe. When cast across stream and retrieved in jerks 6 inches to a foot in length, the flaunting, tempting liveliness of the tail makes trout hop on it in a hurry.

Marabous are tied in a variety of solid colors and color combinations as shown later on in this chapter, and a number of tyers in various parts of the country have added innovations of their own, for their particular area. An outstanding one is the silver garland, tied by Polly Rosborough of Chiloquin, Oregon, for rainbows. This is a weighted marabou with blue and white wings and silver tinsel body, and is a terrific fish getter for almost any species where such a streamer might be feasible at all.

With both muddler and marabou being such great flies it was only a matter of time before they were put together in a single tie. Dan Bailey of Livingston, Montana, and his partner, Red Monical, did just that, producing the now renowned maribou-muddler. They first tied this fly with the regular muddler dressing, but using a white marabou wing instead of turkey feather wing. Some big fish were taken on it, and then other colors in marabou wings were tried. On one occasion I arrived at the Chimehuin River in Argentina with half a dozen black marabou muddlers in my fly book, in hook sizes No. 4, 2 and 1/0. I also had white marabou muddlers, brown marabou muddlers and gray marabou muddlers in great numbers. I tried the black one first, and fish piled into it. They tore it apart in a hurry. Charles Radziwill and Bebe Anchorena, who were fishing with me, each borrowed one from me, and the trout took those apart, too. We tried other colors, and took only the occasional fish. Back went the black marabou, and wham, we had hit after hit. Yet another time, when the three of us fished the Rio Grande on Tierra del Fuego, it was the gray marabou muddler that got the hits from the big, silver-bright sea-run brown trout that were in the river.

The gray marabou also proved itself on the Missouri River in Montana, when Gene Anderegg of Ridgewood, New Jersey, used a 1/0 to land a walloping 10-pound brown.

So all the marabou muddlers pay off; and size does not seem to make too much difference. I've caught some very large fish on a No. 4, and others on a 1/0.

Another marrying of successful patterns produced the spuddler. Dan Bailey and Red Monical had both used the spruce-fly streamer to take many large trout. They had both noticed that it did more damage when fished on a sinking line. On the other hand, the muddler seemed best when fished on a floating line. They decided to combine the dressing of both flies, with the accent on copying the sculpin minnow which the muddler basically represents—a minnow that lives under the rocks in rivers and lakes. The spuddler has the flattened bucktail head of the muddler, and the bucktail hackle. The wing is the same barred wing used in the spruce fly, and the tail is black bucktail. The body is light tan wool. Like the marabou muddlers, the spuddler proved itself immediately, and has been one of the great producers of recent years.

Bucktails are usually made of deerhair which is hollow, and therefore they float very well even when tied on large hooks. In fact sometimes it is necessary to give the rod tip a hard jerk to pull the bucktail under the surface.

Of all the hairs used for bucktails, the deerhair seems to have the most sparkle, looks better in the water, and deerhair wings do not seem to wrap around the hook as easily as do

This 1/0 platinum blonde, a white bucktail with wings 3½ inches long, has proved one of the best flies in the author's collection for really big trout.

some of the other hairs used in tying bucktail flies. In this regard, both streamer flies and bucktails should be examined frequently during casting, to be sure that the wings have not wrapped around the bend of the hook, as this destroys both appearance and action, and a fly so entangled will seldom draw a strike. When wings hang up in this manner, I pull the hair or feather upwards from the hook, where they are tied to it. This helps for a while at least, to make the wings ride high and wide, free of the bend of the hook.

Many flies designed for fresh water have proven equally efficient in the salt, and conversely a number of streamers and bucktails designed for fishing the ocean flats have turned out to be highly effective in fresh water, especially for big trout and salmon. One big white bucktail, the platinum blonde, and an equally big fly made of yellow bucktail, called the honey blonde, have proven just about the best flies I have ever used for really big trout.

They were originally tied for striped bass and in an effort to make the fly large and extra long-winged, one piece of bucktail was tied on top of the 1/0 hook and immediately behind the eye, and another length of bucktail was tied just in front of the bend of the hook. Over a long number of years it has continued to be a terrific number for stripers and has also proven a great fly for big trout. In the Chimehuin River in Argentina I have taken many brown trout from 10 to 18 pounds on a 1/0 platinum blonde; and my friend Bebe Anchorena used a honey blonde to land a 24-pound brown there. The blondes are also great for sea trout. Everywhere they are fished they produce bigger than usual fish.

Similarly, big multiwing streamers with three and four feathers on each side of the 1/0 hook are sure attractions for the big boys. These streamers work in the water, closing in on the hook when the angler strips line, spreading out again as he stops the retrieve, so that they appear to breathe. They are used in salt water with telling effect and while many a freshwater angler will look at them askance, they surely do have the power to bring hits from big trout, too.

The first time I produced those big flies at the Chimehuin River in Argentina, I brought down the house.

"What's that, your shaving brush?" howled my friend Jorge Donovan.

"Funny, eh?" I said. "Just wait!"

"We use small flies," said Jorge. "A big bundle like that will

A multiwing streamer on a 1/0 hook that produced laughs—and giant trout—in Argentina.

These two rainbows couldn't turn down the author's 3-inch red-hackled streamer with yellow wings.

scare them out of the river. They'll run up into Lake Huechulaufquen and hide on the bottom."

"Wait a while," I said again.

I was using a 9-foot rod, a WF-8-F line and a 14-foot leader, starting with a 30-pound butt section and tapered down to a 4-pound-test tippet. I threw that big bucktail across the current at the head of the pool and started it back. I had only taken three 2-foot-long strips of line, when something hit that fly so hard that it almost knocked the rod out of my hand. It was something big.

That baby turned it on for a downstream dash that made the water fly from the speeding line. Then he showed himself, a beautiful brown trout that jumped 2 feet in the air and seemed to hang there as if pinned up. And that's what I thought. "What a pin-up, and I'll take it!"

After fifteen minutes I got him in, took the hook from the corner of his mouth and gently put him back again.

"What are you doing?" asked Jorge.

"I'm releasing him," I said. "He was a great fighter."

"Releasing a 10-pound fish," said Bebe Anchorena. "That's good."

"But what am I doing, just standing here?" he said suddenly. "How many of those flies do you have?"

"Cut me in, too," grinned Jorge.

We used those big flies down there in Argentina for a month of fishing. We took big brown trout and rainbows and landlocked salmon with them, and in the Rio Grande River on Tierra del Fuego we caught sea-run brown trout that hit them like a trip-hammer every time one of those big streamers was pulled across their noses.

While big streamers and bucktails are the answer in big water for larger than average fish, the smaller, more sparsely tied ones will pay off best in clear and shallow water. There, the lightest presentation possible with a small fly will get results when a big fly might chase the fish out in a hurry. Nevertheless, some of these streamers manage to have a bulky enough look to tempt good-sized fish. Some of the long-winged flies used in Maine are tied on tandem hooks and are designed to look like the smelt upon which the landlocks feed. They have been proven flies for this game fish for a long time, and practically all the blue-winged ties in this group are good, with the supervisor probably being the best known, and the Wilson special, while not so well known, being equally as good for getting hits.

In either bucktail or streamer the Mickey Finn is a good early-season fly, and is also good in discolored water . . . as indeed are almost all the yellow or black flies.

A well-stocked streamer and bucktail book will include most of the following:

STREAMERS, *hook sizes 6 to 12, long shank*

BLACK GHOST	WILSON'S SPECIAL
GRAY GHOST	MICKEY FINN
YORK'S KENNEBAGO	RED AND YELLOW
LADY GHOST	RED AND WHITE
BLACK NOSED DACE	RED AND BARRED YELLOW WINGS
COLONEL FULLER	YELLOW AND WHITE
SUPERVISOR	BLACK AND WHITE

MULTIWING STREAMERS, *hook sizes 1 and 1/0*

RED AND WHITE	BLACK AND WHITE
RED AND YELLOW	BLACK HACKLE BARRED ORANGE WING
YELLOW AND BARRED YELLOW WINGS	

MARABOU STREAMERS, *hook sizes 6 to 12, long shank*

BLACK	WHITE
RED	BLACK AND YELLOW
YELLOW	RED AND YELLOW

BUCKTAILS, *hook sizes 6 to 12, long shank*

BLACK PRINCE	BLACK AND WHITE
PRINCE CHARLIE	RED AND WHITE
BROWN AND YELLOW	RED AND YELLOW
BROWN AND WHITE	MICKEY FINN

BLONDE BUCKTAILS, *hook size 1/0*

PLATINUM BLONDE	STRAWBERRY BLONDE
HONEY BLONDE	ARGENTINE BLONDE
BLACK BLONDE	

MUDDLER MINNOW, *hook sizes 1/0, 2, 4, 6, 8, 10*

BROWN MUDDLER	WHITE MUDDLER (MISSOULIAN SPOOK)
YELLOW MUDDLER	

MARABOU MUDDLERS, *hook sizes 1/0, 2, 4, 6*

WHITE	GRAY
BROWN	BLACK

If you want to catch lunker trout, use big streamer flies. When a trout reaches 2½ to 3 pounds, he has done with midges, freshwater shrimp and other small fry. He wants to gulp down something big enough to make his stomach sac press against his sides. Occasionally a 4-pounder will take a size 10 hairwing and once in a while he might even go for a size 18 or 20. But generally speaking, trout that big don't play for peanuts. They want the works.

Streamers bring out the yen for meat in these big boys and with the right presentation and retrieve an angler can get strikes from hook-jawed old busters that weigh in up in the heavyweight division. They are so hungry for substantial food that even if their stomachs are stuffed tighter than a Pennsylvania food locker the day after deer season, they still will grab another minnow that they can't even swallow and will swim around with the tail sticking out of their mouths, waiting for the swallowed part to dissolve so they can handle the rest. And believe it or not, those big-eyed aquatic so-and-sos, with that remnant of a partly digested meal still protruding from their throats, will hit a streamer. When I opened up one 4½-pound lunker last year, what did I find? Two field mice each about 5 inches long, two minnows each about 4 inches long, and one 5-inch minnow with its tail just showing in the trout's throat. Here was this jasper making like the filling of a knockwurst and he wants a bucktail, yet!

Three excellent freshwater streamers (top to bottom): grey ghost, grizzly, royal coachman. *Courtesy of The Orvis Co.*

In streamer fishing the handling of the retrieve means defeat or success. You must make the lure imitate the actions of the natural food upon which the trout feed, so that they go for it totally unsuspecting. Streamer fishing calls for rod tip work and line manipulation that will make the fly out there act like a minnow. It should be retrieved in short jerks to make it look like a minnow darting erratically around the pool, or in longer strips to ape a more leisurely swim. A lure that is allowed to sink and is then played very slowly can be made to look like a minnow nosing the bottom for food and an extra-fast top-water retrieve makes the artificial dash across the surface, faking a natural minnow that is rushing along the top, trying to escape some great, toothy-mawed 5-pounder.

The angler should try all types of bringbacks until he discovers just which one will do the best job that day. I usually start with the cast across the current, mend the line, then let the fly float downstream broadside and without any motion. When it reaches the end of the float and starts to swim my way, I impart 6-inch jerks to it, then when it has finally swung in directly below me, I bring it back my way slowly and evenly for about 3 feet, then pick it up for the next cast. You can expect a thudding hit at any stage of that play.

Another effective cast and retrieve is upstream and across, bringing the fly back in 2-foot-long jerks, fast, right to the rod tip. Often a fish will follow such a retrieve and hit it just as the angler is about to pick it up for the next cast. And sometimes in a low clear stream it is a good move to cast directly upstream. This cast requires the same care and stealth in approach as does dry-fly fishing, but often such a throw and a slowly retrieved, sparsely tied bucktail will take trout when all other methods fail.

One of the fish-teasin'est ways of all is to figure where a fish should be lying in the current, cast the fly to that spot and instead of bringing it back all the way, just retrieve it a foot or two, then let it float downstream again, retrieve it a foot or so again, and repeat the whole procedure. It takes patience, but it's usually worth the effort in bringing hits that won't seem to come by other methods just then.

That retrieve paid heavy dividends one day when I fished the East Branch of the Antietam River with Bob Wishard of Waynesboro, Pennsylvania. The stream meandered through lush meadows, and at the bends the current had cut under the banks, making deep holes and swell hiding places for trout. At such a bend a brush pile provided shelter for fish. I watched Bob work a yellow and brown streamer in and out of one of those spooky-looking spots, giving it action that made it perform for all the world like a small minnow lying there just above the log jam and darting upstream, then dropping back, waiting for food to come to it in the current. Bob teased a trout so much with that retrieve that at last it zoomed up from out of that black hole and hit the fly so hard he was carried into the air by the force of his rush. As soon as he fell in again, he jumped and landed on top of the brush, snapped the leader and lay there on a big log, flapping, and finally slipped back into the water.

Bob's face was white.

"With all that water around, he has to jump on that bunch of logs!" he grumbled. "That trout weighed 3 pounds at least."

Later we both took a couple of good fish in the same way, by assuming that there was a lunker under every log pile, and teasing them out with a streamer.

During the spring when the streams are high and roily, and after rains during the summer, streamers are fairly commonly used by Eastern anglers, but few of them are used at any other time. Yet even when the water has dropped and is clear and a hundred anglers are walking along the banks of a 30-foot-wide Eastern river, a wide-awake trouter can get hits with a streamer. In clear water, a sparsely tied bucktail on a number 10 or even a 12 hook is very effective when used with a leader tapered down to a 5X tippet. These thinly clad numbers tied with wings of black and white, brown and white, blue and white, and brown and yellow, will do a swell job of making lazy trout hit.

In discolored water, on the other hand, all yellow, all brown or all black seem to show up best. Once on Beaver Creek in Maryland, the water turned so brown following a heavy downpour that we were ready to quit fishing.

"Sometimes I've caught trout in very muddy water with this fly," said Bill Snyder, holding up a brown hackle.

"Not in water this muddy," I said.

Bill tossed his fly midway out in the pool. A fish shot up through that muddy mess and took the fly like he had seen it through gin-clear water. Bill was so surprised he struck too hard and left the fly in the trout's mouth. But he had proved his point. I grubbed into my streamer box and brought out an all-yellow number, tied it on and was in business at the first hole upstream. A 14-incher roared up and knocked that yellow Sally silly. In the next hour we landed nine fish.

After that I took three dark colors and held them in the water, then took a couple of other flies with neutral colors and held them beside the dark ones. The yellow, brown and black showed up five times more plainly.

To fish streamers the angler needs a bigger rod than is used for dry-fly fishing but it is not necessary to go into the heavy equipment that some fishermen seem to think. Using a small streamer in a low, clear stream, an 8-foot rod weighing 4 ounces, with an DT-5-F line and a 10-foot leader tapered down to as low as 4X will do a workmanlike job. The tippet may be upped to 3X or 2X depending on the size of fish you are getting hits from. Sometimes when the line is being stripped, a big trout will sock the streamer, and the combined pressure of the pull and the hit will break the leader. So with a light leader you stand the chance of losing a few fish, but you will get more strikes, too.

The larger streamers are difficult to cast on a small rod and with a long, fine leader, and in order to throw them effectively, an 8½-foot rod weighing as much as 4¾ ounces is needed, and should be fitted with a WF-7-F line. The 10-foot leader should start off with a heavy butt section and then fade down to a 4X tippet (*see* TACKLE). Just before and right at dark, an even heavier leader is all right as in the evening light the trout don't seem to be scared by the larger tippet diameter.

Hook sizes in streamers should range from 12 all the way down to 1/0. Many times it is the size of the fly rather than the color that seems to make the difference between hits and no hits, so the streamer fisherman should carry a large assortment of both colors and sizes. Some day it will pay off heavily.

Out West, trout fishermen have always favored big wet flies and wooly worms, and with these they catch plenty of big trout. Yet if these same fellows would use streamers, I believe they would find the size of their fish increasing.

I well remember the day I introduced a Montana fishing pal to streamers. Len Kinkie had fished dries, and wets and nymphs, but the big black ghost I presented to him scared him.

"What is it?" he said. "Trimming for a gal's hat?"

"Trimming for a trout," I assured him.

It was just before dark. Len went up to the fast water at the top of the 300-foot pool while I worked down toward the tail. I was busily casting when I heard a shout. My head snapped around in time to see Len walking towards the shore, rod held high. Out in the current a great trout jumped clear and threw the hook.

"That was the biggest trout I've ever hooked," Len told me

later. "He was 10 pounds. I know now what you mean about streamers."

Speaking of big streamers and big fish always makes me think of a certain pool on the Yellowstone River. If I'm within a couple of hundred miles of it, regardless of time or inconvenience, I'll head for it pronto. From that pool I've taken enough big trout—and put most of them back—that if they were laid end to end they would reach from Denver to the Rio Grande.

The last time I waded out into that pool was 4:00 p.m. on October 19, my last day of fishing before heading east. As always, I was expecting to sink my barbs into a 16- or 17-pounder.

Since I was sure there would be some big fish working there just before dark, I tied on a 2X tippet. I started at the head of the pool, dropping a size 1/0 white marabou 20 feet out in the fast water and letting it float a bit before bringing it back in

Three top producers for big trout (top to bottom): the muddler, the spruce fly and the spuddler. The last is a combination of the top two patterns created by Dan Bailey and Red Monical.

fast, foot-long jerks. I lengthened the second throw 2 feet. And the next one another 2 feet. When I had 50 feet of line out, I floated it through and waded down to about where it had swung across on that last cast. Then I started the series of casts again. That way I was covering all of the holding water.

The first cast on the next series brought a strike when the marabou was only 20 feet away. That rany hit almost on top and threw water 3 feet high when he took. Then he hung there for a second, heavy, and then my rod tip snapped back and the flyless leader shot high in the air. He had broken me off on the hit.

I tested the leader and put on another marabou. I started the series of casts from where I was. This time it took three casts and then again I almost jumped out of my waders when a hook-beaked beezer poked his nose out and clapped his mandibles at me. He missed the fly but he didn't miss giving me the cold chills. He looked bigger than the other.

I rested him for three or four minutes only, and then sent the fly over the spot where he had been and once again a fish had it, and once again the tip bowed down and stayed there a minute and then flaunted another flyless leader in my face.

I burned then! I was sure that every one of those fish went over 5 pounds. I put on a 1X tippet, cast again and once more got the same treatment. And that one took my last marabou.

I cut off the 1X, leaving just the heavier part of the tapered leader, and tied on a yellow and brown streamer. On the first cast a big baby out there took, rolled on the leader, and once again I was fit to be tied. The sun was away down, peeping over the top of the Gallatins, shadows already across the river, and back of me I heard a deer bleat.

This time I cut that 12-foot leader in half. I must have been up to at least 8-pound test after all that clipping.

While I was tying on a muddler, a fish rose 30 feet in front of me. I cast and he was waiting there with his mouth wide open. I didn't have time to strike because he started off so fast. He slashed across the fast water, then ran down with it for 30 feet and came out in a going-away jump. All I could see was a dark blob down there and as I dropped the rod tip he fell back in and went away again, fast.

He did everything a trout should do to get off. But somehow I gradually started to gain on him. He came upstream and I reeled fast to keep him coming, to get fly line back on the reel. When I got him close, he jumped right in front of me and threw water in my face and then went off again in a slashing drive across current, and then swirled on top and started to shake his head back and forth.

At that nasty maneuver I gave line in a hurry. Then he hung there in the current and I couldn't make him bat an eye. It was a draw for a couple of minutes and then I fooled him. I suddenly gave him slack and he slipped down with the current, and while he was wondering what happened, I tightened up and pulled him off balance and got him coming my way. He tried to get his head again but I held him and skidded him sideways now, in close, and up on top and into the net. He weighed 3¼ pounds, a nice fish to end the season.

As I waded ashore with him, I heard the sound of a riser out there in the current back of me. It made a noise like the thud of a rock falling on frozen ground. I wanted to go back but it was too dark.

"I'll get you next year," I said aloud. "I'll start fishing right here and I'll use a size 1/0 muddler, or maybe a white marabou."

The Big Hole demon, named for one of the nation's top trout streams, was designed by a Montana rancher.

Two views of the marabou muddler. Top fly is fresh, unwetted. Bottom view shows how the fly takes on appearance of a minnow when wetted.

Proof of the abilities of the marabou muddler: Red Monical, left, and Dan Bailey, each with a 4-pound brown trout taken from the Yellowstone River, Montana.

The author with a 6-pound, 8-ounce brown trout taken on a muddler in the Missouri River, Montana. *Photo by Bill Browning.*

Because I know it's big flies those big lunkers want.

A recent streamer-type fly that has had great success is the Big Hole demon, first tied in 1964 by rancher Nick Naranchi, of Twin Bridges, Montana. This fine fly looks something like a low-water wooly worm, and it brings lots of hits from big trout. It is fished across current and allowed to drift free for several feet, then a slow jerk is given to make it look alive and make it swim across the current in an enticing manner. However, most strikes come when the demon is floating still.

Dan Bailey ties two versions of the pattern, one with black and badger body, one with black and furnace body. Both are good. I use them on hook sizes 2, 4, 6, and down to number 10. Like all good patterns, this one was soon carried far and wide, to scenes far from the Big Hole River, for which the fly was named. Bebe Anchorena fished Montana the summer of 1965, and he took a couple of dozen Big Hole demons back to Argentina with him, and there he and Charles Radziwill cashed in with them, landing sea trout to 10 pounds.

There are many long-known streamers and bucktails that are temporarily forgotten because of the success of some new fly. Last year I broke out one such, the Bailey bi-fly, and fished it with such success that I won't forget it again. It can be used either wet or dry, but I have the best luck when I fish it as a streamer.

In general, trout fishing must be done with great quiet, and therefore the popping bug is seldom considered a good trout fly. Yet even big brown trout, smartest and scariest of them all, like a big popper, properly administered in the right place.

Two winters ago, while fishing the Chimehuin River in Argentina. I was taking a string of 6-, 8- and 10-pound fish on large streamers, enjoying the best trout fishing I've ever had in my life. But I knew there were bigger ones there. Bebe Anchorena and Jorge Donovan of Buenos Aires, who were fishing with me, had told me about the heft of some of those trout.

"Every year," said Jorge, "someone catches brown trout up to 25 pounds here in this river."

"Last year a friend of mine caught a 26-pounder," said Bebe. "He was plug casting with a spoon."

Suddenly I thought of popping bugs. I wondered. And I

tried. I got out a big popper, one with a total length of 5 inches, from eye of the hook to end of tail.

It was a rough day. The water on the lake above was white-capped and dark clouds blotted out the mountains and raced over the low hills. It was a rough day to tie into a rough fish, and that was what I wanted to do. Here in the river the water was bouncing with 6-inch waves, and I thought how perfect a spot this was to use a big bug, because it had the bulk a big brownie would like and the waves would not allow too loud a pop, to maybe scare off a suspicious fish.

I cast that big popping bug across current 70 feet, bringing the rod tip almost down to the water so the wind wouldn't blow the bug off course. I let it drift for maybe 10 feet, then retrieved it slowly, in foot-long pulls, trying to make the bug skip softly along. Suddenly I saw a big brown shape out there standing on its head. The rod tip went down violently and the reel began to sing and I was into a big trout. He went 8½ pounds.

I didn't see the next one because he hit in the middle of an incoming wave that still wore a frothy top. But I felt the strike more than the other one. It was a sort of double hit, as if he turned and missed and then took a second try. Or maybe he was hooked the first time, then turned fast and yanked his head around as he did. Anyway, I had all I could handle for the next ten minutes weathering his first frantic fight. Then it turned into a slug fest and it was fifteen minutes before I slipped him ashore, a good quarter of a mile downstream. He was a 10-pounder.

"Give me one of those poppers," said Jorge, who had been going right along with me.

"Me, too," said Bebe.

I handed a popper to each of them, and they left on the run for the next pool.

I had only brought three poppers with me, not expecting to use poppers on trout, so that left me with only the one I had been using. I decided to save it for some special occasion when I thought there might be an extra-big fish around. That occasion came only a couple of days later. I had fished down river for a good half mile without a hit. Then I came to a pool that

Here's an 18½-pound brown trout that fell for a popping bug.

was so fishy looking that there just had to be a big trout in there.

Out came that big popper. On the third cast I saw a great fish in back of the bug, his cavernous mouth open. I saw him bring his upper mandible down. I struck. Three quarters of an hour later I landed that baby, an 18½-pound brown trout that was 35 inches long and had a girth of 22 inches. A few days later I took a 15-pounder on the same bug.

Those were the two biggest fish of the trip. Popping bugs? You bet!

CHAPTER/8

LANDING BASS ON THE FLY

WHETHER LAKE OR RIVER DWELLERS, BOTH SMALL-mouth and largemouth black bass are great fly-rod fish, mostly because they feed on so many different forms of life that can readily be matched with artificials. And they have such tremendous appetites that while they may sometimes get selective and go for one dish only, they can still be had by matching the hatch, whatever it is.

They like frogs, the different types of minnows such as shiners, darters, chubs and small catfish. They eat leeches, nymphs, small eels, natural flies, and all kinds of things that fall into the water, such as ants, worms, bugs, even mice and small snakes. And one of their favorite snacks is old pinchnose the hellgramite. The largemouth is such a stuffer that when hunger pangs assail him he's sudden death to almost any living thing that comes near him. He'll eat his nearest and dearest relatives, and has even been known to snatch a squirrel running along a log in the water, and to take birds of assorted sizes.

With such a wide variety of items to match or imitate, the bass fisherman should have a well stocked fly box and when he's so armed, he's certain at some time or other to have fine sport. There will be days, of course, as with any kind of fishing, when hits are few and far between, and a fellow should have gone to the movies, or "stood in bed"; but in general, with the right equipment plus a little thought and the right technique, he can have a banner day with bass.

And because one or the other of the basses is found reasonably close to almost any spot you can name in the United States and Canada, the bass fills a mighty void for the thousands of avid fly-rodders. The largemouth does more than his share to provide sport by moving into brackish water in sounds, bays and river mouths; and there, with that touch of salt to spark his fight, he seems greater than ever.

If I were to choose a single fly-rod artificial for both smallmouth and largemouth black bass, it would be a popping bug. A popper does something special to a bass as it makes a popping sound, caused by water action against the collar.

Probably the best-working model is the bug made of balsa wood. This has lightness for casting and for effective lure play, even in large sizes. It can be popped or slid or skidded across the surface, or pulled under, according to the way it is constructed, and generally can be played with real zip and pep so as to appear to be something very much alive. Other materials may be more durable, but none performs with the same lifelike actions as does the balsa wood popper.

The new plastic popping bugs, however, while a little heavier per size, also do a workmanlike job and are more durable and retain their finish better. And in Southern canals, tiny poppers made of either balsa, plastic or cork, all with rubber legs, get a great play from fishermen out for bream but taking bass on the side.

Because bass are found around weed beds so often, there are now quite a number of weedless poppers on the market, and they are good because they give the angler the confidence to cast into grass patches and among lily pads, knowing he will not hang up and will be able to play the popper properly. It will "walk" across the grass and lily pads, and that's where some mighty nice bass are often lying.

Popping bugs vary greatly in size, from the little bream getters just mentioned, which are sometimes only the size of a thumbnail, to whopping big foolers that are primarily designed

The Phillip's weedless wiggle popper is a bass getter in weeds and lily pads.

for the big maws of the largemouth but are frequently just as effective for smallmouths.

The action is built into a popper by the tyer, according to the way he wants it to work. Some are designed to be played with loud pops, while others are planned to make little noise—hence are often called "sliders"—and are meant to be just pulled across the surface, rather than popped.

One of the best bugs for largemouth, and smallmouth, too, is the skipping bug, first tied of cork by the writer back in the late '30s for striped bass. I soon found that it was ideal for freshwater bass. Its long, round body lies flat on the water when not being popped, the weight of the hook held up by the deer-hair tail so the bug floats level on the surface. When you give it a twitch it looks like a wounded minnow trying to swim away. I now have it made of balsa wood in three sizes, 3/0 for big largemouth bass, 1/0 for both largemouth and smallmouth, and on a #1 long-shank hook for smaller smallmouth. The best colors are red head with the balance of the body yellow, and a yellow tail; red head with white body and tail; all white; and all yellow.

When the skipping bug hits the surface, it's best to let it sit for a few minutes, then give it a slight pop, then let it stay still there maybe twenty seconds, then another pop, and then bring it back in a series of pops until it is close enough to pick up for the next cast. A bass will hit at any point in this retrieve, either when the bug is moving or when it is lying motionless on the surface.

With this, as with any popper, it's important to tune in on the bass' wave length. Don't pop the bug so hard that it will scare him. When a bug hits the water a bass usually swims away for several feet, then turns and gives it the eye. Then a slight pop interests him and he moves in. Another pop and he's ready. Sometimes a doubtful bass will wait until your series of pops has convinced him that thing is getting away and then he'll charge and take. You can't taunt him too much.

Actual-size photograph of two typical popping bugs, showing how they vary in size. The big one is called "The Thing," designed to get large-mouth bass; its tiny companion is a Phillips "peewee popper" for small bass and panfish.

Even when he's half asleep you can make him mad enough to come out, if you keep popping the bug lightly, time and again, over his hole in the grass, his cave under a tree, his lair under an old dock. When you tease him like that it is not long before he gets his dorsal fin up and charges, so hard and fervently that sometimes he'll knock the bug a couple of feet into the air, open his wide mouth and make a fair catch of that high-kicked, buggy punt.

Another bug I first tied back in the early '40s, this one aimed at smallmouth, is the spouter. You seldom find this one on the market, but many bass-bug fishermen have tried it and found it so good that they make their own. It is a great bug for river fishing, its face shaped to cut into the current like the bow of of a boat, and with slanting shoulders, so that when you give it a pop, jets of water shoot up. It picks up easily and casts well, having a minimum of wind resistance. The spouter is made on a No. 1 3X long hook with cork body 5/8 inch in diameter by 1 inch long, in each case with a feathery tail. I like it in robin's egg blue, for smallmouth, and all yellow for largemouth, but all brown, brown with yellow tail, and all yellow are also good.

Yellow seems to be one of the best colors to use for bass, but robin's egg blue is also good, especially for smallmouth. And black is greatly overlooked. Black has always brought me plenty of strikes, and yet there are probably fewer professionally made poppers in black than in any other color. Combination colors that pay off are the bugs with head of red on a yellow body, red on white, and blue on white. These bugs have the face and maybe a quarter-inch of color painted all around the head part of the bug, then the rest of the body and usually the tail of deer hair are in the other shade.

An excellent strike getter is the all-black popper with yellow dots all over it, and another one is all white with black dots on sides and back. There is considerable doubt in my mind that the bass ever see those fancy designs on the sides and backs of bugs, but the fishermen like them, both the tyer and the buyer, and they do catch fish.

The fisherman who goes for bass with streamers and bucktails should stock his fly book with a wide assortment as to both

A favorite fly for largemouth black bass is the professor, which can be used with or without a spinner.

color and size. Bass are sometimes quite selective, and the angler should be equipped with several of each of certain basic patterns, so that if he loses a couple he will still have more of what those fish are looking for.

Larger editions of the trout flies, usually tied on No. 2 hooks, are excellent bass streamers. I believe the essential difference is that, in general, the more sparsely dressed fly is better for bass. Many bucktails are tied with so much hair that the wing looks dead, and acts that way, too. Even with good rod and line manipulation it still doesn't have the dash to get hits. But a sparsely dressed bucktail with hair tapered to a point at the end of the wings to give it a minnow-like appearance, results in some slamming strikes. Bucktails seem to expand somewhat in the water and these lightly dressed flies then take on added stature. Some of the best luck I have ever had with bass came to an ordinary white bucktail, sparsely tied on a No. 2 hook.

Similarly, too many feathers in the wings of streamers make the fly appear too bulky in most smallmouth water and scare the fish off rather than enticing them into striking. However, even though the dressing may be skimpy, considerable length is good in these bass flies.

The standard all-time successful colors are the winners in bass streamers and bucktails. One of the best of all is a blue and white bucktail, the top half blue and the lower half white.

The all white, the all yellow, the brown and white, and the black and white are all good producers. The yellow is especially good in discolored or roily water, as are the black and the brown. Black is a universally good color for both smallmouth and largemouth bass and in waters where black leeches occur as a natural food, then the black marabou will produce plenty of action.

The muddler minnow, designed for trout, has turned out to be a great fly for bass. Smallmouth black bass must see it as a grasshopper, or a stone cat that lives under the rocks in the river, or a river runner, darter, or the sculpin for which the imitation was first tied. The muddler can look like any of these. It may also look like a very small mouse. No wonder those smallmouth go for it in a big way.

In a river the muddler is fished in the same way for smallmouth as it would be for trout. Throw an S-cast across current, let the fly sink a bit, an inch or two beneath the surface, then start it back straight across current in short, fast jerks, and keep it coming until it is close enough to pick up for your next cast. If that doesn't bring hits, try dropping it out there across the current and letting it float along without motion, then as it starts to swing across the current, make slow pulls of a couple of feet, which speeds the fly. Then for the last part of the retrieve, give foot-long jerks until the fly swings below you, then bring it upstream in those same jerks until you wish to pick it up for the next cast. Nothing gets you action better than trying different types of retrieves, faster or slower, dead floats, fast jerks, slow jerks. A well-mixed bag of tricks gets you the bunting.

While dry flies are not widely used for bass, there are certain situations when smallmouths will knock the feathers off them, and occasionally the largemouths, too, will go for a big dry.

When you're after smallmouths in rivers, a size 6 dry fished as it would be handled for trout, with accent on the perfect float, will often produce wonderful results. Many smallmouths are found in little meadow runs that hardly seem big enough to hold fish, yet from such places I have taken smallmouths up to 3 pounds, and it is fun with a light outfit and small flies.

As in trout fishing, this kind of water calls for a quiet approach and careful delivery and to fish these small waterways I use an 8-foot rod, a DT-5-F line and a leader tapered to a 3-pound-test point, or roughly, a 4X tippet. Dry flies that work well are the standard patterns of royal coachman, black gnat, light Cahill, ginger quill, and the hairwing dries, all on size 6, 8, 10 and 12 hooks.

As is the case with dry flies, only a handful of anglers ever use nymphs for bass, but when the occasion calls for them, and when properly played, nymphs are good items for smallmouth. Only a few patterns will be needed in the bass fisherman's book, however, because if the bass are hitting nymphs it will usually be either the large gray nymph, or a large black one tied on a No. 4 hook. This particular one matches the hellgramite on which bass feed so avidly and brings thudding strikes. And nymphs tied to represent the large salmon flies, trout flies and willow flies of the West are also good with smallmouth.

When bass go deep during the heat of a summer day, or when the opposite is true—the air is chilled and the water cold in spring or fall—a sinking line will help to get the fly down where the fish lie. Even a chilly smallmouth hates to see a good-looking fly go past without telling it just who is boss. In the shallower parts of the rivers, in water from 4 to 10 foot depth, the Scientific Anglers Wet Head sinking/floating line (*see* FLY LINES) will get the fly down and the floating section will enable you to mend the line and to pick up the sinking head that much more easily. The same applies in lake fishing.

When bass are hitting on top, I'd rather use a popping bug, and if they're just below the surface, then my choice is a streamer. But there are plenty of times when the fish are lying deep and seem to need something to stir them up, and at such times there is nothing quite like the fly and spinner combination to produce results. This tandem pair is designed to look like a minnow, with the flashy spoon to catch a dormant bass' attention and get him moving.

It takes a good stout rod to throw such a fly because nothing but a strong tip would stand the constant strain of lifting the heavy lure from the water and casting it repeatedly. Perhaps this is one reason that this oldtime favorite of bass fishermen is so seldom used today. In many places it is next to impossible to buy ready-made flies of this kind. Yet I remember one day last summer on a northern Ontario lake when I tried everything in the book without any luck, and then dug that old spinner rigged with a Colonel Fuller wet fly out of my box. It had been lying there for a couple of years, unused. But that day it brought the previously lazy smallmouth roaring up for it, to give me one of my best days of the season.

Even when it is not possible to find the ready-made flies, it is easy enough to purchase small spinners of the type used in both trout and bass fishing and to attach a favorite fly to them. The spinners should be in size No. 2 for clear water, or No. 3 for roily or muddly water. Bronze, silver or gold color is a matter of seeming indifference. It is the flash that counts. Sometimes, especially when the water is very heavy or discolored, a tandem spinner will attract notice and bring strikes.

Flies to be used with these spinners should be tied on hooks with a straight eye, as a turned-down eye will not allow the fly to ride freely, but instead forces it to one side, thus preventing good action.

Some of the most successful flies to combine with spinners are listed below. All are wet flies, tied on 1/0 hooks; 2/0 hooks are satisfactory in many cases, but the extra size is not necessary and extra size means extra weight, making the fly just that much heavier to throw.

PATTERNS FOR FLY AND SPINNER COMBINATIONS

Hook sizes 8, 10, 12

COLONEL FULLER	ROYAL COACHMAN
LORD BALTIMORE	COACHMAN
BROWN HACKLE	BLACK GNAT
GRAY HACKLE	RED AND WHITE STREAMER
YELLOW SALLY	BROWN AND WHITE STREAMER
PROFESSOR	COLONEL BATES

With all the spinner combinations, the retrieve should be slow and steady, so that the fly swims, drops, swims, drops, while the spinner gives out the glint to draw the eye of the fish to the wounded minnow which I suspect this combination represents. Sometimes if this fails to catch their eye, a smooth, slow retrieve will stir them. The important thing is that the spinner blade be moving from the time it enters the water until it is lifted from it.

FISHING FOR SMALLMOUTH BLACK BASS

Two of the best smallmouths I've ever caught came to big poppers. One was taken from an Ontario lake only a few acres in size, one evening when I dropped a yellow popping bug on the mirrored surface and popped it only once. While the tiny waves were just starting to roll out from it, I had a strike that tossed water all around and out came a big-headed, pot-bellied smallmouth that was ready for just about anything. It took me a long time to get him in. He weighed 5¼ pounds, one of the biggest smallmouth black bass I've ever seen. When we got in to the dock, I looked down his throat. A broad tail was sticking out.

"Look," I said to Frank Bentz who was fishing with me. "Full to overflowing, and he still socks a bug."

I took a pair of pliers and clamped down on that protruding tail and carefully pulled out the half-decomposed carcass. It was 7 inches long, what was left of a bullhead.

"They sure like big things to eat," I said. "And this shows that you can make them mad by working a big popper, too."

"That fish had to be mad, all right," Frank agreed. "The way he was packed he couldn't have swallowed a no-see-um."

A year later I was fishing with Frank again, with the same model bug, and for the same species, smallmouth black bass. We were with Fred Narvel at Port Deposit, Maryland, and we were fishing the Susquehanna River below the Conowingo Dam. We had been working the shoreline with poppers and getting enough fair-sized fish to get a big bang out of it.

Then I put on an extra-big popper and the minute it dropped, in close to the shore, it looked as if a landmine had exploded. Then, as my nerves jolted back into their grooves and my eyes stopped spinning, I saw the shape of a great, bronze-backed fish emerging above the splashes of water, a long, wide, ferocious smallmouth, the biggest of all.

Types of popping bugs smallmouth black bass will hit. This 3-pounder was bug happy and struck three times before being hooked.

That was a fight, too, because he was as powerful as he looked, with the spunk of a great fighting species to back him up. But I finally brought him to net. He weighed 6½ pounds, the largest smallmouth I've ever taken.

The greatest charm of fishing with poppers is that they bring the bass within sight of the angler as it hits. The popping bug lets him in on the whole works. He has the fun of manipulating the bug to coax the fish to it, then he gets a bang out of the strike, right there in plain view, and then the excitement of fighting the fish near the surface.

But the bug must be worked right to produce results. A popping bug, especially a big one, without proper play, is as impotent as a sea cucumber. Most novices at the popper game just throw the bug out and bring it back at once in a series of pops, maybe for 5 or 6 feet, and then pick it up and cast again. And usually they rip the line off the water so hard that they scare the scales off any nearby fish. Bringing it back so fast doesn't give the fish time to get to it and the undue surface commotion discourages him from even trying. Most fish, on seeing a bug drop to the surface, swim away and then turn to see what's happening. If they see the bug resting quietly there, or making only a slight dent in the surface, they'll usually swim back to see what's cooking, and that's when the angler has his chance. And unfortunately, that's the time the novice chooses to rip the line off the water, and then the fish is suspicious for sure. In fact, he's convinced that all is not as it should be.

But an angler who knows how to put a popping bug through its paces can make it talk the right language to make that bass come up and sock it, make him so mad he wants to grab it and smash it flat. So the popper should be rested quietly a moment, then popped gently, then brought back in a slow retrieve of interspersed pops and rests. If that doesn't work, then try a faster retrieve: Make the bug act like a minnow skipping across the surface. Use small pops across the top. Use a big, hard pop now and then, one that really kicks up a commotion and makes a big fish think that there's something he wants.

But always remember that there is plenty of attraction for bass, both big and small, in a still lure. Especially in hot weather, the slower the play the better. The bug should be stopped dead and allowed to lie on the surface for as long as half a minute. Sixty per cent of all strikes come when the bug is not moving, but resting quietly on the surface.

While it is hard to choose between the two, I believe that it requires just a shade more finesse to fish for smallmouth than it does for largemouth. It's true that as summer wanes and fall moves in, the smallmouth bass really go on a feeding binge and during this splurge they wage the best fight of their careers. So that at such a time their behavior is a little more erratic than that of the largemouth. I remember one day in particular when I drove in on the Virginia side of the Potomac River, about twenty miles from Washington, parked the car and began to wade upstream. The water was seldom more than waist deep over the whole river and only occasionally was it necessary to wade around a deep hole. I loafed along, using a popping bug, casting only to risers. With arm-length strips of the line I brought the bug back across the surface as fast as I could, barely popping it, imparting more of a skid than a real pop, keeping the bug moving without a real pause at all.

The first smallmouth that hit fell on that fast-moving bug so hard he almost knocked the rod from my hands. And in the next two hours about fifteen more bass did the same thing. Then they slacked off and passed up not only that retrieve but every other kind of retrieve I tried.

Then I noticed that there had been a change in the way the fish were rising. Earlier, they had been dimpling the surface, but now they were leaping all the way out of the water. I soon saw why. Snake doctors were flying about hovering a few inches above the surface. Those bass were jumping for them. So I put on a 2X tippet and tied on a spentwing Adams dry, size 6.

That turned the tables. They hit it hard and often and for the next hour I had the time of my life floating that big dry over them. But at last that ceased to be the medicine, too. The fish went down, and even though I moved upstream to show my flies to new and less wary bass, I couldn't connect. Yet I knew they were around.

Then I thought of an old-time trick that often sets reluctant trout on fire. I tied on a big spider fly and tossed that small powderpuff out about 50 feet. I imparted quick jerks to it as

I brought it back, made it jump across the current for 2 or 3 feet at a time, then let it sit still for a few seconds, then gave it the business again. Soon I had a 3-pounder chasing that fly, all but turning himself inside out in his efforts to get it. So I stopped the fly altogether and wham! he had it. He smothered the fly with spray and when the hook went home he came out, red eyed as a mad bull, and once again I was in business. For half an hour, from then until dark, I had the time of my life fishing spiders.

Time and again when for one reason or another, the bass have been down, I've taken them by using that varied, jerky retrieve with spiders, variants and big hairwing flies, not only on rivers but on lakes and ponds as well. A fly played in that manner seems to bring out a playful spirit in bass. They like to chase a windblown natural across the surface, like a puppy after a ball, or a cat playing with a string. Sometimes I've found them with five or six naturals in their mouths, not swallowed, just sticking there. So apparently it's not the food but just the game's the thing, with smallmouths.

Hair frogs are great top-water lures for smallmouth black bass. Although it is little used these days, I think that Joe Messenger's famous hair frog, tied many, many years ago, has probably caught more smallmouth bass than any other single lure. Fished fast across the surface, it looks like a swimming frog. Smallmouth tear into it with wild abandon. Very similar to it is another great hair bug called the Weberfoot, after its designer, my friend Walt Weber, wildlife artist for the *National Geographic Magazine*. This bug is also fished in fast, foot-long jerks across the surface, with many changes of speed to interest fish that are not coming good. The body is shaped like a frog, the legs slanting backwards from the body and bound with thread and lacquered about half an inch from the end, so they look like feet. When you strip the bug the legs pump back and forth, giving a very lifelike action. Eyes are painted on the bug and the whole result is a very juicy-looking morsel. I like the No. 2 and No. 1 hook size for smallmouth, and the 1/0 regular shank for largemouth.

When fishing a hair frog, or any other hair bug, the angler should always have a good supply on hand, as they soon become wet and then they are hard to cast and lose their buoyant action, start dragging their feet, so they lack the fire to make a smallmouth forget his cunning and go for them hard.

Many anglers grease the underside of the hair frog before starting to fish, and this keeps the frog from becoming soggy for quite a while. If you do only have one and it becomes wet, you can often squeeze most of the water out and return it to some of its original life.

As mentioned earlier, when I find that the bass are not coming to a popper, I usually turn to streamers. I recall one such day on the Susquehanna below the Conowingo Dam when we had used poppers for some time and although we had taken the odd bass, we were surely not setting the world on fire. Then we turned to streamers. I tied on a fly with a 3-inch-long yellow wing and a brown body, on a No. 1 hook.

I started casting it in among the rocks, dropping it less than a foot from shore and bringing it back straight across current, fast, in foot-long jumps. The long feathers really had action, flipping back and forth in the current. I cast for five minutes without a strike, then the whole tribe of Susquehanna smallmouths seemed to be located along about a hundred yards of shoreline and each one of them made at my fly. They just about tore the feathers off the hook. My partner was having the same experience. We never were sure just what those smallmouths figured the streamers to be—maybe they thought they were small walleyes, or catfish or sauger, or even chub, or some of the saltwater minnows strayed four miles from tidewater. Or maybe just those flaunting feathers brought them roaring up.

And certainly the way the streamer is played makes the difference, as I remember another day on the same river, when every strike came when the fly was played in the exact opposite to the method just described.

Frank Bentz and I had fished all morning without taking anything more than a couple of 10-inchers. But fish were moving because as we waded and cast to the shoreline, we would now and then see the wave put up by a good sized fish as he got out of there.

We had tried almost everything in the box, and finally Frank was starting all over again, with a white bucktail on a size 4 hook. He made a cast, let the fly drift free in the current, and turned to say something to me. Bang! A 2-pound smallmouth latched onto that drifting streamer and busted for the ceiling. Frank landed that one. We kept on fishing. No more action.

Then Frank turned to me.

"Maybe they want it just fished like a wet fly, without any action," he said.

"Give it a try," I agreed. "After all, that other one hit while the fly was floating with the current."

And it turned out that was what they wanted that day. They wanted their streamers without any action. We both fished that way and both got some nice bass. So there's nothing that beats trying new ways as well as new flies, to get to bass that are not cooperating.

Even when an angler thinks he knows just what the fish are going to hit, it always pays to watch just what's going on in the water. Once while fishing near Point of Rocks, on the Potomac, Walt Weber and I were using our favorite popping bugs, but with little success. It was a still, hot day. The glides, slides and runs looked dead calm, only the bounce of the riffles giving any life to the surface of the river. There wasn't a sign of fish life.

Yet when we waded in the shallower water we could see the waves that several bass made as they went out ahead of us.

"They're here," said Walt. "They just aren't hitting."

At that moment we both saw a couple of swirls along the shoreline, close by. Those fish didn't break through the surface, they just pushed it up.

"They're bulging," I said. "Just like trout."

"Nymphing!" said Walt, and we both dove for our tackle boxes.

We added an extra 2 feet of 2X tippet to the end of our leaders and then greased the leaders down to within 4 inches of the end. Then we put on gray nymphs tied on No. 8 hooks.

Walt made the first cast, to one of those fish we had spotted. He dropped the nymph 3 feet above the bulge and let it float free with the current. Down it came. Our eyes were glued on the end of the floating leader and just under it we could picture the nymph, 2 or 3 inches below the surface, jiggling around a little in the current, lifelike.

Then the forward motion of the leader stopped and it seemed as if a giant hand had grabbed it and pulled it forward.

"He's there! He's on!" yelled Walt, striking.

A 2-pound tiger-striped smallmouth came out and walked across the surface on his tail. He splashed back in and dashed away for 20 feet, then came out in an end-over-end leap. He tore down the shoreline, then cut out below us, headed for deeper water. When he hit the fast current, he jumped again. Then he hung there in the current, resting.

Walt kept the pressure on and finally pulled his head our way and got him moving. That stubborn fish dashed for shore and jumped again in water so shallow that he must have bumped his belly on the bottom. But at last Walt got him in. He was only the first of a nice string we took on those gray nymphs.

Since smallmouths live mostly in clear-water lakes and rivers, and have eyes like a hawk, they present a special problem during the bright part of the day. In the shallows, particularly, they can spot motion in a hurry, and fishing for them there calls for just as careful an approach as fishing for trout. The angler who wants to connect in such water must work cautiously, avoid noise or excessive commotion in the boat or in wading.

The value of being quiet when fly-rodding for bass was convincingly demonstrated to me one summer when half a dozen of us who lived in Baltimore used to go to the Upper Potomac near Shepherdstown, West Virginia, for weekends of smallmouth fishing. Usually we would line up in the river and start down, six abreast, flinging flies in all directions. We caught plenty of fish because there were plenty of them in there—and solely for that reason, I believe. Because six men fishing together in a stream make a lot of commotion. But the fish we caught were mostly 8 and 9 inches long, with a few up to 15 inches.

It was fun, for there is nothing dull about the fight of even that size of smallmouth. But we wished we would catch some larger ones occasionally.

"There are no big ones in here," said one of the boys.

"Want to bet on that?" asked Walt Weber. "I'll bet we could come out here on a week day, just a couple of us, when the river is quiet, and take some good fish."

Bets were laid, and later that week Walt and I slipped out there. We eased into the river quietly, waded carefully, avoiding excessive grinding of gravel under our boots, and made no false motions for wary big boys to spot. There was no one on the river but ourselves.

We took several smallmouths apiece in the 2-, 3- and 4-pound class. And in almost any water where the small ones are found, you can count on some hard-hitting bigger ones, too, if you get there at the right time and fish the right way.

In large rivers such as the Potomac, the Shenandoah in Virginia, the Great Cacapon in West Virginia, the shorelines are frequently big producing areas. To avoid spooking the fish that are lying or feeding alongshore, the angler should stay well out from the shore, at least 50 feet, and work slowly downstream, casting directly across current, in to the shore. The fly will go downstream in the current, then swing in below with plenty of real-looking action. A fly cast directly downstream, as would be the case if the angler were wading inshore and casting to fish just below him, would look lifeless. The fly should be retrieved in slow, even strips, and brought well in before being picked up for the next cast.

When smallmouths are feeding in the shallows along the shore of a lake, as they often do on summer mornings or evenings, then a quiet, stealthy approach is doubly important. Always when a fish is in shallow water he is warier than at other times. He knows he is open to attack from many angles, so he swims and feeds with both eyes cocked, ready to shoot off to safety. At such times a fairly long cast is advisable, both to reach the spot where you know there is a fish, and to avoid frightening any that might happen to be between you and the known smallmouth.

"What do you call a long cast?" one angler asked me.

"Anywhere from 65 to 70 feet," I said.

"How about these 100-foot casts you hear people talking about?" he wanted to know.

"There's such a thing as casting too far," I told him. "For efficient fly or bug play and for a quick strike, and for line work in general, I'd say that 55 to 70 feet would be the best distance to cast. Over 80 feet the strike impulse takes too long to get to the fish and he may spit out the fly before he's hooked. And the greater the distance away, the harder it is to see the flash of a fish as he goes for the lure, and so you may strike too late."

In other words, the shorter the cast, the more control the angler has over line and fly, and the easier it is for him to hook his fish. So he has to judge the conditions and cast accordingly, remembering always that the shorter cast is surer and easier to handle.

Often on rivers I creep up close enough to get off casts of only 40 feet. And if I were to choose one over-all perfect casting distance, I would take 50 feet. At that distance you have control, it's hard for the fish to see you but fairly easy for you to see him.

Another important thing to remember in clear-water fishing for smallmouths is that the terminal tackle should be light. Going light on fly leaders for bass means tapering down to 3X, which works very well with dry flies and nymphs on rivers. Generally it is better to go a bit heavier when using streamers or bucktails on big water. A hard strike from a smallmouth while the lure is being retrieved quickly across current will snap the leader where it is tied to the fly, if the tippet is too light.

On such big water there are usually swirls and runs, broken surfaces and bubbles which tend to prevent the bass from seeing the leader too readily anyway. Then a slightly heavier tippet is called for—say 4-pound test. But there is seldom, if ever, any need to put on a heavier leader than that. A 4-pound-test tippet will hold almost any smallmouth in existence, and the finer the calibration of the last section of the leader, the better action can be given to the fly. A stiff, heavy leader end makes the streamer appear dead and will certainly be spotted in a hurry by a suspicious bass.

And the bass leader should be tapered just as carefully as the trout leader; in fact, a properly tapered leader is all the more important in casting the big flies and poppers used for bass.

While the smallmouth is undoubtedly one of the readiest hitters, there are times when they cross you up, and for no apparent reason refuse to hit.

Don Gapen and I ran into such a situation in a little lake on an island in Lake Superior, near Nipigon, Ontario. This was not smallmouth country, but Don knew where there were some bass in a lake and he frequently took guests from his nearby resort to this lake for a change from trout and northern pike fishing. But that day we cast poppers for an hour without a hit. We tried bucktails, streamers, nymphs, dry flies. Don put on a spinner and fly combination and tried that. Nothing happened. We tried fast retrieves, slow retrieves, with equal lack of success. We went back to popping bugs again, hoping to stir up those lethargic bass.

"It's been pretty hot," said Don. "But still, we should get a hit or two, at least."

We were both sitting there feeling pretty disconsolate, and as we sat, Don had left his popper lying on the surface of the water about 50 feet out from the boat. It must have lain there a full minute, and then he started to retrieve it.

"Bam!"

A two-pound smallmouth came roaring out, clamped down on that popper and the fight was on.

After he had landed that one, Don threw the popper out again and I did the same with mine, and then we just sat there and grinned. Don pointed to his watch.

"We'll give them a full minute," he said. "That's what they need. Time. We haven't been waiting long enough."

If you've ever sat and waited for a bass to hit, while you watched the second hand of a wristwatch make a full circuit of 60 seconds, you know that a minute can seem like an hour. But that's what we did. And it paid off. And has paid off many more times, with lazy bass.

"They must have been down there looking at the bugs all the time," said Don. "But they're lazy with the heat and it takes quite a while for them to make up their minds to hit."

"Well, we can wait," I said. "It's never too long to wait for smallmouth."

Later in the day, when air and water had cooled a little, those bass returned to their normal willing form and knocked the spots off our poppers and for the last half-hour before dark we were mixed up with a bunch of wild-eyed bass that didn't care what kind of temptation we offered. They took everything, to remind us once again that in spite of their peculiar behavior earlier, they were the same old rambunctious, hard-hitting, high-jumping smallmouths that make anglers all over the United States and Canada just as wild-eyed as they are.

FISHING FOR LARGEMOUTH BLACK BASS

Probably more words have been written about the largemouth black bass than about any other fish, except, perhaps, the trout. It's not because they are harder to make hit, or that they wage a tougher fight, or that they jump higher, or bore deeper, or shake their heads more than others. It's because of two things—wherever an angler lives in the U.S.A., he can find them nearby; and wherever he finds them they are ready takers of lures. They are the fish kids cut their teeth on. They are the fish, even more than sunnies, that most anglers catch first.

While the largemouth goes by many different names, there's never really any question as to who he is. He's the same forthright guy everywhere, a buster with a great hunger, with eyes larger than his very big stomach. He has an appetite that will make him try to swallow anything from a mouse to a manatee. The hungrier he gets, the madder he gets, and when he's mad he looks mad all over. His scales stick out, his fins beat violently, his lower jaw juts out more than usual, and his eyes get as red as a mad bull's. He bristles. He is full of a hot-headed desire to knock the heck out of anything that goes by. So your popping bug, or other feathery fooler is near, and boy, oh boy, does he sock it!

The farther south the largemouth is found, the bigger he gets. Wherever he isn't ice-bound, he feeds most of the year round, and down in lower Georgia and Florida he is sitting at the dinner table all of the time. They grow big in Texas, too, and that state rightly boasts of the outsize hunks of bassy fish-flesh that swim its waters. This was brought home to me once when I fished with Andy Anderson of the Houston *Press*. That day Andy and I were casting away, talking up a storm and in general having a good old get-together.

"Gosh!" cried Andy, suddenly. "Did you see that?"

I looked in time to see him with one foot on the gunwale,

one arm on a tree branch, like he was going to climb up to get away from something.

"What?" I stammered, thinking of snakes and sea serpents.

Andy pointed. I looked, and where he was pointing I could still see the receding waves that could only have been pushed up by a monster bass.

"Come down out of that tree," I said, "and cast back there."

It was a tough place to put a bug but Andy did it. In fact he did it eleven times, and then, deep down, something moved. Two small whirlpools showed on the surface, about 2 feet apart.

"He'll hit soon," I said. "Throw on back. He just swirled down deep."

"Probably just a little one," said Andy.

"Little!" I shouted. "Did you see how far apart those little whirlpools were? Only a big bass makes swirls like that."

My excitement was beginning to get Andy. His next cast was a bit off line but he brought it carefully back, tried again and made a bullseye. The bug had hardly lit before the water flew apart as that big bass rammed his wide open mug through the surface, inhaled the bug, turned and tore across the top, headed for the sanctuary of a maze of criss-crossed tree branches just under the surface. Andy put the heat on, leaned back on his rod, and held. The tip bounced down to the surface, hung there, then as the bass slowed, the pressure brought him to the surface and Andy got him coming our way. He looked like 20 pounds to me.

Even when I put the net under him and lifted him into the boat, he still looked that big.

"A fair fish," said Andy. "Let's put him back."

"I don't mind putting him back," I replied. "But what size do you call a big fish, in Texas?"

"Wal," said Andy. "We call anything over 15 pounds a big fish. This one's only about 9."

I kept mum because I didn't want Andy to know that any largemouth over 5 pounds seemed very big to me. But this was Texas.

When he does get over 10 pounds, the largemouth seems to be all mouth and gut. His maw looks as big as the entrance to the Luray Caverns. And when he's big like that he gets a

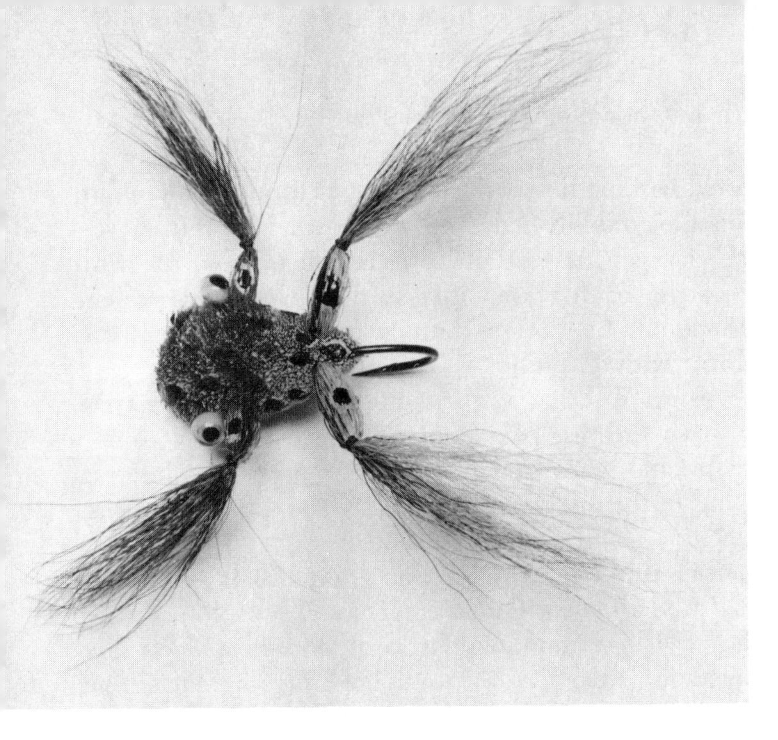

Largemouths go for a wide variety of lures, including frogs like the Jaylure hairfrog (above), tied by Larry Austin, and the realistic Jaylure hairmouse (below).

bit lazy, often basking like a walrus, or lying around moping in the shade of a log or a lily pad. On hot days when the sun moves around, he changes his position just enough to keep up with his shade patch, making even that small move under protest and you imagine you can see him grumpily wipe the sweat from his brow with a limp fin.

In order to make such a lazy bass hit, a lure must be played very slowly—in the case of a popping bug, with long pauses between pops, and many changes of pace to arouse his interest or anger; and in the case of a streamer, with a tempting, flirting action.

But when he is hungry, you just can't take the fly away from him. And if he's a brackish-water largemouth, as well as being hungry, he's twice as rambunctious as usual. There's no more evil-tempered fish than the bigmouth in brackish water. The sea seems to add a little salt to his disposition, and when an angler disturbs his slumbers or merely interrupts his train of thought as he lies among the weeds, he may expect that fish to come up with wide-open mouth to fix that pesky noise maker. He'll even come back a second time if he's mad enough. And it isn't hard to make him mad enough.

Many times I have fished Currituck Sound out of Poplar Branch, North Carolina, working the islands and little lakes among the marshes. The fish in there always seem ready, to the point that they'll almost climb a bush to get at a lure. On one trip there, I saw the swirl of a big fish right against a bank.

"He's grabbed a soft crab," I thought.

My guide eased me into casting distance. My cast started off all right, but it went too far and hung on the reeds that grew up from the water, directly above where the fish had struck. I pulled back with the rod, the bug came loose and jumped a foot onto a single reed, then slipped 3 or 4 inches down it. I pulled back again, and up the reed went the bug, like it had hands. That bass came out then for that bug and I fancied I could hear his jaws bang together as he tried and missed. When my nerves stopped jumping I pulled some more and that bug started swinging, monkey like, from reed to reed. And below it, sticking his ugly old head out and following it, was that bass. He kept after it for 6 feet, and then it fell to the water. He busted it quick and as I set the hook he jumped, fell over a bunch of floating grass and pulled free.

I sat down till my heart began to give an all quiet signal again. Then I cast back there, just to see if perhaps that 12-pounder was still anxious for that bug. He was. He took it on the first cast, as soon as it hit the water, and I landed him that time. He weighed 7 pounds 5 ounces, a far cry from the 12 pounds my bulging eyes had imagined him to be. But he was still a good, walloping big largemouth.

Largemouth are easy to finger. No use to waste time working stretches of flat beach, unbroken sandy places, muddy flats devoid of vegetation or cover. Old bigmouth is out with the things he likes to eat. He's hanging around under or alongside moored boats, docks, logs, fallen trees, channel markers, rafts, pilings, drop-offs, grass beds, both secure and floating along banks and under rocks. Once in Shirley Mill Pond in Virginia, Moses Nunnally showed me just how accurately the largemouth can be spotted. Moses took me out on the pond and pointed out what he called "hurdles."

"We put a pile of cedar bushes down there, held by four poles to keep them from floating away," he explained. "Looks something like an underwater race track hurdle, and it provides just the sort of spot where bass like to hang out. Cast 4 feet beyond that stake to the left, and exactly 2 feet out from it. That's where he'll be."

My cast wasn't quite exact, but it was close. I didn't even have time to pop the bug. There was a swirl and I struck. A big, wide mouth showed for a minute, then the big bug flew back at me. I had only nicked him.

"Too bad," said Moses. "A 6-pounder." He started the motor. "But there's another one right over here."

We moved farther down the shore.

"See that lap?" said Moses.

"What's a lap?" I wanted to know.

"It's the top half of a tree," he explained. "Cut off so it falls in the water. Makes a swell place for fish to hide."

"That one?" I asked, pointing to a freshly downed tree lying against the shore.

"No," said Moses. "The one beyond that. That's a new one

that you are looking at. Next year it will be just right. There are about 200 of them in the pond right now, a few that fell naturally, but most of them we chopped."

"Put the bug right in beside it," he went on. "Bob lives there."

Seeing the look I gave him, Moses laughed. "Bob's a 7-pound bass," he explained. "I know him so well I have a name for him. Of course there's just a chance he won't hit, but he's there."

Bob was there. And Bob hit. He was a well-stacked 7-pounds, a top-conditioned largemouth.

We had drifted a considerable distance from the lap when I put him back but Moses told me that he'd go right back there, and be there the next time we came by.

"Suppose we had put him back farther away," I said. "How far would he travel to get back to where he lives?"

"I know two bass named Peggy and Jock," he said. "They used to live on a point down the lake. Each time I caught them there I'd carry them to the other end of the pond in the live well, and then release them. But the next time I came past their home point, there they would be.

"I caught them so often," he added, "that I guess they began to wonder where their home really was. They moved down the lake where I was always putting them back, and now I catch them there and bring them back to the point, and they swim right back down the lake again."

"Just a couple of mixed up kids!" I laughed.

But there was nothing mixed up about the way Moses could spot those fish, and that's the way largemouth are—if you know where they like to live, and if there are fish in there at all, they'll be where you expect them to be.

Largemouth go for a big lure. Especially the weighty old-timers can't be bothered with small stuff. They only stir their stumpy fins for an article of food big enough to bulge their bellies. They like the large popping bugs and streamers and bucktails, and they like streamer-spinner and bucktail-spinner combinations. But while these big lures bring lots of hits, the angler must use caution in presenting and playing them. When the fly hits the surface, the nearby bass will start swimming away, but invariably he will turn back after a bit and look to see what has fallen there. If the lure is quiet, like a bug that has dropped and is resting, he will come back and generally grab it. Sometimes if he is a little suspicious, a slight quiver of the bug will chase his fears away. But always, after making the cast, be sure to rest it awhile before beginning to play it—whether using streamer or popping bug.

In my book the all-time greatest bass bug, the one I think is a mile ahead of any other for largemouth, is the gerbubble bug, invented in the late 1920s by Tom Loving of Baltimore, Maryland. Because it is difficult to make, and because the pattern has seldom appeared in print, this wonderful bug is little used. It's one I think every bass fisherman should try. The gerbubble bug picks up lightly, pops well, sits low in the water, and the fringe-like hackles on the sides and the flirting tail make it a potent bit of medicine for bass. Loving tied it on a No. 2/0 hook with cork body 9/16 inches high, 11/16 inches wide and 7/8 inches long. It has hackle fringes projecting from the sides, and a feathery hackled tail. He painted his bugs an overall brown with red, white or yellow tiny circles or dots here and there; or all white, or all yellow, with the same added small eyes and circles, and matching feathers. This makes the bug look more natural than some of the bright colors painted on many bugs, and which I think are designed to dazzle the angler rather than the bass.

Another bug that can look like many different kinds of food to a bass is "The Thing." This is a bug that features five moosemane legs, each 3 inches long, on the top side of the cork body. When you throw it out and it lights on the surface, the legs are all straight up. As you watch, they fall on the surface, slowly, on either side of the cork body. It looks for all the world like a bird alighting on the water and folding its wings. Sometimes I think the small fish flee before it, believing it to be a fish hawk. But it's something else again when you show it to a lunker. He'll sink his fangs into it. Some of the biggest bass ever landed in Virginia and Maryland waters have hit The Thing.

A number of commercially tied popping bugs feature a fine wire weedless attachment, looking like two delicate legs extending back under the body from just below the face. When these wires hit the reeds or heavy grass they ride the bug up so the hook doesn't catch on these obstacles. But you can maneuver any of the good poppers in such weedy spots if you handle them carefully. When you cast a popper in to a stand of upthrust reeds, play it very slowly as it nears each single reed. This brings the head of the bug up against the reed, and as you pull gently the hook will move out and the whole bug will get safely by.

With the bug, a good half-minute rest before giving it the first pop pays off, especially during the warm months. The majority of strikes come when the bug is not moving, but resting quietly on the surface. Sometimes a bass will see a lure coming through the air, move under it and grab it as soon as it hits, but usually they want to look it over carefully before picking up their knives and forks. Glutton-like, they want to bolt it down in a hurry, but gourmand-like, they want to savor it a bit, and they want to be sure it's not tainted meat.

A streamer should be allowed to sink almost to the bottom in shallow water, or a good long time if it's deeper, before it is started back. And even if the first cast doesn't produce, a second, or a third, back to the same spot will bring a hit. The largemouth is not the hardest fish to make hit a fly but he can go down, like any other fish, and being the stubborn creature he is, when a bigmouth is down, he's really down.

Even a veteran angler usually fishes far too fast. One quick cast, a fast retrieve, and away he goes to the next likely spot, never realizing that the fast retrieve gets the lure out of there too soon, maybe just when the fish is getting interested. A bass wants to think things over a bit, he wants his suspicions lulled, he wants to be convinced that the fly is really something good to eat.

During the hot months the lure can hardly be played slowly enough. I've waited a full minute, and never less than half a minute, before giving a popping bug action. It seems an hour, when you want hits, but it's that way or else.

School bass behave quite differently from the singles. At Welaka on the St. John's River in Florida, schools of largemouth cut the surface up as they feed on shad minnows, and along with the bass, sticking their long, slender snouts out and feeding at the same trough are beaucoup needlefish. They like shad minnows, too.

"A.P." Oliver knows the first name of every bass in that area. Besides being a fine angler, an excellent guide, and a student of fish behavior, A.P. is fun to fish with. Not much misses his keen eye and usually when other fishermen are drawing blanks, A.P. is boating fish.

When I fished with A.P. we were ninety miles from the river mouth, yet there was still tidal action. We cut the motor and soon saw fish working a short way off.

"Do they always school here?" I asked.

"Generally from October to April," A.P. said. "But in 1952 they were thick around here all year."

We were close to the breaking school now. I cast a popping bug to a spot where I had seen a rise. By the time the bug hit the surface, I saw top-water disturbance only 10 feet away.

"They move fast," said A.P. "You gotta get to them in a hurry."

But before I could even pop that bug, a 2-pounder hit and came on out, shaking his head so hard that he threw the insecurely hooked tenite bug a foot into the air. When it hit the water again, another bass was waiting and gobbled it fast, jumped, and also threw the bug. I looked at the hook, but the fault wasn't there. It was my fault.

I cast and had another hit, and this time I pulled in a 3-pound fish. As I took the hook out, an inch-long shad minnow pulled out of his mouth, then another, and another, all fresh.

"Can you beat that!" I said. "Here's a guy stuffed to the hilt, so full that he's making like a machine grinding hamburgers, and he still wants his plate refilled!"

I threw him back into the water and when he hit he disgorged at least half a dozen more shad minnows. These last were a bit more of the chum variety—a bit used, so to speak.

Another school showed suddenly, thrashing the top 20 feet away. They sounded, and I cast uptide from where they had showed.

"That's the wrong place," A.P. advised. "Cast downtide from the fish. They follow the shad minnows that swim with the tide, and hit them from behind."

Pick up a bass by the lower lip and he stops struggling and stays quiet as long as you hold him that way. *Photo by Leon Kesteloo.*

Sure enough, they showed again 10 feet farther downtide, going away from us. A.P. started the motor. My nerves jumped.

"Hey!" I shouted. "Hadn't we better row after them? The motor will put them down."

"Not these school bass," said A.P. "It doesn't work that way here. The motor doesn't scare them, but if I were to cut it and start rowing, then they would go down."

It was hard to believe, but that's the way it is.

"Look," I said. "It's raining over there."

A white line showed on the surface a hundred yards away where raindrops were slapping hard into the water.

"That's bass," A.P. said. "Look at them feed."

The disturbance was in a straight line for a hundred feet and altogether there must have been two acres of water jumping up. As we came nearer we saw that the water was being splashed a couple of inches high as the bass, completely beserk, rammed open-mouthed into tightly packed, frenzied schools of shad minnows. We could hear the sizzling sound when A.P. cut the motor, and now and then we saw a minnow knocked high in the air. It was vicious. These might be school fish, but they were the same old extra-hungry, extra-big eaters, the same old largemouth black bass.

Then everything went down and here and there patches of foam were left, so it looked like the circus grounds after the tents are down and gone, the scattered pieces of paper, the bits of cardboard cups.

We left the school fish then and worked the shoreline for big stuff under stumps and floating vegetation. And while the school fish were mostly small, there are some bass in that river that will pry your eyelids wide open. You never know what will happen, or when. It's bass fishing that keeps you guessing, and it certainly keeps you casting because if you want action, the school fish will furnish that, and if you want size, the huge hunks along the shoreline will provide that.

Bass school all over the South, in the TVA lakes, in big rivers in Texas, and in the bigger lakes and rivers of Florida. On Lake Okeechobee they are continually moving into the bays and along the shoreline to spawn. For nine months of the year they keep moving in, furnish fishing, spawn, and then go back to the big part of the lake where it is hard to find them, hard to get a hit.

On one trip to Lake Okeechobee with Captain Bill Johnston of Clewiston, we took his charter boat, the Seven Seas, towed a couple of skiffs, and ran down to Moonshine Bay. The water was from 2 to 5 feet deep and reeds stuck up everywhere and pepper grass lay on the surface in great patches. This type of fishing called for a weedless attachment so I tied on a popping bug that was ready rigged that way. It had rubber legs, a yellow tenite body, white bucktail tail. I cast it out, and started it walking across the surface. It looked alive and it didn't walk very far before a mite of a bass flew up and hit it. That bigmouthed youngster wasn't 8 inches long.

We worked all the open spaces in the reeds, all the little pockets that looked bassy enough to hold 10-pounders. We fished for fifteen minutes without a strike aside from that junior edition. Then I dropped the bug on the pepper grass and a five-pounder tore up and engulfed it and dove for the bottom.

After that almost every time we dropped a lure on that pepper grass we had a hit. The bass would come up, grab the bug, jump once, then dive and tangle in the grass. We would have to row over, catch hold of the leader and pull gently, bringing up a huge wad of grass with each fish. Half the time the bass would be entirely covered with grass and weeds and wouldn't even kick as we took the hook out and dropped them back in. With their heads buried in all that greenery they must have thought they were hidden from us.

The next day Bill took us to Fisheating Creek, also near Clewiston. It was a bassy looking place, pretty enough to make us want to take pictures of it, with or without fish. There were great live oaks with wide limbs dripping with Spanish moss. Rimming the creek were huge cypress trees, thin trunked at the top, fringed with leaves, and tapering outward fast at the butt, like the skirts of a Seminole squaw. On the ground, all around, were cypress knees. The early sun slanted through the trees, sifting through the hanging tendrils of moss and cutting through the leaves in shafts. The morning mist rose from the water like incense, giving the whole thing a cathedral atmosphere.

But we shook our heads briskly and soon shapes of huge bass covered the picture, shattered the calm. We were bass hungry. We dashed for the water. Bill and Hoite Agey took the boat and Dave Roberts and I slipped upstream along the shore. Dave eased into the first nice looking bit of water and I went on until I came to a round pool rimmed with water hyacinths. It looked like what I wanted.

On my first cast, the big yellow popper had hardly hit the water before the surface was smashed into a thousand particles. A bigmouth jumped, shaking his head, gill covers flaring outward, red gills showing, the big yellow bug showing, too, in the corner of his mouth. He was a 5-pounder and fought like double that. I took three others from that pool before moving upstream.

Fisheating Creek lazed through bottom land in a million twists and turns. I had to wade the creek a dozen times and still wasn't very far from where we had parked. The fishing was terrific.

I stayed at it till dark and had to use my flashlight to get back to the car.

As we put our rods away, we talked over the day.

"Best bass fishing I've had in a long, long time," I said. "I even had to kick them aside as I waded."

"Yah!" said Hoite. "I can see you kicking bass out of the way."

"No fooling," I said. "Once I felt one bump into my leg and I kicked him."

Hoite laughed. "The next time you feel something bump into you in those hyacinths," he said, "brush it aside with a 15-foot pole. That was a cottonmouth you kicked, for sure."

In the autumn, in the colder parts of the country, largemouth seem to go on orgies of eating everything within reach, everything they can stuff down their wide throats, as if to store up fat to tide them over the winter months. For a while, then, they seem to hit harder and fight harder, and for the angler it is one of the best times of year to be out. The bass lose a lot of their summer sluggishness then, and are ready and willing to chase after a fly. They hit so hard and so often that the lucky fisherman who is in on those days comes to believe that he has discovered the all time secret of catching bass. And then the next day they are down, and he begins to understand. This was their last mighty binge, just before curtains, and as the cold continues to work on them, only a deep, slow-moving streamer or bucktail will get any response at all.

BRACKISH WATER LARGEMOUTH

Where largemouth black bass go into brackish water they provide anglers with some extra-special sport. I remember one day not long ago when I fished for largemouth at Currituck Sound, out of Bertha, North Carolina. Met Lupton, who was guiding me, jockeyed the skiff broadside to a small island fringed with reeds and grasses.

"This bank is loaded with bass," he said.

I made a false cast, then shot the line out. The leader went over a clump of reeds that rose from the shallow water close to shore, and the gerbubble bug landed with a splat on the surface back of them. I lifted the rod tip. The leader pulled across the reeds and the popper rose from the surface, climbing one of the stalks like something alive. There was a swirl under it and I almost struck. I pulled again, gently, hoping the bug would fall on the water. Instead it swung out into the air as the leader slid across yet another reed. I could see water movement as the bass followed. Then the bug dropped to the surface. Water flew. I struck and missed.

I cast right back and again the bug went over the reeds. As I started the retrieve it swung from reed to reed as if it were a monkey traveling the jungle lanes. I gave an extra-hard jerk and the bug landed on the surface 2 feet from the reeds. There was a walloping hit. I lifted the rod and felt him.

He busted out in the air, a bulldog of a bass close to 6 pounds. He fell back in and swept along the bank as if looking for something sharp on which to cut the leader. He jumped again, and when he fell back in I pulled back with the rod and turned him. He came our way slowly, doggedly, then made another lunge and came halfway out of the water. He was tiring and I used the butt of the rod to keep him coming. Met grabbed him by the lower lip and lifted him up to remove the hook. We let him go.

The brackish-water largemouth is widespread throughout the country in a thin band wherever salt and fresh water meet, a great gamefish overlooked by many anglers. They are in tidewater and below, wherever a river floods down lots of fresh water into the salt, or in sounds where winds move salt water into a freshwater area. The upper part of the Chesapeake Bay is a good place for them because the mighty Susquehanna pours in there. Nearby, the Elk and Northeast rivers are veritable pipelines of fresh water pushing well out into the bay, and all this sweet water spreads out and mingles with the salt over the famed Susquehanna flats. Another good spot is where the tidewater pushing in through Oregon Inlet is moved by winds up into Currituck, Albemarle and Pamlico sounds in North Carolina, and as far as Back Bay, Virginia. Still further south the brackish-water largemouth finds suitable habitat in the mysterious, mangrove-studded bays of the Florida coast where the freshwater streams of the Everglades pour into the Gulf of Mexico. Wherever you find this mixture of salt water and fresh in comparative shallows, within the range of the largemouth, there you find him adapting himself to the brackish water. The salt brings him an extra supply of minnows, baitfish, shrimps, crabs and small eels.

Too much fresh water moves the brackish bass a bit farther toward the salt, but too much salt can do them real harm. In 1935 a hurricane brought the sea rolling over the Outer Banks of North Carolina into Currituck Sound. The brine killed off a lot of bass. But within a few years, as the salinity of the water returned to normal (about 4½ percent) there he was again, that hard-hitting, bug-eyed, devil-may-care, ever-hungry slammer.

In sounds and marshes and along the mainland and islands, these brackish-water bass run 1½ to 2½ pounds, with a sprinkling of 4- and 5-pounders, and a few weighing 7 and 8. Ten-pounders are taken occasionally but they are few and far between. Regardless of size, their strike, especially to a surface lure, is a rocker. A touch of salt gives the largemouth extra ginger, makes him more of a gamefish.

Practically everywhere within their habitat, 25, 50, 75 and even 100 fish may be caught in a day. Fishing alone in Currituck Sound, I once took 32 bass without moving the skiff. I just worked the water 5 feet deep between two islands. Another time when I was at Currituck with Walt Weber, *National Geographic* wildlife artist, we took turns fishing and landed 75 bass in one day on one single gerbubble bug. On two different occasions we each took 100 bass. All, of course, were returned to the water.

Good brackish-water bass fishing begins in mid-April in most places and continues until the first part of October. If it stays warm in the northern part of their range, the fish will continue to hit, but when colder weather chills the water they go deep and become sluggish. May is perhaps the best month in their northern range, and that's a good time to be out in the marshes. As you cast you see the long-billed marsh wren, a tiny wooer, rise straight up 10 feet in the air on fast-beating wings, singing his mating song; then, overcome by it all, sink back down to his perch on a reed. You hear the chattering cry of the clapper rail, the raspy wail of a galinule. Add all that to the swirls you see as bass break and feed.

Since brackish-water bass usually inhabit the shallows, you often have a problem with dingy water. Strong winds roll up waves that sweep the bottom and stir the mud. But there's a way to overcome this. Search out heavier growths of weeds that reach right to the surface. Dotted here and there within these patches of weeds you'll often find spots that are bare of vegetation. Within these protected circles the water will be clear.

While they will hit many kinds of lures, top-water and subsurface, the nature of the bass's home grounds makes the fly-rod popper the most effective lure of all. You can work a fly-rod popper in around reeds, close along the bank, around mounds of mud and grass, and back into little bays and coves amid the irregular growth of swamp sedge. It goes in there easily, floats on the water, responds lightly to rod and line play, and is easy to get out again without hanging up, because of the wide gape of the hook.

In spite of the fact that these bass have plenty of water to move about in, they run true to form by taking up residence in certain spots, migrating only with the rise and fall of wind-controlled tides. You'll find them off points, which they seem to use as feeding stations, around duck blinds, where they are often just resting in the shade. They move to cooler spots when the sun goes around, half asleep, but not so sleepy that they'll miss a well-placed bug offered with a minimum of commotion. They lie along the edges of weed beds, under rocks, and all manner of floating live boxes, logs or downed trees. You find them almost anywhere they can locate something to lean against or on which to scratch their backs.

There is little use in fishing long, flat stretches where the bottom is smooth and without the cover that bass like. Unless you see fish working, it's usually unproductive to fish a fly in water 6 feet or more deep. The exceptions are the guts that run like a network of veins through the marshes. In them the water may be 6 or 7 feet deep, but you'll find largemouth lurking close along the upslope of the banks. In many places you can put on hip boots and walk the banks of the guts, streams and man-made canals, watching for risers and casting ahead to good-looking spots. Such places often hold large bass.

One of the most effective ways of bringing hits is to drop a bug as close as possible to tuckahoes and lily pads. It's fun to drop your offering smack on top of a lily pad, let it sit a moment, then yank it off. Suddenly, before it has gone a foot, there's often a resounding strike. Bass seem to think that anything sitting on a lily pad is something good to eat.

During the hot months poppers should be played very slowly. Bass evidently feel the heat, and, like people, don't want to move around too much or too fast. In the summer the best fishing is from daybreak on for a couple of hours, and again a couple of hours before dark. Things are cooler then, the bass more active. In the cooler weather of early spring and autumn, a faster retrieve often does better. In the fall the fish are on the prod, feeding heavily to store up energy for the cold days ahead. Cast in to a dock, boat or bank, let the bug sit still when it hits, then give it a single pop, then start it back in a series of pops, fast all the way until you pick it up for the next cast. One payoff retrieve is to cast 50 feet or less, raise the rod tip as high as you can and make short strips of the line. The bug comes part way out of the water, sways from side to side, tail swishing. It's a beautiful and tantalizing-looking bug just then, and no wonder it makes bass tingle all over and rush up and strike.

Regardless of the speed of your retrieve, always remember to let the bug sit that first few seconds after it hits the water. I've watched bass from a dock when other anglers were casting to them. When the bug lands, the bass will slowly swim 4 or 5 feet away, then stop, turn, and eye the resting bug. The angler gives it a slight pop. The bass beats his fins a bit more rapidly. He's casing that thing up there. He wants to be sure it's what he thinks it is. Another slight pop eases his doubts and he rushes for it.

When bass go down and spurn the best surface offerings, you can sometimes save the day by tying on a bucktail or streamer in red and white, red and yellow, blue and white, all brown, all yellow or all white. I like them on hooks that range from 1/0 through No. 1 and No. 2. Cast these to the same places you would drop a bug, keep the rod tip high on the retrieve in shallow water, and bring the fly back in slow, foot-long jerks. This seems to be the best all-round retrieve for streamers and bucktails, but if it brings no strikes, then experiment a little. Try a fast, even retrieve, make the fly dart forward in erratic jerks, start it back slowly, then speed it up. Mix up your offerings until you find the retrieve they will hit. The strip method of retrieve is best for this because it enables you to bring the fly back at any speed—slow, fast, extra fast. You have control of the line at all times and you are always ready for the strike or the pickup for the next cast.

CHAPTER/9

INSHORE SALTWATER FLY FISHING

LIGHT TACKLE FISHING IN THE SALT IS STILL NEW ENOUGH that the fisherman who goes after ocean swimmers with a fly rod attracts plenty of attention. Yet the true story of saltwater fly fishing goes back a long way. A book entitled *Fly Fishing in Salt and Fresh Water,* published in 1851 in England, mentions the taking of whiting, pollock, mackerel, bass and gray mullet on flies. To merit such mention, fly fishing in the salt must have been conducted well in advance of the publication date of this book. And why not? The art of fly fishing got its start in the freshwaters of England, and had been practiced there for centuries. It makes sense that some adventurous angler would take his salmon outfit to the salty bays, lagoons and inlets and shallows to see what was there that might hit his flies. Who actually hooked and landed the first salty fish on a fly will probably never be known.

On the American scene, *Salt Water Sportsman Magazine* reports that Genio Scott, author of *Fishing in American Waters,* wrote of fly fishing for stripers in 1875. Only a few years later, according to Tarleton H. Bean, who wrote the chapters on marine basses for the book *The Basses, Fresh Water and Marine* (edited by Louis Rhead and published in 1905), members of the famous striped bass clubs of the New England coast now and then used flies, sometimes trolling them, and other times casting them into a strong current, "using a considerable length of line and manipulating it on the surface of the water." They used gaudy flies and black-bass tackle.

At an equally early date, around 1875, at least one fly fisherman was taking shad on trout flies below tidewater on the Susquehanna River, as was reported in Baltimore newspapers.

In his book *Camping and Cruising in Florida,* published in 1884, Dr. James A. Henshall says that in 1878 he fished the vicinity of Fort Capron, Florida, and took "crevalle of 5 pounds, sea trout of 10 pounds, redfish of 5 pounds, bluefish of 4 pounds, "snooks" or sergentfish of 6 pounds, ladyfish of 2 pounds, and tarpon of 10 pounds" all on flies. This comes close to giving him the honor of landing the first saltwater fish on a fly in U.S. Continental waters.

Not long afterwards, Frank S. Pinckney wrote a book called *Tarpon or Silver King,* published in 1888, in which he says that Dr. George Trowbridge of New York had caught a baby tarpon weighing 1 pound 3 ounces on a fly. That puts Trowbridge right up there on the heels of Dr. Henshall.

Around 1900 the Dimocks, A.W. and Julian, father and son, caught tarpon regularly on flies, and Julian took some of the greatest pictures ever made of leaping tarpon, pictures that are phenomenal when you consider the equipment available in those days. The Dimock's fine *Book of the Tarpon* is a delight to read.

To my personal knowledge, Tom Loving of Baltimore began to consistently take shad on flies in the 1920s, and by 1922 was tying flies especially for shad, striped bass and brackish-water largemouth black bass.

Another fly-rod pioneer, Colonel L.S. Thompson of Red Bank, New Jersey, fished at Long Key in 1926, with Captain J.T. Harrod, one of Florida's greatest guides. The Colonel caught plenty of tarpon to 20 pounds, using royal coachman flies, and he also latched onto a couple of bonefish, although, as J.T. says: "We thought it was an accident, so we didn't try for bonefish but instead concentrated on the tarpon."

Two of the earliest bonefish bucktails—the Frankee-Belle (top) and the Phillips bonefish bucktail, both on 1/0 hooks.

By the time the now renowned Rod & Reel Club of Miami Beach, Florida, was started in 1928, some of its members had already taken tarpon on a fly, and snook in the shallow waters of Florida Bay and the canals around Miami. Two of the earlier fly fishermen who did a valuable job in bringing the shallow saltwater fishing possibilities to the attention of fly-rodders were Red Greb and Homer Rhode, of Miami. And far out on the West Coast, pioneer Oregon fly-rod men were working out ties for the imported stripers and shad, as well as the resident silver and king salmon.

But these were lone riders, and it was not until 1947 that the main body of fly fishermen came awake to the knowledge that in the salt was a whole new world for them to explore, and that, as a result of that upsurge in fly fishing the salt, commercially tied saltwater flies began to appear. Since then a standard set of flies has evolved, all of which do a good job in the ocean shallows, and in some cases over the ocean deeps as well.

Saltwater fish seldom, if ever, feed on real flies which have fallen to the surface of the ocean, and there is no aquatic hatch similar to that of a freshwater stream or lake, and therefore there are no dry flies tied for salt water. Rather, flies for the briny have been designed to imitate such common forms of ocean-going fish food as minnows, crabs, shrimp, small worms of the ocean, sand fleas, and so on, and saltwater fly fishing is therefore almost entirely confined to streamers, bucktails and popping bugs.

Most saltwater streamers are tied with three or four saddle hackle feathers on each side of the hook, so that as the streamer is retrieved in foot-long jerks, the feathers will work, closing each time a strip is made, and flaring outwards again when the pull is stopped. These flies, known as "breathers," are often as much as 5 inches in overall length, tied on 3/0 hooks.

The breathers are good numbers for tarpon, striped bass, channel bass, snook, jack crevalle, big snappers, ladyfish, and many other less commonly sought game fish of the seas. Smaller editions of the same breather flies, tied on a 1/0 hook, are also used for bonefish when the fish are in fairly deep water, this hook having sufficient weight to get down to them. But when bonefish are in very shallow water, a bucktail tied on a No. 1 hook, or even a No. 2 hook, will float better, and not catch on the bottom so readily. And when the fish are feeding on extremely low tide, then even lighter hooks, as small as No. 4, are used.

In the Bahamas the flats are extremely shallow at low tide. When bonefish come up on them to feed there is often so little water that their backs are sticking out. A fly tied on a heavy hook would sink too rapidly and catch on the bottom, so the No. 2 or No. 4 hooks are in order. In some cases, anglers even use Palmer-tied flies there, so that the hackle makes a shield sufficient to prevent the point of the hook from hanging up on weeds or coral.

Another tie which solves some of the problems of fishing the very shallow flats is a pink shrimp. These little numbers, on a No. 4 hook, are tied with the hair wrapped around the

The shrimp fly, a top taker of bonefish and permit, is tied in three sizes, for varying depths of water.

Blonde flies are among the best in salt water. Left, top to bottom: platinum blonde, Argentine blonde, black blonde. Right, top to bottom: honey blonde, pink blonde, strawberry blonde.

body of the hook and enough of it protruding underneath to make it almost weedless. It floats high in the water, and is perfect for shallow flats.

Like the bonefish, other saltwater species require different flies according to the water in which the angler is fishing for them. Snook in deep water take the bigger bucktails and streamers, but in canals, when they are feeding on schools of small minnows, herding them into the bank and then striking into them open-mouthed—then a small, inch-long bucktail on a No. 1 hook most nearly matches the minnows. Some enormous snook have been taken on such small bucktails. And in like manner, the flies designed for tarpon vary considerably in size. Fishing for baby tarpon, from 2 to 20 pounds, calls for a 1/0 hook, while for their bigger brothers, the 3/0 is better and if you are going to tangle with 100-pound or better tarpon, you should go to the 4/0 or 5/0 hook.

Poppers are potent lures for almost every saltwater species, in one circumstance or another, and because of the thrill the angler gets when he sees some big, hard-hitting ocean fish sock a surface lure, they are widely used. Some poppers are built so they will skip across the water making plenty of commotion, looking like a small fish jumping and tailwalking in an effort to escape some predatory monster that is on his trail. Others have cork bodies and bullet noses and are called sliders because they go along the top without noise. These are good in canals and in tight spots such as openings in the mangroves where a hard-popped bug might scare the fish.

One of the best producers for snook is the 3/0 skipping bug. There is something about the action, the noise of the pops, the look of the wounded minnow, of this bug, that gets a quick response from big snook. They fly out from under overhanging mangrove limbs, or from under a log, and take this surface fooler with a lunge and a clank of formidable jaws.

In addition to these special designs for salt water, practically all the freshwater designs for bugs have been brought to the sea, the only alteration being that they are tied on heavier hooks to combat the crushing power of saltwater gangsters' hard-mouthed jaws.

In the early days of saltwater fishing, because of the rust

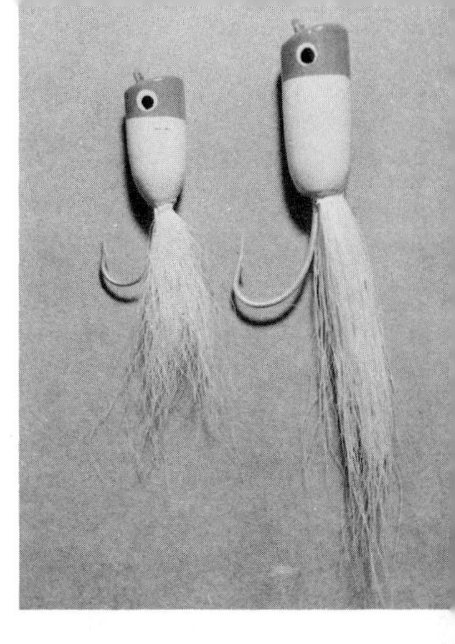

The famous skipping bug, first tied by the author to simulate the action of a baitfish running away form a charging gamefish. Skipping bug at right is on 3/0 hook. The one at left, on a 1/0 hook, is a prime favorite for baby tarpon up to 20 pounds, as well as many other species in both salt and fresh water.

problem, all these flies were tied on Z-nickel hooks, but rust proofing has now made many of the lighter hooks suitable, too.

As with freshwater flies, color is always a point of argument. It seems that the color which is good one day may be totally ignored the next. And saltwater fish being the obstreperous hitters they are, will sock almost anything that is offered them, at one time or another, further confusing the issue.

But in general, the same color combinations which have proven fish getters in fresh water are emerging as the standbys for salt. Barred rock wings are good in streamers, as are red and yellow, red and white, yellow and white, and brown and white. Plain yellow and plain white in the bucktails are universally good. And so are small white bucktails in any of a number of variations of trim, from a few hairs of blue on top to a few of brown.

Orange has come on strong as a saltwater color, and the combination of red and orange, as in the strawberry blonde fly, has proven to be great for many saltwater fish, including the spotted sea trout, ladyfish, snook, redfish, jacks and both baby and big tarpon.

Below are listed some of the best-known flies and poppers for all types of saltwater fishing.

SALTWATER FLIES

FRANKEE-BELLE BONEFISH FLY

HACKLE None
BODY Yellow chenille
WINGS Barred rock over white feather, 1½ inches long, one on each side of hook
THROAT White bucktail under hook and going back ½ inch beyond bend of hook
HOOK 1/0

PHILLIPS BONEFISH BUCKTAIL

HACKLE White, two feathers about 5 inches long
BODY Brown chenille
WINGS Brown over white bucktail, 1½ inches long
HOOK No. 4 for water 5 inches to 1 foot deep. 1/0 for water 1 to 2 feet. Deeper–3/0

HAGEN SANDS BONEFISH FLY

HACKLE None
BODY None
WINGS Yellow and barred rock, two on each side of hook White bucktail tied on under feathers, all on top of hook shank
HEAD Built-up and eyed
HOOK 1/0

BILL SMITH FLIES

GLADY-I TARPON STREAMER

HACKLE Saddle hackle, 4 inches long, wrapped around, tied off with red thread
BODY None
WINGS Saddle hackles 4 inches long, three on each side of hook, flared outward, dull sides together
HOOK 5/0

This fly is tied with red hackle and white wings, red hackle and yellow wings, red hackle and orange wings, blue hackle and white wings, and all blue. The last two are especially good for big snook.

SALTUS BONEFISH AND PERMIT FLY

HACKLE	White
BODY	Orange thread wrapped sparsely around hook shank to within 1/4 inch of bend
WINGS	Ostrich wings over white bucktail, 2 1/2 inches long
HOOK	1/0

TIM-REP (permit spelled backwards)
BONEFISH AND PERMIT FLY

HACKLE	White
BODY	Orange thread wrapped sparsely around hook shank to within 1/4 inch of bend
WINGS	Ostrich wings over white bucktail, 2 1/2 inches long
HOOK	3/0

TED WILLIAMS TARPON STREAMER

HACKLE	Red
BODY	None
WINGS	4 1/2-inch saddle hackles, three to a side, yellow or white
HOOK	5/0

TED WILLIAMS BONEFISH FLY

HACKLE	Brown
BODY	White chenille
WINGS	2-inch white bucktail
HOOK	1/0

PHILLIPS MULTIWING STREAMER

HACKLE	Two feathers about 5 inches long
BODY	White chenille
WINGS	Eight feathers atop hook, four to a side, flared outward
HOOK	1/0

This fly is tied with red hackle and white wings, red hackle and yellow wings, red hackle and barred rock wings.

PHILLIPS PINK SHRIMP

HACKLE	Pink hackle tied Palmer over body
HOOD	Pink bucktail
BODY	Silver oval tinsel
TAIL	Pink bucktail
HOOK	No. 2, 4, 6, 1/0

The body is weighted under the hook with two rows of lead.

BLONDE FLIES

HACKLE	None
BODY	Silver tinsel wrapped around hook shank
WINGS	One 3-inch bucktail tied in just behind the hook eye. One 3-inch bucktail tied at the bend of the hook. Both are tied on top of the hook shank
HOOKS	1/0, 3/0, and, for big tarpon, 5/0

THE FRY FLY

HACKLE	None
BODY	White chenille built up in shoulders behind hook eye and tapered down to bend of hook
TAIL	White chenille
HOOK	No. 2, 4, 6, 1/0

THE HORROR

HACKLE	None
BODY	Yellow chenille, ½-inch long. There is a ⅛-inch wrap of chenille behind bucktail wing, which assures a steady wing that covers point of hook
WINGS	Brown bucktail, 1½ inches long, coming out from under chenille body ½ inch from hook eye and protruding ¾ inch beyond bend of hook. When cast and worked, the hook rides up, does not snag on bottom in shallow water.

CONNECTICUT RIVER SHAD FLY #1

BODY	Flat silver tinsel

WINGS Red-dyed duck feathers, 1/4 inch wide, tied upright at middle of shank
HOOK 1/0 with red bead ahead of hook

CONNECTICUT RIVER SHAD FLY #2

BODY Flat silver tinsel
WINGS Orange-dyed duck feather, 1/4 inch long
TAIL Orange-dyed duck feather, 1 inch long
HOOK 1/0 with red bead ahead of hook

SUSQUEHANNA SHAD FLY

BODY White chenille with silver tinsel ribbing
WINGS White bucktail
TAIL Golden pheasant tippet
HOOK No. 8 long

TOM LOVING'S ORIGINAL SHAD FLY
(tied with one or two hooks)

HACKLE None
BODY White chenille with black ribbing
WINGS Single white bucktail wing, 1 inch long
HOOK SIZES 6 to 12

PACIFIC COAST SHAD FLY

BODY Red wool, gold tinsel ribbing
WINGS Black bucktail, 1 1/4 inches long
HACKLE White bucktail, 2 inches long, under hook
HEAD Black
HOOK 2X, short

HAROLD GIBBS STRIPER FLY

BODY Silver, no tag
WINGS White bucktail, 3 inches long, fairly full, 1 1/2-inch bright blue feather as cheek, tapering to point, each side. Shorter cheek (tied over blue feathers) of brown feather with white rib, 3/4 inch long.
HEAD Painted yellow eyes with small black dot for pupil

GALLASCH SAILFISH FLY #1

BODY	White dylite, 1 inch long, 3/4 inch diameter, small flat face with body tapering to larger diameter at back
TAIL	White saddle hackles, 5 to 6 inches long
HOOK	7/0

GALLASCH SAILFISH FLY #2

BODY	White dylite, 1 inch long, 3/4 inch diameter, large flat face with body tapering to smaller diameter at back
TAIL	White saddle hackles, 5 to 6 inches long
HOOK	7/0

GALLASCH TARPON AND REDFISH STREAMER FLIES (also used for sailfish)

GALLASCH TARPON STREAMER #1 (Red and White)

BODY	White chenille, 3/4 inch long, wisp of bucktail comes out of chenille to just beyond bend of hook
HACKLE	Red
WINGS	White saddle hackle, 5 inches long, 3 feathers on each side of hook, tied to flair outwards
HOOK	3/0 (with wings 4 inches long); 5/0 (with wings 5 inches long)

GALLASCH TARPON STREAMER #2 (Red and Yellow)

BODY	Yellow chenille, 3/4 inch long, wisp of bucktail comes out from chenille to just beyond bend of hook
HACKLE	Red
WINGS	Yellow saddle hackle, 5 inches long, 3 feathers on each side of hook, tied to flair outwards
HOOK	3/0 (with wings 4 inches long); 5/0 (with wings 5 inches long)

GALLASCH TARPON STREAMER #3 (Red and Orange)

BODY	Orange chenille, 3/4 inch long, wisp of orange bucktail comes out from chenille to just beyond bend of hook

HACKLE Red

WINGS Orange saddle hackle, 5 inches long, 3 feathers on each side of hook, tied to flair outwards

HOOK 3/0 (with wings 4 inches long); 5/0 (with wings 5 inches long)

WEB ROBINSON BILLFISH FLY

BODY White dylite, 1 inch long, 3/4 inch diameter, flat underside, concave face painted red

TAIL White saddle hackle, 6 each side, 5 inches long

HOOK 6/0, placed to ride upright from body

LEE WULFF'S BILLFISH FLY, THE SEA WULFF

WINGS Long, white and yellow

HACKLE Red and yellow

HOOK Tandem, 4/0 separated by less than a shank's length of 100-pound test nylon

SKIPPING BUG

BODY Balsa wood, face slanted down and back from top

TAIL Same color as body

HOOK With 1/0 hook, body is 1 inch long with 1/2 inch diameter face and tail 2 1/2 inches long

2/0 with body 1 1/4 inches long with 5/8 inch diameter face and tail 3 1/4 inches long

3/0 with body 1 1/2 inches long with 5/8 inch diameter face and tail 3 1/2 inches long

COLOR All white, yellow, pink or black. Combinations of red and white, red and yellow, blue and white. The red or blue is at the front of the bug, 1/2 inch wide from the face

Specifications for saltwater fly-fishing tackle are included in the chapter on equipment in this book, but I think it worthwhile to outline them briefly here, with special reference to the species being dealt with.

Anyone who has a good bass-bug rod, properly lined, is reasonably well equipped to fly fish the salt. But as recommended in the rod chapter, earlier, the ideal is a 9- or 9½-foot rod with slow action that comes right down into the grip. The slow action is needed to handle the large, wind-resistant lures commonly used in saltwater fly fishing, to wait for them to travel slowly rearwards, complete the loop at the end of the backcast, and then have the power to make the forward throw. A stiff, fast-action rod snaps back too soon for this slow back loop and the line will drop and power is lost. Also, with a stiff rod the caster will have to make several casts in order to get out sufficient line and such repeated false casts are very tiring, especially in wind, which is often a hazard on saltwater flats. A slow rod enables him to get off a quick toss to an oncoming fish without loss of time.

I like the 9½-foot stick better than the 9-footer. The added length gives greater height on the backcast, making for a better throw; and the length comes in handy when playing the lure in extremely shallow water. By holding the rod high you can often prevent the fly from catching on the bottom and keep it swimming in a couple of inches of water. You can bring the line in better, keep it coming until both line and leader are out of the water and only the fly resting on the surface. Then the added height of the rod helps as you give a backward and upward flip of your wrist, for the backcast for the next throw. The fly leaves the water without a ripple.

Because of the lighter tip of the 9½-foot stick you can impart better action to fly or popping bug, make them do tricks that would be impossible with a stiffer, heavier tip. And with many shallow-water swimmers fly action is very important in getting strikes. With this rod I use a WF-8-F almost all the time. This light line can be dropped on the surface far more quietly than the heavier WF-9-F, and this makes a difference. I remember one day when there was a bit of a wind up so I was using a WF-9-F. When the wind dropped I kept on using it. I cast to several fish and noticed that they shied off, giving me the eye and then swimming slowly away. The fly was not falling too close to them, I was using a 14-foot leader, so at last I figured that it had to be the sound of the line hitting the surface that was alerting them. I put on a reel loaded with a WF-8-F line and right away began to get hits. This is important to remember. In the salt fish are scary, and sometimes more scary than those in fresh water. Take advantage of everything you can to make your presentation quiet and easy.

As mentioned earlier, in the tackle chapter of this book, the stiff rods show their value when anglers go for 100-pound tarpon, and some that go near the 200-pound mark. The present fly rod record is 151 pounds, a fish caught by Pan American airways pilot Stu Apte of Miami, an avid saltwater angler. Because the 12-pound-test hard nylon leader tippets used for this fishing are so strong, the big tarpon will tow the skiff, and when they get deep or lie still, as they sometimes do, this is the rod needed to pull them and pump them and get them in. The same applies with the fly-rod technique for taking sailfish and striped marlin. You must have a stick or you just can't get these fish in.

These two rods are, to me, the only ones you need for saltwater fly fishing. The slow action alone does the job except for the few anglers who go for the extra-big fish.

The lining of these big rods is all important. A level line will not shoot well, and a double taper is so light on the end that it will fold up in the wind. But a WF-8-F forward taper (for explanation of this and other line-diameter terms, see section on LINES) will bring out everything that is in the rod. You can shoot the head of the line and the weight up front will pull the shooting line after it. It is possible to pick up 35 feet of line and shoot an additional 35 feet, all with only one backcast. It takes the work out of fishing and an angler who uses this equipment can fish all day with pleasure. Yet if he were to try to pick up, say 50 feet of line, false cast it a couple of times, and heave it out, his arm would fall off by the end of the day.

Generally the lines used for saltwater fly fishing will be the WF-8-F and the WF-9-F, and sometimes, according to the rod, the WF-10-F (*see* LINES IN TACKLE CHAPTER). Sinking lines also have their place in the salt. Care should be taken to select the proper sinking line for the depth of water you are going to fish. The Hi-Density line will sink in its entirety, getting the line down in a hurry. Scientific Anglers' Wet-Head, sinking/floating line, is good for fishing in water from 4 to 12 feet deep because the first 30 feet of the line will sink while the remainder, the shooting or running line, will float. If you want to be ready for all eventualities you should have reels loaded with both, in your gear.

The tapered leader is an important adjunct to the WF-9-F line. The leader should start with a 30-pound-test nylon butt section, then taper, in an overall length of 12 feet, through 20, 15, 12 and 10 to whatever fineness is desired on the tippet. For big tarpon and snook, most fishermen who go for them use a 12-pound-test tippet. For fish like channel bass and stripers, a 10-pound-test tippet assures enough strikes and has the strength to withstand the weight and rough tactics of these great fighters. For bonefish and ladyfish, tippets are tapered as low as 6- and sometimes 4-pound test. In all cases, the butt section and the tippet section should be longer than the other parts of the leader—the butt section because it will help the casting by the added stiffness near the fly line; and the tippet because the long, finer nylon allows the angler to give more action to the fly and also keeps the fish from seeing the leader.

Because so many of the briny speedsters make long runs, a saltwater reel should carry at least 200 yards of backing as well as the fly line. Some of these fast-running fish would break the leader or the rod tip if they weren't allowed to run. Most of the larger freshwater reels, and practically all of the good Atlantic salmon reels, are large enough to hold this much backing.

For general saltwater fishing this backing is usually 250 yards of 18-pound-test nylon squidding line; while for big tarpon and other huge fish the backing is usually a couple hundred yards of 30-pound-test dacron. The reason for the difference in backing is that when you fish the shallows a fish may run your line or backing around a sea fan, sponge or bit of coral, and the stretch of the nylon squidding line is then an asset, giving enough that in many cases it prevents the fish from snapping the tippet. The 30-pound-test dacron has practically no stretch and so is a help when you have to lift and pull a heavy fish.

The saltwater fly reel should have a smooth, strong drag. A reel which has practically no drag would let the fish run on and on, in spite of such finger drag as you might apply. Applying the drag manually may be alright for veterans, but for the average angler who only goes out for a few weeks out of the year, fishing will be much more productive and much more fun if he has a reel with a good drag.

I've seen big tarpon swim and feed, hardly knowing they were hooked on lighter gear. The thing that makes a fish work is a drag of 5 or 6 pounds, keeping relentless pressure on him. Even then it takes a long time to land a big fish.

With bonefish, on the other hand, I like to use a very light drag, just enough to keep the fish from getting away from the pressure, to keep him from making a loop and getting slack line. I get a big bang out of that first all-out run for the deep, across the shallow flat, wide open, busting down everything in front of him. A stout drag would bring him in more quickly, but I'd miss the fun of the run.

Other species such as spotted seatrout, ladyfish, cuda, small snappers to 7 pounds, jack crevalle to 7 or 8 pounds, and such swimmers, also do not call for a very heavy drag.

In all cases, however, the drag must be matched to the weight of the leader tippet being used. Most saltwater fly casters use a 6- or 8-pound-test leader tippet for bonefish and other shallow-water swimmers, and seldom go above 12-pound test. For bonefish and permit, I like to use a 6-pound-test tippet on smooth flats where there are not many obstacles. On flats where there are sea fans and coral, I go to 8- or 10-pound-test tippets.

With such species as tarpon, snook and ladyfish, the danger to the tippet comes from the fraying or cutting power of the fish rather than from breakage, and that's a hazard you have to face regardless of the weight of the tippet. I remember one 150-pound tarpon (estimated), that I fought for an hour and a half. He finally frayed through the knot of the 12-inch trace at the eye of the fly. That knot was made of 80-pound-test nylon leader material. This 12-inch length of 60-, 80- or 100-pound-test nylon is widely used when the angler is out after big tarpon, billfish, amberjack, sharks, dolphin and Allison tuna. It is far better than a length of wire, which often twists and then breaks as a result of the wild antics of these fish. Wire, however, is often used for barracuda and bluefish, a 6-inch length of No. 4 or 5 wire being sufficient to defeat the sharp teeth.

Many fishing clubs list two classifications under Fly Fishing—*Fly, Light,* which stipulates a leader tippet of not more than 12-pound test; and *Fly, Heavy,* which permits a 12-pound test tippet plus 12 inches of any leader material. This is where the trace of heavy nylon comes in, to defeat the fraying action of tarpon, ladyfish, snook, sailfish and marlin.

Since salty fish are highly individual in their reactions, the playing of the lure is important, and only experience teaches exactly what each fish wants under varying conditions. But basic to all lure play, regardless of the end result being sought, is the strip method of retrieve. The strip enables the fisherman to bring the fly back in jerks to match the action of a swimming minnow, shrimp or crab. With this method he can give the fly a 6-inch pull or bring it forward a foot. He can slow or speed the retrieve or stop it altogether, and yet he will always have a line that is good and tight for the strike or for the pickup.

In Northeastern waters, the striped bass is probably the choice of fly-rod possibilities. Hard hitting, slashing and rambunctious, he moves into the shallows of coastal areas all the way from New England to northern Florida, and cruises the shores in 3 to 4 feet of water, an ideal target for flies.

Saltwater fishermen who've fished for striped bass know that they are rough and tumble hitters and ready feeders. They are famous for their gluttonous orgies in schools of bait. But go for those same stripers in shallow bays and see what happens. Approach them when a school is breaking the surface after bait fish. A few casts, a few fish caught, and down go the works. You can hang around hopefully watching the gulls and waiting for them to come up again. Sometimes they do, but more often than not it's curtains for the day. Like all their salty brothers, striped bass take some fancy fishing when they are within reach of light-tackle lures.

Once while I was fishing at Fox Island on the Chesapeake with Howard Cox of Cincinnati, we found the right timing on that score. Fishing off the southeast corner of the island, we each took a couple of 4-pounders with popping bugs, and then the water went flat. No action at all, where twenty minutes before fish had been all over the place. I strolled across the 400 feet to the other side of the island. The tide was running good and there was a 12-foot-deep channel just 20 feet out. My first cast brought a hit and I landed a 6-pounder. Howard came hurrying over then, and we took two more fish before that batch went down like a fallen cake in an oven, and for the same reason—too much noise.

We went back to the other side. This time we each took one fish. We sashayed back again to the other side. One fish there, this time, and the next two treks were barren. Those resident fish didn't like strangers any more, so they had taken off for more peaceful waters.

In the Chesapeake Bay area, where they are known as rockfish or simply as "rock," stripers feed along the salt marshes looking for soft crabs, minnows and schools of alewives. The bigger ones work singly or in pairs, and now and then a school of smaller fish will sweep by. All a guy needs is a pair of hip boots for walking the muddy banks, a landing net, and proper fly equipment. He wants to have big popping bugs and 5-inch-long streamers or bucktails for flies, because big stripers like a big mouthful and the smaller ones will hit a lure almost as big as themselves, anyway, so why quibble?

There is some of this kind of fishing along the New Jersey marshes, with weakfish to be caught as an extra dividend on the same junket.

In the sounds, inlets, bays and bights of the Chesapeake, rock also work up on the flats on either side of the channels to feed. Usually they are active on the flats from three-quarters of the way in on the tide through the high water to three-quarters of the way out, but there is so much variation in this,

The author, with fly rod and popping bug, gets striper action wading the shores of little bays.

in different areas, that the only way to be sure of hitting it right is either to fish regardless of tide, or to find a local angler who knows the score and be advised by him. In the summer, in most places, the best time for stripers is at dawn and again at dusk, and many charter boat captains never go after them until after dark.

Fly fishing is still new enough to startle the old timers in the Chesapeake area. I remember fishing one evening near Gwynn's Island, Virginia, a spot where the fish come up on the flats to feed in about 4 feet of water, making for wonderful streamer-fly and popping-bug fishing.

As I cast, I heard the crunk, crunk, crunk of an oar working in the stern of a skiff. A Negro waterman came sculling around the point just below where I had thrown the popper.

"Hey!" I yelled. "Hold it a minute."

My bug was sitting there on top of the water, right in his path, and I had an idea that a big striper was lying down there eyeing it. I popped the bug once, then let it stay still. Then I popped it again.

His boat drifting with the tide, the homeward bound sculler watched this peculiar behavior with amazement.

Then that fish took. I set the hook and had my hands full of bouncing fly rod, whirling reel handle and roughhouse striper. We had it hot and heavy for ten minutes, and all the time that oysterman stood there motionless in his skiff, leaning on his oar, goggle-eyed. As I finally lifted the 8-pound striper aboard, he shook his head.

"You sho' got som'p'n der," he admired. "What bait you got, Cap'n?"

He sculled up close and I held up the big tenite bug for him to see.

He looked at it in silence for a full minute. Then, "He eat DAT?" he asked incredulously. And as he sculled away, shaking his head from side to side, I could hear him muttering to himself.

"Dey eat DAT! Dem rock eat DAT!"

Dem rock'll eat any good fly-rod lure you put in front of them.

New England surfmen have made a fine study of the huge

An all-white 3/0 skipping bug got this 29-pound, 6-ounce striped bass, a fly-rod world record on 12-pound-test leader tippet.

stripers that come their way and the lures they take, and those boys, who are really experts at heavyweight fishing, know the answer. Big striped bass like a big mouthful, and by mouthful they mean a plug that measures 12 to 14 inches in length.

The only chance a fly-rod man has for a really big fish, then, is to use the biggest popper he can throw and then make as much disturbance with it as possible, in an effort to convince nearby stripers that here it is, something big and lively and good to eat. In other words, the flyman has to sell the sizzle, not the steak.

And the way to make the sizzle sound like pure champagne popping, to a striper, is to throw a 5- or 6-inch-long skipping bug out in the vicinity of a big bull striper and then give it a couple of hardest pops you can impart to it. Then pull the entire bug beneath the surface and with a hard yank bring it along below the surface for a couple of feet. This makes the bug throw up a burst of bubbles, big, loud and disturbing enough to bring any striper within a hundred feet zooming over to investigate. Then, after that, let the bug sit quietly on the surface for at least a half-minute, time enough for the fish to get over to it, then give it a very quiet pop, then a series of hard pops.

If a striper doesn't hit, then give that underwater pull again, and if that doesn't work, there just aren't any stripers around.

The reader may think that I am being too explicit in outlining every move of the bug play, but that technique has paid off for me many times and on one occasion attracted the two biggest stripers I have ever been lucky enough to hook. It was at Coos Bay, Oregon, and we were cruising along while I cast a big white balsa-wood popper against the shoreline rocks where the water was about 3 feet deep.

I would let the popper sit still a second, then give it a hard pull, one that yanked it under the surface and kept it coming for a foot before it bobbed to the top. It put up a combination of pop and bursting bubbles that could be seen for quite a distance. Any nearby striper was almost sure to see that commotion and come over to find out what was happening. So then I let the bug sit still and waited for one to investigate.

When I thought enough time had elapsed for any fish within

100 feet to arrive on the spot, I gave the bug a slight pop, just enough to make it look alive, like a real bug struggling. Then I let it stay quiet for half a minute, then dented the surface with a quick, loud pop.

That was the one that talked turkey. A great swirl came up under the bug and made it bounce. Before I had time to get set I saw the blurred shape of a huge fish as he came halfway out, took that bug on the go, and raced for the deep water. He was 100 feet away before I got over the shock of the strike. Then my fingers began to tingle as the blood came back into them and I got into that fight. That was the most shocking and powerful strike I ever had.

And this was a big fish. He kept going for 200 feet, out to deep water, and then he went down. He must have gone down 50 feet, then leveled and headed for the Pacific like a tramp steamer, slow but strong and steady. Maybe I'd never stop him!

I tightened the drag on the big single-action salmon reel I was using, put a bend in the 9½-foot rod and hung on. I gave line, pumped some in, gave line again, and got it back. I knew that as far as equipment went, I had the best and that if anything gave it would be the 12-pound-test nylon tippet. Unless, of course, he stripped me down to the reel, and in that case he might break the 14-pound-test nylon squidding line I was using as backing for the fly line.

Finally after three-quarters of an hour, he surfaced, 60 feet from the boat. His dorsal fin came out.

I heard a shout from the captain, and then Chan Brown and Don Harger, both of whom were with me at the time, gasped.

"It's bigger than the other one," the captain said. "It must be 35 pounds."

We all got a good look at its broad back and could even see the stripes along its sides. Then it dove and after a bit the hook came out and the popper drifted to the top.

I felt like a deflated balloon. That was a tough fish to lose. But it was a great fish to have on, too, and I was somewhat consoled by the fact that I already had a nice fly-rod striper in the boat, a 29-pound 6-ounces that I had caught on that same popping bug just an hour before, using exactly that same series of pops, rests and retrieves. That was a record on a fly for almost twenty years. Then, in 1966 Russell Chatham of Black Point, California, took one that weighed 36 pounds 6 ouncer, on a fly outfit with 15-pound-test tippet. This is the new world record, but mine still holds up in the 12-pound-test tippet class.

Many waters that are good for stripers are also good for shad. Shad run into East Coast freshwater rivers from Florida to Nova Scotia, the most famous shad rivers of the East being the St. John's in Florida, the Susquehanna in Maryland, the Potomac in the same state, and the Connecticut River in Connecticut. They are also found on the West Coast, in some of the Oregon rivers, having been transplanted from the East and planted in Pacific waters in 1879.

The shad, sometimes called white shad, bears the Latin tag *Alosa sapidissima,* while the hickory shad, a close relative (also called Taylor herring) is *Alosa mediocris,* not nearly as good a fish from the sportsman's point of view. Both are anadromous, being saltwater fish that ascend freshwater rivers to spawn. They usually enter the rivers in March or April and stay until May or June before once again heading back to the salt. Once there they go straight on out and disappear in the depths beyond the continental shelf.

But while in the rivers they hit a fly hard and if they miss it, as they often do, they keep going for it, giving it thumping strikes all the way in to the boat. Or once hooked, they dart off downstream in a wild dash, then cut across current, and they usually come up with some good jumps during the fight. It may take as long as 20 minutes to land a 6-pound shad, and that while using a 9½-foot fly rod and a leader tapered to a 6-pound-test tippet. The biggest fish are the roe shad, running as high as 8 pounds, while the males are smaller, usually reaching a top of 3 to 3½ pounds.

Shad have been called the poor man's salmon and with some justification. They come up the river like salmon, in runs. They spread out in the pools like salmon. And they take a small fly like salmon. Their fight is not as swift, their jumps not as violent or as high, but they are dogged and will sometimes take longer to land.

A lot of shad are taken trolling with a fly rod and fly, but the fun of shad fishing is in casting for them. Usually it takes moving current to put them in the mood to hit, but when you catch a run heading upstream, you are in for some great fishing. The best pitch for shad is to cast across current, allow the fly to sink about a foot, and then bring it back in even, 2-foot-long jerks, slowly, but steadily. The shad will come to the top as they roll at the fly and will often miss, but back they will come, keeping on striking and each time they hit, it will numb your fingers.

Once with Fred Narvel on the Susquehanna River below the Conowingo Dam we were anchored, and casting in to the shore where shad often travel as they move upstream. We had caught three or four fish, using small white bucktails, but things had quieted down and we were just about to move. Then both Fred and I had hits at once. These were bigger fish, too, and we were hard at it for the next ten minutes before bringing them in to net. They were each about 5 pounds. And no sooner had we got our flies back in the water than we both had hits again. This kept up until we thought it was never going to stop, and when finally those fish went on and left us, they left us with our tongues hanging out. That is the only time I ever caught two fish with a single hook. As I put the net down to bring in one of my fish and pulled upwards, I discovered two fish in the net. A small buck had been travelling with the hooked roe shad and had even followed it into the net. We had often seen a couple of bucks on either side of a roe fish, pressing against it, so we knew what had happened. Those fish were ready to spawn and those eager bucks were trying to hurry nature's process along.

We had it that day, such fishing as you dream about.

Shad have a strange way of working their jaws when hooked. They keep opening and closing their mouths as if trying to work the hook loose, and that is what they eventually do. Their cheek covers are paper thin, and if hooked there it is only a short time before they have made a big hole there, and have worked the hook through their cheeks.

Shad will hit many flies, small bucktails, wet flies, even Atlantic salmon flies, and especially the shad flies such as the Connecticut River shad fly, described earlier, and those tied for other well-known rivers.

The hickory shad has habits much like those of his big brother. He comes into the same rivers, but in greater numbers, and more often. And when a run of hickory shad hits a river there is plenty of action because these fish really go for flies. They reach a top weight of 3 pounds, they jump often when hooked, and they put up a good fight, but nothing like that of the true shad. They have one habit that detracts from their fight and that keeps them from being truly great fighters —they will run straight upstream to the boat, making it easy to pull them in and net them. But a hickory will jump as many as six or seven times, and their hard strike alone is worth going for. They sock a fly so hard they almost knock the rod from your hands.

Hickory shad are not good to eat and their bodies are laced and interlaced with bones, but their roe is very good, finer and tastier, many people consider, than that of the shad.

With the advent of the new sinking lines (*see* TACKLE) the fly man now has a much better chance of taking shad. It should be remembered that the leader must be kept down to about 6 feet in length so the fly will stay down. When you use a 10- or 12-foot length the current pushes the light leader and the fly upward and away from the lie of the shad. The short leader keeps the fly down where the fish are.

Big tarpon react to poppers in much the same way as big stripers do. A small popper may get a small one but more than likely it will go unnoticed by the whoppers. Yet with a single pop of a big bug, the angler can turn that same big tarpon from as far away as 80 feet.

From 5 inches to 200 pounds, tarpon, more than any other saltwater fish, fall for a well-placed fly or bug. A 6-inch tarpon will hit as boldy, jump and fight with the same abandon, in miniature, as his full-grown pappy. And the little fellows will frequently hit just as big and bright a lure, too, the only reason for using the smaller one being that the babies sometimes are difficult to hook with a large lure.

In the Tamiami Trail Canal and along the Flamingo Road

Canal near Homestead, Florida, schools of these tarpon, moving along and feeding with the tide, provide some of the most exciting small fish angling to be found anywhere. The fish range in size from 2 to 20 pounds, with a few as big as 30 pounds. In the autumn, after the spawning season, there are often schools of them as small as 8 inches in length, and these make wonderful decorative mounts.

On one trip to Flamingo, I was fishing with Curt Gowdy, TV sports announcer, when we got into a school of those tiny fellows.

"I've never seen such small tarpon," said Curt, when we spied them rolling in West Lake. "What fly will take them?"

"Try one of those small bream popping bugs," I suggested. "They'll hit on top, and that should be just about the right size."

It was. Curt's first cast got a hit and we watched that 8-inch-long silver kinglet leap and turn on a really good scrap for his size.

Later, in the Tamiami Trail Canal, we connected with some of his 30-pound brothers and had the same sport on a grander scale.

Often in these canals it is necessary to run or drive in order to keep ahead of the fish, so quickly do they move down the narrow canal. So the fishermen tear along, running, casting, getting hits and landing fish or losing them. Then back into the car again, and the same thing all over again, sometimes for several miles, until the school either goes down under the constant pounding of flies and poppers, or disappears with the tide.

Many times, bonefishermen working the banks in Florida Bay will see schools of tarpon circling or just lying still in the great holes that are spotted like lakes through the banks. Here, where the water is 8 or 10 feet deep, is another ideal spot for baby tarpon, and it is much easier to land one in this open water than in the jungle-infested canals. If a school is worked carefully it is sometimes possible to land as many as four or five fish before they take it on the lam.

Back in the shallow bays of this same area, in the spring, the tarpon may be seen spawning, eight or ten fish swimming

The author cradles the fly rod on which he took this 38-pound tarpon. Captain Rolie Hollenbeck holding fish, Louis Mowbray at right. *Photo by Charles C. Ebbets.*

slowly around in a 20-foot-wide circle, the female dropping the roe and the trailing males fertilizing it with their milt. Although it seems a shame to interrupt such an important process of nature, a light-tackle fisherman can have a picnic with these fish. A fly or lure dropped along the edge of the circle will usually pull out a big fish in a hurry, big enough that when he comes out of the water all hell breaks loose. And then his terror strikes his milling mates and off they go in headlong

And the other extreme—Curt Gowdy, well-known TV sportscaster, with a baby tarpon taken from a brackish-water canal in Florida.

flight. And more than likely the hooked fish is right with them and the angler is reeling in an empty line.

A baby tarpon hits hard and fast and the angler must strike at the flash of the fish below the lure, if he hopes to hook him. The big fish, on the other hand, are slow and deliberate takers. A big tarpon sucks in the fly. He comes up with his mouth wide open and as he is usually pointing at the boat, an immediate strike would pull the fly right out of his mouth. So the angler must stand there and look down that great maw and hold still until the tarpon turns, before setting the hook.

If the angler wishes to stick to the 12-pound-test "light" tippet, as designated by many angling clubs, he can get plenty of hits from big tarpon, but it's extremely unlikely that he will land one. The hard mouth and jaws, the rough scales and fins of the bigger tarpon, fish of 100 to 150 pounds, will almost always fray through the light tippet. You can't just pull such a big fish in, it usually means a one- to three-hour battle to get him boatside. Usually the leader tippet will fray through, often within the first half hour of the fight. I've fought some of those big boys as long as 3½ hours on the 12-pound-test leader tippet, but every time they eventually frayed through the leader point. As long ago as 1947 Captain Jimmie Albright of Islamorada on the Florida Keys, told me that he didn't think that anyone could land a tarpon of 100 pounds or better on the 12-pound-test tippet. He was very close to right. Since that time, up until now, 1968, only one tarpon, weighing 100 pounds even, has been landed on that light tippet. The fish was taken by Oliver Coffee, a member of the Miami Beach Rod and Reel Club.

Many large ones, however, have been taken on fly tackle with the addition of the 12-inch trace of heavier material, under the *Fly, Heavy* classification mentioned earlier.

One of the best things about fishing for these big tarpon on the Florida Keys is the fact that you generally see the fish before you cast. You drop your fly a few feet in front of him, let it sink a foot, then start a very slow, foot-long retrieve. Big tarpon appear to be moving at a leisurely pace, but don't let that fool you. Once your fly has hit and they want it, they get there in a hurry.

When the fish has the fly and has turned, to either side, or down, hit him hard, once, twice, three or four times. It seems to me that big tarpon are far easier to hook than are baby tarpon from 1 to 20 pounds. Those babies are so fast that all you see is a flash of silver, and when you see that flash you must strike right then. Big tarpon are just as scary as the small fish you generally find in smooth or confined waters. You must approach them carefully and quietly, don't wave your arms around. Don't drop the fly in back of a tarpon. If you do, you'll see him get out of there in a hurry. Another point is to avoid "lining" the fish. Lining a tarpon means throwing the line and fly well beyond the oncoming fish. He will often see the line and follow it right to the boat, spot you, and flush. Judge your distance so your retrieve will bring the fly right in front of him, a good 3 or 4 feet, to give him time to zoom up and take.

When you are fishing for big tarpon your drag should be set at about 5 pounds. Keep it there. Hold the rod tip up, which adds more drag. Don't let that fish get a breath of air. Keep the pressure on all the time, except to drop the rod tip when he jumps. Dropping the tip keeps the fish from falling on a tight line and breaking or fraying it. So bow to the tarpon and you have a better chance of landing him. Fight that fish with everything you have. Tarpon have a trick of rolling up and gulping for air. You want to keep them from doing that, but if your fish does succeed in his try, then the best thing to do is to try to hold him up there, make him fight to get back down again. This really slows him, more than anything you can do. So lay back on the rod and hold tight, keep that rod high and the fish up. There are no half measures with 100-pound tarpon. If you fight him like this you will be surprised how quickly you can land such a big fish. It is possible to bring to boat a tarpon of 50 pounds in 15 minutes, an 80-pounder in 20 minutes, a 100-pounder in 30 minutes. The bigger ones seem to take longer. I once landed one that went 119 pounds in 54 minutes. My biggest on a fly, weighing 148 pounds 8 ounces, took an even 2 hours.

In the past few years saltwater fly fishermen have been taking sailfish, both the Atlantic and the Pacific varieties—and

Baby tarpon, 1 to 20 pounds, are often found in canals. Anglers fishing from the banks can have lots of fun with these small, acrobatic, silver kings. *Courtesy Florida News Bureau.*

also striped marlin on flies. Fishing on the Caiman II at Pinas Bay, Panama, the late Dr. Webster Robinson of Key West, Florida, worked out a technique for this kind of fly fishing, and in January, 1961, he took the first sailfish ever known to have been taken on a fly. He had always felt that such a thing could be done, and knowing the habits and reactions of sailfish to bait, he concluded that you could tease them into getting mad enough to come within easy reach of a fly. He rigged up a hookless bait and trolled it from an outrigger. Instead of clipping the line directly to the clothespin, he placed a metal ring there and ran the line through that, so the person on the trolling rod, in this case, Mrs. Robinson, could freely reel the hookless bait in or drop it back.

Using this technique, the angler starts trolling with the bait about 50 feet astern. When a fish shows and hits the bait, the motion of the boat pulls it away from him. The fish comes back, hits, and again the hookless bait is pulled from his mouth. By this time he's mad, so the hookless bait is slowly reeled in, closer and closer, and all the time the maddened sail keeps following and hitting at it, sometimes coming half way out. Suddenly there he is, only 30 feet from the boat, out to the side. The Captain throws the motor out of gear, to conform with angling regulations which stipulate that the cast must be made from a standing boat, and the angler makes his cast. The frustrated sail will usually pile all over his offering.

The fly Web Robinson used was a big white popping bug with a tail of white saddle hackle feathers, tied on a 6/0 hook. To cast this wind-resistant fly he used a 9-foot glass fly rod weighing 6 ounces, a WF-8-F fly line, and a leader tapered down to a 12-pound-test tippet, plus 12 inches of vinyl-covered wire to keep the tough mouth and bill of the fish from fraying the leader tippet. On this tackle he landed more than a dozen Pacific sailfish up to 97 pounds. Later he used the same technique to bring striped marlin within casting range, at Baja California. He landed two, the largest going 145 pounds, a great fish on any tackle, a real feat on fly gear.

With this technique you do not have to make long casts to get to the fish, usually only 30 to 35 feet, sometimes less; and as the fish is usually off to the side, under the outrigger,

Three-pound baby tarpon is carefully returned to the water (not thrown), to live and fight another day. *Courtesy Florida News Bureau.*

The author with the 148-pound, 8-ounce tarpon he took on a fly off Little Torch Key, Florida, while guided by Captain Stu Apte. *Courtesy Florida State News Bureau.*

The original fly-rod popping bug used by Webster Robinson to take sailfish on a fly. In the water the bug looks much like a squid.

Big saltwater popper tied by Bill Gallasch, of Richmond, Virginia, for sailfish.

you can easily get off your backcast free of the rigging. The one thing you must remember is to hold your strike until the fish has turned his head, one way or the other, or down, or you will pull the fly out of his mouth. It's not always easy to hold your strike when a billfish sticks his bill out at your bait, or makes a terrific splash as he takes.

Billfish are fast, and when they run they put sufficient extra pressure of water on a line such as the WF-10-F, which has a heavy belly, that they may pop the 12-pound-test leader tippet. To avoid this, Web Robinson used only the front taper of an 8 line, cutting off the running or shooting line altogether and tying that front section to the backing. This way there is a lot less water resistance.

Quite a number of Atlantic and Pacific sailfish have now been landed on flies. Lee Cuddy of Miami, Florida, has taken both species on this gear, his biggest a fine 115-pound 8-ounce Pacific sail caught at Pinas Bay, Panama.

Many other fish besides the billfish will come to the hookless bait and be vulnerable to a cast fly . . . fish like 40-pound dog-tooth snappers, or amberjack, and such salty swimmers. The close-up view afforded the angler in this type of fishing will stay with him for a long time, and bring him back for more.

It's surprising what fish will hit big streamers and poppers in the salt. When found in suitable water even such deep-water fish as the snappers offer superlative sport. The strike of an 8-pound snapper or grouper to a popping bug is something to long remember. I got into some red-hot snapper fishing one day when I was out with Captain Vic Barothy. We started casting along the shoreline, throwing our poppers in to the edge of the mangroves.

"There should be a lot of snappers in here," said Vic. "And a few snook."

We covered 50 feet, then 100 feet. No snapper. No snook. No nothing.

"It's flatter than a cowboy's stomach," said Vic in disappointment.

"You're righ—" I started, and just then the water foamed up under my bug. I struck and was into a strong fish. I tightened and pulled back but that powerhouse kept on until he

Dr. Webster Robinson, who pioneered fly fishing for sailfish and marlin, casts to a marlin at Cabo San Lucas, Baja California.

The striped marlin takes the bug.

As the fish jumps you can see the bug in the scissors of his mouth.

Dr. Webster Robinson's fine 145-pound striped marlin taken on a fly at Cabo San Lucas, Baja California.

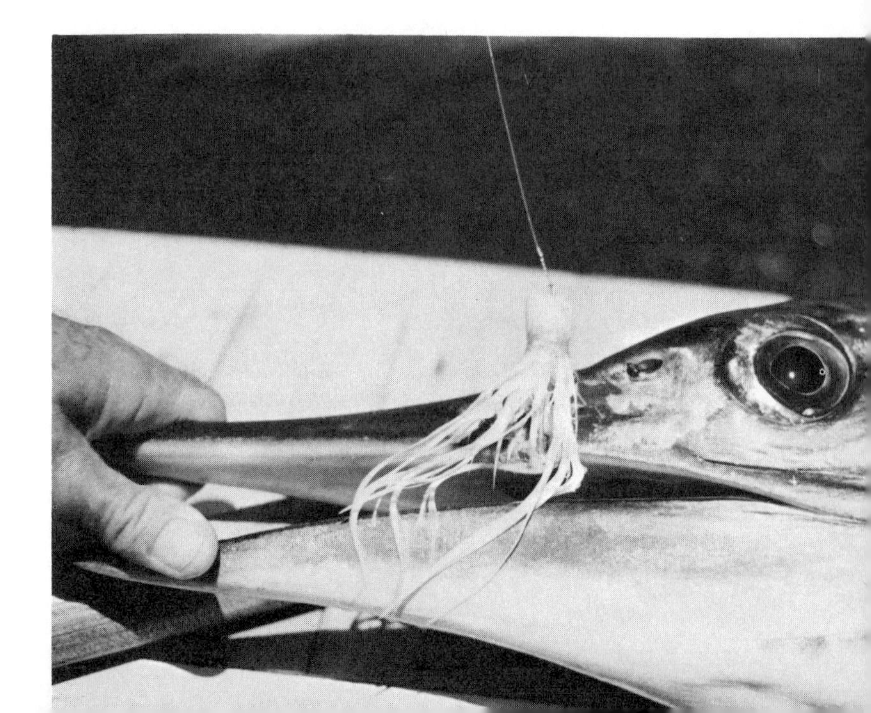

hit the mangrove roots so hard he climbed up them a foot out of water.

"Gosh! What's that?" I cried, as he cut me off on the mangroves.

"That was a small snapper," said Vic.

"Small!" I snorted. "He'd go 10 pounds."

"Well," said Vic, "that's small compared to some of the horses I've seen hereabouts. Let me show you my secret way of catching those snappers. Something I learned as a boy, back on the Michigan trout streams."

He threw the popper into a hole under the limbs of a sizable mangrove and let it sit there for at least half a minute. He looked at the sky, whistled gently to himself.

"Why 'Home on The Range'?" I asked. "And why don't you pop that bug?"

"'Home on The Range' because I'm thinking of fried fish," said Vic. "And I'm going to pop that bug now."

He gave it a small pop and immediately water flew high. This time that underwater Brahma bull charged right at us, went under the boat, and Vic had to make time to get the tip of the rod across the bow so the fish wouldn't break it. It went deep, then, and stayed there for ten minutes, swimming slowly away, but Vic kept his rod bent almost double and that pressure stopped him, then moved him up and up towards the surface. We saw him then. He was a hefty, 5-pound mangrove snapper.

"Don't lose him, Vic," I said.

"Not if I can help it," answered Vic. "He'll make a couple nice fillets."

He pulled the struggling fish backwards right into the net I was holding in the water.

"Your turn," said Vic.

I tossed my bug shoreward and watched it hit a foot out from the trees. I didn't move it.

"Wait," Vic said. "Wait till all those little circles of waves around the bug have died away. Then give it a pop."

I looked into the water. Deep down I saw a dim shadow. I gave the bug a pop. The shadow moved higher. I popped the bug again.

Up came the shadow, turned into a shape, turned into a great, wide open mouth. The mouth made a loud slurping noise. I watched the bug disappear down that throat and saw the fish turn. Then I struck and struck and kept striking. Each time I'd hit, the rod tip would bend down almost to the water, but all the while, between strikes, the reel click kept grinding away like an alarm clock in a still room, loud and slow. That snapper wasn't even swimming fast. He was descending into a hole under the mangroves where he wanted to rest and enjoy that tenite bug. He didn't even know he was hooked.

I laid back on the rod, grabbed the reel handle with one hand, the line just above the spool with the other, and froze. It stopped him for a second. Then he gave a tail swipe that sent up a swirl like a great spring boiling up. After that he shot forward like an arrow, plunged through the mangrove roots and broke off. I reeled in the line and looked at the 10-pound-test tippet. You could see where the rough root had frayed through it. In a way I was glad, because I knew that if I had stopped him he would either have put a set in my fly rod or busted it for keeps.

"Look," said Vic, pointing.

The big yellow popper was drifting on the surface. That fish had got rid of it. As we looked, an even bigger shadow than before came up and socked that free floating bug. He hit it hard, knocked it 3 inches into the air.

"Let's get out of here," I said. "Let's get out of here before a big one comes up and socks this boat."

A different type of hitter to a floating popping bug is the jack crevalle. These far-ranging, fast-traveling school fish slash into a popper as if they had a long held and abiding hatred for it. When a 10-pounder hits like that you feel as if someone has dropped a boulder on your rod.

Jacks will powder a streamer, too, and with both streamers and poppers, they, in common with many other school fish, like a fast retrieve. The big, solitary jacks that sometimes hang out along the drop-off to a channel are just as ready hitters to a well placed lure, and pound for pound I'd stack these big fellows, along with their cousins the horse-eye jacks, against anything that swims.

The ferocious barracuda which has the reputation of walloping anything he sees, including your hand or foot if it is within reach, is particularly hard to take on a fly or lure when he comes onto the flats. He won't charge you, he'll run from you. I well remember the first time I ever worked a salty flat alone and on foot. I was peering 80 feet ahead through the gin-clear water when something big and dark caught my eye. It didn't seem to be moving. "Only a log that's drifted ashore," I told myself.

Then that log turned toward me, and my head suddenly felt as if someone had grabbed a handful of my scalp. That hulk was five feet long, with a long snout and black spots and black tail. It was a barracuda and it must have weighed 40 pounds.

Almost without realizing what I was doing, I shot the fly out and dropped it a foot in front of that ugly fish with the doglike teeth. He didn't move at first, just lay there. Remembering that I'd been told that barracuda like a fast retrieve, I started to strip, in quick, foot-long jerks. And then, like a jet, that baby went into action. He churned the water and sand as he launched himself, and all at once, when the fly was only 15 feet away from me, I wondered whether he was after the fly or my legs.

I wanted out. I turned and ran, mentally feeling those fangs at my ankles every step of the way. When I hit the shore and still had my underpinnings I stopped and looked back. That cuda was going to sea as fast as I had come ashore.

Where another fish is concerned, cuda are both ruthless and fearless. Once on Judy Island, off Key Largo, Florida, I hooked a 14-incher, and while I was playing it a 15-incher jumped him and with one bite cut him neatly in two and made off with the lower half. Another time a 20-pounder chased a bonefish I had hooked, followed it in close to the boat, and bit that 8-pound bonefish in half right under my nose. In spite of their savagery, however, those mean and forthright feeders are smart hombres when they suspect a man is near. Even in deep water, although big catches are often made by trollers, the barracuda is not an easy mark once he has a halfway even chance to learn something about anglers. For instance, those which hang out around the Keys lighthouses in comparatively deep water. I once told Captain Vic Barothy that I thought they should be easy to take.

"Practically never catch 'em," he said. "They are fished so heavily around those lighthouses that they're onto the game. You can't sneak up on them. Not ever. They always see you first."

So when you cast a fly to a barracuda in the shallows, you are working on a fish that is as suspicious as a Dominiquer rooster in a fly tyer's yard. However stealthily you move up on him, he's looking you right in the eye when you get close enough to cast. However fine you taper your leader tippet, he'll see you start your cast and he'll swim slowly away. You have to stay up late to outwit a barracuda.

Once hooked, he's a worthy fighter and your troubles are not over. He's a sprinter, and for a short distance is amazingly fast. He takes to the air in high and wide leaps and each time he comes out, he looks all teeth and those teeth are working on your leader. If you want enough excitement to last for quite a while, put in the time necessary to hook a good-sized barracuda in shallow water.

Popping bugs, and particularly the skipping bug, account for many ocean fish, not only inshore but on the reefs and in the ocean lanes. It is possible to cast your bugs out over 40 or 50 feet of water and by popping, popping, time and again, get amberjack up, and once they are up they go for the bug with blazing eyes and open mouth. Other fish will be attracted by the noise and swim over to see what is making the commotion and they, too, will hit: big mangrove snappers, muttonfish; and such restless species as the jacks will zero in in schools and tear the bugs to pieces. Offshore the dolphin in particular likes popping bugs. Any time you see a floating crate or a dense carpet of sargassum weed, or a floating tree, it is worth a cast.

The fact that popping bugs and such lures may be played noisily now and again with rich reward, does not mean that even on those occasions other noises have any part in saltwater fly fishing. The angler who roars up to an ocean flat or into a channel or bay he hopes to fish, with outboard motor at full speed, or who bumps oars on the bottom of the boat, or clanks his tackle box around, is going a long way towards defeating himself before he even starts. Talk as loudly as he likes, yes, but he should remember that fish hear through earstones which pick up vibrations from the water, not from the air. Any noise offered to a fish should be doled out deliberately and with malice aforethought.

The bonefish and permit, in particular, call for an enormous amount of care and quiet in approach. No brown trout was ever spookier than a bonefish in 6 or 8 inches of water.

The bonefish is one of the few gamefish which have survived unchanged since prehistoric times, and he seems to have retained his primeval wildness along with the body features that link him with the past. His large eyes have clear, plasticlike coverings which evidently allow him to see in many directions, even, I suspect, backwards. And when he's scared, he's gone with a single thrust of his forked tail, badge of a fast swimmer.

His Latin name is *Albula vulpes,* which means "white fox," and believe me, that's an understatement. When you go for him in shallow water you'll find that he's foxier than any Renard ever thought of being. You get so keyed up when you creep up on him that you don't see, hear or think of anything but that waving tail fin. You want him more than anything. And to get him takes a combination of iron nerves, careful stalk, delicate, accurate casting, enticing retrieve, fast rod and line manipulation, quick strike at the right time, and sensitive perception of the fish's runs, darts and struggles to escape.

When a bonefish hits and starts off, he goes so fast that almost anything can happen. The line stripped in as the retrieve was made to tempt him to take that fly, is gone in a hurry. It catches on the reel, or the rod butt, or the buttons of the angler's clothing. It jams under his feet, catches on parts of the boat or goes around the fisherman's neck. Any one of those accidents inevitably results in the leader snapping.

Or, instead of taking off for deep water, which is his usual procedure, the perverse bonefish may get a notion that he can hide among the mangroves. So he heads for shore and thoroughly tangles the line in a thousand tough mangrove shoots. The chance of landing a bonefish that has got into the mangrove roots is one in a million, but that's what makes bonefishing fun. You never know what will happen next, and the only thing you're sure about is that you have just a ghost of a chance of getting your fish.

And then a beginner steps up and takes a bonefish on the first 20-foot cast he makes.

"It's easy," he says. "They're overrated."

But try this beginner out for size a year later, after he's had all manner of bonefish things happen to him, and the story will be different.

"They're the dang-gangest things on fins," he'll say. "Chain lightning. I lost one today that looked like 18 pounds. Would have been a world record. That fish ran out all 700 feet of my line in a couple of seconds flat, and kept right on going. He just stripped me."

For me, the most exciting part of bonefishing with a fly is stalking the fish. It's a combination of hunting and fishing. Bonefish come onto the shallow-water flats to feed on shrimp, crabs and small minnows. They flit across the shallow flats like ghosts, every sense alert, knowing that in such thin water they're vulnerable to attack from birds as well as sharks and barracuda. So when an angler eases up on a bonefish that is tailing, mudding or swimming in water less than 2 feet deep, everything must be right. One mistake will send him charging for the sanctuary of deep water.

The fish usually feed into the tide, sniffing out their prey and sucking crabs and worms from holes in the sand. It was their habit of nuzzling into and under grasses, sandy mounds and coral that once made people think that bonefish were bottom feeders and wouldn't take a lure. But bonefish feed on sight, too, and when they flush their prey they go after it as it speeds away. They chase minnows, shrimps and crabs relentlessly. And it is this trick of chasing fleeing food that makes the bonefish the great fly-rod fish he is.

When bonefish aren't feeding, it's even more nerve wracking to fish for them. Sometimes schools of fifty or more may be seen sweeping across a flat, pushing the water before them in a wave. When they're doing that, the angler may as well put his rod down and relax, because a nervous, spooky bonefish isn't

Spotting a tailing bonefish in shallow water.

One of the great moments in all angling—a tailing bonefish, and a fly caster putting his fly right on the nose of the shallow-water speedster. Polaroid glasses help angler see under water. *Courtesy Florida State News Bureau.*

going to take a lure. And the harder he is fished, the more spooky he's going to get. Even fishing one stretch of water too hard and too often will either put the bones off completely or make them so jumpy they won't take. I've stood in one place on a Key Largo flat, facing seaward, right in the path of bonefish swimming in to feed, and have taken one after another. Yet when that same flat has been fished heavily for several days, the bonefish disappeared and didn't come back until that area had been "rested" for a few days.

Once when I was fishing with John Hunter of Hollidaysburg, Pennsylvania, we saw a good example of this. We staked the boat in water a foot deep, and saw fish working along the flat, coming our way. Some were tailing and others were just swimming slowly. One school of twenty stopped about 60 feet away and fanned lazily with their pectoral fins.

"Get after them, John," I said.

His first cast caused a bonefish stampede—not away, but towards the fly. One outdistanced the others and grabbed the fly. John set the hook and that bonefish beat it across the flat, sending the others fleeing in all directions. Yet by the time that

5-pounder was landed and we were ready to cast again, all those bonefish were back. Before we left that flat we had landed seven, lost three, and had had innumerable strikes. Those fish, swimming over a sandy bottom and in crystal clear water, certainly saw us, but showed no signs of being afraid.

They learned quickly. Two days later we went back there and this time we spooked bonefish right and left. They flushed at the line in the air, at our motions as we false cast, at the sound of feet scraping in the bottom of the skiff, even at the grinding of the poling pole in the sand. We came out of that cove without taking a single fish. Those babies had been to school.

The taking of bonefish on artificial flies dates back only to 1947. Prior to that time several anglers had reported catching bonefish on flies while fishing for baby tarpon, but they considered it just an accident that a bonefish hit. Then in 1947, while I was attending an Outdoor Writers Association of America convention at St. Petersburg, Allen Corson, Fishing Editor of the Miami *Herald,* told me about bonefish and asked if I thought they could be taken on a fly—fly fishing being my specialty. I opined that it was worth a try, journeyed down

Nothing to do but raise the rod high, hang on and pray! Note the weed and grass picked up by the line—another hazard of bonefishing. *Courtesy Florida State News Bureau.*

to Islamorada, went out with Captain Jimmie Albright, who said right off that he thought it was possible, and took two tailing bonefish on streamer flies. As far as is known, that was the first deliberate effort to take bonefish on flies, and it was successful.

Word soon got around and it wasn't long until the flats were crowded with fly casters, for the bonefish is undoubtedly one of the great gamefish of the world.

For the first-time try for bonefish, the angler should always go with a guide. The guide will know right where the fish are, or at least where they are likely to be. He knows their habits, how to spot them in the water, and the novice angler can cash in on all this knowledge.

On the Florida Keys the cost of a guide, who furnishes skiff and outboards, and of course, his own services, is from $60.00 to $70.00 per day. Guides who use a cruiser and take their fishing parties far back to the less heavily fished flats, towing a skiff or two, charge around $80.00 per day with one skiff. (Two anglers per skiff.) If an extra guide and skiff are wanted, there is an additional charge.

If a man's budget doesn't run to that kind of fishing, and he has a strong-armed friend, he can rent a skiff for $7.50 per day, or a skiff and motor for $10.00 per day, in most places, run out to the flats, and take turns poling each other. Or he can just drive to the shore, park his car and wade out 10 feet and start fishing.

It's difficult to say which is the best way to go for bonefish, wading or in a skiff, but one thing is sure. The higher the angler is above the water, the easier it is to spot the fish. When I'm in a skiff, I'm standing on the seat, and when I'm poling, I'm on the gunwales. I always wish I were on stilts.

Polaroid glasses are an essential part of the bonefisherman's equipment. The Polaroid lens is much better than any other, price regardless, in seeing through the water and spotting fish. And to spot an approaching bonefish quickly means more strikes because then it is possible to get the fly to him quickly, before he sees the angler and becomes suspicious.

A skiff allows the angler to cover more ground, and that's important when the fish are moving. However, there is also

When you pick a bonefish from water, don't touch his gills. Grab him across the back, let your hand go under him and then lift gently with a loose grip. Fish seldom struggle when handled this way. *Courtesy Florida State News Bureau.*

Bonefish flit about like ghosts, reacting to the slightest movement near them. *Courtesy Florida State News Bureau.*

Bonefish tailing (note the tail above the water). *Courtesy Florida State News Bureau.*

more danger of flushing fish and of them seeing you. No matter what, the angler must be on his toes every minute, for he must often cast quickly in unexpected directions.

But in general, there is a fairly definite pattern to this fishing. It is best to have the sun at the angler's back. In such light, and in water 12 to 18 inches deep, the fish show up clearly. Their backs look black, but often the body will appear transparent, especially when they are swimming over a sandy bottom. And sometimes they will take on a yellow-green hue. One angler, Fausto Nieva of Miami, thought the first bonefish he spotted was a grapefruit floating in the water.

Barracuda and sharks also feed on the shallow flats and they fool many a fisherman into casting for them. An unfailing mark of identification of the bonefish, however, is that he is seldom still. A barracuda will lie like a log, just under the surface, and you can tell him by his black tail, too. Sharks, while occasionally managing to look like bonefish, give themselves away by the regular, side-to-side swing of their tails, which is entirely different from the motion of the bonefish.

The appearance of the bonefish soon becomes familiar, and you quickly get hep to their tailing as they feed on the bottom

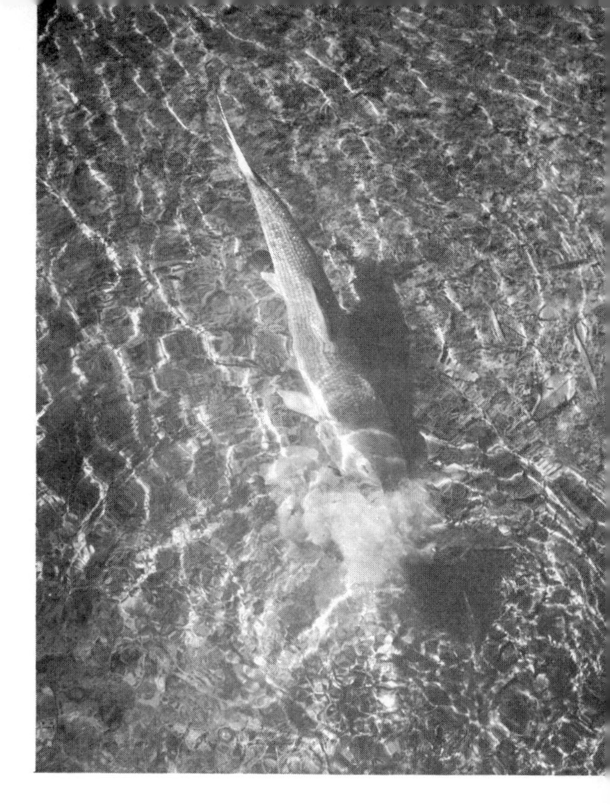

Bonefish mudding (stirring up mud or sand as he searches the bottom for food). *Courtesy Florida State News Bureau.*

and tilt their bodies so that their tails break the surface. Before long it is quite easy to spot the "mud," too, in water too deep for the tail to show. The mud is a puff of sand or mud sent up by the bonefish as he searches the bottom for food. Anglers and guides call this "smoking" because of the likeness of the updrifting mud to the puff a smoker makes as he exhales.

When working on a mudding fish, the angler must remember that the fish moves faster than the smoke—in other words, the feeder is always ahead of the last puff of mud that has come up, and the cast should therefore go a couple of yards in front of that last puff.

Timing is all-important when fish are in shallow water, either tailing or swimming along. The first cast must be right because there is seldom a second chance. This is the time that it pays to wait, to carefully judge the cast. The stories one hears about 100-foot casts are all wet. The average cast to a bonefish is from 45 to 55 feet. Usually casts of 80, 90 or 100 feet are wasted because they offer so many chances for misplay. It's difficult to set the hook when the lure is out so far. By the time the strike gets to the fish, he may even have spit the fly out. And at that distance it is difficult to see either fly or fish very clearly, well enough to judge how the bonefish is reacting to the retrieve. And lure play is very important with bonefish.

I use the strip method of retrieve, as described earlier in this chapter. With that method I can strip 3 feet of line, or an inch. I can make a fast retrieve or a slow one, so slow that line and fly are barely moving. I can stop the fly altogether, and let it sit still while a fish moves up on it, and if I have a hit, I always have a tight line.

When the fly is played that way, it's like pulling a string with the fish on the end of it. On the Key Largo flats one day, I watched George Phillips cast to a bonefish that was cruising slowly along the shore in 12-inch water, some 50 feet away. He threw too far and the fly hit the water a foot beyond the fish so that the leader lay only 6 inches in front of him. George knew that if he didn't get it out of there fast, the fish would run into the tippet and flush. He gave the fly a quick jerk. It shot past the bonefish's nose and stopped 2 feet our side of him. The fish turned fast, swam to the fly, and seemed to nuzzle it. But he didn't take. George gave the line a slow, foot-long pull and the fish stayed right in back of the fly. Then he seemed to lose interest and turned away. But George gave the line another pull. Back came the bone, right behind the fly.

"Get him, George," I said.

He gave the fly a quick, 6-inch jerk, so that it shot forward like a shrimp trying to get away. That was too much for old Mr. Bonefish. He pounced on it. George waited until he felt him, then set the hook, and as the fish turned and started seaward, he set it again and again for good measure.

Once a bonefish is hooked in shallow water, the angler holds the rod up, arms as high as they will go, while the fish runs. There are so many things that the line can wrap around, or the leader catch on. Above all, he must keep his hands away from the reel, for the leader most certainly will snap if he tries to clamp down while the fish is making that first phenomenal run. Always wait until that first run is over before even touching the reel handle, and starting to reel.

If the line wraps around coral or sponge on the bottom, or

Bonefish running! Anglerette holds her rod high —the badge of a veteran bonefisherman. *Courtesy Florida State News Bureau.*

becomes tangled with seaweed, the best way to free it is to wade or pole the boat over to the obstruction, keeping a fairly tight line meanwhile, free the line, then reel up the slack. A hard pull or jerk on the rod when the fish has the line tied up like that will almost always result in a cut leader.

When bonefishermen talk about runs of 350 and 400 feet, doubting Thomases flap their ears. But those unbelievers should see for themselves. The longest-running bonefish I have ever hooked took out 700 feet of line. That powerhouse also proved to be my biggest, an 11-pound, 5½-ounce fish. A 10-pound, 13½-ouncer I took while fishing with Captain Cecil Keith also ran 700 feet. Frankee Albright, who incidentally guided me to the first big one mentioned, reported a 10-pound, 13½-ouncer she took as stripping off 900 feet of line, and even then she had to upstake and take after it. Often a 6- to 7-pound fish runs just as far as the larger ones do.

This distance dash of the bonefish is all the more remarkable when you consider that he's dragging a heavy, forward-tapered WF-8-F fly line plus the backing, which is usually 200 yards of 18-pound-test nylon squidding line. Add all that to the drag already set on the reel and it is easy to see that those fish are pulling a formidable load.

Because of the flighty nature of the bonefish, and the difference in the flats where he is fished, size of fly may make or break the day's fishing. As mentioned in the fly section, flies tied on the 1/0 hook and having wings 2½ to 3 inches long do very well in water from 2 to 4 feet deep, but in shallow water from 8 to 18 inches in depth, a smaller fly does better. More often than not, a large fly cast over the shallows will flush the fish. A small bucktail or streamer tied on a No. 2 or 4 hook, with wings an inch, and not more than an inch and a half long, will not sink as rapidly as the larger fly, won't catch on the bottom as readily, and won't scare a spooky fish as much.

Bonefish will hit almost any fly that is retrieved properly, but those tied with some white in them, either in wings or body, seem to be the most productive. Brown and white is a good color combination, but the good old red and white is still hard to beat. Recently an Atlantic salmon fly featuring junglecock shoulders and a honey-colored wing, and tied on a No. 2 hook, has proven a fine lure for bonefish.

A typical bonefish flat at low tide on ocean side of Florida Keys. Usually there is a lot more coral rock on the ocean side than on the Gulf side flats. In background anglers have anchored their skiff out for enough so falling tide will not leave it high and dry. *Courtesy Florida State News Bureau.*

Hagen Sands is shown with his record catch of a 14-pound, 2-ounce bonefish taken on a fly at Boca Chica Flats, on the Florida Keys.

While fly fishing for bonefish was developed largely along the Florida Keys, the species is found in most of the warm seas, in Hawaii, Africa, Mexico, Bermuda, the Bahamas, Haiti and throughout the West Indies.

Those in the Bahamas and the Caribbean generally average 4 to 6 pounds, with many larger ones in certain spots. You never know when a 12-pounder may chase down and take your fly. The Florida Keys produce at least one bonefish a year that tips the scales to 13 pounds or better; and the largest ever taken anywhere on a fly came from the Keys. This was a 14-pound, 2-ounce fish caught by Hagen Sands of Key West while fishing the Boca Chica flats. The average in the Florida range of the bonefish is a good 7½ pounds; and this weight is closely approximated by the average in the Virgin Islands. The biggest bonefish ever taken on any type of tackle was a whopping 19-pounder taken on bait by Brian W. Batchelor in 1962 at Zululand, South Africa. This fish is now the International Game Fish Association all-tackle record.

What the brown trout is to the dry-fly angler, the bonefish is to the fly-rodder in the salt. There's no easy way to take him, and fly-rodding is probably the hardest of all. But there's a bag full of satisfaction in making an ornery, suspicious, hard-headed bonefish take, and there's great fun in watching him streak seaward, cutting figure eights, or seeing him cross you up and rush the boat.

Once someone said to me, "But they don't jump, do they?"

"Shhh!" I answered quickly. "Don't even mention it. They might hear you. And if bonefish ever started jumping—well, I couldn't stand it."

Just the way he is, he's all any angler could want. When he has stalked the bonefish, avoided all the pitfalls of tricky casting, tense retrieve, suspicious take, and lightning run—when he has fought him through all his tricks and finally brought him to the boat, what does the angler do?

There the bonefish lies, belly up because he's fought until there isn't an ounce of fight left in him. The angler grabs him by the tail, turns him upright, and rocks him gently from side to side. He gives the salty gamester artificial respiration, to put life back in him. Then he turns him loose, for he's a gentleman, and one of the world's greatest gamefish. He deserves to live and roam the salt.

Occasionally you will hear someone say that bonefish are overrated, that they are easy to take. Sometimes they *are* easy, on spinning gear or bait, especially if they are in deeper water. But I'd like to be with that same scoffer when he goes for a bonefish in 6 to 8 inches of water, with a fly. He'll sing another tune.

Some other species, although not quite as easily spooked as the bonefish, demand just as great accuracy in casting. Redfish or channel bass tail like bonefish and they grub so hard as they nose into the grassy bottom that often, despite your most accurate casts, they don't see the fly. They just don't come up for air. You must keep at it, waiting until the fish raises his head to swim to another place, then drop the fly on his nose and watch out.

I watched Charlie Ebbets casting to a school of channel bass one day when we were fishing with Captain Rolie Hollenbeck, out in Florida Bay. Rolie pointed out a dark spot in the water about 60 feet away from us.

"There are about twenty redfish in that school," he said. "Drop the fly right on their noses, because they can't see more than a foot."

Charlie cast. The fly fell 18 inches our side of the school. Those fish never batted an eye. Charlie retrieved and cast again. This time the fly fell 18 inches to our side. He retrieved and again those fish didn't budge.

Once more Charlie hitched up his pants, started false casting, took aim and fired. This time the fly fell right on the snout of a bull redfish. He opened his big maw and the red and yellow streamer shot down it, and as he turned, Charlie struck.

That redfish could shake his head harder, faster and meaner than any pit terrier ever did. He shook the rod tip till I thought the guides would fly off. He stood on his head and tried to rub the hook out, then went off across the flats, not too fast, but steady and strong. He took a couple of hundred feet of line, then stood on his head again. It was so shallow that his tail came out of water, big and broad. Before Charlie finally worked him back and got him close to the boat, we knew he was a big one. He weighed 21 pounds 6 ounces.

Another time I recall, I was with Jimmie Albright, fishing the back country west of Islamorada. I cast to a tailing red several times without result.

"Watch this," said Jimmie. "I'll wake him up."

Jimmie cast and made the fly hit with a splash, hard. He repeated this four times. On the fifth try the red came up and swung on that fly. The sound had made him turn, and there was the fly, and he grabbed it.

A slow-played popper will often attract a big old short-sighted red, too. The popper should be cast so it lights about 5 feet away, not close enough to scare him, then retrieved for a single pop, left to sit quietly for a moment, then a series of pops, rest again, and repeat. The noise will often attract him, and he'll come moseying over.

Bright flies are best as they seem easier for the redfish to see: big streamers with 4- or 5-inch-long wings with breather action. Red hackle with yellow wings, and red hackle with orange wings, are perhaps the two best combinations, but red and white will also pay off. Flies should be on 3/0 hooks.

The redfish that anglers catch in the Bay of Florida and other places along the Keys will run from 5 to 25 pounds, and average out about 10 pounds. You don't see many over 25, but they are there at times.

The snook is another ocean swimmer that will hit a wide variety of lures, but they must each be proffered at the right time.

When they are in canals, feeding on schools of minnows, the small, inch-long bucktail described earlier in this chapter is sure fire. And in June, when the spring migration is on, you find the snook working the beaches. Sometimes from shore you can look out and see closely packed balls of minnows, a big, dark patch, easy to spot. As you watch, you see a patch of white, widening, spreading out like a soft snowball exploding against a black-surfaced road. A snook has struck into that ball of bait. The ranks close in again, then wham! The snowball strikes again. It's something to see. At such a time that same inch-and-a-half-long white bucktail tied on a 1/0 hook will take those snook.

Along the beach apparently the snook are too busy to be readily frightened, and I have seen a fisherman pull one out of a group of bathers who happened to get close to the minnow school. But usually he calls for careful fishing when he is in shallow water. In the Ten Thousand Islands section of the Everglades they often rove the shallows in water from 8 inches to 2 feet deep. One day when I was fishing with Jean Crooks and Jim Nankivell, we spotted a bay that looked like great snook water. We throttled the motor low and started to fish. All along the shore we saw puffs of mud rise.

"Look at that," said Jim. "This place is alive with snook."

We eased along, casting where they had been, but didn't get a hit, yet those puffs of mud kept appearing. We suddenly realized that we were spooking snook, even though we were barely moving and making as little noise as possible. We cut the motor then, but we had to pole the boat a full quarter of a mile before Jim hooked the first fish. After that, still making like Seminoles, we took several nice ones.

A careless, unobservant angler working that water might have thought there were no snook around. And certainly those who fish with running outboard, no matter how far throttled down, may take a fair number of fish in a day by covering sufficient water; but if those same fishermen would cut the motor and fish the area quietly, they would do better. As it is, they take a fish or two, and chase the others off.

Probably some of the most exciting snook fishing of all is to be found by casting a popper along the mangroves back in the Everglades. Usually it is still-water fishing, and suddenly as the popper moves along, the angler sees a great brown shape under it, and bang, the water flies as he takes. Snook are buffalo strong, and when a big one heads for the iron-fingered mangrove roots it's usually on its way to cutting the leader—and freedom.

Not to be overlooked by the fly fishermen are the snook that frequently hang out around bridges, often right in the heart of town. A big, breather-type streamer will bring them up to sock it with determination. Or a popping bug brought playfully back across a current of running tide will raise their ever-ready tempers to the boiling point so they just have to whack it.

Snook conduct their fight very much like largemouth black bass, only they hit harder, grow bigger, and are much stronger. They just don't come in without a rough fight. They are willing strikers to flies, and I think they sometimes show a slight preference for a fly that has a little bit of blue in it—streamers and bucktails with blue wings, or a blue body with a white wing. But they also hit the red and yellow, and red and white combinations; and I have taken many snook on the blonde fly patterns.

One of the best days of snook fishing I ever had was on the Sibun River in British Honduras, with Vic Barothy. I had a 3/0 skipping bug on and was dropping it every 2 feet, smack against the mangrove roots, into the small coves, under high outthrust mangrove limbs, as we moved along. I threw one that went far back in. I popped it once. There was such a swirl and splash of water back in there that I thought a jaguar was pawing at that bug, but I felt nothing. I popped the bug out from under those limbs and as soon as it saw daylight a snook busted it so hard that I felt it to my heels. I struck and out he came, out and out, that is, further and further, and still I didn't see all of him. He was long, thick, and deep. He finally cleared the water.

"My golly!" breathed Vic. "What a snook!"

I couldn't talk. I hung on and watched water jump up from the line as the fish headed for the middle of the river. He got out there, then swiveled and headed back. I had a bit of slack line after that fast turn, but I got tight and put more drag on in an effort to keep him out of the mangroves. I might just as well have tried to stop a manatee. He dashed in and cut me off, and I'd had it.

"Do you know how big that snook was?" Vic said, in a whisper. "Forty pounds!"

Snook are great hitters to popping bugs. Once he makes up his mind about it he has only one idea: pulverize that thing!

It pays to mix up your retrieves when you are after snook. With streamers the slow, foot-long pull seems to be what they like. I always start off with this unless I see a fish close in and want to get the fly in front of him in a hurry. Then I give a long, hard jerk, or several, which often does the job. I usually speed up the retrieve when the fly nears the boat and often this brings last-minute hits, practically beside the skiff, all of which are startling, to say the least.

I like to play a popping bug slowly. In confined places, like a shallow cover, or under mangrove limbs, make the pops light. Too hard a pop will flush the fish. In the open the loudness doesn't matter so much. Always, when you want to bring the bug back in for the next cast, speed it up and impart a series of short pops. It really pays off to keep fishing the bug or fly all the way in.

Snook hit well after dark, and when a 12- or 15-pounder clamps down on your surface lure out there in the dark of the night, it's something you'll never forget. If you're not a snook man already, you will be, from there on out.

Because of the tremendous numbers of saltwater fish, as compared to the freshwater species, the angler who takes his fly rod into the salt always has a chance of getting into something new and different. Perhaps the species which are consistent fly takers could be boiled down to a dozen, but there are half a hundred more that are, at one time or another, within reach of a fly.

Many an angler out for bonefish and other shallow water cruisers and having a bad day, has made a desultory cast to a shark and found himself tied to a new and startling experience.

By nature sharks are killers. Their savagery is legend. One sniff of blood will send them charging recklessly to slash and bite and tear at any wounded creature. They will snatch big hunks of flesh from a still living body, piscatorial or otherwise, and practically every deep-sea angler has seen sharks chew the flesh off the entire length of a hooked fish while it was being played. To watch some of those pelagic sharks in their own element is enough to raise a crop of chills that reach bumper size. The 25-foot jumps of the great mako, the peculiar leaps of the spinner shark, the tremendous power of the thrashing, slashing hammerhead—these are ferocious and awesome sights at close quarters.

However cruel and relentless these live torpedoes may be out in the deep, the picture is different when smaller editions of their species come into the shallows. Then they are on the alert for foes, and they don't like too much noise and commotion. As they criuse the shallows at river mouths, in bays, across bonefish flats, looking for food, they come within reach of the fly caster and they put up a fight that compares favorably with that of almost any gamefish. So much so that not only are anglers showing more interest in them, but fishing tournaments are beginning to include several species on their list of eligible fish.

These small sharks furnish a lot of fun, year round, and inexpensively, too. On most of the Florida Keys a fisherman can park his car within a few feet of the ocean, wade out to knee-deep water and be in business. Many times when other more publicized fish are down deep and won't hit, sharks will come in to prowl and feed. If you don't want to wade, it's easy to rent a skiff and go for them that way. And if you're fishing with a guide, you can often save an otherwise dull day when fishing is slow, by working on the sharks you see.

However you go for them, in the shallow waters of most of

Bonnet shark, belonging to the hammerhead family, is a consistent taker of small streamers, bucktails or popping bugs. He puts up a very good fight, makes long runs. Because of the position of his mouth, the leader rubs against the tough and rough skin around his head and often frays through. There is nothing the angler can do to prevent this. *Courtesy Miami News Bureau, Charles C. Ebbets.*

the warm seas you will see sharks and they will hit a fly if it is put to them right. On a good shark day you might encounter small hammerhead, bonnet or shovelnose, lemon, lesser black-tipped, dusky and many other kinds. All of them will hit flies. The only exception is the nurse shark, a lazy, reddish fellow that limps across the flats looking for a sandy patch in which to lie down and sleep. You can come right up on him and poke him with an oar and I have seen a guide rudely awaken one from its nap by grabbing it by the tail and raising it clear of the water. Many an angler takes a kick at one of these lazy beasts that happens to get in his way while he is bonefishing.

Using your feet to boot a shark is probably a very reckless gesture, however, unless you are mighty sure it is a nurse shark. After one try at it, I got over the habit. I was wading one of the flats on Key Largo, and after fighting a big bonefish for a long time had just got him in close and was reaching down to lift him out of the water. Then I saw a 9-foot shark, appearing from nowhere, it seemed, zooming for my hooked bonefish. I yanked back with the rod tip to pull the bonefish away from him. The motion scared him, and he turned, not 2 feet in front of me.

I raised my foot and let him have it. The 300-pound lemon shark got out of there as if he had a hot coal burning him. That was a $150 kick because the bonefish took top prize of an outboard motor in the fly casting division of the Metropolitan Miami Fishing Tournament. But right after that kick I found myself wondering how I'd look wading the flats without a right foot. And since then I've always been careful to count ten before kicking any sharks. Not only are they loaded with very workmanlike teeth, but they even carry extras back in their mouths.

While sharks will come quite close before they scare, and are therefore easy targets, still a certain amount of stealth and quietness will bring more strikes. The cast should be made so that the fly falls within 2 feet of the shark as they are remarkably short-sighted. Then when the shark has moved up so that the fly is just 3 or 4 inches in front of him, bring it along very slowly—or rapidly if the shark happens to be moving fast. At any rate, just fast enough to keep it right on his nose, so to speak. Sharks will often follow for 15 or 20 feet before hitting, and sometimes they will come up and look you right in the eye and then swim away, but you'll get enough of them for thrills.

Sometimes if the cast is off a bit and the fly falls about 6 feet from the shark, he will turn and rush in that direction, and when he gets in the general vicinity he will start swimming in a circle, sniffing like a hound dog, trying to find that fly. And because his eyesight isn't in the same league with his wonderful nose, the best thing to do is to pick the fly up again and cast back there, making it hit hard so he'll hear it, swim over and see it, and take.

When a surface bug is being used for sharks, it should be retrieved slowly, with pops, jerks and rests. The top-water bug is a potent shark finder especially in channels and along the deeper water off the flats. Start popping one and before you know it there will be three or four sharks lurking and ready for action. A bit of lure play, and they usually grab the popper quickly.

It is a mistake to think that a shark has to turn on its side to feed. It's true that the mouth is well under the nose, but when chasing small fish it doesn't have time to turn, it merely pushes its snout forward and brings the mouth into striking position. So don't hesitate to use a surface bug for sharks. They'll take it as they would a small, fleeing fish, or a shrimp that is floating on top, or a wounded minnow struggling on the surface.

When first hooked, most sharks turn on a burst of speed and sometimes they make runs of amazing length. Once Ted Williams and I were fishing Key Largo for bonefish when we both spotted a good-sized shark coming our way. Ted dropped his fly 3 feet in front of it, let it sink, and as the shark neared it, pulled the fly up, an inch in front of his nose.

The shark didn't break his stride, but opened his mouth, gave a spurt upward, stuck his upper mandible forward and clamped down on that poor, unsuspecting fly. Ted set the hook and 20 pounds of black-tipped shark twisted around and ran down the shoreline in 7 inches of water, going in a straight line, like a homer on the way, tossing mud and water a foot high. He went for 400 feet and then headed seaward and went another 50 feet before he slowed down enough to let Ted put the rod to work. I don't believe either of us had ever seen a shark go as fast as that one did, or as far. Ted lost him later, when he frayed through the 6-pound-test tippet.

Sharks have such tough hides that they will fray through even 12- or 15-pound-test nylon leader tippets; so the angler may expect to land only about one out of sixteen unless he uses an extra-heavy tippet, such as a 6- or 8-inch length of No. 5 wire or 12 inches of heavy nylon, 30-pound test being big enough for sharks up to 50 pounds in weight, and 60-pound test for very large ones.

CHAPTER/10

CHUMMING AND OFFSHORE FLY FISHING

WHEN YOU FLY FISH THE SALT THERE ARE MANY FISH that ordinarily would not come within reach but which can be coaxed up to hit a fly, by the use of chum.

Chumming is the process of throwing out on the surface some food which the fish might like, and thus attracting them to or near the surface where the fly can be presented to them. In the Chesapeake Bay and many other places, striped bass fishermen have long chummed with shrimp, pouring them overboard until a heavy slick is formed, into which the stripers eventually work. In many of the bays where there are crab canning plants, there is a more or less constant flow of natural chum in the waste that is dumped, and fishing is frequently very good in those areas. Another natural chum that attracts fish is spread out in the water when oyster tongers stir the bottom, and the fly caster who anchors downtide from them and casts his fly in the general direction of the oysterman has a good chance of coming up with stripers that are there feeding on the tidbits pushed up by the tongs.

In Bermuda, where chumming is common because of the deep water around the island, one of the favorite chums is hog-mouthed fry, an inch-long, silvery minnow that is all head and mouth, as his name implies. A handful of these fry thrown on the surface will usually bring a concentration of gray snapper and yellowtail and other reef dwellers to feed, and once they start to feed, a well-placed bucktail tied to match the fry, will usually get hits.

Fly casting into a chum line doesn't call for any particular skill because the fish are not usually far away and will stay in the one area. It does, however, demand extreme care with equipment. Everything must be right, from the knots in the leader to the mechanics of the drag on the reel. Even hook points should be thoroughly sharpened. Some terrific fish come to the chum line, strong fish and fast fish and long-running fish, and to be prepared for their maneuvers everything must be in the angler's favor when he fights these ocean roustabouts.

In almost all chum fishing, and especially when fishing for snappers, no motion is given to the fly, as these canny and sharp eyed "sea lawyers" are seldom taken in by a trick. The fly must be allowed to float along with the fry, looking just like it, at the mercy of the tide. The slightest movement, and a snapper will spot it as a phony. He may tear right up to it in his wild feeding, and then, at the last second he will slam on the brakes and give it the old cold eye. But let it float "dead" with the rest of the fry, and the angler is in for some fun. Gray snappers are very strong fish and usually they dive straight for the bottom and cut the leader on the rocks.

After the chum line has been out a while, it will extend far downtide and cruising fish, crossing it, will turn and follow it to the boat, feeding as they come, grabbing the hogmouthed fry avidly and moving in fast on the source of supply.

The first time I chum-fished in Bermuda, we anchored the big Aquarium boat, the *Iridio,* about 10 miles offshore, over 60 feet of water. In no time, our chum line pulled in a large school of yellowtails, so many that the water around them appeared yellow. They were big for the species, 5- and 6-pound fish that worked through the chum, sucking it in as if they had magnets in their bellies.

A fry fly, with white chenille body, tied on a size 2 hook, matches the real fry used in chumming for yellowtail and mackerel.

A fry fly did the trick.

We dropped them into the floating chum and whammie, a big yellowtail would smash into them like a blow from a hammer.

Yet even so, once in a while those sharp-eyed babies would give us a fit, dashing headlong at the fly, then turning off at the last second, coming so close to taking that we would often strike.

Then far out on the chum line we saw other fish breaking.

"Mackerel!" shouted Brose Gosling.

These were the same fish as the Florida false albacore or little tuna, fish strangely built by nature so that they always have to keep swimming. The gill structure is such that if they stayed still they would die.

Now we saw them slipping through the chum within 30 feet of the boat. They didn't hesitate, but seemed to grab the floating fry at top speed. When they turned, they went far out, then getting a bearing they charged back into the fry. This time we were ready.

Both Brose and I dropped flies in front of them. Fish took both flies at the same time and the two reels went into high. I thought those fish had been traveling at top speed before, but now they really turned it on. They ran 500 feet before we finally stopped them, and it was 20 minutes before we could finally boat that pair. They weighed 7 pounds apiece . . . as nice an example of what the fly-rodder may expect from the chum line, as anything I could name.

Brose Gosling of Bermuda studies a well-earned yellowtail taken on a pink shrimp fly. *Courtesy Bermuda News Bureau.*

Bread is also widely used as chum in Bermuda. There, along the beautiful pink beaches, the gaff topsail pompano often come inshore and can be seen swimming through the curl of the breakers.

These tough bits of fish flesh, also called palometa, have a top weight of 4 pounds and average just under a pound. But they're as strong as little bulls. A 2-pounder can snake out a fly line and a hundred feet of backing before he stops. They feed extensively on sand fleas and nature has equipped them with amazingly sturdy ribs that are built to take a beating as the fish dash ashore in the wake of a receding wave and grab a flea before it can bury itself in the sand. Sometimes the game little pompano are left almost high and dry, flapping their bodies hard to get back to the water. Then they will come in again, their long, black dorsal and anal fins showing dark in the clear green water, just under the crest of the breakers.

They will hit a very small fly and spinner combination as well as an inch-long white or yellow bucktail, and will take almost any of the small spoon-type lures that fit a fly rod. Because of the clearness of the Bermuda water, these all have to ride on the end of a fine tippet, one that tapers down to at most 4-pound test.

When the gaff topsail pompano are first spotted, they can often be taken without chum, but as they are fished they grow a little scary and move into deeper water, and then the bread is crumbled into little balls and thrown out, and this coaxes them back within wading and casting distance.

It used to be that the light-tackle angler was not very welcome on charter boats, largely because when he hooked a big

Gaff topsail pompano caught with fly equipment. *Courtesy Bermuda News Bureau.*

fish it took him so long to land it that the other fishermen sharing the charter became disgruntled. However, in the past few years, more and more light-tackle anglers are using charter boats to go after unusual and sporty catches in the deeps, and when several pool their funds and go together, the charter men are only too glad to have them.

Casting from a charter boat has its hazards because of the superstructure, but usually the backcast can be managed without snagging a mate, an outrigger, or a fellow fisherman, as almost all casts in this kind of fishing are short, seldom more than 50 feet. And since the fish sought by this method are usually close to the boat, feeding on chum, or are school fish like dolphin and are following an already hooked fish, there is no need to hurry the cast.

There are other hazards of fishing the deeper water, too. Sometimes a hooked fish is lost to sharks, and sometimes a fish will dive to the bottom and cut the leader. Or the angler may tie into such a big, seagoing speedster that it just won't stop at all and ends by either snapping the leader or breaking the backing where it is tied to the reel core. But these are pleasant risks to take, with the ever-pleasant chance of coming up with something really unusual.

A lot of this kind of fishing is done on the Florida Keys, where charter boat captains are all "light-tackle minded." Last spring Captain Howard Victor took us out on his boat, the *Cadet,* to look for school dolphin in the line of driftage along the Gulf Stream just off Islamorada. Pete Perinchief of Bermuda was with me, making his first go for dolphin.

"Let's try these big red and yellow streamers," I suggested. "But first, let Vic get the fish in here where we can reach them."

Vic put out a trolling outfit and handed Pete the rod.

"Get one on," he instructed him. "And hold it. Bring it in to about 20 feet from the boat and just keep it there. The whole school will follow and stay with it, and then Joe can cast to them with his fly rod."

Ten minutes later Pete's rod bounced down and he held on while something tore line from the reel, then came out in a beautiful jump—a leaping, rainbow-hued dolphin, about 7 pounds.

Guide Bobby Ray of Bermuda throws chum out as author casts fly to a snapper. *Courtesy Bermuda News Bureau.*

He slipped back in and Pete fought him hard for five minutes, then began to get him in. We could see him out there in the water, and right in back of him were the brilliant yellow, golden and green streaks that told us the rest of the school was zipping around him, staying with the hooked fish.

I false cast line out, dropped the big streamer near Pete's fish. It looked as if the entire school rushed it at once. One socked it hard, and I set the hook and leaned back on the rod.

Three-pound mangrove or gray snapper—lots of fun on a fly. Chum brings them close enough for fly casting. *Courtesy Bermuda News Bureau.*

Out he came in a really high jump, a dolphin that could have been the twin of the one Pete had on. It took me fifteen minutes to land him.

Pete was still holding his hooked fish out there.

"Here," he said, shoving the rod at me and grabbing his own fly rod. "I gotta get in on this."

The school was still there and Pete was into a fish on his first cast, a leaping, jumping powerhouse that looked like flames from a wind-driven fire. He was in and out of the water like something was after him, but he finally tired and Pete got him in. As he released his catch, I brought the decoy in.

"We'll release him, too," I said. "He deserves it."

We hit two more schools in short order and each time we had the same fast action. Then a bit later, as we cruised along a heavy mat of sargasso weed, we saw something dash out from it, right along the top. It hit the bait like a ton of bricks. This was no school dolphin. This was a good big bull.

"He'll go 30 pounds," said Captain Vic.

I had the bait rod at the moment, and that fish kept me tied to it for half an hour. It was touch and go the whole time. Then he began to tire. He surfaced, away out, and right back of him we spotted another shape, something long and brown looking.

"That's another big dolphin," shouted Vic. "Get your fish in closer, Joe, so Pete can put a fly to the other one."

I pulled harder on my now tired fish, and brought him closer. The brown shape followed like a shadow. They were both at 35 feet.

Pete shot the fly out, a perfect cast that dropped the fly two feet in front of that shadow. The dolphin took at once and came out in the most tremendous leap I've ever seen, an arching jump that took him 10 feet in the air and carried him 30 feet across the ocean waves before he lit.

Pete's mouth was open, his eyes gleaming with a mixture of delight and disbelief. I probably had exactly the same look on my face. Never was there such a wonderful sight as that beautiful fish jumping across the ocean. Then I looked to the rear where my fish had been dogging it during all this wild excitement. Suddenly, as if jealous of the show his pal was putting on, he rushed to the top and came out, too, in a straight up jump, and threw the hook. I heaved a sigh and started reeling in, and suddenly, right where my hook was, Pete's fish came up, busted into the sunlight and threw Pete's fly. We reeled in a couple of empty lines.

Pete took three 7-pounders on his fly from the next school that hopped onto the trolled bait. They really punched holes in the ocean, like fast moving sewing machine needles.

"Catching 'em or losing 'em," said Pete, "if there's any better kind of fishing than this, I've yet to see it."

I thought of Pete that winter when I was using a popping bug for dolphin, down in Panama Bay. There are all kinds of strikes to a popping bug, fast ones, slow, majestic ones, sloppy tries, and pinpoint aiming. For pinpointing, the dolphin probably takes the diploma. They like poppers, and when one of those flossy looking numbers comes from under seaweed or a floating log to bop down on a lure, he does it with mathematical precision.

Dolphin are very curious about the noise made by a popper, and on this trip out in Panama Bay I coaxed a whole school of about a dozen 20-pounders out of some driftage to see what was going on. They bore down on that popper like a cavalry charge. The smallest one got there first, but even so the hit was so strong that it pulled the fly line out of my left hand and I had no control over the line until it hit the reel with a bang, and the leader snapped like a strand of spider web. The rest of the school followed that brilliantly hued dolphin as he leaped and leaped, trying to throw the fly, and every now and then another dolphin would jump clear to see what was happening. Then the whole bunch faded under the line of driftage and didn't come out again until we popped the next bug.

Dolphin will hit just about any feathered lure or popper that is tossed to them. But after a couple of fish have been taken from one school with the same fly, they will often stop hitting, as if getting wise to the lure. Then a change of color or pattern will usually stir them up again and put the angler back in business.

In the Florida Keys area, the hot time for this kind of fishing is from about May 25 to the end of the first week in July.

There are some school dolphin around all the time, of course, but they are spotty, and you may lose a lot of time hunting for them before ever getting a cast. But in the spring months they appear in numbers, following the line of sargasso weed, hanging around it and hiding under it, using it for a salty umbrella.

In July these Florida fish work northwards and during the summer they furnish great sport off the North Carolina coast. In Panama Bay, on the other hand, the dolphin continue on into October, following the fallen trees and driftage that float out into the Bay from the rain-swollen rivers.

CHAPTER/11

FLY FISHING FOR ATLANTIC SALMON

THE EATING HABITS OF THE ATLANTIC SALMON HAVE long been the subject of scientific and piscatorial discussion. Many authorities believe that the salmon doesn't eat after it leaves the salt, for the stomach of the fish is always empty when caught in fresh water; and that the fish hits a fly only "from memory"—memory of the days when he was a parr, feeding heavily in the fresh water of the river in which he was born.

Still another school of thought holds that, since salmon do take flies, and that since they are even known to have been caught on worms by poachers, the gastric juices of their stomachs are so strong that food is dissolved instantly and only the juices remain for the angler to discover when he opens the fish.

Once in the tidewater pool of a Newfoundland river, I took a salmon that had the backbone of a capelin in its stomach, all that remained of the smeltlike fish that salmon feed upon in the salt. How long it had been there is the question. Salmon do move in and out of the tidewater pools, getting used to the fresh water before moving up the river. But aside from that one time I have never found anything but a brown slime in the

Atlantic salmon wet flies are among the most beautiful ties. Here are (l. to r.) the blue charm, a low-water fly, size 4; Durham ranger, size 8; and two-hooked thunder and lightening, size 2.

stomachs of any of the salmon I have taken over many years. But whatever the reason, the Atlantic salmon readily hits a well-delivered fly.

Since earliest times salmon have been the fish that made sport fishing, and flies tied away back then are still used and continue to be top strike bringers, as well as being the most beautiful ties known, and the most romantically named . . . flies like the Jock Scott, Durham ranger, blue charm, thunder and lightning, black dose, silver doctor, March brown and many others.

Classic Atlantic salmon flies have the feathers "married," intertwined rather than tied separately like trout flies, and this is such an intricate procedure that they are, of necessity, expensive.

Recently some ties have been made with hair wings, and have found their way into the Atlantic salmon scene and are taking plenty of fish. These flies are not so expensive because they do not have the different kinds of feathers in the wings, nor the elaborate bodies that the classic ties do, but they seem to take their share of fish. For these reasons, that they are cheaper and do take fish, anglers are using them more and more. Such great recent ties as the black, gray, rusty and silver rat

The Rat series of salmon flies are typical of the successful hair flies. They come in black, gray, brown, rusty and silver, in sizes 2, 4, 6, 8, 10. *Courtesy of The Orvis Co.*

have hair wings and are proven salmon takers. Bigger hair flies also take salmon. I carried the great trout fly, the muddler, to Europe with me some years ago and caught a lot of good salmon on it. A bit more on the experimental side, I also tried the 1/0 blondes, especially the platinum and the honey, and these two also took salmon. Strikes didn't come too often to the blondes but generally the fish turned out to be good ones.

Regardless of married feathers or hair wings, it pays to carry a wide assortment of flies with you. For instance, in high water bigger flies are needed, while in low, clear water a small fly is required, not only small in stature but skimpily dressed as well. And because many a salmon river changes overnight as a result of a heavy rain, a wide range of flies is often necessary for one and the same river. And again it pays to know the kind and size of flies suitable for the country in which you will fish for salmon.

In nine years of salmon fishing in Newfoundland, I don't recall ever using a salmon fly bigger than a 2/0. Yet in some of the bigger rivers of Quebec, anglers go as high as 7/0. And in Norway 8/0 and 9/0 salmon flies are used almost every day, and in that country of wild rivers a 4/0 is considered a very small salmon fly.

Until very recently it would have been hard to convince me that there is any real need for a salmon fly as large as the 9/0, or for that matter, for a two-handed rod, but you live and learn, and the more I fish the more I realize how much there is that I don't know. And that July, when I made my first trip to Norway, I found in the heavy, short rivers that drop down like torrents in less than a mile from mountains to sea, just the set of conditions that called for that big equipment.

In the Aaroy River the water was fast and heavy and we tossed our flies out from casting platforms. In order to make pools, many dams, called kjaerr (pronounced she-air), had been constructed. The ends of these dams protruded just enough to make a hazard which could lose you a fish in a hurry. It was those kjaerrs that finally forced me to the extra length of the two-handed rod, but what first made me need one was the 9/0 flies. Trying to cast a 9/0 salmon fly with a 9-foot, 6-ounce fly rod, calls for Paul Bunyan wrists and also an iron hat to protect the back of the angler's head. One hit back there with such a hook and it's hard to say what would happen. You might end up in the river, or spend the rest of your days shadow boxing with emerging May fly hatches.

But the water was so heavy that only those heavy-hooked flies would get down deep in that rushing torrent. And only the long rod would lift the line over the protruding arms of the kjaerrs.

Many of the older salmon flies were tied on double hooks, but, like the big, two-handed rods, except for very special circumstances, these are on the way out. I believe that the single hook drops more lightly and does a better job of hooking the salmon, as with the two-hooked flies the two prongs are apt to work against each other. Some anglers hold the opinion that a two-hooked fly rides better, and gets the fly deeper, but proper presentation can overcome the first problem, and I do not be-

One of the enormous Atlantic salmon flies, size 9/0, used with two-handed rods on Norway's torrential rivers.

lieve that there is enough additional weight in the extra hook to make much difference in sinking the fly.

Low-water flies are used in low, clear pools where a heavily dressed fly would look like a bird falling into the river, far too big for anything but scaring the salmon off their perches. But the low-water flies, with the dressing tied sparsely and only a bit more than halfway back on the shank of the small wire hooks, can be presented lightly and quietly and inconspicuously. For salmon are strange-acting fish in low water. They want small flies, lightly dressed, and carry their liking to such an extreme that they will even hit a bare hook.

Dry flies are very effective for Atlantic salmon in North American waters. The dries are generally tied on No. 6 hooks, making a good big fly that will ride well in heavy water as well as smooth. But it is in the slick parts of the pools that the dry comes into best use.

A No. 6 dry will get you a salmon but you can go much smaller in hook size. Nowadays a dry fly dressed on a No. 12 hook is often used, and some anglers even go to the very light No. 16—which, of course, calls for some fine angling to bring the fish in.

Casting a dry to salmon, when the water has dropped and the fish can be seen in the pools, calls for a cast which will put the fly ahead of the leader on the water. Many times with an upstream cast with a straight leader, the salmon will rise to the floater only to bump the leader with his nose and so knock the fly away. A slack line S-cast, or a curve either to the right or left will overcome this, and give enough good float to overcome the drag problem.

A good stout hook is essential in dry fishing for Atlantic salmon and of course, the smaller the size of the dry fly, the thinner is the hook. But a size 8 or 10 hook will take salmon, especially if there is plenty of room to fight the fish, and many times I have resorted to dries tied on a size 12 hook. The only place there is danger of the salmon giving you trouble by straightening out the hook is when he gets downstream from you in heavy water or strong current. Then a light hook seldom holds a big salmon and the only recourse is to run downstream or go by canoe, following the fish until he has stopped in a pool and the angler has a fair chance to fight it out with him.

It's always a moot point whether it is the size of the fly or the color or the pattern that is of most importance. But the list below should get an angler through most circumstances, if they are carried in a wide assortment of hook sizes, and a stock of the same patterns is carried in the low water flies.

WET FLIES, *hook sizes 12 to 9/0*

BLACK DOSE	MARCH BROWN
BLACK DOCTOR	SILVER GRAY
BLUE CHARM	SILVER DOCTOR
COSSEBOOM	THUNDER AND LIGHTNING
DURHAM RANGER	LOGIE
DUSTY MILLER	JOCK SCOTT
GREEN HIGHLANDER	
MAR LODGE	

DRY FLIES, *hook sizes 6 to 14*

GRAY WULFF	GRAY BIVISIBLE
ROYAL WULFF	BLACK BIVISIBLE
WHITE WULFF	BADGER BIVISIBLE
BROWN BIVISIBLE	PINK LADY

All the salmon flies in the world will not help the angler if his trip does not coincide with the run of fish in the river to which he is going. Salmon are anadromous—that is, they are born in the fresh water, live there for a couple of years, go to sea for various lengths of time (from one or two to five or more years) then return to spawn in their native river. Usually the date of this spawning run into any given river, be it in Newfoundland, Maine or Norway, varies only a day or two from year to year, but occasionally natural conditions will hold back the run—as in 1954, for example, when an unusually large number of icebergs along the Newfoundland coast delayed the season there as much as ten days in some rivers.

Part of the joy of salmon fishing is the thrill of being in on that spring dash to the spawning beds far up-river. I know of no wilder, more fascinating or more thrilling sight than that of a salmon run passing through a pool, the fish jumping clear of the water, cutting the surface, dashing, darting, and going on up. They come in waves, bucking the relentless rush of the river, and while they are on the move it is no use to offer them a fly.

Then it is important to know the spot that is their first stopping place on that drive upstream. For instance, in Newfoundland, salmon enter the Humber River and don't stop, or at least don't come within the angler's reach, until they hit the Big Falls Pool, twenty miles above the town of Deer Lake. Once they reach that pool, however, the fishing is fabulous.

Occasionally, if the water drops during this upstream run, the salmon will be confined to pools, patiently waiting for rain, and the consequent rise of the river, before moving again to pools farther up. In such "staying pools" salmon will rise like a rocket to a fly.

While the first run salmon usually head for an upstream pool some distance from the mouth of the river, later runs will stop lower down, too, probably because the water is lower by that time. The Humber is an example in point—the early run goes straight to the Big Falls Pool, but later on, in late July, salmon begin to stop in all the pools. So to get in on first rate fishing, the salmon angler must know all the details about the river where he plans to fish.

There is a big difference in the way a salmon fights when he is hooked in the shallow water of a staying pool, and when he is hooked in heavy water. In the former case, he will seldom leave the pool. I remember one time on Harry's Brook, Newfoundland, hanging a salmon that weighed 15 pounds, in a pool the size of a tennis court. He tore that pool into bits, zipping across and back, catercornering. He was in and out of the air, throwing water high and wide. It was unleashed fury, turned loose on a pinpoint. But he wouldn't leave that pool, even though a dash through the shallow, rock-strewn rapids below would most certainly have resulted in a cut leader.

On the other hand, when the water in the rivers is fast and the salmon comes upstream in the spring run-off, he goes like a shooting star. A run of 200 or 300 feet is nothing, and in such water the angler must often follow a big salmon for considerable distance before landing it. A lot depends on the drag you have on your reel. Too light a drag will allow him to make long runs. If you are using a reel with a good, smooth drag and have a heavy enough leader, say 12-pound test, you can put quite a bit of pressure on and beat your salmon in fast time. Never give the fish a chance to rest, instead keep at him, lay back on the rod, get below him and pull him downstream, and soon he will tire and you can get him in.

I was in on a double exhibition of how much it means to have a reel with good drag, one day last summer. When you get an old brute of a salmon in fast water you need a fly reel with a good, smooth drag, one that you can set at 5 pounds pull and forget it. Last summer my wife, Mary, and I flew Pan American to Oslo, and then went up to the famous Alta River in arctic Norway. This particular day we were fishing a pool on the Sautso Beat, where you can cast from shore. The pool was long, the water fast, and at the end was a rapids that would scare you. At the side of it a deep backwater prevented the angler from following a fish downstream. Any salmon we hooked here would have to be kept in the pool. If he once hit those rapids, the weight of a big fish would be too much even for the 20-pound-test tippets we were using. We'd have to hold them, and as the salmon in the Alta average between 23 and 27 pounds, we knew we had our work cut out for us.

I started at the head of the pool and worked down, using a dusty miller, the top fly on the Alta, tied on a 4/0 hook. I went down about 10 feet without a strike. Then I laid the fly straight across current for 65 feet. I mended the line, got ready to mend again, and then I felt the line stop and then the powerful surge of a heavy fish. I kept from striking, let the downstream belly of the line pull the fly into the corner of his mouth. The line came up to the top, and there he was, only halfway out, but big!

We had it hot and heavy and he made one run that almost took him out of the pool but I pulled the rod in to my bank and got him out of the fast current and into a bit of slower water down near the end of the pool. I kept a tight line and walked down, reeling fast, and then he ran upstream and I followed him up. The pressure of the drag began to tell. After he made a series of lunges on the surface I got his head turned and pulled him in to the shallow water, where I could gaff him. He was in the mid-thirties, I knew.

As soon as I had him in, Mary had started fishing up at the top of the pool. Now I heard a faint cry wafted down on the wind over the roar of the river. I looked up. Mary was fighting a fish.

"He's big," she told me when I got up there. "I saw him take, 50 feet out."

The fish raced across to the other side, then back towards us again, then headed downstream as if he were a jet on a runway, about to take off. Mary pulled her 9½-foot rod towards the bank, held it there. It swept the fish out of the current and he came upstream a bit, then stopped and laid there, still.

"I'm going down," said Mary. "I want to get the fly line back on the reel."

Reeling as she walked, she moved below him and pulled back hard. That started him moving again, and he came up and halfway out. It was a very big salmon.

Mary was right on him. She followed him upstream and fought him there for ten minutes. He started down, facing into the current, letting the water push him, gaining line by sheer weight, even against the strong drag of the No. 3 Fin Nor fly reel. Then he suddenly rushed right at our shore, swirled in 2 feet of water and took off across the pool like he was never going to stop. He ran for 200 feet and then bored into the current over there, broadside to us, a mighty salmon not about to give up.

Again Mary pulled her rod towards our shore, holding it downstream, and the pressure of the current on the line, the pull of the long fly rod, the steady drag of that reel, turned the salmon and he came slowly across current again, on top now. Thirty feet out from us he faced the heavy current again and with powerful thrusts and beats of his big, broad tail, gaining a foot each time, pushed his way towards the middle of the pool. After thirty minutes had passed Mary had him in to within only 20 feet. He rolled on top, turned completely over, swirled again, and this time floated for a couple of feet, still. Mary moved her rod shorewards, walked back five feet,

Mrs. Joe Brooks took this 39-pound, 12-ounce Atlantic salmon in the Alta River, Norway, using a 4/0 silver gray and 20-pound-test leader tippet, on a 9½-foot bamboo rod and Fin-Nor #2 reel. It took half hour to land him.

Joe Brooks watches Bing Crosby make a cast in the Derwent River in England, as the two fished for Atlantic salmon for ABC-TV cameras while filming a show for the American Sportsman series.

and pulled the fish over my waiting gaff. I got him, carried him well back and put him down. He weighed 39 pounds 12 ounces.

The usual way of fishing a fly for Atlantic salmon is to cast across current, let the fly float along motionless until it has swung through below the angler. Sometimes the fly is kept moving throughout the entire journey, by working the rod tip, thus imparting small jerks to the fly as it travels. If the

Etienne de Ganay of Paris with 37-pound Atlantic salmon taken from the Aaroy River, Norway, while using a 9/0 Jock Scott, and a 14-foot, two-handed salmon rod.

salmon rises to this delivery, and refuses, then the fly is changed, from a light to a darker one, or from one size to another. Then the cast is made again, perhaps starting with a shorter throw, in case the fish has moved upstream on the strike, and then with successively longer casts to and beyond the point of the original strike, in case he has dropped downstream.

By mending the line you can slow the float of the fly, keep it broadside out there in the current, making it easier for the salmon to take.

The novice salmon fisherman must steel himself so that he doesn't strike when a salmon rises to take his fly. Let him have it. He will hook himself. Generally they take and zoom upstream, putting a belly in the line, which then pulls the fly into the scissors of the mouth. If you don't feel a fish, let the fly float on through, rest him for a while, and try again.

Usually there is very good reason for the refusal of the fish in the first place. Either the fly zipped past his lie too fast, headed downstream by the bellying line, or it wasn't the right pattern or size, and so on. But once he has shown interest, it is usually possible to produce a fly that will get him.

This was the method I always used until some years ago when I read a book by Jock Scott called *Greased Line Fishing*

Two Atlantic salmon dry flies—the gray bivisible (left) and the pink lady on size 8 hooks.

for Salmon. It was first published in 1895 and was a description of a way of angling with a wet fly for salmon, as advocated by Arthur Wood, one of England's most famous salmon fishermen. That book changed my whole way of wet-fly fishing for salmon and I have never gone back to the old way. I am thoroughly convinced that with this method the angler will get more hits and hook more fish.

The whole thing boils down to the theory that the reason a salmon rises to a fly and then refuses is that the fly is not presented in the proper manner. Wood contended that when the angler cast the fly across current, the current caught the line and pulled the fly downstream too fast and in the wrong position for the salmon. His remedy was to grease the line so that it would float well, make the cast, then mend the line upstream and at the same time keep the rod ahead of the line so that the fly would proceed downstream broadside to the fish. He suggested that the reason the salmon hit when the fly was making its final swing below the angler was that the fly was then broadside to the fish, and that the salmon like the fly to be at all times in that position. He further said that a fly presented by the greased line method would hook the salmon on the first rise and that each strike would find the hook embedded in the corner of the salmon's mouth.

Let me tabulate the main points of the book before I go into my own first adventure with its theories.

1. The salmon likes to see the fly coming downstream broadside. He likes to see the whole fly, not just a passing flash. Salmon often refuse a fly offered with usual fishing methods because the fly is going too fast or is presented so that only the tail of the fly is visible to the fish.
2. The fly should travel more downstream than across so it will have a natural float—wobbling, swimming, rising and falling with the play of the eddies exactly as would an insect or minnow in trouble. To achieve this action, the fly must be fished on a slack line, so that there is no tension behind it.
3. On a slack line, the fly floats naturally right into the salmon's mouth and the current helps to push it farther back towards the throat. The slack line is swept downstream by the current, and this automatically draws the hook into the corner of the fish's mouth—the most secure hold that is possible. A mere pull toward the bank, a "tightening" rather than a strike, is all that is needed to hook the fish.
4. The way to meet all the requirements above, is to cast a slack line and lead the line downstream with the rod tip slightly in advance, letting it drift naturally.

I determined to give Mr. Wood's technique a thorough tryout, and so did my fishing partner, Charlie.

At Grant's Pool on the Serpentine, it was plain at once that it was going to be tough to make fish hit. The river was low and clear. When it's like that, the salmon have a habit of sitting it out, waiting for higher water, and disdaining even the best dressed flies. We needed rain to pep up the fish and put them in a striking mood. Yet it looked like a perfect proving ground for Wood's theories, because Wood first devised this method of angling for just such low, clear conditions.

But first I had promised Charlie a lesson in line mending, because the whole Wood method depends on the proper execution of the mend. And since it's practically impossible to mend

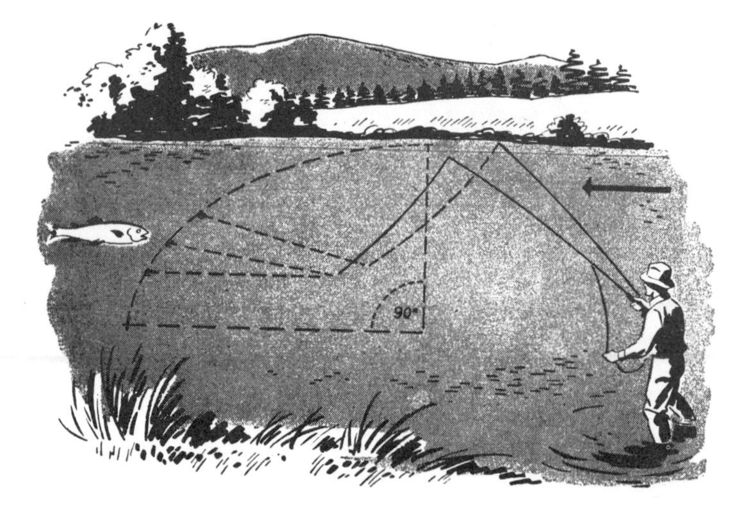

A sunken salmon fly ordinarily is fished like this. It moves at mid depth, more across than downstream, offers a tail-end view to the fish, floats un-
A sunken salmon fly ordinarily is fished like this. It moves at mid-depth,
naturally. Salmon often rise to the offering, then refuse it.

a logy, sinking line, the line should be greased first. Hence the term—greased line fishing. A greased line is lighter, more buoyant. You can cast it easily, drop the fly lightly. And it makes it simpler to keep the fly drifting just beneath the surface, where it should be.

Most dry-fly trout fishermen mend their lines to avoid drag and control the fly. I always mend mine wherever the current between me and the fly will belly the line. If the line is mended properly, you are ready to strike quickly, or to pick up smoothly for another cast. There's less water disturbance, too, and less chance of scaring the fish. I explained to Charlie that the mend is made by casting across the stream, pointing the arm and rod horizontally toward the fly, then, with a fairly stiff arm, rolling the line upstream with a half-circle sweep of the rod. It's a sort of side-arm roll cast, across as well as upstream. The line flips upstream in an arc between the fly and the rod tip. Wood called it a "pick up and put down."

"But what do I do if the current between me and the fly happens to be slower instead of faster than the water out there where the fly is floating?" Charlie asked.

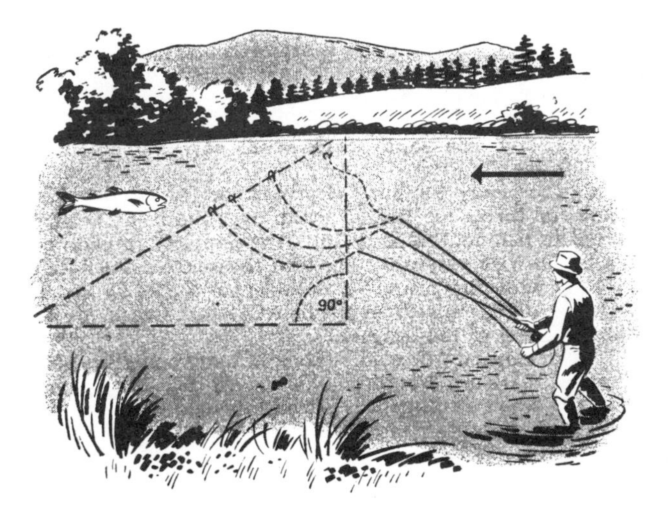

In greased-line fishing, the fly travels just under the surface on a slack line, moves downstream in a natural, easy drift, and presents a broadside view to the fish.

"Simple. Mend the fly downstream," I said.

I left him then, executing a very capable line mend, and started for the Dump Pool, four miles below.

As I stripped line off my reel to make my first cast, I recited what I'd learned by heart—the key to greased line fishing.

"The line is used as a float for, and controlling agent of, the fly; it keeps the fly just below the surface and controls its path in such a way that it swims diagonally down and across the stream, entirely free from the slightest pull of the line. . . . [Thus] the fly rides in a natural manner, and the fish, having taken, is soundly hooked."

Well, the line was well greased and would float as high as a balsa wood popper on a millpond. The next step was to get that natural float, free from the pull of the line. I'd have to throw a slack line. I could do that by throwing harder than I needed for the distance and pulling back with the rod at the end of the cast. The line would fall in a series of S's, with plenty of slack.

Then what? Lead the line downstream with the rod, Wood said. That way, any fish facing upstream would get a broadside

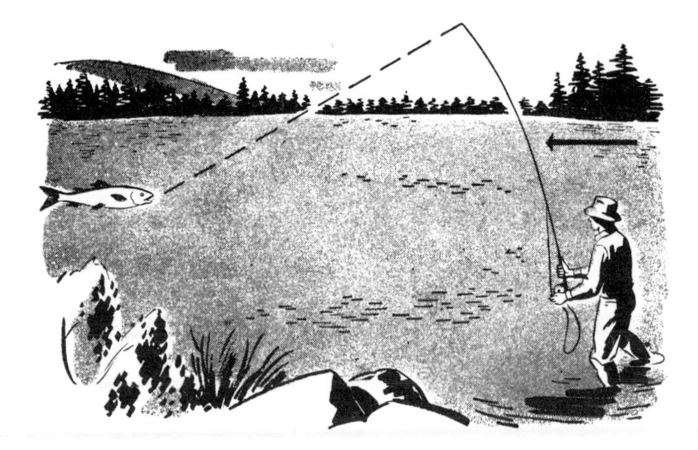

It's easy to jerk the fly right out of a salmon's mouth by trying to set the hook with an upward flip of the rod tip.

view of the fly. And that's the way they like to see it—not tearing across the surface a mile a minute, scaring the spots off every grilse and salmon in the stream. It's that long, diagonal float before the fly swings in below the angler that gets the fish.

I soft-footed into position and made a cast. The line shot across the current and the fly, a number 6, landed, floated a couple of feet, and then the line started to belly. I mended it and again led it down with the rod tip slightly in advance. I knew as I watched, that any salmon seeing its downward

The old Scot's method is to let the fish charge ahead with the fly, keep the rod low, then sweep the line in sideways.

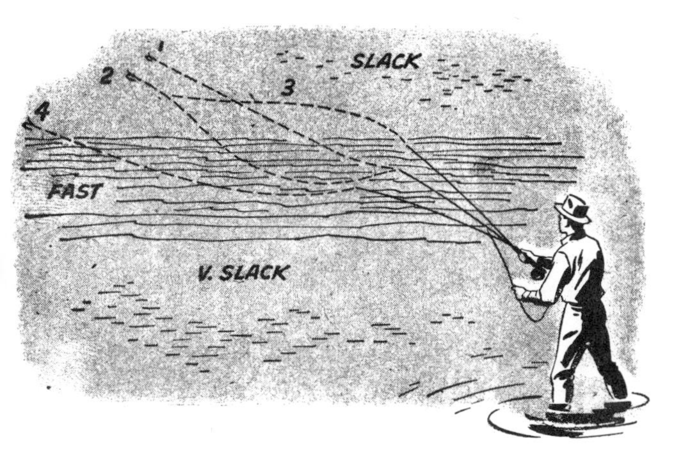

Here's a common problem that line mending solves. The cast, made to slack water, crosses a fast current, 1. That causes the line to belly, 2. So flip to 3 for a natural drift to 4.

journey would be viewing it broadside.

The fly swept on, apparently unnoticed. I mended line a second time as it started to belly again, and a moment later I saw a flash, down deep. I struck automatically, felt a mere tick of the hook on the salmon's lip, and then nothing. Ruefully I remembered the Scotsman's admonition not to "strike." That the fly is taken broadside by the salmon as he comes up from below to meet it, and the force of his rush invariably carries some of the line and leader upstream with him. This causes the line to belly and pulls the leader across his mouth and

When the fly itself is cast to fast water, 1, it will loop down ahead of line on slack water, 2. Save it with a roll of the line to 3, so that you get a long natural drift to 4.

the fly into the angle of his jaw. As the fish takes, the pull of the current will be enough strike to send the barb home.

"Wait until you see the line being held or pulled on the surface of the water and then tighten by moving the rod in toward your bank, but do not on any account strike," is the way Wood put it. In other words, if you allow the fish plenty of time to take the fly and roll it around in its mouth, the hook will go home as a result of a mere "pull" towards your bank.

A few minutes later, in new water, I made my second cast. Once again I mended when the line bellied—and a moment later I saw that familiar flash. Then I felt a shocking, thudding strike and saw 15 pounds of Atlantic salmon burst out into the sunshine, land 10 feet further away, and nip off downstream.

Wood was right. The salmon had taken on his first rise. And when I finally beached that seagoing powerhouse, I took the fly from the *corner* of his mouth. Again Wood had scored.

The Atlantic salmon's habit of taking a fly and rolling it around in its mouth was what made Wood realize the need for slowness in the strike. Occasionally he even went so far as to give slack line after he'd seen a fish take. It was his retort to the age-old debate on whether or not salmon eat after they reach the sweet water. Wood claimed he had seen them take naturals at this time, and believed that salmon crush the flies, extract the juices, and eject the carcasses.

I apply this phase of the greased line method, slightly modified, to angling for bonefish. The bonefish has a peculiar mouth, equipped with crushers well back in the throat, and when it takes a fly it throws it back into these crushers. I give slack line at the moment of the take and wait until I see the line moving and actually feel the fish before I strike. Every fish taken that way has the hook in the corner of his mouth.

I landed four more salmon that day, using this new-found method, and Tom White, my guide, and I, were in fine spirits when we headed back to camp.

At the Admiral Pool, next day, I found a good chance to try another of Wood's theories. A fish was rising right out in front of me, just a little upstream. I'd always had trouble taking a fish that lay upstream from me like that. I usually ended by having to go above him to get a hit. Now I made a cast, mended the line at once, led with the rod tip, and so showed that baby the fly broadside. He hit hard and fifteen minutes later I beached him. Within half an hour I landed three more salmon, and all had hit flies placed directly opposite me on the stream. That used to be a dead area for me because the line would belly as soon as it hit the water and pull the fly out of there too fast for a fish to get to it.

Then I started to miss strikes. I was striking too soon and taking the fly away from the fish. I remembered the "pull and tighten" instructions given in the Wood method, but still I only nicked fish or missed them altogether. I began to grow frantic, started to throw the fly any old way, and then noticed that my guide was looking at me.

"Slow down, old boy," I said to myself. "You're slipping up somewhere in this new technique."

I finally decided that I was holding too tight a line to begin with, and wasn't keeping the rod high enough so that when I saw the fish start to take I could drop the rod tip and give more slack. So I tried that. I watched the next fish come for the fly, fed a foot of line through the guides to be sure of slack, and as the fish took, I just pulled the rod in toward the bank. It worked and business began to pick up.

Then something happened. I saw a fish rise about 40 feet across the pool. I cast a couple of times, but while I mended the line twice before the fly reached him, it didn't seem to go over that fish properly. The fly would drag over that spot, zipping downstream headfirst, much too fast.

I soon discovered why. A strong breeze was blowing my leader and fly straight downstream, and I was getting plenty of belly even before the current got in its deadly work. To avoid that upstream drift, I brought the rod tip down hard at the end of the cast to within a couple of feet of the surface. That sent the fly out under the wind and right to where I wanted it. One mend was all I needed and that salmon went for the fly like a kid for his Christmas presents.

Wood even adjusted the quickness of the strike to the size of the hook he was using. For example, he used large No. 1 flies in the cold, heavy run-off of early season. In the summer months he turned to the sparsely tied low water flies on little No. 10 and 12 hooks. The warmer the water, the smaller the hook used. Anyone who has fished salmon in low water and has resorted to clipping the feathers even from low water flies will understand Wood's crowning experiment with flies and hook size . . . he fished hooks without any feathers at all, merely a little color painted on. Jock Scott saw the great Scotsman use these flies and take salmon with them, and in his dour manner named them baldy, the blueshank and the redshank.

Wood contended that salmon feel and eject a large hook, No. 1 to 4, in a hurry, and when he used these sizes he tightened up very quickly. That's what I call putting the finger on the salmon.

I practically always use a floating line for Atlantic salmon, but in very high water the sinking/floating line (*see* TACKLE) is made to order. As previously described, this line allows you to manipulate the floating part of the line, while the head goes out and down, putting the fly right in front of the fish. With this line then, you are able to fish in the same manner as with a floater: cast across stream, mend the line, let the fly float until it starts across current, mend again, then let it swing through and stop in the water below, then retrieve.

Dry-fly fishing for salmon comes into its own after the first run-off of water through the rivers. Then, when the pools are low and clear, a dry fly is tops. There's nothing in fishing quite like the rise of a salmon to a dry fly unless perhaps it's the roll of a 100-pound tarpon to a popping bug.

Generally the dry is fished just as it would be for trout, up and straight across. Some dry-fly anglers allow the fly to float down below them, sink it, and then retrieve it in short jerks, just under the surface. This method will take the odd salmon, just as it will take the odd trout, but it's more or less accidental and a wet fly properly fished would take more salmon.

In small streams salmon fishermen must go into very fine tackle and fish with extreme quiet and care. A 15-foot leader tapered down to a 4-foot section of 6-pound-test nylon will fall lightly and not scare the fish. For, although salmon may stay right in plain view of the angler, so that they appear not to have scared, once they have been put down by carelessness or sloppy casting, they're down and just lying there staring at him, with no intention of hitting.

CHAPTER / 12

THE LANDLOCKED SALMON

LANDLOCKED SALMON ARE OF THE SAME SPECIES AS Atlantic salmon, but have either become area bound without access to the sea, or have lost the migratory urge which makes the Atlantic salmon perform his phenomenal ocean to river migration.

The landlocked are both limited and widespread in habitat, as they have been planted in many lakes beyond their original home waters. But wherever they are found, they provide fast and exciting fly rod sport. My own first encounter with the species was at Kennebago, Maine. I was casting the Little Kennebago River and had a hit to my streamer fly, and then out came a bright, silvery colored number in a series of jumps so fast that I thought it must be a whole school of fish. I couldn't believe that a single salmon could jump up such a storm. Since that day, so many years ago, I have caught many landlocked in widely scattered waters, and all of them kick up the same turmoil.

They are now found in many Northern Hemisphere spots, from Maine and New York to Northern Ontario, Quebec, (where they are called ouananiche), Newfoundland and Labrador. They have been transplanted to New Zealand and Argentina, with great success. But most of these fish, wherever they are found, originated with stock from Sebago Lake in the Rangeley Lakes section of Maine, and the scientific name comes from this origin—*Salmo salar sebago.*

Many of the time-honored landlocked salmon flies also originated in the Rangeleys, Kennebago, Mooselookmeguntic and Moosehead Lake fishing camps. Smelt comprise the main food item on the landlocked salmon menu in Maine, and many of the flies simulate the smelt in one way or another. The supervisor is probably the outstanding example of this tie and will probably get more hits than any other artificial in the books. But the gray ghost, green ghost, dark tiger and many Atlantic salmon flies will also take them, and when they are hitting well they can be caught on almost any type of fly, from nymphs through the wet flies and dries, as well as on streamers and bucktails. Best dries are the gray Wulff, white Wulff, royal coachman Wulff, green drake, gray hackle with yellow body, and the black gnat, all in sizes 14 to 8.

The Grand Lake Stream area in Maine was at one time a choice landlocked salmon fly fishing spot. The lake itself was usually fished by trolling, but wide-awake fly casters watched for risers and cast both wets and dries with great success. And the stream below the lake, running into Big Lake, three miles below, furnished wonderful dry-fly fishing. On one trip there I recall taking several landlocked salmon over 4 pounds apiece on a green drake, size 12. We fished dries for them much as we would for trout, working the pools carefully, and finding them in the same places as we would have found rainbows or browns. They responded, however, with typical salmon spontaneity, and busted skyward with the usual spectacular aerial activity of the family. And wherever he has been transplanted, the landlocked salmon has carried on the traditions of his forebear, the Atlantic salmon, earning his reputation as a rip-snorting game fish with plenty on the ball.

The most successful retrieve when fishing streamers for landlocks, in either lake or river, is a slow, foot-long pull back. Again, it will pay to cast a streamer or bucktail out, when fishing a river, and let it float without motion, riding the current just a few inches under the surface. Many times such fly play

Joe Brooks (left) and David Wayne admire a fine 8-pound landlocked salmon taken from the Traful River, Argentina, while filming a picture for ABC-TV's American Sportsman show.

pays off in a thumping strike. And sometimes, if such a float does not bring any response, the fish can be stirred up with a fast, foot-long strip just at the end of the float, making the streamer leap forward. Then the force of the current pulls the fly to the surface, or just under the surface, and the angler will see the fish as he takes, banging into it with authority.

Nothing beats trying, and working hard with different speeds, lengths of jerks, and different levels of retrieve. As long as the fish are hitting a certain bringback, that is the one to stick to, but when hits fall off, then other methods are called for.

Wet flies, nymphs and dries are all fished the same way for landlocked salmon as they are for trout. Nymphs may be allowed to float motionless, or be given action by allowing them to sink, then bringing them up in short jerks. A wet fly is allowed to swing on down without motion, then retrieved, or it may be given short jerks to make it look like a downed insect struggling along. Dries are fished up or up and across stream with the same care to avoid drag as if they were being fished for brownies.

When fishing a dry on lakes, however, the dry fly should always be given action. A dry fly cast out and left to sit there seldom brings a strike. In order to attract a nearby fish and create an urge for that fly, it must jump, shake, shiver and run across the top. Fishing a dry that way for landlocks can be lots of fun.

The landlocked salmon is indistinguishable in appearance from the Atlantic salmon, but does not grow as big. The top fish listed on world record charts is a 22-pound 8-ouncer caught in Sebago Lake, Maine, in 1907, by Edward Blakely. However, it is known that several larger ones have been taken in the Traful River in Argentina, where the landlocked salmon has taken on with tremendous success. Pictures and log books there list four fish over 24 pounds, none of which, however, was entered for world record.

The Traful River is probably the greatest landlocked salmon water in the world today. From Sebago Lake stock planted there in 1903, the species has now spread out over such a wide area that today they can be taken in many lakes and streams in the Nahuel Huapi, Lanin and Futalaufquen National Parks.

In the Compomento Pool in the Traful, the salmon may be seen lying in plain view, sometimes within 25 feet of the wading fisherman. When I first went into that pool, I started at the top and used the drop system of casting which I had often used for Atlantic salmon. I would throw the fly out for about 15 feet, then lengthen the throw by a couple of feet each succeeding cast. Then, when I had finished that drop, I would walk downstream for 20 feet, and start all over again.

But my fishing companions, Jorge Donovan and Bebe Anchorena, soon advised me of the different procedure used in Argentinian waters.

"Down here they don't stay in the heads of the pools," Jorge said. "Start in the middle of the pool. They will be from there down to the end."

"We don't use that casting system, either," said Bebe. "We just cast across stream and let the fly swing down in the current. Then we move a few feet down with each cast."

When I reached the middle of the pool I saw some fish facing into the current and only 30 feet out from me. The water was so clear that I was afraid I would scare them but the first float over those babies brought one roaring up for the blue charm I had on, and he took hard.

He fought all the way, with runs, jumps, pulls, tugs and dashes. He did everything but give up—but I finally landed him.

That trip we fished the Traful from one end to the other and it was like something out of a dream. We took fish from every pool, fish that went from 3 to 12 pounds and averaged around 7½ pounds. That was real fishing, even though some days the fish were choosy and we didn't do too well, and had to really work to get them to hit. But we kept at it and showed them a million flies, and found enough that they liked.

At that time, which was March, they would not hit dry flies, but probably would have done so earlier in the season when the water was lower and warmer. Dr. Cornelio Donovan of Buenos Aires, father of my friend Jorge, holds the record for landlocked salmon on a dry in the Traful, a 12-pounder.

On a stormy day at the end of our fishing trip, we fished the boca where the river pours out of Lake Traful. Dark clouds hung low over the lake and you could see the rain up there, but as happens so often in Argentina, the clouds stayed there and didn't come rushing down on us to spoil our fishing.

The salmon were lying out there facing the outlet from the lake, in a semicircle. I went out waist deep in the water and started casting. No strikes. I turned and cast to my right, but still no strikes. Then on the other side of the outlet, I noticed the current pouring past a rock wall that rose straight up. It looked like a perfect lie for salmon. I waded carefully over to within casting range. I put a size 8 honey fly on and threw it right up against that rock. It floated for a yard, then everything stopped. I raised the rod tip and felt the fish. He dashed up along that rock, then veered off towards the middle of the lake. He came my way and jumped almost in my face. He looked as long as a canoe paddle.

I dropped the rod tip fast, then pulled it up again as he fell back in and headed downstream, going at least 50 per.

He went through the fast water at the head of the pool, he steamed through the 200-foot length of it into the next pool. I started to wade ashore, holding the rod high, with one eye glued on the diminishing line on the reel. I kept a tight line, hit shore, and headed after the fish. He stopped then and I reeled fast as I walked down to him. He was in the middle of the pool, lying doggo. I got below him finally and pulled back and started him going again. He jumped three times in a row. He sprinted to the head of the pool, and went into the white water, but he was tiring now and I stopped him and turned him and reeled him back my way. He fought back there for five minutes more and then I skidded him ashore. He weighed 9½ pounds, a wonderful fish, as sleek as a new shine.

Until the last day, that was the top fish of the whole trip. Then on the last day all of us tangled with great fish, and finally just as we were about to quit, Bebe got one that beat mine.

I had finished my pool, and walked up to where he was.

"What luck?" I asked.

He held up the fly he had been using. It was a 4-inch-long platinum blonde, a big bucktail tied on a 1/0 hook, a fly we had used with great success on brown trout.

"It's driving them wild," he said. "They jump on it, hit it with their tails. They hit it like they hate it. So far I've landed four salmon from this one pool on this fly."

He waded out a bit farther then, and made a 50-foot cast. The fly had hardly landed before a long, silvery shape slashed up and hit. This fish was a runner, he ran 150 feet in 10 seconds, flung himself out of the water in an astounding leap, then ran right back our way. Bebe was reeling up a fit trying to gain back the slack line the sudden turn of the fish had caused, and he finally made it. Then the fish came right out, not 30 feet away. He looked very big.

He fought and fought. He jumped nine times. He made several more runs, shorter, but with lots of zip. Bebe finally skidded him ashore. He weighed 12 pounds 8 ounces, the largest of the trip.

On a later visit to the Traful, Bebe and I had rare sport using the 1/0 platinum blonde, casting it across the pool and bringing it back in quick jerks as fast as we could. To get hits we had to really yank the line back through the guides, making the rod tip bounce up for several inches with each strip. We made the flies zip through the surface water, and that did it; we couldn't have gotten the flies away from those landlocks if we had wanted to. It was far from classic fishing, but I can tell you one thing, it was certainly a lot of fun.

During the same visit I tried an Adams hackle skating spider, with 2-inch-long hackles, tied on a No. 12 hook. I used an 8½-foot rod to skate the spider, and greased my fly line and the leader, too, all the way down to where it was tied to the fly. I had already put plenty of silacone dressing on the flies. I got into the Compomento Pool and cast the skater straight across the still surface for 60 feet. With rod held high I started making that fly dance its way across the slow current. I gave it a foot-long jerk, let it sit still, then a 2-foot-long jerk, then a series of inch-long jerks, let it sit still, then started it my way with more of those inch-long jerks. I saw him coming. A streak, then a silvery arrow, and he hit that fly and I was into him. He took me all over the pool and made some amazing jumps. I finally landed him, a fine 7-pound 8-ounce landlocked salmon who liked his skaters moving smartly along.

In any of the waters in which the landlocked salmon is found, the best fly rod is the 8½-footer, with a WF-7-F fly line. The leader should be tapered to a 3X tippet in most cases, but in low, clear water a 4X will bring more hits. On the other hand, in fairly heavy water, a 2X tippet that has a breaking point of 6.3 pounds will be small enough in diameter to get strikes, and still strong enough to withstand the fight of the fish.

Many times, in a small stream, an 8-foot, 4-ounce rod would do an entirely satisfactory job, but as the streamer fly is the payoff one for most landlocked salmon, the bigger rod is the better one for all around fishing. And when moving into small water with the big rod, it is still possible to lighten the tackle by reducing the size of the tippet. And as the tippet is the weakest part of the fly man's equipment, the caster can go as fine as he likes in that department. One thing to remember, however, is that with a large rod and a very light tippet, the strike should be very gentle, a mere lifting of the tip, or the fly may be snapped off where it is tied to the leader.

CHAPTER/13

TROUT THAT GO TO SEA

IT SEEMS THAT JUST ABOUT ANYWHERE THAT TROUT LIVE in a coastal river, they have the urge to go down to the sea, live there for various lengths of time, then return to their native river to spawn. Because they feed heavily in the well-stocked larder of the ocean, they grow rapidly in the salt, and because they range the great open spaces of the seas, they become strong, swift and sure of themselves. When they return to the rivers they are far from the timid fish that first poked their small noses into the briny. They are at their peak, with extra heft and extra zip, all wrapped up in the bright silver coat that is the badge of the sea.

These sea-run species are widespread enough to furnish good fishing in many places. The steelhead of the Pacific coast, the sea-run brook trout of Newfoundland and the New England coast, the sea-run cutthroat of the Pacific northwest, the sea-run brown trout of the European coast from Spain to the Arctic waters of Norway, the sea-run browns of near-Antarctica, in Argentina's Tierra del Fuego and the sea-run char found all across the top of Canada, and in the Arctic Ocean from Labrador to Norway and to the island of Spitsbergen. All these sea-going trout are ready hitters to flies. They are real battlers, packing a special sailor's punch to furnish some of the greatest sport the angler will find anywhere.

STEELHEAD

In America, the steelhead is the outstanding fish of this kind. The steelhead is a rainbow that goes to sea, and more specifically it is the rainbow of the Pacific coast. From California to Alaska, these tidal rovers slip downstream into the sea each year, stay there for periods that vary from one to four months, then journey back into the sweet water of the coastal waters, and head on up to distant spawning beds. They travel amazing distances, and it is nothing to catch them 100 miles upstream from the salt. When they first come in they are bright silver, readily identifiable, but after being in the river for a while, they resume their original familiar rainbow colors.

Before planning a trip to the Pacific coast for steelhead, it is essential to contact someone who is right on the river that the angler plans to fish, or who at least knows the general area thoroughly—an outdoor editor of the local newspaper, for instance, or the game and fish department authorities, as the steelhead is strictly a periodic fish.

There are what are known as "summer runs" and "winter runs" and each comes at a certain specific time in each special river, sometimes only a week apart—but if the run is not in, the fish just are not there. The Kalama in Washington, the Deschutes in Oregon and the Klamath in northern California are early rivers with summer runs working in around September 15th and continuing into the fall. The early-run fish are usually small (called half-pounders by anglers), weighing from half a pound up to 3 or 4 pounds. The average weight increases as the run continues, with more 5- and 6-pounders, and the bigger fish coming in late. With the exception of a few rivers, there are seldom any really big fish in the early runs. However, the Deschutes is one river that holds some big fish as early as mid-September. It was from this river that former Governor of Nevada Morley Griswold took his world record steelhead on a fly, a wonderful 28-pounder.

But in general, the winter-run steelhead are much bigger than the earlier ones, with many 20-pounders being taken on flies. They are real busters and in the high water of the winter months they are something to handle.

A famous big-fish river is the Babine in British Columbia. Bill McGuire, Director of Research and Development for Eddie Bauer, Expedition Outfitters of Seattle, Washington, first introduced me to the Babine, and I have gone there every year since, around the end of September when the run is heavy. The biggest steelhead ever taken from the Babine was a 47-pound, 8-ounce fish caught by the Indians in a net. The largest known to have been taken on a fly weighed 26 pounds. Last year I watched Don Ives of Seattle, one of our party, take one that was very close to that. He was fishing a shallow riffle where rocks protruded some 50 feet from shore. Out there the water deepened and went scurrying along over what we knew was a bottom covered with round rocks. It looked like a great holding place for steelhead.

Don dropped his fly only 20 feet out, let it float through, picked it up and landed the next one about 3 feet farther out. Seconds later the rod dipped down and stayed there, and I saw a steelhead bust out in a blaze of crimson. He jetted down the pool so fast I was glad I was ashore or he would have run me down. Don had to follow him down to the end of the pool, but he gained line as he went and finally beached the steelhead, as beautiful a fish as I've ever seen. His bullet-shaped head tapered back into a thick, deep body, and he sported a tail like a shovel. Tints of brilliant red shone on his gill covers and streaked down his sides. He weighed 23 pounds, a whale of a steelie.

These big fish come 200 miles from the sea via the Skeena River Watershed, which produces some of the biggest known steelhead for its two main rivers, the Babine and the Kispiox. Both rivers hold enormous fish, with the nod going a bit to the Kispiox.

Sinking lines are used almost exclusively for steelheading. The Scientific Anglers Wet-Head, with 30 feet that sinks while the balance of the line floats (*see* TACKLE), makes a perfect steelhead line. You can cast out, know that your fly is near the bottom, and still be able to mend the shooting part of the line to keep the fly working down the pool. A line which sinks entirely will often be pushed out of the current and sometimes end up, fly and all, right at your feet. The steelhead hardly gets a glance at it before it is pulled away from his lie.

Another thing I like about the sinking line for steelhead is that you don't need to use a weighted fly; you don't get the nice feel of a smooth cast with a weighted fly.

In order to really capitalize on a sinking line the angler should use a short leader, not more than 6 feet in length. When the leader is longer, say 10 or 12 feet, the fly line still sinks, all right, but the long, comparatively light leader rises in the water, pushed by the current, and this moves the fly higher in the water and defeats your purpose.

Sometimes there are too many fishermen for the pool or riffle on a steelhead river and then it is that the line forms from the right. A fisherman will get into position at the top of the riffle and start casting across current, fishing his fly down through that float. Then he will move down a couple of feet in the riffle and make his next cast. After a few moves, the next angler will take his position and he, too, will start casting. There could be as many as eight or ten men in a riffle at one time. The procedure is that as soon as an angler catches a fish he backs out of line and starts again at the rear of the parade. It works very well, and in that manner a lot of fishermen can work the same water and with success. Once the first man reaches the end of the riffle, he scrambles out and goes off to another run, or back he goes to the end of the line and again awaits his turn.

But when it is possible, I like to work a steelhead pool or riffle by the "drop system" used by many Atlantic salmon anglers. I cast the fly out 25 feet and fish it through the pool, pick it up and send it out on the next cast 2 or 3 feet farther out, and so on until I am casting far out and covering a lot of holding water. Then I move down 10 feet and start all over again.

Fish out each float until the fly has swung through and come to a stop below you in the current. Some steelheaders start it back fast, right then, getting it in to pick up for the next cast. Others bring it upstream in foot-long pulls for 3 or 4 feet before increasing the speed to pick it up. This is up to the individual. But after getting quite a few strikes as I made that retrieve of a few feet, I stick with that method.

Every fly fisherman who is after steelhead should use a shooting basket. The shooting basket, strapped around your waist with the open basket mouth in front of you, allows you to strip in line in a hurry—and it seems that it can't come in fast enough to satisfy a steelheader. He wants to pick up and get his fly out there again in a hurry. When ready to strip line, you tuck your rod under your arm, clamping it tightly to your side with your elbow, and then, with both hands free you can strip in the line, hand over hand, into the basket, so it drops in coils, one upon the other. When you make your next cast the shooting line will lift out nicely, coil after coil and shoot on out.

Most steelheaders who are fishing big rivers use a 9- or 9½-foot rod weighing about 6 ounces. These are usually slow-action sticks and can handle the Wet Head, WF-10-F/S line just described, or do equally well with the WF-10-S, the all-sinking high-density line used in slower, deeper rivers where you want the entire line to sink.

Steelhead will occasionally take a dry fly in a low, clear river —for instance, in the early fall when the summer fish are in,

Selection of steelhead flies. Top: black demon. Second row, l. to r.: Babine special, Al's special. Bottom row, l. to r.: Palmer special, Skykomish sunrise. Steelhead flies mimic salmon eggs.

but for the most part fishing for this species is done almost entirely with wet flies.

There are a multitude of good-producing steelhead flies that have been evolved over the years by the top tyers and anglers of the West, flies to fit the food of the steelhead and to fit the various rivers. Over the wide range of the fish, from California to Alaska, probably more steelhead are caught on flies tied to match salmon eggs, upon which the species feeds. They feature pink, orange or red bodies, and white, pink or red hackles. Some tyers make the bodies of bright gantron yarn, others of dark grey, and still others of yellow and various color combinations. Size varies from No. 12 all the way to the big 1/0. Some tyers even go to 2/0 and 3/0 because the heavier hook gets the fly down. Weighted flies are also widely used.

One of my own favorites is the Babine Special, tied by Bill McGuire. While he first tied it on No. 4 and No. 6 hooks, those of us who use it regularly on the Babine now like it on a 1/0; and that makes sense because the steelhead in the Babine average 15 pounds and you want a good stout hook to hold them.

WET FLIES FOR STEELHEAD, *hook sizes 2, 4, 6, 8, 1/0*

THOR	ORLEANS BARBER
VAN LUVEN	BLACK OPTIC
BROWN'S EAK	RED OPTIC
QUEEN BESS	COCK ROBIN OPTIC
NORWEGIAN MOUSTACHE	UMPQUA
KALAMA SPECIAL	DUSTY MILLER
GOLDEN DEMON	ALASKA MARY ANN
CUMMING'S SPECIAL	CARSON
AL'S SPECIAL	MCGINTY
BOBBIE DUNN	POLAR SHRIMP
SKYKOMISH SUNRISE	DRAIN 20
BABINE SPECIAL	PALMER'S SPECIAL

Many different kinds of dry flies are used for steelhead, usually well-known patterns that were designed for Atlantic salmon and big trout. These are a few of the consistent producers:

DRY FLIES FOR STEELHEAD, *hook sizes 6 to 12*	
BROWN BIVISIBLE	GRAY WULFF
GRAY BIVISIBLE	BLACK WULFF
PINK LADY	GRIZZLY WULFF
ADAMS	

SEA-RUN CUTTHROAT

Another Pacific coast trout that goes to sea is the cutthroat, the "native" of the West. The cutthroat stays only a short time in the salt and sometimes remains in the fresh water as much as three years before making another sojourn, but there are enough of them that make the trip each year to provide plenty of sporty fly fishing in coastal rivers in Oregon, Washington, British Columbia, and on up into Alaska.

Ejnar Madsen, proprietor of Norlakes Lodge, on the Babine River, British Columbia, nets an 18-pound steelhead for Bill McGuire of Seattle, Washington.

They usually go to sea in the spring months, from March on into May, returning in late August and moving up the rivers in September and October. Even after that relatively short stay in the seawater, they come back dressed in brighter colors and filled with a lot of extra vinegar. The cutthroat that has been to sea is commonly called blueback, or harvest trout, and although the average weight is only about a pound and a half, the fight is so much better than that put up by the resident fish that they hardly seem to be the same species. They hit a fly hard and jump as often as four times before finally coming to net.

Bluebacks are just as avid fly hitters as the regular cutthroat. They sock all the standard ties in the wet flies, plus the steelhead flies, and small red and white bucktails tied on No. 6 hooks. Another sure-fire bet with them is the Harger sea shrimp, tied by Don Harger of Salem, Oregon, a long-time blueblack enthusiast.

The first time I got into a sea-run cutthroat was twenty years ago when I was fishing the Nestucca with Don. That fish was a rodful of dynamite. He tore the surface apart, made short, fast runs, dogged plunges, and did a lot of good hard pulling. He was a 2-pound sea-run cutthroat that made me a fan right then.

Leigh Perkins, President of the Orvis Company, encountered spectacular fishing for this species in Alaska. They hit well all day, tore flies apart. They averaged about 2 pounds.

The sea-going cutthroat is not as plentiful as some of the other migratory species but if you know where they are, you'll get there fast.

The rod best suited to throwing these flies at the blueback is an 8-footer with an DT-5-F line and a leader tapered down to 4-pound-test tippet.

SEA-RUN BROOK TROUT

On the opposite side of the continent another native trout, the brook trout of Newfoundland, also goes to sea and returns to provide anglers with some sensational fishing. These seagoing fish are the true Eastern brook trout, *Salvelinus fontinalis,* the native trout of the Eastern states, also called speckled trout, squaretail and brook trout. In Newfoundland they are commonly referred to by the lowly name of "mud trout" because of their habit of lying over mud in ponds and in the backwaters of rivers.

Many Newfoundland brookies remain in their native streams, but just as many more for some unknown reason head for the salt in March and April, stay for periods of one to three months, then return to the rivers in July and August to spawn. Usually they stay over in the river, then, until the next spring. Strangely enough, those fish that stay at home, stay regardless of size, and the same applies to those that go to sea—fish as small as 7 inches make the ocean trip, come back into the rivers and spawn.

The fish work into the rivers in runs, the smaller males first, then the big hens. So thick are these runs that sometimes the bottom of the river appears to be black with them. Like all sea run trout, when they first come in they are bright silver and will hit a fly with a wallop, and being the strong fish they are, they make a rodful for quite a while. Catches of 12-pounders used to be common in the Fox Island and Serpentine Rivers.

Sea-run brookies like salmon flies to the point that many a salmon fisherman has cussed them out when he was working over a good salmon and smaller sea trout kept hitting his fly. I remember my own first encounter with them, very vividly.

Jim Young of Flat Bay, Newfoundland, was guiding me on the Serpentine River. That morning I was working on a nice salmon that had come to my mar lodge and refused. As I rested him and changed to a black dose, Jim pointed to a dark patch down towards the middle of the pool.

"A school of seatrout have moved in since yesterday," he said.

I barely glanced in their direction. I was after salmon.

I had a hit on my first cast, the short one with which I usually start each series of casts to cover a salmon pool. I waited for the fish to take off or jump but this one stayed deep, shot across the pool, came back to the middle of it, made a hole in the ranks of the sea trout Jim had showed me, and then hung down there, sulking. I batted on the butt of the rod grip and yanked back to try to dislodge that salmon from his perch and he came up to the top and started thrashing around.

"Seatrout!" shouted Jim.

Ten minutes later I got him in. He was a 5-pounder, strong and then some.

I made the next cast and was into another brookie. After landing this 5-pounder, I looked at my black dose. It was just about torn apart. I wanted to catch some more of those sea-run brookies but I didn't want to give up a good salmon fly for each two I took.

"Will they hit streamers?" I asked.

"You bet," said Jim.

I tied a No. 6, red and white streamer, on the end of the 6-pound-test tippet. They tore that one up too.

Each time I would hang a fish, the black patch would dissolve, then when I landed the fighting fish, they would reform their ranks.

"I'm going to try a dry fly," I said to Jim.

"They'll hit that, too," he answered.

I was casting straight across stream and I sent a royal Wulff over the patch. Two fish came up for that floater and one got there first. Again I had a good, stirring fight, this time a bit longer because he was big enough that on that size 10 dry-fly hook I had to play him easy.

These fish were ready. In this short time I had taken them on Atlantic salmon flies, streamers, and dry flies. What more could you want?

While usually, as on that day, they'll hit almost anything you offer, the best wet flies for Newfoundland are the silver doctor, Parmarchene belle, cowdung, black Zulu, gray hackle, brown hackle, professor, quill Gordon, and the Traverse Brook seatrout fly. All should be carried in hook sizes from 4 to 12.

There are not too many ways to fish a wet fly, but to counteract that there are many different sizes and kinds of wet flies, and as it sometimes seems to be size and color, rather than action, that makes these fish hit, the wet-fly angler can still get plenty of variety into his offerings to the trout.

The red and white, black and white, all black and all white bucktails are tops, and the famous muddler minnow is away up front as usual, as a strike bringer. The black, white and yellow marabous are excellent producers and the gray ghost and royal coachman streamers all produce plenty of hits. Streamers and bucktails deliver best when they are cast straight across stream and then brought back in foot-long jerks with a pause between jerks, so that the fly floats downstream 8 to 12 inches with each pause. Sometimes the retrieve is begun almost the moment the fly hits the water, and at other times it can be allowed to float a few feet before starting it back. Similarly, variety should be added to the retrieve if the fish are not coming the way they should. Sometimes I use a slow retrieve on the first half of the bring back, then if I do not get a hit I speed it up on the theory that if a trout is following, but not hitting, he will think the fly is going to escape, and will sock it at once. And if they are still slow in hitting, I make the fly literally jump across the surface, and often that will wake them up.

Dry-fly fishing for sea-run brook trout is just like dry-fly fishing for any trout. The cast is made up and across, or straight up, and care should be taken to avoid drag and to avoid slapping the line down hard on the pool. The best dries for Newfoundland are the royal Wulff, gray Wulff, grizzly Wulff, the old reliable gray hackle, the brown hackle, the brown bivisible and the black bivisible, all tied on hook sizes 8 to 12.

The ideal rod for sea-run brook trout is an 8-foot rod that weighs 4 to 4¼ ounces. The matching line should be a DT-5-F and the leader should be tapered from a heavy butt section to a 4- or 5-pound-test tippet.

Any reel that is large enough to hold 100 feet of backing is big enough for brook trout as they do not wage a long-running fight. But since many times the angler is fishing for them in rivers where he just might hang a salmon, it is just as well to use an Atlantic salmon reel with enough capacity for the fly line and 100 yards of 14-pound-test nylon squidding line for backing. Then he is ready if he should latch onto something big.

Besides Newfoundland rivers, there are a number of eastern coastal rivers in the United States and Canada where a certain number of native brook trout go to sea and return full of fight, and while they do not move in the same big and consistent runs as those in Newfoundland, they do provide some wonderful sport for those anglers who know about them. Hal Lyman, publisher of the *Salt Water Sportsman,* has taken them on Cape Cod for years, and while the largest I have ever taken in those waters was about a pound and a half, Hal has caught them as large as 4 pounds in streams only 20 feet across.

Sea-run brook trout can be taken in the salt, too, when they hang about the entrances of the rivers into which they plan to run. Sometimes they remain around the inlets for as long as two weeks before entering, and then a cast made right across the river mouth where it enters the salt, or a fly drifted along either edge of the current, is an almost sure strike getter. Occasionally, too, they can be spotted in the open salt by water commotion, such as a wave put up by moving fish; or blind casting in shallow bays and estuaries will get them.

Because the fish feed a great deal on a small fish called capelin almost any streamer tied to represent these 6-inch-long smeltlike bait fish will usually do a job.

For big water such as is often found around the mouths of rivers or in the estuaries themselves, it is advisable to step the tackle up to an 8½-foot rod with a WF-7-F line. This will throw the bigger flies with less effort than the smaller outfit, especially if there is some wind blowing. The same 12-foot leader, tapered down to a 6-pound-test tippet will handle the strikes even from the saltiest of the trout.

SEA-RUN BROWN TROUT

Sea-run brown trout cover a far wider range than any other member of the family that noses into the salt. They are the seatrout of Europe, extending from above the Arctic Circle in Norway, all the way down to Spain. They are found in Iceland, and over here on the North American continent they are taken in Newfoundland and down as far as Connecticut. And due to foresighted stocking of the species in Tierra del Fuego in 1935, there are now great numbers of brownies down there, many of which definitely go to sea and return to run up the Fuegian rivers to spawn.

Wherever they are found, they are great fighters, and in most places they also reach great weights. Swedish anglers come up with some in the 20- to 22-pound class, they weigh slightly less in Iceland, and in Newfoundland 18-pounders have been taken. In the New England States the brown trout that go to sea do not seem to reach very large sizes, mostly 1½ to 2 pounds being the average, and there are not too many of them. Only occasionally a 4-pounder is reported. In Argentina, originally not even a natural territory for them, they go up to the 20-pound mark. And in New Zealand at South Island, 15-pounders are taken on flies, usually at night.

In Norway seatrout are such favorites that they vie with salmon in popularity and fancy prices are paid for a "beat" on water into which the seatrout will run. Norwegians use dry flies almost exclusively for seatrout, mostly the same patterns that take Atlantic salmon, big flies that are good floaters, like the Wulff patterns and a Norwegian tie that is a big black hackled tie with hair wings, also black, on a No. 6 hook.

In Norway the seatrout usually come into the rivers about July 1 and continue coming until August 15—and this is the die-hard trout fisherman's heaven because at that time of year it never gets darker than dusk and the fishing often goes on until 2:00 or 3:00 A.M.

The first place I ever fished for seatrout in Norway was the Aaroy River, just above the point where it pours into the fjord. It's big water and you wouldn't expect those sea run fish to be very difficult. But my host, Andre de Ganay, who was leasing the river, soon put me straight on that point.

"You won't get a hit until you go down to a 4X tippet," he said. "These fish are just as alert and scary as brown trout in fresh water."

Just for the sake of experiment, I tried a 3X—and Andre had a couple of fish on while I got never a strike. I soon changed to a 4X and got into the action.

Later I fished the Jan Fasmer beat on the Laerdal River, which plays host to a sensational influx of seatrout.

"They come in on August 1st," I was told. "We only fish them in the mornings and at night. During the bright part of the day they just won't hit."

The morning of August 1st I stood at the tail of a pool. Trout were rising everywhere I looked. I dropped my black Norwegian seatrout fly out there and watched it float down over the spot where a trout had showed. There he was. I raised the rod tip and the hook went home and then he came out, about a 3-pounder that lit and ran and jumped and shook his head and raced up and down that pool like a seal was after him. After ten minutes he slowed and I began to bring him in. He came peacefully enough until he was 15 feet away, then he turned and with hard lunges of his tail shot out of the shallows like he had seen a mink. He went all the way to the middle of the pool before he stopped and then I pulled his head around and this time brought him in and skidded him up on shore. He was as streamlined as any fish I'd seen, bright silver, and he had several sea lice near his pectoral fin, a sure sign that he was just in from the salty water of the fjord.

That morning and the next three mornings and evenings were among my most wonderful days astream.

The Aurland is another great seatrout river. While my friend Bebe Anchorena and I took a few when we fished there during the daylight hours for Atlantic salmon, the action only really started at dusk. By 8 o'clock you could see an angler across the river from you, but while you could see his casting arm move, you couldn't see the rod. Then there would be a splash as a seatrout hit the air, and from the actions of the angler on the bank you could follow the fight to its conclusion. It's eerie fishing in the half dark, but great!

There is terrific fishing for seatrout in some rivers of the British Isles, where they are often found in great numbers, although on the whole they are somewhat smaller than those in Norway. In Britain, as in Norway, many anglers go for seatrout at night, but if you hit a dark, overcast day, with low clouds racing across the hills, that's a good time to get out.

Seatrout are suspicious of a falling leaf, a heavy step on the bank, or a waving fly rod. I remember once on the Teifi River in Wales, when I moved very cautiously in to the tail of a pool, stood there a few minutes without moving, then raised my arm to cast. Thirty feet up the pool, in water only about 12 inches deep, I saw the swirl of water as several seatrout got out of there. I went back ashore and walked carefully and slowly up the pool. Halfway up I looked down and saw about a dozen trout, plainly, in water about 4 feet deep. Just to see what would happen I pushed my arm and rod out over them. There was a flurry and suddenly they were gone. My only hope now was up at the top where fast water riffled in. I stopped 60 feet short, got quietly into the water and moved cautiously out 10 feet. I stopped and waited a good five minutes, then made my cast. My fly dropped on the edge of the fast current and bobbed down, floating high and fancy. There he was. He took that size 14 blue dun and dashed down the pool, really moving, turned in the tail water, came back and jumped out in front of me. He lit running and suddenly he was in the fast water and he kept going upstream, wrapped my leader around an upjutting branch and broke me off.

Once in Scotland on the Oykel River I had a night of seatrout fishing that I'll never forget. Fish were breaking all over the pool. It was so dark that I could barely make out the spots where they showed. There was little wind, so I tied on a size 12 light Cahill and cast it out. I couldn't see it in the dark, and that gives you a funny feeling. You are tense, conscious of every movement around you, of the noises of the night, all magnified a thousand times, it seems. Then there was a hard strike, a throw of water out where that fly was, and I struck and had him. He jumped a dozen times and fought hard, but I finally got him in, a nice pound and a half fish.

I fished that pool for another hour. Sometimes a fish would break out there and I'd strike, only to find that the fish that rose was yards away from my fly. Every time you strike like that you down all the nearby fish, so you just have to wait until they begin to rise again.

Generally at night fishermen use a somewhat bigger fly, say about a No. 10, and up the leader tippet a bit. In the dark you can do this and still get hits.

In the British Isles there are many spate rivers, streams which drop quickly in the spring and early summer and only have enough water in them after a heavy rain to allow the seatrout to ascend. The trout run up the rivers and stop in pools here and there, before finally ending their journey in

After a long battle, a hefty sea-run brown trout is brought in by Bebe Anchorena on fly tackle in the Rio Grande, Tierra del Fuego.

the loch above. In the lochs they provide great sport. Loch Inagh, near Ashworth Castle in County Mayo, is famous for its seatrout. My wife, Mary, and I had some excellent fishing there for trout that averaged about a pound and a half. We started off with Atlantic salmon flies. I took one on a No. 8 silver doctor, and Mary landed one on a No. 6 thunder and lightning, but things were slow. Then I tied on a No. 10 muddler. Fish after fish piled into it and we wound up the morning with some fine fishing.

Seatrout will take practically any of the popular Atlantic salmon flies and will hit many small bucktails and streamers. Yet, fishlike, they will cross you up sometimes. The big blonde flies and the Phillips multiwing streamers with which I have caught many big sea-run brown trout in Tierra del Fuego, didn't do a thing for me in the British Isles, and not much more in Norway.

One river in the British Isles where I have come up with some good seatrout as I fished for Atlantic salmon, is the Derwent, in Cumberland. In this river some seatrout have been taken up to 20 pounds, and fairly frequently they run to 10 or 11.

On the whole, you catch most of your European seatrout while you are fishing for salmon, and so are using a heavier leader tippet than you would for resident brown trout—and it is just as well, when you get into a big seatrout, because I believe that they will outfight a salmon of comparable size.

You certainly need the bigger tippets when you go for seatrout at the other end of the world: in the Rio Grande River, on the Argentine side of Tierra del Fuego.

Sea-run brown trout begin to ascend the Rio Grande River in mid-January and keep coming up until the middle of February, with stragglers showing even later than that. They also come into the Rio Gallegos, further north where it empties from the mainland into the Magellan Straits near the town of Gallegos, and in that wonderful river they show the same preference for streamers and bucktails.

Jorge Donovan, Bebe Anchorena and I hit the Rio Grande on Charlie Menendez Behety's ranch when the run was really pouring into the river. On my third cast something hit the fast-moving red and yellow streamer and threw a shock into me. But I recovered in time, and when the first flurry of excitement was over, I knew I was into a big and powerful fish. He gave a couple of those head swings from side to side, a thing I always like because only heavy fish do that. Then he went downstream like a runaway pacer, really turning it on. He went 400 feet, a long run for any fish. At last he stopped and hung down there in the current still pulling line off the reel, slowly but surely. I had to get out of the river and run down the bank trying to get line back, and as I ran, that obliging cuss started to run up. So we met halfway and I got a tight line on him. But he cut downstream again, this time for 300 feet, and once again I went after him, but this time he felt mean and made me come all the way. I went below him and pulled back on the rod and pulled him backwards a bit, and that made him mad and off he went upstream in a hurry.

But that hard pull licked him. He slowed and I soon was pulling him backwards again, then completely over, and then I reeled him in towards shore, got the butt of the leader to the rod tip, and then I walked back from the edge of the water and skidded him up on a small sand spit. He looked bigger than a small balloon, so I reached down and got a grip in his gills and carried him ashore. He weighed 12 pounds.

He was a beautiful fish, silver all over, with his dots showing up near his shoulders. I wasn't too sure at first but what he was a rainbow, or an Atlantic salmon, or a landlocked salmon, but he was thicker through the peduncle, and as he faded the brownie marks stood out distinctly.

We took many sea-run brown trout weighing from 10 to 16 pounds in both the Rio Gallegos and the Rio Grande, a few on size 4 and size 6 Atlantic salmon flies, but the big streamers and bucktails did far better, especially the platinum blonde and the honey blonde, the red hackle, white wing streamer, gray hackle with yellow wings, and red hackle with yellow wings, all on number 1 and 1/0 hooks.

We used both 8½- and 9-foot rods, but mostly leaned to the 9-footers because of the wind. With the 8½-foot rods we used a WF-7-F line; and with the 9-footers, a WF-8-F line, to bring out the action of the matching stick. It blows a lot down there and we needed those big sticks to get out the large streamers we were using. Even the slightest breeze is an obstacle with those big flies.

The author with his 10-pound sea-run brown trout taken from the Rio Grande, Tierra del Fuego, on a red and yellow streamer.

CHAPTER / 14

FLY FISHING FOR PANFISH

PANFISH COMPRISE A WIDE VARIETY OF SMALL FISH THAT are no longer than the width of a frying pan. Mostly they are members of the sunfish family, but there are some which are not, and for this book I am including the black and silver crappie, a bit larger, but still eligible for the group.

You find these fish in canals, ponds, lakes, rivers, streams, and in fact anywhere there is water enough for them to swim. They bear some of the most euphonious names in fishdom—stumpknocker, shellcracker, pumpkinseed, longear sunfish, as well as the more commonly called black crappie, silver crappie, yellowbreast, yellow perch or ring perch, sunnies, rock bass, warmouth and green sunfish, and bluegills—all classed together most places as bream, pronounced "brim" in the South, and named panfish in other localities.

One or more of the group will be found in every state of the Union but they reach their peak in the Southern states where living conditions are right up their alley. And standing right on the edge of the alley are thousands of eager fishermen throwing everything in the book at them.

Fly casting for panfish does not usually call for any particularly careful presentation, but because the fly must be dropped in holes in the grass beds, pockets along banks, and under tree limbs, it does call for accuracy, and a good handling of the retrieve. In open water a light 7½-foot or 8-foot fly rod would be ideal, with an DT-4-F or DT-5-F fly line, and a 6-foot leader tapered down to a 4-pound-test tippet. But in the majority of situations where panfish are found, there are so many obstructions that a longer stick does a better job. The 8½- or even 9-footer gives the added length needed to drop the fly just right among the grasses and helps lift it from holes and over stumps and outjutting limbs and such hazards where a shorter rod might very well hang the caster up. With the 8½-foot rod, a DT-7-F or WF-7-F line is in order, while the 9-footer needs a WF-8-F. The 4-pound-test tippet is strong enough to take the shock of the strike with this type of outfit.

For this fishing I like the slow-action rod because it can handle the wind-resistant bugs better than a fast stick; and also because with the slow-action rod you can use a slightly lighter line, a WF-7-F, for instance, on a slow 9-foot rod, as compared to a WF-8-F on a fast one. The lighter line makes for lighter presentation, which even with a panfish will get you more strikes.

Panfish feed on everything from night crawlers to crawfish to grubs to corn kernels, and the fly fisherman can be pretty safe in offering them almost anything in his box. But the country-wide favorite with angler and bream alike is the small popping bug, preferably with rubber legs. That's the one that stings them. That's the one that really takes panfish.

The countrywide favorite panfish lure is the small popping bug, preferably with rubber legs.

The fishermen probably like it because it rides the surface and doesn't hang up; and for whatever reason the fish likes it, he socks it hard.

Besides the small poppers, panfish will also hit the little fly-rod lures, the small spoons and wobblers that can be purchased in any tackle store. A small fly such as the size 12 white miller or a black gnat or yellow Sally, with a very small bladed spinner (size 1 or size 0) is a good combination. And the very small fly-rod spoons, about half an inch in length with hook size 8 or 10, and in gold, silver, black or green, are good bream takers.

Bigger members of the panfish family, such as the ring perch or crappies, will hit relatively large drone-type spoons, those designated as 0 and 00. But any of the heavier or underwater lures are only satisfactory when fished in open, unobstructed waters. And most ponds and places in lakes where bream "use" are full of grass and logs and tree branches, so that underwater lures are fouled up most of the time.

In cold water, however, when the bream are not hitting well, a fly and spinner or spoon-type lure, retrieved in slow, even strips—the slower the better—will often bring them out after it.

And even though bream are happy-go-lucky hitters, a knowledge of fish lies will help fill the creel with them, just as with other fish. For instance, the crappie is usually a deep-lying fish. So the fly should be allowed to sink anywhere from 2 to 4 feet, before starting the retrieve. Otherwise, unless he is rising to feed on something on the surface, he will not see it.

Virginia is one of the best states for bream fishermen. Besides the many old mill ponds which are found throughout the state, there is an ever-increasing number of man-made ponds being developed, and these are crawling with sporty little panfish as well as some of the biggest largemouth black bass to be found anywhere.

While there is no closed season on bass and panfish in impounded water, newly built lakes and ponds are stocked with adult fish in the autumn and the water is not opened for fishing until the following June. This gives the fish a chance to spawn before being exposed to fishing. Largemouth black bass

Fish rise on Virginia Pond as fly casters use small popping bugs for bream. *Photo by Leon Kesterloo.*

and bluegills are stocked first, then in the second year silver and black crappies are added.

Florida is also fortunate in the number of panfish available to fly fishermen. In some of the canals in the southern part of the state, it seems as if there must be millions of bream, all working, all striking on top as they feed. A popper dropped along the reeds near the shore—as near as it is possible to drop it—is almost sure to disappear with a "sput" as a bream, usually a bluegill, has it.

In Florida the silver crappie are called "specs," and when the run of specs is on, everyone for miles around turns out and the fishing is something hard to believe. Such a run occurs in the Kissimmee River near Lake Okeechobee and here the

A good mess of crappies, a favorite panfish. *Photo by Leon Kesterloo.*

fly-rod man usually mops up as he can place a fly into holes in the reeds and grass where other lures soon get fouled up.

Years ago, in Minnesota, I used to take yellow perch on flies, in Big Deer Lake in Itasca County. They were nice, firm fish, delicious eating, and good scrappers. And later I took the same little fish in the East, this time in brackish and even salty water, along with their cousins the white perch.

In the spring great runs of white perch enter Eastern coastal rivers and so vicious are these small fish, sometimes only 6 to 12 inches long, that they will hit a plug as long as they are. They are a set-up for a small bucktail or a fly and spinner combination. In fact when they are in the rivers they will hit just about anything. And many times in the bays or sounds they will even hit a popping bug.

The same goes for the yellow perch. They, too, will hit flies or poppers. Of the two, you will find more yellow perch in sweet water, while in the salt or brackish water there seem to be about even numbers of these fine little fish.

Yes, they're a far cry from the great gamefish, but it is good to go for those little panfish sometimes, in a contemplative mood. And before long you begin to have a different view of the small gamesters. Because they are game, they fight hard for their size, and none of them give up easily. They fight to the finish. Let yourself go—for panfish. You'll like it lots.

CHAPTER/15

STREAM MANNERS AND SAFETY

THE FLY FISHERMAN SHOULD, AND USUALLY DOES, LEAD the field in his regard for stream manners. It doesn't take many trips to a trout stream to discover that "Do as you would be done by" is practical as well as polite.

In trout fishing there are certain time-honored rules of behavior, and as they are readily applicable to stream fishing, it doesn't take long for the novice to learn them, either from friendly advice or just plain first-hand experience and observation. It stands to reason that a man fishing a dry fly upstream is not going to appreciate seeing another angler step into the same pool above him . . . in other words, cut him off from the pattern he has laid out for fishing that pool.

I remember one occasion when I had inched my way across a treacherous rapids in order to get to the ideal spot from which to cast to a riser I had spotted. I had crept up on him carefully, then stood there motionless for several minutes to let the wave subside, that I had put up with my wading. I wanted everything to be right because this was a big-looking fish.

Then, just as I was about to cast, a fisherman suddenly appeared from the woods at the head of the pool, waved an arm at me and splashed in and started to cast. The trout I had been stalking so carefully pushed up a wave a mile high as he headed for shelter. No one caught any fish out of that pool. Yet if that brash though friendly fisherman had only stopped to think, both of us might have taken trout. I could have had my try for that big one, and gone on to the next pool, and he could have come in behind me fifteen minutes later and probably caught fish, too.

For it is surprising how quickly trout forget. They have short memories and even when the water is fairly heavily fished, an angler who uses a careful approach can usually make contact with a properly presented fly.

If a second angler must fish that same pool, then he should certainly come in at the lower stretches, the only exception being a very large pool, say 400 feet long, where it is reasonable to go in at the head, even though another angler may be fishing the tail of the pool or the middle, or vice versa. In that long a pool there is usually room for two or three rods.

When moving up or downstream it is always best to walk well back from the banks of the stream so as not to disturb the fish for others. Another of my bitter memories is of a friend from the East who discovered me on my favorite dry-fly river, the Big Hole, in Montana, last summer. I was again working up on a nice trout that was feeding just under an overhanging bank, where the current came around a curve. Suddenly I heard a loud halloo and looked up from the pinpoint spot to which I was casting. There was my friend, waving his arms joyfully, full of good fellowship.

"I've been looking for you all up and down the river," he yelled. "Sure am glad I found you."

I couldn't reciprocate in kind! There he was, standing immediately above that fish, thumping his feet gladly, so that even if the trout had not been able to see him silhouetted against the sky, it could certainly hear him. It was the end of a good day's fishing, and also of a great friendship. Never come out on the bank above a fish!

Even when quitting a pool, the angler should move quietly, making as little disturbance as he can, so that the fish will settle as soon as possible, for the next comer.

Of course, it is easier to practice good stream manners in the western part of the country than in the East. Out there the trout streams are more numerous, and there are comparatively few fishermen. But even on crowded Eastern waters it shouldn't be necessary to behave as a crowd of anglers did on one occasion I witnessed on Beaver Creek in Maryland.

I was watching a fly caster working his way along a pool, when only 5 feet from shore he hooked a trout. While he was fighting it, fishermen seemed to appear suddenly from all directions, as if alerted by radio beam. They threw flies over that man's head, under his raised arms. Spoons whizzed past his ears. Everyone seemed to expect to catch fish, just because he had hooked one, when all the while his hooked fish had, of course, stirred up the pool so much that all the other trout were hiding under rocks on the bottom.

Finally one of the over-anxious anglers did whoop: "I've got one!"

What he had was the first fisherman's line, and in the resultant tangle the fly fisherman lost his trout, and again no one got a fish.

Not to discredit my native Maryland, the Maryland State Game and Fish Association was one of the first to post streams with a code of stream manners, and it did plenty of good. With the exception of a few cases such as just described, Maryland stream manners today are something for trout fishermen of other states to strive for. And certainly if sportsmen's groups do not look after such niceties of fishing, then it is up to the State Game and Fish Commissions to do so.

Another important phase of stream manners which all too many of us leave to "the other fellow," is the angler's treatment of the stream he is fishing, and the land around it. The fisherman should regard it as his privilege, not his right, to fish on private property. Permission should always be sought from the owner, and the property should be treated, not as so many are apt to say "as if it were your own," but rather, definitely as if it were not your own but someone else's and you were there on sufferance. Gates should be carefully closed, field crops treated with respect, and trash should be properly taken care of. John McDonald, *Fortune Magazine* editor and crack fly fisherman, has a word for some of the sights the fly fisherman comes upon on his trek up a stream—"wilderness slums," he calls them, and it's an apt description of the slovenly mess of old tin cans, beer bottles and scraps of paper so often scattered to the winds by careless people who should never be allowed out of a cage. And these are usually the very ones who will wonder why, when next time the farmer says "No" when they want to fish.

Particularly in the western part of the country, the angler should always treat cattle with respect. I know of one ranch in Colorado where anglers booed at, waved at and chased and otherwise disturbed the cattle, which had been gentled in preparation for showing at livestock fairs, until the rancher finally had to post his land. Except in very rare instances, cattle will not annoy the angler, if he does not annoy them. And to be sure, for his own safety, that he is not entering a field with one of those very rare instances, he should obtain the rancher's permission. No rancher will knowingly allow him to go into such a danger spot.

One of the best examples of good farmer-sportsman relations may be seen on 23-mile-long Spring Creek, which runs through Lewistown, Montana. There is not a single "posted" sign along its entire length. Instead there are notices erected by the ranchers, telling anglers where to park their cars, and the ranchers have cleared such parking spots wherever there is an entrance to the river. Not to be outdone by the ranchers, the Lewistown sportsmen, led by Nate Mane and Hash Nelson, have erected stiles over all the fences, in order to prevent damage, and have painted them white so the fishermen can readily see them.

That is one stream where everyone, rancher and angler alike, is happy.

Another thing which all fishermen should remember is that the other fellow may be out for his only day astream in the whole year. It doesn't hurt to give him a chance, give him the big end of the bargain, the best part of the pool, tell him what flies you've had luck with that day, where the fish are and where they are hitting. I don't think such everyday politeness has ever cost me a fish, in all my years of fishing. And a little effort on the part of each angler, in that way, will eventually pay off in big dividends in the overall picture of stream etiquette.

While lakes are much wider and roomier than rivers, the same laws of fishing etiquette apply—when a fisherman hooks a fish in a certain spot, other anglers should not immediately crowd over, hampering his fishing, and probably scaring any other fish that may be around. Give him room—and take room for yourself.

Even with a whole ocean to fish in, I have seen some horrible things happen in the salt. One time I was knee deep on a Key Largo, Florida, flat, stalking a particularly large bonefish that was tailing up a fit in his search for food. The very way he was working showed that he was hungry, and I felt that my chances were good if I could just get close enough to put the fly in front of him. For 100 feet I sneaked along, putting each foot down carefully, so as not to make a noise in the water, or grind coral rock beneath my feet. Then I was ready. He was just 50 feet away from me, his tail still waving in the sunlight, quite unaware of any danger. I got my fly in the air, started the backcast—but I never completed it. Just at that moment a skiff hit the edge of the flat, with motor going full blast. Within seconds the bonefish was pushing a big wave in front of him as he sped for the deep.

A few minutes later, when that carefree outboarder asked me if I was catching anything, I couldn't even answer. He probably thought that I was dumb. It's all right with me, I think he was dumb, in a different way. Any fisherman who has fished at all, or read about fishing, should know better than to roar into shallow water with a motor going full blast, and not expect to spook fish. And it's twice as bad to spook them for the other fellow as for himself.

This business of motors in shallow water has become so serious in the salt that there's a whole tribe of fishermen who probably don't know that to the fly fisherman (or other casting enthusiast) they are known as "barracuda people," as if they were little men from outer space, scarcely human. These are the boys who troll through water so shallow that they are always either dredging the bottom with the propeller or hooking up their trolling outfits on rocks and weeds. They catch barracuda —sure—but if they would move out beyond the edge of the flats, where the water is a little deeper, they would catch more barracuda and bigger barracuda, and would not run all the bonefish out of the shallows, and then light tackle anglers would be able to enjoy their sport, too.

Similarly, when anglers are trolling, either in fresh or salt water, and see a caster working the shoreline, they should give him a wide berth. The caster does not cover nearly so much ground as the troller, and therefore should be entitled to at least a polite amount of room around him, in which to wave his rod.

SAFETY IN FISHING

Most of the good fishing spots in the United States are also the natural habitat of poisonous snakes. Rattlers are found in various areas—the diamondback in Florida, the mountain rattler in Pennsylvania, the small rattlers of the Rocky Mountains in most of the Western states. The Florida rattler is deadly, the others often extremely dangerous, and fishermen should learn to watch their steps at all times, especially along river banks or rocky ledges. In the South, the cottonmouth moccasin and coral snake are also hazards in certain places, and all Southern snakes seem to carry more venom than Northern ones. The copperhead is another menace throughout the central part of the country.

So, while snakes usually become fewer as man moves in, still there are enough to worry about even in the more settled areas, if it is the natural habitat of any of the above species.

In Florida, when fishing canals, special attention should be given to watching for cottonmouth moccasins. The cottonmouth is a baleful looking, white-throated, yellow-eyed, chunky crawler. He travels as easily under water as above, and can strike under water, too. Although there are occasional stories about moccasins attacking a boat and being fended off with an oar, on the whole these creatures are sluggish and will not bother the angler unless he inadvertently steps on or otherwise disturbs one.

The angler who is fishing on foot should always scan the ground carefully, look under bushes before stepping up beside them, and listen for the rustle of a snake going through grass, or the warning signal of the tail-wagging rattler.

While the cottonmouth is seldom found near salt water, the same cannot be said for the rattler. Rattlesnakes have been found swimming far offshore in the ocean, and only two years ago, the great golfer and fishing enthusiast, Sammy Snead, killed one that measured 7 feet in length. It was swimming 5 miles offshore from Miami. Another was killed as it swam ashore at Islamorada. And as such stories are heard fairly frequently, it always pays to watch for them on any of the keys as well as on the mainland. The Florida rattler is the most dangerous of all American snakes.

The coral snake is probably more venomous, as far as the potency of the venom goes, but fortunately this snake has such a small jaw, and the fangs are set so far back that it would be almost impossible for one to bite an adult who was conscious, as the snake would have to chew its way into a finger or toe in order to get a hold and inject the poison.

During the dry season in mountain areas, snakes frequently move in near the water, and in both Maryland and Pennsylvania I have seen mountain rattlers and copperheads along trout streams, yet I have never heard of a fisherman being struck by one. However, perhaps like myself, they see a snake and immediately go in the opposite direction, because there might very well be another one around.

Most snakes do not want to strike, they want to get away, and will, unless the angler crowds them.

SAFETY IN WADING STREAMS AND LAKES

Wading is fun, whether in lake, ocean or trout stream, but its main attraction is that it enables you to reach fish that you never could get to otherwise. You can wade to position yourself for a better presentation of the fly. The difference of a foot or two counts a lot in getting hits.

When you wade, remember that position does not apply

only to your place in the stream, but also to the things in back of you. Don't wade in a spot where there is a low bank and a lot of sky for background. The fish will see your waving arm and rod and they will not like what they see. Try to find a stand in front of brush or a high bank so that you blend into the background and your movements are not so noticeable.

When moving from one casting position to another, in lake or stream, the wader should always go with feet slightly spread, for better balance, "pushing" the feet along, probing, instead of stepping out as he would on dry land where he can see what is in front of him. He must feel his way along so as not to step into a hole or trip over an unsuspected rock.

This is not only for safety. It is also for quiet, so you will not disturb the nearby fish. To wade fast, you must push your legs hard against the current, stirring up waves and making noise in the water as well as grinding gravel underfoot, and that's all that is needed to tell a fish to get out of there. So swing your legs slowly as you move along, and put your feet down gently. In very shallow water it often helps to raise the foot high, out of the water completely, and slip it in again toe first, so that there is no noise whatever.

Wading can be dangerous unless the angler is constantly on the alert and understands the nature of the surroundings. In big rivers it is easy to become so engrossed in a rising fish as to wade too deep, or move downstream with the current into deeper water and then find that returning against the current is difficult—and perhaps be able to discover no downstream path to the shallows. In such case, the most perilous moment is when you have to turn to go back. As you turn, you must at some time present the full width of your body to the current, and this is the moment when the heavy push of the water can force you off-balance. For this reason you should always make the turn into the current, so you can lean into it, rather than having the full force of the water hit your back. As an example: you are standing sideways to the current, the water pushing against your left leg. To make a turn so you can face in the opposite direction and head for shore, move the upstream foot toe slightly around, then bring the downstream foot along the bottom and upstream about a foot. Ease around this way until both feet are headed upstream, and keep repeating until you are facing shore. Now you can move straight ahead, or wade slightly downstream, to feel less pressure from the current, and work your way in to shore or to shallower water.

You can add a great deal to your comfort and safety in wading by studying the water a bit before you step in. The varying coloration of the water will tell you a lot about what is underneath, and about the depth of the water. Rocks will usually show brown, while the greenish or deep blue cast of deeper water will warn you not to venture out there. If there are many upjutting rocks, remember that there is usually an eddy in back of a rock and you can take advantage of such eddies to give yourself a rest from fighting a fast current. Gravel is often pushed into these eddies by the current and these bits of gravel bed make it easy wading, giving you a firm footing. Sometimes you can make your way across the entire stream with little effort simply by stepping in the eddies behind rocks, from one gravel patch to another.

When it becomes necessary to cross a stretch of fast water, if you do not carry a conventional wading staff you can always improvise one from a stout stick picked up alongside the stream. Use the staff on the upstream side, pushing it down firmly into the gravel a couple of feet ahead of you, then bringing the upstream foot to it, then the downstream foot. Keep repeating this as you work your way across. Never use the wading staff downstream from you, as the force of the current will push you down on it and make wading more difficult rather than easier. When you reach the other bank, lay the staff down there where you can find it if you should come back this way.

When using a wading staff, remember to plant your feet very firmly when you are crossing a fast riffle, where the water strikes you below the knees. Place each foot firmly down, then twist the foot from side to side until you have a good firm base, then do the same thing with the other one.

Even in shallow water you can hurt yourself quite badly if you lose your balance and fall on rocks, hitting your head or breaking a bone, or at least getting some bad bruises. I remember once standing on some wet rocks 5 feet back from the river, talking to a friend. The friend stuck out his hand in a

Angler uses a stout stick as a wading staff to help him cross heavy water.

gesture and just like that he fell, like a shot. Fortunately he didn't get hurt but he could easily have banged his head on the rocks. So watch your step when you wade and when you walk along the edge of a river or lake.

Either in the water or on the bank you can also come a cropper when you step carelessly on a fairly large rock which turns out to be loosely imbedded in the gravel, so it teeters and throws you. Test each rock before you step on it, both for teetering and for slipperiness. It may save you a dunking.

Another thing to watch when wading is the gravel that piles up along a pool, pushed there by heavy water in the spring. The gravel slopes down into the pool and you can wade out without realizing that the base is getting shakier, and then the gravel slides and in you go, feet first. It seems to dissolve right out from under you. If you feel the gravel beginning to give beneath your feet, the best thing you can do is start digging with those feet, giving short, hard pushes, as fast as you can, really scrambling for shore.

If you should wash into the pool, your reactions must depend on the size and depth of the pool, its length, and how much current there is. If you lose touch with the bottom, try to float and swim with the current towards the nearest bank. Always swim down and across, never into the current, as that would tire you quickly. The same thing applies in wading—it is much easier to wade down and across, than to fight your way into the current as you cross.

When you fish with a companion, the bigger man should always take the upstream position when crossing a river, so he breaks the current and the downstream man can take his hand and more or less walk in the eddy, only a yard downstream from him. If one man slips, the other can hold him up. With several people crossing the river in this manner you can make it through some really heavy water.

The easiest wading is in water about waist deep. In a smooth, even flow, even if it is fast, you can work your way along without much fear of losing your balance, because you are so deep in the water. If you should get into spots that are deeper yet, you can often walk on tip-toe, slanting towards the shore, bouncing along, sometimes moving a couple of feet, then touching down and giving a push, then on and into shallow water.

Balance is everything in wading. Generally when I am wading I hold my arms out on either side, for better balance, and then if I start to fall I use my rod, pushing it hard to the side needed to right myself. It is surprising how the force of the rod against the air will stop a fall. Similarly, in deeper water, or just wading across current, I sometimes place the rod into the water on the downstream side, so the entire rod, right up to the reel seat, is submerged. If I slip, a quick push of the rod down hard into the water, or forward or back, as the case may be, provides the leverage to let me regain my balance. Or if I am wading along and suddenly start to fall, I slap the rod down hard into the water and push, and again, the resistance of the rod to the water keeps me upright. Don't do this in water only a few inches

The author shows how you can use your rod below the surface to help maintain your balance while wading a big river.

deep, of course, where you might break the rod on rocks; but if you are out to a 2- or 3-foot depth it doesn't hurt the rod in any way. The use of the rod while wading has saved me many times from a fall.

There has always been a considerable amount of discussion as to the safety of hip boots as compared to chest-high waders. I believe that chest-high waders, worn with a belt, provide the safest, most comfortable gear for wading. Converse-Hodgman waders come with belt loops, and the angler should be sure to use them. Cinch your belt in tightly; if you should fall, this keeps the water from pouring into them. It would be harder to swim with hip boots as there would be nothing to prevent them from filling rapidly. Of course, with hippers you are not going to be out so deep, so the hazard is not as great. But be sure to look the water over carefully before wading out, even with hip boots.

In either case, felt soles will add considerably to your safety. Wet felt clings to rocks, even slippery ones. Wet rubber slides off wet rock and will send you flying.

SALTWATER WADING

In salt water, careful wading will also get you more fish. Wading the shallow flats for bonefish and other inshore salty swimmers calls for a stealthy approach, so, just as you do in fresh water, swing your legs as you wade, to avoid pushing out waves. Probe the bottom carefully with each foot, to find rocks which might crunch and signal your approach, or which might trip you if you are moving along hurriedly. If you spot a fish and need to chase him to get within casting range, pick up your foot from the water, then slide it back in, toe pointed, to make a minimum of water disturbance and noise.

Always wear polaroid glasses, which enable you to see the bottom as well as to pick out fish more readily; and wade with the sun at your back if possible, as that, too, makes for easier seeing. If possible you should also move with the waves or current that is pushed along in shallow water by the wind. Fish like to work into such a current, so they can nose into the water for the delicious scent of shrimp or crabs or other palate ticklers.

Above all, never wade barefoot. The hazards on the salty bottom are not serious but can be very uncomfortable. Once when we were on a houseboat trip to a remote key, we were wading a sandy beach, looking for bonefish. Our guide, who was wading barefoot, suddenly cried out and raised a blood-dripping foot from the water. He had stepped on the sharp lip of a submerged conch shell and it had sliced a long, jagged cut across the bottom of his instep. We had to give up the trip and head home to find a doctor.

Another hazard frequently met in the salt is the sea urchin, which has long, needle-sharp spikes sticking out from a round, black body, spikes which can penetrate a sole or the side of a canvas shoe. And yet another danger to watch for is sharp, jagged, upjutting coral rock. In some areas you may also encounter stingrays. Once as I walked along a sandy beach I saw a bonefish tailing 100 feet out. Without thinking I ran through the shallow water to get within casting range. Suddenly, not a foot on either side of me, two big clouds of mud came up as two stingrays got out of there. I had run right between them. I was lucky that time. If you wade in areas where there are stingrays or whiprays, you should always push your feet along the bottom. If you plunge along, as I did that time, and your foot comes down on top of a ray, his natural reaction is to lash upwards with his long tail, on which there is a barb dripping with poison. It makes a wound which is very painful and slow in healing. You might well end up in a hospital for quite some time.

Occasionally as you wade a bonefish flat or the edges of the mangroves looking for snook or baby tarpon, you run into some very treacherous muck, a bottom that is so soft that you sink down for several feet, sometimes to your waist. If you get into one of these quagmires, take your time. You will have to pull out one foot and advance it towards harder bottom, get it planted, then pull out the other, and so on. Never try to take too long a step or it will throw you off balance. Slow and easy does it, and you will make it to hard ground.

In many places where an angler walks in the water or along the banks of salty marshes looking for stripers there are some boggy areas, but the main hazard is potholes, and you should be always alert for these, to avoid a bad fall or a broken leg.

SUN AND INSECTS

With all the sunburn lotions on the market, there is no need for even the one-day-a-year angler to be burned to a crisp. Yet year after year, around fishing camps and holiday resorts, dozens of people spoil their own sport by not preparing for wind and sun. Every fisherman should apply some kind of protection before starting out, and at least twice more during the day. Then, even though he may be pink at sundown, he will not really burn or blister and can enjoy the next day's angling, too. The same thing applies to combatting the various insects such as mosquitoes, sand flies, chiggers and black flies that lie in wait for those who venture into the out of doors. There are plenty of excellent repellants now on the market, some in cream form as well as liquid or spray, which will keep most of them under control. It is also a good thing to remember that old Florida watchword: brush the mosquitoes off arm or face, and they won't bother you. But slap them and draw blood, and the whole works will descend on the unhappy angler with jabbing stingers.

There's a good deal of truth in those words.

CHAPTER/16

CLOTHING

CLOTHING FOR FISHING SHOULD BE SELECTED FROM TWO viewpoints—comfort to the angler, and invisibility to the fish. For instance, most fishermen are thoroughly convinced that on a bonefish flat an angler who is wearing a white shirt will be spotted by his wary prey far more readily than one who is wearing a darker color. And I believe that the same things applies with trout—a white or bright red shirt will be seen by an eagle-eyed brownie or a suspicious rainbow when a more subdued color might go unnoticed. A somber hue such as khaki is best for any fishing, and patterned materials also seem to blend into the surroundings to provide protective coloration to the angler.

Especially in the North and West, shirts should have long sleeves, because they can readily be rolled up for comfort, if necessary, but there are many times when because of sun, cold or insects, a short sleeve would be extremely impracticable. For the same reasons, the lightweight, brimmed type of khaki hat in common use is much the best for all kinds of fishing. They protect the ears and back of the neck from the sun, and shade the eyes, too. The billed caps are good as far as the eye shade is concerned, but they leave the ears and neck exposed,

Clothing of khaki or other subdued hue has best chance of not being seen by sharp-eyed trout and other fish. Patterned materials, which blend into surroundings, are also good.

Ideal trout fishing gear. Chest-high, felt-soled waders allow the angler to go into deep water. The belt at the waist holds waders comfortably firm and helps prevent rubbing, and also prevents water from running down inside if the angler should happen to fall in. Short vest stays clear of the water, even in deep wading. Note that the net attaches comfortably to a loop at the back of the vest, so it hangs out of the way while fishing but can easily be slung forward to net a fish.

and the angler may get a very painful burn in those two areas.

For saltwater fishing, long cotton slacks and ankle socks will guard against sunburn on the legs, and rubber-soled sneakers are a must in boats, and are equally good for wading, if the angler does not plan to use waders.

For wading freshwater rivers, if the weather is likely to be cool, then woolen underwear should be worn along with either lightweight jeans or slacks, or heavier woolen slacks if the temperature of the water is very cold, as in some Western rivers. For long trips in variable weather, it is best to carry woolen underwear and both types of top pants—light ones for the cooler days and evening fishing, and the lighter ones for the warmer times of day.

Wading gear is probably the most important part of the trout fisherman's outfit. The old-time hobnailed wading shoes are rapidly disappearing because the hobs were often knocked out and it was necessary to carry a shoemaker's kit along to keep them in repair . . . so few fishermen still use this type of shoe. Many anglers now wear stockingfoot waders, with a wool sock over the rubber foot, and then a shoe with a felt sole. These are comfortably light, but they are a lot of trouble to put on and after fishing there is the additional problem of caring for the wet socks, so gradually the real trouters are turning to the boot-type wader, again with a felt sole, and preferably chest-high waders. On certain Eastern streams the hip boot in the same style is sufficient, but generally there is at least once in the day when the angler wants to get to a better depth in order to reach a fish, and that's when the chest-high waders pay off. They are also warmer in cold weather. And, of course, they are practically a necessity in most of the big trout streams, bass rivers and salmon waters.

These waders are higher priced than the hip boots or the stockingfoot waders, but in the long run they pay for themselves as they wear well, do not tear easily on brush or fences, and if turned inside out after each time used, to allow the insides to dry thoroughly of the condensed moisture which forms inside from body heat, then they will last for years.

In all cases, the soles should be made of felt, as rubber becomes so slick in fresh water that it is dangerous.

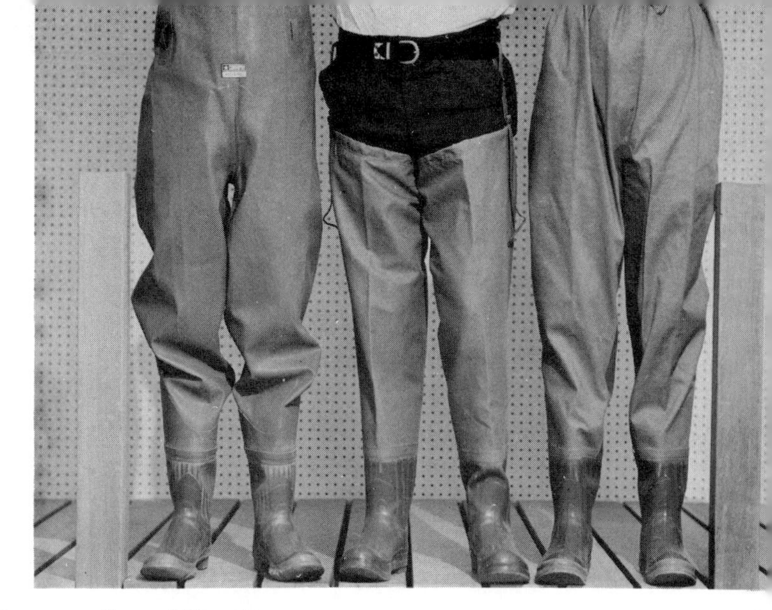

Three types of wading gear (from left): chest-high waders with rubber soles (not recommended for stream fishing); felt-soled hip boots; and waist-high, felt-soled waders—all made by the Converse-Hodgman Company. Felt soles provide the surest footing on slippery rocks. *Courtesy Abercrombie & Fitch Co.*

On the other hand, rubber is best for saltwater wading, where the fisherman is traveling over mud, sand, coral and weed beds. Here again, chest-high waders are essential in most places in order to get out deep enough to reach fish. In the warmer, tropical waters, however, many anglers "wade wet"—that is, they wear blue jeans or slacks of some kind, and rubber-soled sneakers, or if they can obtain them, the old army jungle boot, which can sometimes still be found in army surplus stores. However, ankle-height tennis shoes are a fair substitute. These shoes must be thoroughly rinsed in fresh water after wading or they become "smelly" from the decayed salt-water vegetation and muck.

Most chest-high waders are quite full in the body, and they will feel much more comfortable if a belt is worn around the outside. This helps to keep water out, if the angler should happen to fall in, and it is also very restful, acting as a prop around the middle and really takes some of the strain out of a long day of wading. It also keeps the waders firmly in position, preventing rubbing at the knees, as very loose waders are inclined to do.

Juan Jose Silvestre Blaquier, of Buenos Aires, one of Argentina's leading fly casters, doesn't believe in waders. Heavy underwear keeps him just as warm as waders do, he says. He wears woolen socks, and rope-soled shoes.

Occasionally everyone runs into some friend who has developed a special wading outfit which he considers to be far above all others, and if it is comfortable, then that's the thing to wear. In Argentina, one angler I met, Juan Blaquier, wades in heavy long drawers, with walking shorts over them, plus woolen stockings and rope soled alpargatas, and Mr. Blaquier claims that even when wet, the wool is just as warm and comfortable as waders would be. I would question the point in really cold mountain streams, but in Argentine rivers it seems to be quite comfortable.

The fishing vest is the second most important part of the trout or salmon fisherman's clothing. Vests should have plenty of pockets for storing all the accoutrements of fly fishing—a pocket for fly buoy, one for clippers, another for leader boxes, line dressing, various boxes of flies, and so on. The short vests are by far the best because they stay clear of the water at all times, while the longer jacket style will get wet.

Some of the short vests now have a creel attachment which is more compact and easier to carry than the old fashioned cane

For saltwater wading, rubber-soled Converse-Hodgman chest-high waders or hip boots provide good footing. For skiff fishing, the Deck Star, a rubber-soled canvas shoe, is excellent.

creel. These are light bags which zip on and off at the lower edge of the vest, and have the outside fashioned of mesh in order to let air in to the fish. Their only drawback is that they will not hold an extra-large fish, but to counteract that the angler can carry a large plastic bag such as is used in deep freeze lockers, and which will fold compactly into any pocket. Then if he catches a 4-pounder he can put it in the plastic bag and stuff the whole thing in the large pocket at the back of the vest. This pocket, incidentally, is large enough to hold a couple of sandwiches and even a pint thermos of coffee.

The angler who is clad in waders and fishing vest is fairly well protected against rain, but it is always a good idea to tote along one of the new, roll-up raincoats and matching hat. The hood type is not so good for fishing because the hood cuts off sounds, and these are an essential part of fishing, particularly for trout. A fish might break and would not be heard by the fisherman who wears a hood, but the hat will give the same protection and still allow him to hear the right noises.

Generally he will not be fishing in a heavy downpour, but if caught out in such a heavy rain, even the trees do not give complete protection, and then a raincoat is invaluable. The Converse-Hodgman parka jacket is easily carried in the back pocket of the vest and can be slipped on when rain comes. It also keeps you warm. When a storm catches an angler astream, he should go ashore and sit down under some low bushes—not big trees. The low bushes will provide good protection from the rain and will not attract lightning or blow over.

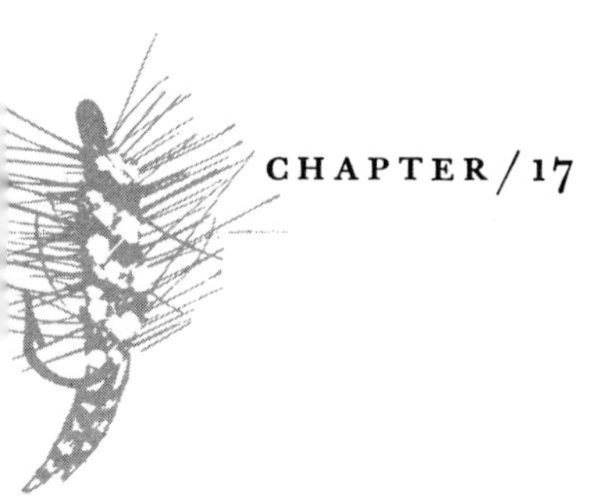

CHAPTER / 17

KNOTS

THE THREE MOST IMPORTANT KNOTS INVOLVED IN FLY fishing are the blood knot which joints the leader sections together, the clinch knot, which ties the fly to the tippet, and the nail knot, which attaches the leader to the line. Drawings showing how to tie these knots are on the following pages. It should be noted that with the blood knot, joining the leader sections together, there should be at least six turns on each side, to prevent the knot from slipping. And with the clinch knot, tying the fly to the tippet, I make at least ten turns of the leader around itself, before tightening up. This is particularly important when nylon is used, as it will slip more easily than gut. Extreme care should be used in making ties with synthetic materials.

The nail knot, described on page 377, is of great help in achieving a smooth, streamlined connection between fly line and backing, or fly line and leader. This flat-lying knot will move freely through small guides and can be tied much more quickly than older splicing methods. Once the nail knot has been mastered, it can be tied in a couple of minutes.

Other knots of importance are the Turle knot and the dropper knot for wet flies, drawings for which are also shown here.

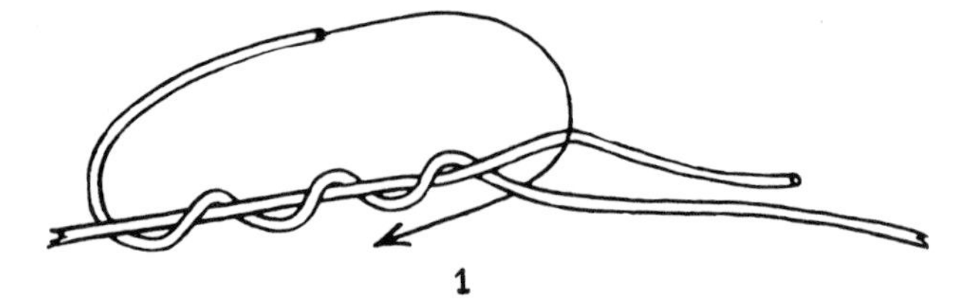

1

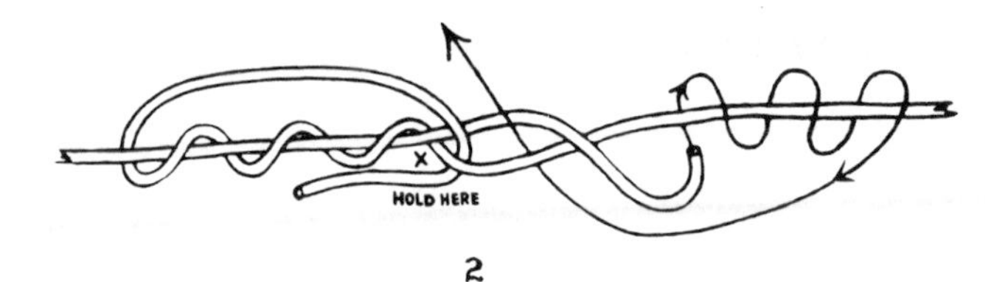

2

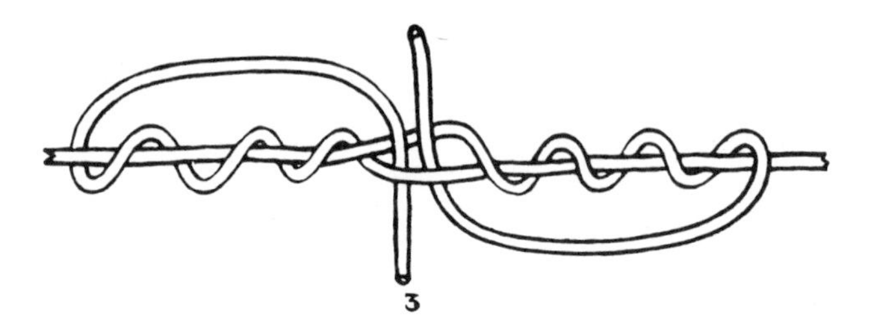

3

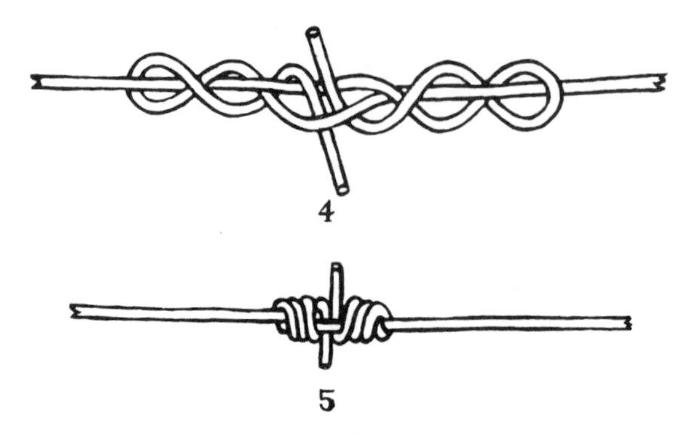

4

5

Blood Knot *to join leader sections together.*
Overlap two ends of leader sections and wrap one end six times around the other, (shown only three times in simplified drawing, Fig. 1; author recommends at least six times). Bring the end back, slip it down in front of first cross-over and hold between fingers, as indicated by X in Fig. 2. Repeat this with other end, as in Fig. 2. Bring end back and slip it up through center opening. These ends serve as locks. Slowly pull the two outer ends simultaneously so that coils form figure eights along trunk lines, as in Fig. 4. Pull tight, bringing the coils snugly against each other, as in Fig 5.

CLINCH KNOT *to tie tippet to fly.*
Pass end of the leader through eye of the hook toward the bend. Pull it back and wrap it around itself at least ten turns (only four turns are shown in simplified illustration, but author recommends ten). Bring end back to hook and slip it up through opening between hook and first cross-over, as in Fig. 1. The end serves as a lock. Pull tippet against fly until coils are tight against eye, as in Fig. 2.

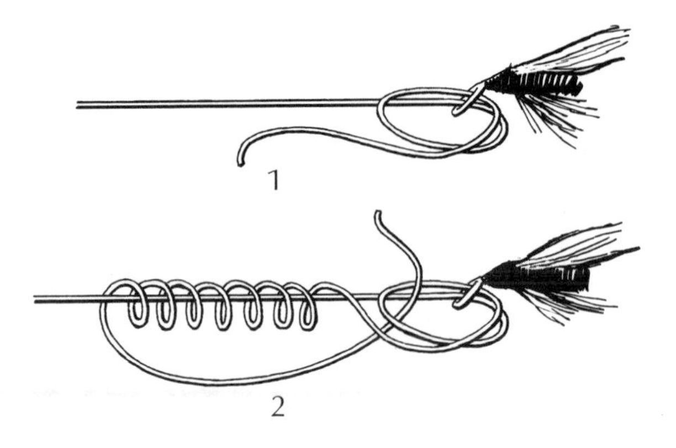

DOUBLE CLINCH KNOT

Pass the end of the leader through the eye of the hook twice, instead of only once. Allow enough line to wrap around itself at least seven times. Push the end through the loop which has been formed immediately ahead of the eye of the hook. Carefully and evenly pull tight and snip off the protruding end. This knot very seldom slips.

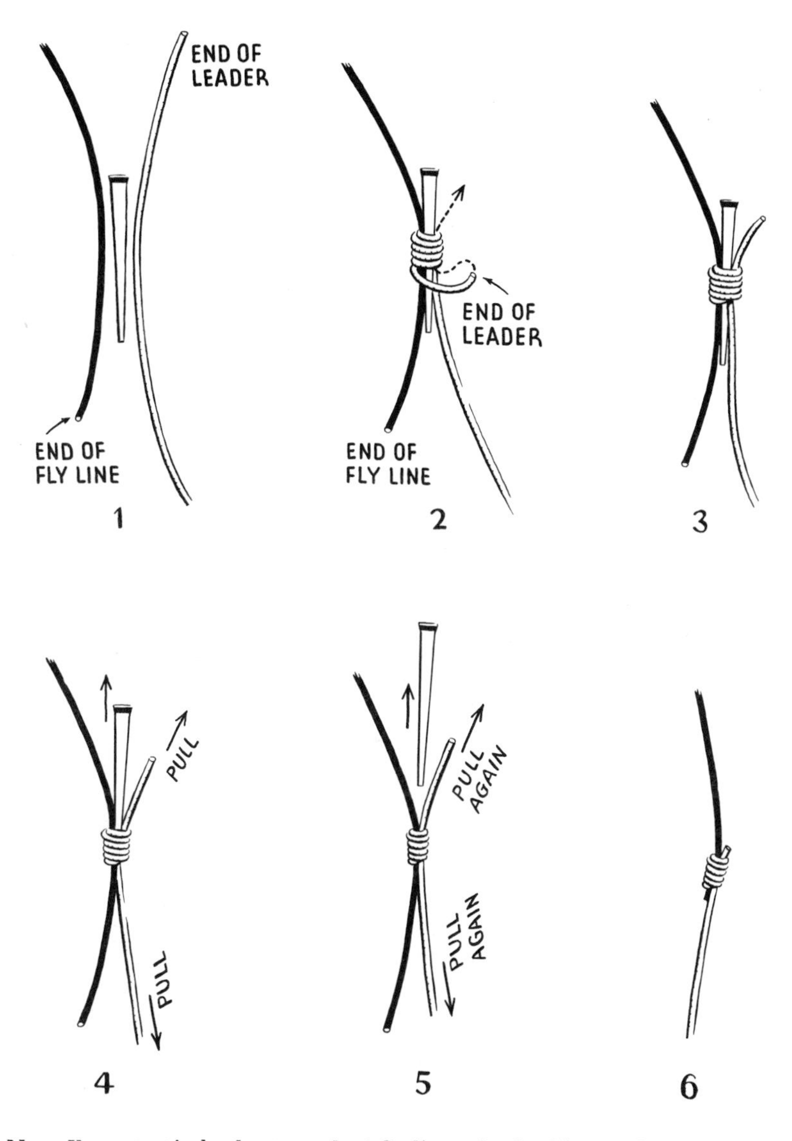

NAIL KNOT *to tie leader to end of fly line, also backing to fly line.* Hold tapered nail, line and leader with fingers in position shown in Fig. 1. Then wind leader downward around nail, line and itself six times, and run end of leader up under loops. Pull both ends of leader tight. Slip knot down nail, tightening by pulling both ends of leader as it goes. Slip nail out and retighten by again pulling leader ends. Then pull line and leader tight to secure final knot. Clip end of line and leader close to knot and soften end of line by breaking fibers with end of nail or fingernail.

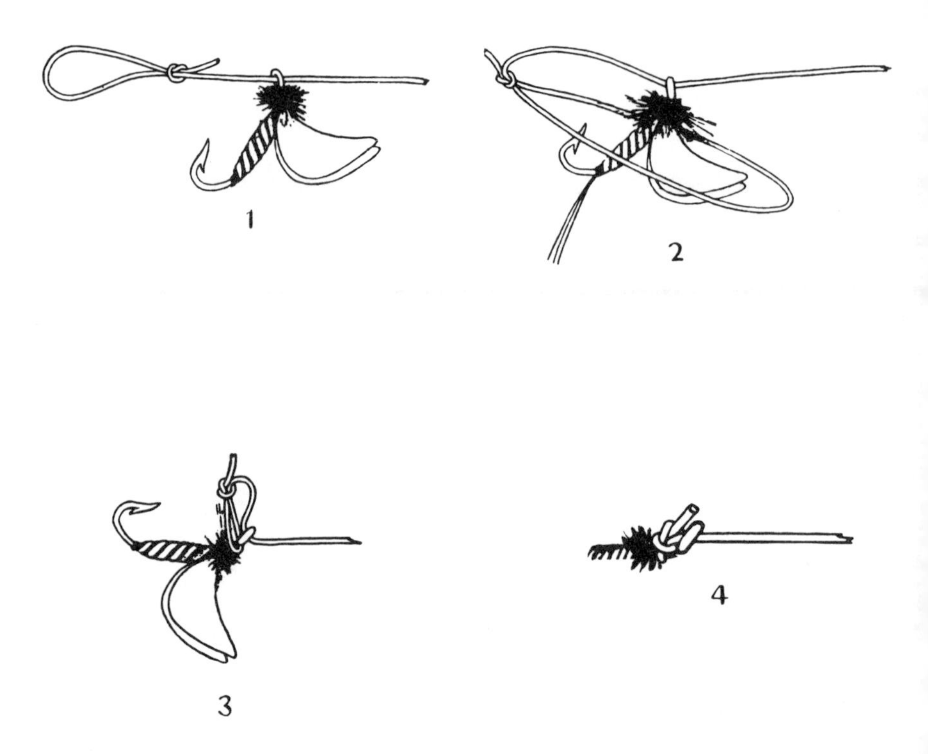

Turle Knot *to tie fly to leader.*
Run end of the leader through eye of the hook toward the bend. Make a "single running" knot in the leader end, as in Fig. 1. Slip fly through loop. Fig. 2, until loop rests on neck of fly. With the loop tight against the neck of the fly, pull on the leader until knot has slipped down and is tight against neck of fly, Figs. 3 and 4.

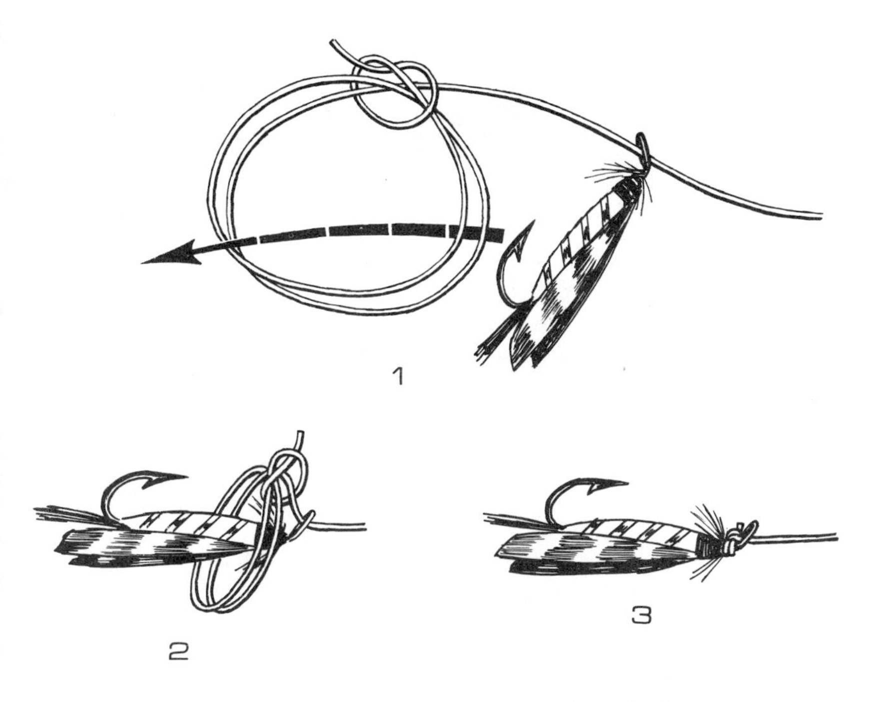

DOUBLE TURLE KNOT, *a stronger knot for tying fly to leader.*
Pass the end of the leader through the eye of the fly and let the fly drop well out of the way. Make two loops at the end of the leader, each about an inch in diameter. Tie the loops together with an overhand knot and pull it tight, Fig. 1. Now bring the fly down, pass it through the loops and bring the eye against the knot, Fig. 2. Pull on the leader gently, slowly tightening the two loops on the shank of the hook just behind the eye, Fig. 3.

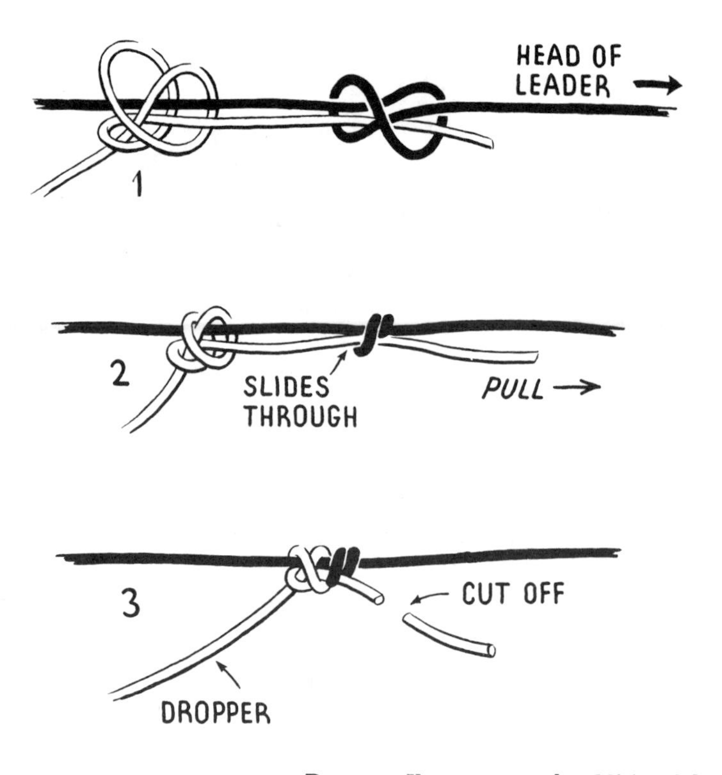

DROPPER KNOT *to attach additional leaders for wet flies.*

Loop dropper around leader twice, then place end through loops, as in Fig. 1. Then pull end to tighten knot and pull up against loops in leader as in Figs. 2 and 3.

ALBRIGHT KNOT

This knot is very good for tying leader to line, usually the line being of greater diameter; and also for attaching a shock leader to a lighter one, as for instance when fishing for large tarpon, sailfish and other species which fray through or cut a small leader tippet. Make a loop in the end of the heavier line, then bring the lighter line through the loop and make 10 or 12 winds. Now bring the end of the light line through the front loop. Hold both this line and the line which is already going into the loop in your right hand. Holding the loop and wrapped line tightly with the fingers of the left hand, pull up evenly until tight.

SOURCES OF FLIES
AND FLY-TYING MATERIALS

This list includes fly tyers—individuals and companies—who sell fly-tying materials in many widely scattered parts of the country. Certainly some who are equally worthy of mention have been overlooked because the list is necessarily limited to those companies or individuals with whom I have had some contact. However, it does contain the names of some of the greatest fly tyers in the world, and the reader may safely purchase flies or materials from these sources with the assurance that he will receive top-grade products.

CALIFORNIA

NEWT BALCH
127 East Third Street
Duarte, Calif.
Flies, retail.

MRS. WAYNE BUSEK
805 West Tulare Avenue
Visalia, Calif.
Flies, retail.

JENSEN'S SPORTING GOODS
2391 North Lake Avenue
Altadena, Calif.
Flies, fly tying materials, retail.

ED LANDRY
3822 Ocean View
Montrose, Calif.
Flies, fly tying materials, retail.

JED WELSH
835 East Hill
Long Beach, Calif.
Flies, fly tying materials, retail.

COLORADO

HANK ROBERTS
Roberts Fishing Tackle
1636 Pearl Street
Boulder, Colo.
Flies, wholesale and retail.

SURE STRIKE COMPANY
130 South Federal
Denver 19, Colo.
Flies, fly tying materials, wholesale and retail.

FLORIDA

CAPTAIN BILL SMITH
Box 1
Islamorada, Fla.

EDDIE RICHARDSON
Islamorada, Fla.

IDAHO

GLENN L. EVANS COMPANY
Caldwell, Idaho
Flies, fly tying materials, wholesale and retail.

RUEL STAYNER
Stayner Sporting Goods
Twin Falls, Idaho

SHOSHONE INC.
108 East 40th Street
Boise, Idaho

ILLINOIS

SUN FEATHER COMPANY
1244 South Kedzie Avenue
Chicago 23, Ill.
Fly tying materials, feathers, wholesale.

TACK-L-TYERS
939 M, Chicago Avenue
Evanston, Ill.
Flies, wholesale.

INDIANA

AGAR BUG COMPANY
P. O. Box 65
Butler, Ind.
Popping bugs, wholesale.

IOWA

LACEY GEE
The Wapsi Company
Independence, Iowa
Flies, wholesale and retail.

MAINE

PERCY TACKLE COMPANY
204 Federal Street
Portland, Maine
Flies, wholesale and retail.

FOSTER'S SALMON FLIES
Westfield, Maine

MINNESOTA

GAPEN FLY COMPANY
2335 Main Street
Anoka, Minn. 55303

HERTERS, INC.
Waseca, Minn.
Flies, fly tying materials, wholesale and retail.

MONTANA

PAT BARNES
Barnes Fly Shop
West Yellowstone, Mont.
Flies, fly tying materials, wholesale and retail.

DAN BAILEY
Bailey's Fly Shop
Livingston, Mont.
Flies, fly tying materials, wholesale and retail.

MERTON PARKS
Parks Fly Shop
Gardiner, Mont.
Flies, fly tying materials, wholesale and retail.

POTTS FLIES
Missoula, Mont.
Flies, wholesale and retail.

FRITZ PRITCHARD
Palace Hotel
Missoula, Mont.
Flies, custom-tied.

BUD LILLY'S FLY SHOP
West Yellowstone, Mont.

NEW YORK

ABERCROMBIE & FITCH COMPANY
Madison Avenue & 45th Street
New York 17, N. Y.
Flies, retail.

LAURENCE AUSTIN
L. Austin & Son
1627 University Avenue
Bronx 53, N. Y.
Flies, wholesale and retail.

ELVERTON CLARK
Flylyte Tackle
Lake Placid, N. Y.
Flies, retail.

HARRY AND ELSIE DARBEE
Livingston Manor, N. Y.
Flies, wholesale and retail.

JIM DEREN
Anglers' Roost
Chrysler Building
New York 17, N. Y.
Flies, retail.

WALTER AND WINNIE DETTE
Roscoe, N. Y.
Flies, wholesale and retail.

ARTHUR FLICK
Westkill Tavern Club
Westkill, N. Y.
Fly tyer, wholesale and retail.

WILLIAM MILLS & SON
21 Park Place
New York 7, N. Y.
Flies, retail.

ALEX ROGAN
9311-34th Road
Jackson Heights, N. Y.
Flies, wholesale and retail.

M. SCHWARTZ & SONS, INC.
321 East 3rd Street
New York 9, N. Y.
Fly tying materials for tackle manufacturers, feathers, chenille.

HELEN SHAW
246 East 46th Street
New York 17, N. Y.
Flies, wholesale and retail.

NORTH CAROLINA

CE-BET TACKLE COMPANY
2409 Chapel Hill Road
Durham, N. C.
Fly rod poppers, wholesale.

OREGON

EARL POULSEN
Poulsen Brothers
1222 North East Alberta Street
Portland, Oreg.
Flies, wholesale and retail.

E. H. (POLLY) ROSBOROUGH
Chilaquin, Oreg.
Flies, retail.

WESTERN TACKLE COMPANY
1711 South East Hawthorne
Portland, Oreg.
Flies, wholesale and retail.

PENNSYLVANIA

WILLIAM BENNETT
P.U.C. Capitol
Harrisburg, Pa.
Flies, custom-tied.

JIM CHESNEYS
Carlisle, Pa.
Flies, custom-tied.

STAN COOPER & SON
609 Main Street
Plymouth, Pa.
Flies, wholesale and retail.

WALTER DURGIN
York, Pa.
Flies, custom-tied.

GEORGE HARVEY
State College, Pa.
Flies, custom-tied.

E. Hille
335 Rose Street
Williamsport, Pa.
Flies, feathers, wholesale and retail.

Mrs. Charles Knier
Harrisburg, Pa.
Flies, custom-tied.

Joe Knoss
Carlisle, Pa.
Flies, custom-tied.

H. J. Null
Doylestown, Pa.
Fly tying materials, wholesale.

Clayton Peters
Lykens, Pa.
Flies, custom-tied.

The Phillips Fly & Tackle Co.
Alexandria, Pa.
Flies, wholesale.

Mac Pittinger
Carlisle, Pa.
Flies, custom-tied.

Don Shiner
525 West 5th Street
Nascopeck, Pa.
Flies, retail.

Ross Trimmer
122 Arch Street
Carlisle, Pa.
Flies, custom-tied.

Ed Koch
3 High Street
Boiling Springs, Pa.
Custom tied flies.

Tony Skilton
311 Front Street
Boiling Springs, Pa.
Custom tied flies.

RHODE ISLAND

Rube Cross
606 Public Street
Providence, R. I.
Flies, wholesale and retail.

TENNESSEE

Peckinpaugh & Company
612 Cypress Street
Chattanooga 3, Tenn.
Popping bugs, nymphs, streamers, wholesale.

VERMONT

The Orvis Company
Manchester, Vt.
Flies, retail.

VIRGINIA

William Gallasch
3137 West Cary Street
Richmond, Va.
Streamer flies, popping bugs.

WASHINGTON

Danielson Fly Manufacturing Co.
Seattle 5, Wash.
Flies, fly tying materials, wholesale.

McCoy Tackle Company
Des Moines, Wash.
Flies, wholesale.

Roy Patrick
2237 Eastlake Avenue
Seattle, Wash.
Custom-tied flies, fly tying materials, retail.

Bob Roberts
226 East Viewridge
Everett, Wash.
Flies, wholesale.

Shoff Fishing Tackle Company
Kent, Wash.
Flies, fly tying materials, wholesale and retail.

TERRY TIED FLIES
220 South Custer
Spokane, Wash.
Custom tied flies.

WISCONSIN

MARATHON BAIT COMPANY
840 Henrietta Avenue
Wausau, Wis.
Fly tying material, bugs, wholesale and retail.

THE WEBER LIFELIKE FLY COMPANY
113 Ellis Street
Stevens Point, Wis.
Flies, wholesale.

INDEX

Aaroy River, Norway, 10, 11, 299, 307, 337
ABC-TV American Sportsman series, 306, 319
Adams fly, 91, 93, 331
Adams skating spider, 93, 120, 323
Adams spentwing fly, 93, 191
Admiral Pool, Newfoundland, 314
Africa, 274
Agey, Hoite, 211
Alaska, 326, 330, 331, 332
Alaska Mary Ann fly, 330
Albemarle Sound, North Carolina, 213
Albright, Captain Jimmie, 247, 266
Albright, Frankee, 272
Albright knot, 381
Alder nymph, 126, 138
Alexandria fly, 124, 126
Alexandria, Pennsylvania, 146
Allison tuna, 234
Al's special fly, 329, 330
Alta River, Norway, 303, 305
Amberjack, 234, 254, 260
American Fishing Tackle Manufacturers Association (AFTMA), 18
Anaconda, Montana, 112
Anadromous fish (*see* Spawning fish)
Anchorena, Bebe, 20–22, 160, 162, 164, 175–178, 321–322, 338, 340, 341
Anderegg, Gene, 160
Anderson, Andy, 199–200
Ant, imitation of, 78
  black flying, 79, 81, 91, 115, 145, 153
  fishing for trout with, 145–150
  in high altitude lakes, 147, 150
  wet, 79
Antarctica, 325
Antietam River, Pennsylvania, 168
Apte, Stu, 231, 252
Arctic waters, 325, 336
Argentina, 120, 141, 159, 162, 164, 175–178, 317–318, 320–323, 325, 337, 341, 370, 371
Argentine blonde bucktail, 166, 221
Atherton, John, 118, 120
Atlantic salmon:
  casting, *diagrams,* 310–312, 313
  feeding habits of, 296, 314
  fishing for, 101, 116–117, 146–147, 296–316
    Arthur Wood's method of, 308–316
  run of, 301–302
  tackle for, 6, 10–12, 24, 299–300, 315–316
Atlantic salmon flies, 116, 120, 242, 272, 297–301, 315–316, 341, 342
  double hook, 299
  dry, 300, 301, 308, 316
  featherless, 316
  hairwing, 297–298
  for landlocked salmon, 120, 164, 318
  married feathers, 297, 298
  patterns, *listed,* 93, 301
  wet, 146, 297, 301, 308
Aurland, Norway, 338
Austin, Larry, 201

Babine River, British Columbia, 327, 331
Babine special fly, 329, 330
Back Bay, Virginia, 213
Badger bivisible fly, 92, 301
Badger hackle skating spider, 93, 120
Badger spider, 93, 120
Badger variant fly, 92, 115
Badger yellow rubber-bodied hackle fly, 127
Bahamas, 220, 274
Bailey, Dan, 34, 62, 83–84, 136–137, 146, 159, 160, 171, 174, 175
Bailey's bi-fly, 90, 92, 115, 125, 175
Bailey's May fly nymph, 136

Baja California, 250, 255, 256
Baltimore, Maryland, 39, 195, 205, 218
Bamboo, 5, 12–13, 22, 23, 24
Barothy, Captain Vic, 36, 254, 257–258, 260, 278–279
Barracuda, 38, 233, 234, 259–268
Bass:
- color preference of, 183, 184–185, 187
- fly fishing for, 179–216
- how to pick up, 208
- selective feeding of, 179, 184
- striped (*see* Striped bass)
- where to find, 180

Bass, fishing for, 179–216
- with bucktail, 183–185, 204, 212
- bulging, 194
- double haul in, 59
- with dry fly, 185–186, 191
- with fly and spinner, 84, 186–188, 204
  - patterns, *listed,* 187
- in hot weather, 190, 198–199
- matching the hatch in, 179
- with nymph, 186, 194–195
- with popping bug, 8, 39–40, 85, 180–184, 188–191, 198–199, 202, 204, 214
- with spider, 191–192
- with streamer, 8, 183–185, 193, 204–205, 212
- striped (*see* Striped bass, fishing for)

Bass, flies for:
- bucktail, 183–184, 204, 212
- dry (*see* Dry flies, for bass)
- fly and spinner (*see* Bass, fishing for, with fly and spinner)
- nymph (*see* Nymph flies, for bass)
- popping bug (*see* Bass, fishing for, with popping bug)
- streamer (*See* streamer flies, for bass)

Bass, largemouth black, 180, 181, 185, 199–216, 346
- brackish water, 39–40, 202, 212–216
  - where to find, 213, 214–215
- diet of, 179
- fishing for, 199–216
  - in grassy water, 202–203, 210, 214
  - in hot weather, 206, 214
  - with popping bug, 181, 186, 204–205, 214
  - retrieve, 206, 215, 216
  - for schools of, 206–207, 209–10
- tackle for, 8, 35, 37
- where to find, 199, 202–203, 209

Bass, smallmouth black, 180, 181, 183, 185–187, 188–199
- feeding habits of, 191
- fishing for, 188–199
  - casting for, 196–197
  - with popping bug, 188–191
  - retrieve, 187–188, 190–192, 198
  - in shallow water, 194–195, 196
  - tackle for, 8, 24, 35, 37, 197
- where to find, 195

Basses, Fresh Water and Marine, The (ed., Rhead), 217
Batchelor, Brian W., 274
Bauer, Eddie, 327
Bean, Tarleton H., 217
Beaver Creek, Maryland, 30, 169, 352
Beaverkill fly, 127
Beetle, imitation of, 78, 145
- faking, 153
- fishing for trout with, 150–153

Behety, Charlie Menendez, 341
Bentz, Frank, 188, 193
Bermuda, 9, 274, 286, 288, 289
Bermuda chub, 38
Bertha, North Carolina, 212
Bi-fly orange fly, 92
Bi-fly patterns, 90, 92, 115, 125
Bi-fly yellow fly, 92
Big Blackfoot River, Montana, 31
Big Deer Lake, Minnesota, 348
Big Falls Pool, Newfoundland, 302
Big Hole demon streamer-type fly, 173, 175
Big Hole River, Montana, 31, 59, 98, 175, 351
Big Hunting Creek, Maryland, 67
Big Lake, Maine, 318
Bill Smith flies, 224
Billfish, 229, 234, 254
Bivisible fly patterns, 90, 92, 93

Black ant, 145–150
Black bear orange rubber-bodied hair hackle fly, 127
Black bear rubber-bodied hair hackle fly, 127
Black beetle, 151, 152, 153
Black bivisible fly, 92, 93, 301, 335
Black blonde bucktail, 166, 221
Black bucktail, 158, 334
Black crapple (*see* Crappie, black)
Black creeper nymph, 135
Black and dark olive nymph, 139
Black demon fly, 329
Black doctor fly, 301
Black dose fly, 297, 301, 333, 334
Black fibber fly, 128
Black flat-bodied nymph, 138
Black flying ant, 79, 81, 91, 115, 145, 153
Black fur ant, 145
Black ghost streamer, 82, 165, 170
Black gnat fly, 80, 91, 93, 107–108, 122, 126, 132, 153, 158, 186, 187, 318, 346
Black hackle barred orange wing multiwing streamer, 165
Black jassid fly, 145
Black marabou muddler, 160, 166
Black marabou streamer, 165, 185, 335
Black May fly nymph, 138
Black midge, 135
Black mossback nymph, 139
Black nosed dace streamer, 165
Black nymph, 136, 138, 186
Black optic fly, 330
Black and orange nymph, 138
Black Point, California, 241
Black prince bucktail, 165
Black prince fly, 92, 126
Black quill fly, 91, 126
Black quill midge snow fly, 127
Black and red ant, 148, 149
Black skating spider, 93, 120
Black spider, 93
Black steamer, 158
Black and white bucktail, 165, 185, 334
Black and white multiwing streamer, 165
Black and white streamer, 165
Black wooly worm fly, 127
Black Wulff fly, 92, 93, 115, 331
Black and yellow marabou streamer, 165
Black and yellow nymph, 136, 138
Black Zulu fly, 334
Blakely, Edward, 320
Blaquier, Juan Jose Silvestre, 370, 371
Blond Wulff fly, 92
Blonde bucktail patterns, *listed,* 166
Blonde flies, 221, 226, 278, 298, 341
Blood knot, 34, 373, 374
Blue bottle fly, 127
Blue charm fly, 297, 301, 321
Blue dun fly, 91, 126, 127
Blue dun spenturing fly, 93
Blue quill fly, 91
Blue quill midge snow fly, 127
Blue variant fly, 92
Blue and white bucktail, 184, 216
Blueback trout (*see* Cutthroat trout, sea-run)
Bluefish, 38, 234
Bluegill, 344, 347
Boats, chartered, 266, 289–290
Bobbie Dunn fly, 330
Boca Chica Flats, Florida Keys, 274
Bonefish:
  description of, 261–262, 268
  mudding or tailing, 262, 263, 264, 268–269
  size of, 274
  where to find, 273–274
Bonefish, fishing for, 3, 218, 244, 261–275, 354, 362–363, 365
  casting, 269–270
  cost of, 266
  flies for, 219, 220, 221, 224, 225, 272
  glasses for, 264, 266
  greased line, 314
  retrieve, 270–272
  tackle for, 6, 10, 29, 36, 38, 232
Bonito, 38
Book of the Tarpon (Dimocks), 218
Boyd, Bill, 74
Breadcrust nymph, 135
Bream, 37, 180 (*see also* Panfish, relation to Bream)

Breather flies (*see* Streamer flies, breather)
British Columbia, 327, 331
British Honduras, 278
British Isles, 338, 339–340, 341
Brook trout, 37, 124
  coasters, 117–118, 124
  sea-run, 37, 116, 325, 332–336
Brookies (*see* Brook trout)
Brooks, Mary (Mrs. Joe), 149, 150, 303–305, 341
Brown badger bivisible fly, 92
Brown beetle, 151
Brown bivisible fly, 93, 301, 331, 335
Brown bomber nymph, 135
Brown, Chan, 240
Brown drake nymph, 136, 138
Brown hackle fly, 122, 124, 126, 187, 334, 335
Brown hackle, peacock fly, 91, 127
Brown hackle, yellow fly, 91, 127
Brown jassid fly, 145
Brown marabou muddler, 160, 166
Brown May fly nymph, 138
Brown muddler minnow bucktail, 166
Brown rubber-bodied hair hackle fly, 127
Brown spider, 93
Brown trout, 51, 62, 72, 100, 104, 118, 120, 164, 174, 175–178, 365
  sea-run, 160, 164, 325, 336–343
  tackle for, 29, 30–31, 35, 37
Brown and white bucktail, 165, 185
Brown and white streamer, 187
Brown Wulff fly, 115
Brown and yellow bucktail, 165
Brown's Eak fly, 330
Bucktail, fishing with (*see* Streamer, fishing with)
Bucktail flies, 83, 90
  for bass, 183–184, 204, 212, 216
  blonde patterns, *listed,* 166
  for bonefish, 219, 220
  for brown trout, 162
  color of, 158, 184–185
  description of, 158–162
  fishing for trout with, 158–175
  for landlocked salmon, 164, 322
  to match chum, 286
  muddler minnow, 90, 159, 171, 172, 173, 174, 185, 334
    patterns, *listed,* 166
  patterns, *listed,* 165–166
    for salt water, 224–229
  for rainbow trout, 162, 164
  for salt water, 161, 277, 278
  for shad, 242
  for snook, 222, 277, 278
  sparsely tied, 164, 168, 169, 186
  for striped bass, 162
Buddy Mite nymph, 128, 137
Buenos Aires, 27, 175, 321, 370
"Butterfly Fishing," 118

Cabo San Lucas, Baja California, 255, 256
Caddis larva, 135
Caddis nymph, 136, 137, 138, 139
Cahill fly, 127, 339
Cahill quill fly, 91
California, 326, 330
Campomento Pool, Argentina, 320, 323
Camping and Cruising in Florida (Henshall), 218
Canada, 124, 180, 199, 325, 335
Canadian flies, 124, 125
Canyon Creek Ranch, Montana, 116
Cape Cod, Massachusetts, 336
Caribbean Sea, 274
Carlisle, Pennsylvania, 119
Carmichael's indispensable fly, 115
Carson fly, 330
Casting, fly, 39–76
  advances techniques, 48–64, 69–76
  for beginners, 40–47, 66–67
  beyond 60 feet, 21, 26, 39–40, 56, 176, 196
  drag (*see* Drag)
  drop system of, 101, 130, 171–172, 320, 328
  false, 8, 17, 25, 33, 39, 42, 45, 61, 75, 101, 230
  grip used for, 40–41, 65
  from hemmed in position, 47, 50–51, 53, 55, 59, 57–68, 70
  landing fish, 133
  mending line, 50–51, 97, 307, 308, 309, 310, 313, 314, 316

retrieve, 47, 64–65, 120, 121, 167–168, 185, 190–192, 196, 197, 198, 206, 239–240, 247, 248, 279, 281, 318–319, 345, 346
in salt water, 8–10, 59
shooting line, 25, 42, 46–48, 61, 62, 64, 75, 231, 329
short line, 102
stripping line, 42, 46, 48, 59, 64, 170, 329
for retrieve, 47, 65, 113, 234, 261
in strong wind, 21, 47, 56, 60, 61–62, 64, 69
tackle for, 5–12, 29–32, 52–55, 69, 71
theory of, 5, 65–67
tournament, 25, 59
trick, 50, 51, 52, 69–70
upstream, 65, 67, 101, 121, 129, 146, 154, 168, 300
wrist action for, 42–43, 45, 48, 68, 69, 70
Casts, 39–76
across-current, 129, 146, 147, 168, 185, 303, 306, 308, 310, 316
aerial roll, 51, 57, 59
back, 7–10, 25, 41–45, 70
backhand, 48, 70
bow and arrow, 69–70
change of direction, 49–51, 101
curve, 51–53, 72, 300
double haul, 21, 59–62, 120
downwind, 62–64
forward, 8, 41–46, 47
horizontal, 64, 68, 72, 101
pick-up, 41–42, 44, 56, 57
roll, 21, 54–59, 65, 70
S–, 48–49, 96, 97, 100, 185, 300
serpentine (*see* Casts, S–)
short throw, 47
side arm, 47
tight bow, 60–61, 62
up and across stream, 101, 121, 128–129, 130, 131, 146, 168
Channel bass, 38, 232, 275–277
flies for, 220, 276–277
Charlie White Lake, Montana, 149
Chatham, Russell, 241
Chartered boats, 266, 289–290
Cheat River, West Virginia, 70
Chesapeake Bay, 39, 213, 235, 237, 285
Chicago, Illinois, 72
Chiloquin, Oregon, 159
Chimehuin River, Argentina, 159, 162, 175
Chumming:
with bucktail, 289
in deep salt water, 285–295
definition of, 285
with fly and spinner, 289
with popping bug, 294
season for, 294–295
with streamer, 290, 291
tackle for, 289–290
tippet strength, *table,* 38
Cincinnati, Ohio, 235
Cinnamon ant, 145
Clewiston, Florida, 210
Clinch knot, 33, 373, 375
double clinch, 376
Clinton, Montana, 144
Clothing, 365–372
color of, 365, 366
for salt water, 368, 369, 371
vest, 367, 371–372
wading gear, 361–362, 367, 368–372
Coachman fly, 84, 91, 123, 124, 126, 127, 158, 187
Coachman Trude fly, 92
Coster trout (*see* Brook trout, coasters)
Cock robin optic fly, 330
Coffee, Oliver, 247
Colonel Bates fly, 187
Colonel Fuller fly, 127, 187
streamer, 165
Color:
of clothes, 365, 366
of leader, 33
of line, 28
preference of bass, 183, 184–185, 187
Colorado, 31, 50, 73, 125, 353
Columbia River, Clark Fork of, 144
Connecticut, 241, 336
Connecticut River, Connecticut, 241
Connecticut River shad fly, numbers 1 and 2, 226–227, 242–243

Conowingo Dam, Maryland, 188, 193, 242
Converse-Hodgman parka jacket, 372
Converse-Hodgman waders, 361, 369, 371
Coos Bay, Oregon, 239
Corson, Allen, 265
Cosseboom fly, 301
Cowdung fly, 124, 334
Cox, Howard, 235
Crappie, 344, 346, 347, 348
  black, 344, 347
  silver, 344, 347
Cream May fly nymph, 136
Cream nymph, 135
Crescent Lake, Montana, 116
Crooks, Jean, 277
Crosby, Bing, 306
Cross guinea nymph, 136, 139
Cuba, 36
Cuddy, Lee, 254
Cumming's special fly, 330
Currituck Sound, North Carolina, 202, 212, 213, 214
Cutthroat trout, 37, 116, 148
  blueback (*see* Cutthroat trout, sea-run)
  harvest (*see* Cutthroat trout, sea-run)
  sea-run, 37, 325, 331–332

Dacron fly line, 17–18, 232–233
Daddy long legs, imitation of, 78, 157
Damsel nymph, 135
Dan Bailey's nature nymph patterns, 139
Dan's hopper fly, 92
Dark Cahill fly, 91
Dark Edson bucktail, 83
Dark Hendrickson nymph, 135
Dark Montreal fly, 124
Dark mossback nymph, 136, 137, 139
Dark olive nymph, 136, 139
Dark olive and yellow nymph, 139
Dark tiger streamer, 318
Deck Star shoe, 371
Deer Lake, Newfoundland, 302
de Ganay, André, 10–11, 337
de Ganay, Etienne, 307
Denison fly, 126
Denmark, 157
De Puy, Dick, 104–105
Derwent River, England, 306, 341
Deschutes River, Oregon, 32, 326
Dimocks, A. W., 218
Dimocks, Julian, 218
Dolphin, 3, 38, 234, 260, 290–291, 293–295
Donnelly's light variant fly, 92, 115
Donovan, Dr. Cornelio, 321
Donovan, Jorge, 20–22, 162, 164, 175–178, 321, 341
Drag, 50, 64, 100, 128, 248, 272, 300, 303, 310
  definition of, 94–95
  in reel, 16, 233
Dragon nymph, 135
Drain 20 fly, 330
Dropper knot, 373, 380
Dry flies:
  for bass, 185–186
  buoy solution for, 104, 115
  definition of, 87–90
  favorite, 80, 95
  for lakes, 115–116
  patterns of, *listed*, 91–93
  spentwing, 88
Dry fly fishing:
  for beginners, 94, 97
  casting, 93–95
  in double hatch, 110–112
  at dusk, 98, 105, 107, 111
  in lakes, 110–118
  matching hatch, 87, 110, 115
  in pools and streams, 94–110
  retrieve, 102, 112–113
  tackle for, 6–8, 12, 23, 24, 32, 114
  theory of, 94–95, 97
  for trout, 87–121
DuBois, Don, 32
Dubois, Wyoming, 150
Dump Pool, Newfoundland, 311
Durham ranger fly, 297, 301
Dusty miller fly, 124, 127, 301, 303, 330

East River, Colorado, 31
Eastern fishermen, 169

Eastern streams, 32, 77, 79, 153, 169, 241, 335–336, 348, 352, 368
Ebberts, Charlie, 275–276
Ed Burke nymph, 136, 139
Elliott, Bruce, 144
Elliott, Lee, 112–113
Emigrant Peak, Montana, 149
England, 217, 306, 308
Equipment, matched (*see* Matched equipment)
European coast, 325, 336
Everglades, Florida, 213, 277–278

False albacore, 38, 287
Fasmer, Jan, 337
Fish, species for fly fishing, *listed,* 37–38
Fisheating Creek, Florida, 210, 211
Fishing in American Waters (Scott), 217
Fishing clubs, Fly Fishing classifications of, 234
Fishing Creek, Maryland, 48, 59
Fizzle hair hackle fly, 128
Flamingo Road Canal, Florida, 243–244
Flat Bay, Newfoundland, 333
Flies:
  ant, 78, 145–150
  for Atlantic salmon, 93, 120, 296–316, 334, 341, 342
  for bass, 179–216
  beetle, 78, 150–153
  bucktail, 158–175, 183–184, 204, 212 (*see also* Bucktail flies)
  for chumming, 285–295
  dry, 87–121, 185–186
  for landlocked salmon, 120, 164, 318–324
  listed:
    Atlantic salmon, 93, 301
    dry, 91–93
    landlocked salmon, 94
    nymphs, 138–139
    salt water, 224–229
    with spinner, 187
    steelhead, 330–331
    streamer and bucktail, 165–166
    wet, 126–127
  nymph, 134–143, 186, 194–195
  for panfish, 344–349
  popping bug, 175–176, 180–184, 188–191, 198–199, 202, 204 (*see also* Popping bug flies)
  for salt water, 217–284
  with spinner, 186–188, 204
  streamer, 158–175, 183–184, 193–194, 204–205, 212 (*see also* Streamer flies)
  for trout, 87–121, 325–343
  wet, 122–134
Flight's fancy fly, 127
Floating the fly, 94–97, 100, 125
Floating line (*see* Fly line, floating)
Florida, 199, 206, 209, 213, 218, 219, 234, 241, 244, 259, 274, 277, 287, 295, 347, 354, 355, 356, 364
Florida Bay, Florida, 219, 244, 249, 276
Florida Keys, Florida, 247, 266, 273, 274, 277, 280, 290, 294
Fly buoy, 82, 115
Fly casting, 39–76 (*see also* Casting, fly; Casts)
Fly dressings, 121
Fly Fishing in Salt and Fresh Water, 217
Fly, Heavy classification of fly fishing, 234, 247
Fly, Light classification of fly fishing, 234
Fly line, 17–29
  AFTMA standard weights, *table,* 18
  backing, 14, 15, 232–233, 335
  belly diameter of, 20, 23
  belly length of, 20, 24–26
  care of, 28–29
  color of, 28
  cost of, 22, 23
  cross sections of, showing tapers, 19
  dacron, 17–18, 232–233
  double-taper, 17, 23, 24
  dressing for (*see* Fly line, greasing of)
  floating, 18, 26, 28, 115, 120, 140, 316
  forward taper, 20, 22–23, 56
  greasing of, 26–28, 115, 120, 308–314
  level, 20–23

for long casts, 24–26, 335
nylon, 14, 15, 17, 71, 232–233, 240, 272, 335
with rod, *table,* 22
for salt water, 23, 24, 230–232
shooting of, 25, 42, 46–48, 61, 62, 64, 75, 231, 329
shooting head, 20
silk, 17
sinking, 18, 20, 26, 28, 327–328, 329
universal identification code of AFTMA, 18
Wet Head, 20, 186, 232, 329
Fly patterns (*see also* Flies, *listed*):
bi-flies (*see* Bi-fly patterns)
bivisible, *listed,* 91, 92
hairbodied, 115, 116, 137
hairbug, 79
hairwing (*see* Hairwing fly patterns)
history of, 77–78
listed, 79
spentwing, 93
terrestrials, 78–79, 144–157
variant (*see* Variant fly patterns)
Fly and spinner combination, 84, 289, 346, 348 (*see also* Bass, fishing for, with fly and spinner)
patterns for, *listed,* 187
Fly tyers, 77–86, 124, 136–138, 157, 158–59, 330
sources listed, 382–386
Fontinalis fin fly, 124
Fort Capron, Florida, 218
Fortune Magazine, 352
Fox, Charlie, 78, 120, 153, 154, 156
Fox Island, Maryland, 235
Fox Island River, Newfoundland, 333
Frankee-Belle bonefish fly, 219, 224
Fresh water shrimp nymph, 138
Frog, imitation of, 78, 85, 192–193, 201
Frog Mortar, Maryland, 39
Fry fly, 226, 287
Furnace spider, 93, 120
Futalaufquen National Park, Argentina, 320
Fuzzy bear orange rubber-bodied hair hackle fly, 127
Gaff topsail pompano, 288–289
Gallasch, Bill, 253
Gallasch sailfish fly, numbered 1 and 2, 222
Gallasch tarpon streamer, numbers 1, 2, and 3, 228–229
Gallatin Gateway, Montana, 56
Gallegos, Tierra del Fuego, 341
Gapen, Don, 117–118, 159, 197–198
Gardner, Montana, 83
Gay's grub, 135
Georgetown Lake, Montana, 112
Georgia, 199
Gerbubble bug fly, 205, 212, 214
Gibbs, Harold, 227
Ginger bivisible fly, 92
Ginger quill fly, 91, 93, 124, 126, 127, 186
nymph, 136, 138
Ginger quill midge snow fly, 127
Ginger quill spentwing fly, 93
Ginger spider, 93, 120
Ginger variant fly, 92
Glady-I tarpon streamer, 224
Glass, 5, 12–13, 22, 23–24
Glendivy, Wyoming, 150
Gnome Lake, Montana, 56
Golden demon fly, 330
Golden quill nymph, 135
Goodrich, Jim, 56
Goofus bug fly, 92
Gosling, Brose, 287, 288
Gowdy, Curt, 244, 246
Grand Lake Stream, Maine, 318
Grande stone nymph, 135
Grant's Pool, Newfoundland, 309
Grasshopper, imitation of, 108, 116, 144, 159, 185
Gray bivisible fly, 301, 308, 331
Gray flat-bodied nymph, 138
Gray ghost streamer, 165, 167, 318, 335
Gray ginger bivisible fly, 92
Gray hackle fly, 124, 187, 334, 335
Gray hackle peacock fly, 91
Gray hackle red fly, 91, 122, 127
Gray hackle salmon fly, 116
Gray hackle yellow fly, 91, 122, 126, 318
Gray marabou muddler, 160, 166
Gray May fly nymph, 138

Gray midge hackle fly, 80, 91, 111
Gray nymph, 137, 138, 140, 186, 194–195
Gray snapper (*see* Snapper, mangrove)
Gray spider, 93
Gray Trude fly, 92
Gray wooly worm fly, 127, 148
Gray Wulff fly, 80, 91, 93, 112, 115, 301, 318, 331, 335
Grayling, 37, 150
Greased leader, 151, 152, 194
Greased line fishing, 26–28, 115, 120, 308–314
Greased Line Fishing for Salmon (Scott), 307–308
Great Cacapon River, West Virginia, 196
Greb, Red, 219
Green beetle, 151, 152
Green caddis nymph, 135
Green drake fly, 93, 318
Green ghost streamer, 318
Green highlander fly, 301
Green sunfish, 344
Griswold, Morley, 326
Grizzly bear honey rubber-bodied hair hackle fly, 127
Grizzly bear rubber-bodied hair hackle fly, 127
Grizzly bivisible fly, 92
Grizzly king fly, 127, 158
  Trude, 92
Grizzly streamer, 167
Grizzly Wulff fly, 92, 93, 115, 331, 335
Grouper, 38, 254
Gulf of Mexico, 213
Gulf Stream, 290
Gunnison, Colorado, 73
Gunnison River, Colorado, 31, 104
Gut, 31, 32, 373
Gwynn's Island, Virginia, 237

Hagen Sands bonefish fly, 224
Hair bug fly patterns, 79, 85, 192
Hair frog fly, 192–193, 201
Hair hackle nymph patterns, 125, 128, 137
Hairbodied irresistible fly, 115
Hairwing fly patterns, 89, 90, 92, 108, 115, 186, 192, 297–298
Haiti, 274
Hammerhead (*see* Shark)
Hare's ear fly, 127
Harger, Don, 240, 332
Harger sea shrimp fly, 332
Harold Gibbs striper fly, 227
Harrod, J. T., 218
Harry's Brook, Newfoundland, 302
Harvest trout (*see* Cutthroat trout, sea-run)
Hawaii, 274
Hellgramite, 135, 186
Hendrickson fly, 91
Henshall, Dr. James A., 218
Hewitt, Edward, 118, 119, 120
Hewitt nymphs, 138, 142
Hickory shad (*see* Shad, hickory)
Hi-Density line, 232
Hillgard country, Montana, 56
Hollenbeck, Captain Rolie, 245, 275–276
Homestead, Florida, 244
Honey bear rubber-bodied hair hackle fly, 127
Honey blonde bucktail, 161, 166, 221, 298, 342
Honey skating spider, 93, 120
Hooks, 81–86, 119, 120, 136, 160–162, 187, 216, 220, 222, 223, 286
  double, 297, 299
  sizes (*see* Flies, *listed*)
  straightening out of 81–82, 119, 300
Horror fly, The, 226
Horse-eye jack, 38
Houston *Press,* 199
Humber River, Newfoundland, 302
Hunter, John, 264

Iceland, 336, 337
Inch worm fly, 145
Insects, safety against, in fishing, 318
International Game Fish Association, 274
Iron blue dun fly, 91
Iron blue quill fly, 127
Islamorada, Florida, 247, 266, 290, 356
Isles of Pines, Cuba, 36

Ives, Don, 327

Jack crevalle, 46, 220, 233, 258
Jack's Bass-Houn popping bug, 85
Jassid fly, 78, 95, 153–157
  method of tying, 157
Jaylure hairfrog, 201
Jaylure hairmouse, 201
Jock Scott fly, 80, 297, 301, 307
Joe's hopper fly, 90, 92, 125, 144, 145
Johnston, Captain Bill, 210–211
Judy Island, Florida, 259

Kalama River, Washington, 326
Kalama special fly, 330
Keith, Captain Cecil, 272
Kennebago, Maine, 317, 318
Kentucky, 154
Key Largo, Florida, 259, 264, 270, 282, 283, 354
Kinkie, Len, 46–47, 62, 64, 105, 170
Kispiox River, British Columbia, 327
Kissimmee River, Florida, 347
Kjaerr, 299
Klamath River, California, 326
Knots:
  Albright, 381
  blood, 34, 373, 374
  clinch, 33, 373, 375
    double clinch, 376
  dropper, 373, 380
  nail, 373, 377
  Turle, 373, 378
    double Turle, 379

Labrador, 317, 325
Lady ghost streamer, 165
Lady Mite nymph, 128, 137
Ladyfish, 3, 36, 38, 220, 232, 234
Laerdal River, Norway, 337
Lake Okeechobee, Florida, 209, 210, 347
Lake Superior, 117, 198
Lake of the Woods, Wyoming, 150
Landlocked salmon:
  fishing for, 317–324
  flies for, 120, 164, 318–324
    listed, 93
  tackle for, 24, 323–324
Lanin National Park, Argentina, 320
Laramie River, Wyoming, 50, 150, 151
Laramie spinner fly, 127
Large May fly nymph, 139
Large stone fly nymph, 136, 139
Largemouth black bass (*see* Bass, largemouth black)
Laurin, Montana, 74
Lazy W Cross Ranch, Wyoming, 150
Leader, 29–38, 69, 71, 114, 132, 134, 139, 151, 152, 164, 169, 172, 197, 232
  butt section of, 29–30, 36
  care of, 35–37
  color of, 33
  fine (*see* Tippet, light)
  greasing of, 151, 152, 194
  gut, 32
  heavy, 30, 31
  knotless, 33–34
  length of, 29–30, 114, 120
  light, 32–33
  nylon, 32, 34, 35, 37, 231, 232, 234
  for salt water, 36–37
  sink, 33, 143, 152
  strength of, 29, 34–35
  tapered, 30–31, 114
  thin, 29
  tippet section of (*see* Tippet)
Leadwing coachman fly, 124, 127, 135, 146
Letort cricket fly, 145
Letort hopper fly, 145
Letort River, Pennsylvania, 153
Levering, Paul, 56–57, 95–97
Lewistown, Montana, 84, 353
Light Cahill fly, 75, 91, 93, 110, 124, 126, 127, 135
Light Cahill quill fly, 91
Light Cahill spentwing fly, 93
Light Hendrickson fly, 91
Light mossback nymph, 136, 137, 139
Light olive and cream nymph, 139
Light stone fly, 136
Lightner, Norm, 119
Line (*see* Fly line)

Little Kennebago River, Maine, 317
Little May fly nymph, 137
Little Torch Key, Florida, 252
Livingston, Montana, 51, 62, 83, 136, 159
Logie fly, 301
Long Key, Florida, 218
Longear sunfish, 344
Lord Baltimore fly, 127, 187
Loving, Tom, 39–40, 205, 218
Lupton, Met, 212
Lyman, Hal, 336

Mackerel, 38 (*see also* False albacore)
Madison River, Montana, 31
Madsen, Ejnar, 331
Magellan Straits, 341
Maine, 51, 124, 164, 301, 317, 318, 320
Mane, Nate, 353
Mangrove snapper (*see* Snapper, mangrove)
Manners:
  in salt water, 354–355
  stream, 350–354
Mar lodge fly, 301, 333
Marabou flies (*see* Streamer flies, marabou)
Marabou muddler, 159–160, 174
  patterns, *listed,* 166
March brown fly, 80, 124, 126, 127, 135, 136, 139, 297, 301
Marinaro, Vince, 78, 153–157
Marlin, 3, 6, 38, 231, 234, 250, 255, 256
Maryland, 30, 39, 48, 59, 67, 153, 154, 169, 188, 205, 241, 352, 356
Maryland State Game and Fish Association, 352
Matched equipment, 5–8, 10, 13, 20, 21–25, 30–31, 40, 71, 114, 164, 169–170, 186, 230–233, 240, 241, 284, 299, 316, 323–324, 329, 332, 335, 336, 345
  cost of, 22
  table, 22
McCredie special fly (*see* Pacific coast shad fly)
McDonald, John, 352
McGinty fly, 91, 124, 127, 330
McGuire, Bill, 327, 330, 331
Melrose, Montana, 98, 116
Messenger, Joe, 192
Metropolitan Miami Fishing Tournament, 282
Mexico, 274
Miami, Florida, 268, 356
Miami Beach, Florida, 219
Miami Beach Rod and Reel Club, 219, 247
Miami *Herald,* 265
Michigan, 257
Michigan hopper fly, 92*n.*
Mickey Finn bucktail, 83, 165
Mickey Finn streamer, 165
Midge, imitation of, 83, 115
Midge snow fly patterns, 127
Minnesota, 348
Minnow, imitation of, 78, 124, 158, 159, 167, 168, 174, 181, 184, 186, 188, 190, 220, 222, 234, 309
Missoula, Montana, 125, 139, 144
Missoulian spook muddler minnow bucktail, 166
Missouri, 154
Missouri River, Montana, 160, 174
Mr. Mite nymph, 128, 137
Mite hair hackle flies, 125, 128, 137
Modern Day Fly Code, A (Marinaro), 153
Monical, Red, 152, 159, 160, 171, 174
Montana, 43, 56, 59, 62, 74, 78, 83, 84, 98, 105, 110, 112, 116, 125, 136, 139, 144, 149, 152, 159, 160, 170, 173, 174, 175, 351, 353
Montana nymph, 135, 139
Montana rivers, 31, 74
Montreal fly, 124, 126
Moonshine Bay, Florida, 210
Moosehead Lake, Maine, 318
Mooselookmeguntic, Maine, 51, 318
Mormon girl fly, 127
Mosquito fly, 91, 127
Mosquito larva, 135
Mosquito midge snow fly, 127
Mouse, imitation of, 78, 159, 185, 201
Mowbray, Louis, 245

Mud trout (*see* Brook trout, sea-run)
Muddler minnow bucktail, 90, 159, 171, 172, 173, 174, 185, 334
patterns, *listed,* 166
Multi-colored variant fly, 92
Muttonfish, 260

Nahuel Huapi National Park, Argentina, 320
Nail knot, 373, 377
Nankivell, Jim, 277
Naranchi, Nick, 175
Narvel, Fred, 188, 242
National Geographic Magazine, 192, 214
Navas brown nymph, 141
Nelson, Allen, 148–149
Nelson, Edwin, 42–43, 45, 148–149
Nelson, Hash, 353
Nestucca River, Oregon, 332
Neversink skater, 93, 118, 120
New England, 218, 234, 237, 325, 337
New Jersey, 218, 235
New York, 39, 317
Newfoundland, 116, 296, 298, 301, 302, 309–315, 317, 325, 332–337
Nieva, Fausto, 268
Nipigon, Ontario, 117, 198
Norlakes Lodge, British Columbia, 331
North American continent, 336
North American waters, 300
North Carolina, 202, 212, 213, 214, 295
Northern flies (*see* Canadian flies)
Norway, 10, 11, 298–299, 301, 303, 305, 325, 336, 337–338
Norwegian moustache fly, 330
Nova Scotia, 241
Nunnally, Moses, 203–204
Nylon:
leader, 32, 34, 35, 37, 231, 232, 234
line, 14, 15, 17, 71, 232–233, 240, 272, 335
tippet, 32, 35, 232, 240, 284
Nymph flies, 134–143, 186, 194–195
for bass, 186, 194–195
eastern, 136, 137
flat-bodied, 138
large stone, 136, 139
naturals, 134–136
patterns, *listed,* 138–139
weighted, 135, 139, 142
western, 136
Nymphs, fishing with:
for bass, 186, 194–195
matching hatch in, 140, 141–142
retrieve, 140, 142
tackle for, 7, 23, 24, 139
timing strike in, 142
for trout, 134–143
bulging, 139

Ocean flat fishing, 29
Ohio, 154
Olive dun dark fly, 91
Olive May nymph, 138
Olive quill fly, 127
Olive quill midge snow fly, 127
Olive shrimp nymph, pink stripe, 138
Oliver, "A. P.," 207, 209
Omme River, Denmark, 157
Ontario, Canada, 117, 187, 188, 198, 317
Optic bucktail, 159
Orange and black nymph, 136
Orange wooly worm fly, 127
Oregon, 32, 159, 219, 239, 241, 326, 331, 332
Oregon Inlet, North Carolina, 213
Orleans barber fly, 330
Oslo, Norway, 303
Outdoor Writers Association of America, 265
Outer Banks of North Carolina, 213
Oykel River, Scotland, 339

Pacific coast, 325, 326, 331
Pacific coast shad fly, 227
Pacific Ocean, 240, 241
Pale evening dun fly, 91
Palmer special fly, 329, 330
Palometa (*see* Gaff topsail pompano)
Pamlico Sound, North Carolina, 213
Panama, 250, 254
Panama Bay, 294, 295

Panfish:
- different kinds of, 344
- fishing for, 344–349
  - with fly and spinner, 346, 348
  - with popping bug, 180, 345, 346, 347, 349
- ponds and lakes stocked with, 346–347
- relation to bream, 344
- tackle for, 37, 344–345

Parks, Merton, 83
Parmachene belle fly, 124, 334
Peacock wooly worm fly, 127
Pennsylvania, 39, 53, 78, 107, 119, 132, 146, 153, 154, 168, 355, 356
Perch:
- ring, 344, 346
- white, 348
- yellow, 344, 348, 349

Perinchief, Pete, 290–291, 293–294
Perkins, Leigh, 332
Phillips bonefish bucktail, 219, 224
Phillips fly rod popping bug, 85
Phillips Fly and Tackle Company, Alexandria, Pennsylvania, 146
Phillips, George, 270
Phillips multiwing streamer, 225, 341
Phillips "peewee popper," 182
Phillips pink shrimp fly, 226
Phillips weedless wiggle popping bug, 181
Pinas Bay, Panama, 250, 254
Pinckney, Frank S., 218
Pink blonde fly, 221
Pink lady fly, 91, 301, 308, 331
Pink shrimp fly, 220–222, 226, 288
Platinum blonde bucktail, 161, 166, 221, 298, 322, 323, 342
Point of Rocks, Maryland, 194
Polar shrimp fly, 330
Polaroid glasses, 264, 266, 362
Pompano (*see* Gaff topsail pompano)
Pool:
- fishing head of, 97–99
- fishing tail of, 97–99
- how to fish, 53, 66–67, 97–100

Poplar Branch, North Carolina, 202
Poppers (*see* Popping bug flies)
Popping bug, fishing with:
- for bass (*see* Bass, fishing for, with popping bug)
- for brown trout, 175–178
- for panfish, 180, 345, 346, 347, 349
- for snappers, 254
- for striped bass, 235–240

Popping bug flies:
- balsa wood, 180, 181, 239
- colors of, 183
- cork, 180, 181, 183, 205
- definition of, 180
- plastic, 180
- for salt water, 220, 222, 235–240, 243, 244, 250, 253, 254, 257–259, 276, 278, 279, 294
- skipping bug (*see* Skipping bug fly)
- "sliders," 181, 222
- spouter, 183
- weedless, 85, 180, 181, 205–206, 210

Potomac River, 191, 194, 196, 241
Potts, F. B., 125, 137
Prince Charlie bucktail, 165
Professor fly, 92, 124, 127, 184, 187, 334
Pumphouse Pool, Maryland, 67
Pumpkinseed, 344

Quebec, Canada, 298, 317
Queen Bess fly, 330
Queen of waters fly, 91
Quill Gordon fly, 91, 124, 126, 334

Radziwill, Charles, 27, 160, 175
Rainbow trout, 37, 64, 84, 100, 116, 148, 159, 163, 164, 365
- sea-run (*see* Steelhead trout)

Rangeley Lakes, Maine, 318
Rattlesnake Creek, Pennsylvania, 53
Ray, Bobby, 291
Red ant, 91
Red Bank, New Jersey, 218
Red and barred yellow wings streamer, 165
Red fox fly, 91
Red marabou streamer, 165
Red optic fly, 330

Red, Ray, 73–74
Rew trout (*see* Brook trout)
Red Trude fly, 92
Red variant fly, 91, 92, 93, 115
Red and white bucktail, 165, 216, 332, 334
Red and white multiwing streamer, 165
Red and white streamer, 165, 187, 216, 334
Red and yellow bucktail, 165, 216
Red and yellow marabou streamer, 165
Red and yellow multiwing streamer, 165
Red and yellow streamer, 163, 165, 216, 276, 290, 342, 343
Redfish (*see* Channel bass)
Redman, Duane, 150
Redman, Pete, 150
Reel, 14–17
  Atlantic salmon, 232, 335
  automatic, 14
  care of, 17
  cost of, 16
  for long-running fish, 14, 233, 335
  multiple action, 16
  for salt water, 233
  single action, 16
Renegade fly, 91
Rhead, Louis, 217
Rhode, Homer, 219
Richmond, Virginia, 50, 51
Ridgewood, New Jersey, 160
Ring perch (*see* Perch, ring)
Rio Gallegos River, Tierra del Fuego, 341–342
Rio Grande king fly, 91
Rio Gallegos River, Tierra del Fuego, 21, 160, 164, 340, 341, 342, 343
Roberts, Dave, 211
Roberts fly, 91
Robinson, Dr. Webster, 229, 250, 253, 254, 255, 256
Robinson, Mrs. Webster, 250
Rock (*see* Striped bass, rockfish)
Rock Creek Lodge, Montana, 139, 141, 144
Rock worm fly, 128
Rockfish (*see* Striped bass, rockfish)
Rocky Mountain flies, 124, 125, 136
Rocky Mountain states, 124, 355
Rod, 5–14, 323–324, 342–343, 345
  for Atlantic salmon, 6, 10–12, 24, 299
  bamboo, 5, 12–13, 22, 23, 24
  care of, 14
  fast-action (*see* Rod, stiff-action)
  ferrules of, 13
  glass, 5, 12–13, 22, 23–24
  length of, 6–12, 23–24, 120
  with line, *table,* 22
  matching leader and line with, 6, 8, 10, 13, 22, 24
  medium-action, 6–7
  for practice, 40
  for salt water, 8–10, 18, 20, 24, 230–231
  slow-action, 6–10, 20–21, 230, 329, 345
  stiff-action, 6, 7, 22, 71, 230, 231
  three-piece, 13
  "trick" or "stunt" rods, 12
  two-handed, 6, 10, 11, 298, 299, 300, 307
  two-piece, 13–14
  weight of, 6, 7, 12, 13
  for wind, 8, 12, 24, 114
Rod & Reel Club of Miami Beach, Florida, 219, 247
Rosborough, Polly, 159
Rose, Frank, 74
Royal coachman fly, 80, 91, 93, 106–107, 122, 124, 126, 146, 158, 167, 186, 187, 218, 335
Royal coachman hairwing fly, 148, 152
Royal coachman Trude fly, 92
Royal coachman Wulff fly, 93, 318
Royal Wulff fly, 92, 116, 301, 334, 335
Rubber-bodied hair hackle fly patterns, 127
Ruby River, Montana, 74

Saaby, Sven, 157
Safety in fishing, 355–364
  in rainstorm, 372
  against snakes, 355–356
  against sun and insects, 363–364
  in wading in salt water, 362–363

in wading streams and lakes, 356–362
Sailfish, 3, 6, 38, 231, 234, 248, 250, 253, 254, 255
flies for, 228, 250, 253
St. Ignace Island, Ontario, 117
St. John's River, Florida, 206, 241
St. Petersburg, Florida, 265
Salem, Oregon, 332
Salmon:
Atlantic (*see* Atlantic salmon)
landlocked (*see* Landlocked salmon)
Saltwater flies, 217–229
bucktail (*see* Bucktail flies, for salt water)
description of ties, *listed,* 224–229
hooks for, 220, 222, 223
popping bug (*see* Popping bug flies, for salt water)
special ties, 220, 222
streamer (*see* Streamer flies, for salt water)
Saltwater fly fishing, 217–284
for barracuda (*see* Barracuda)
for bonefish (*see* Bonefish, fishing for)
for channel bass (*see* Channel bass)
for grouper (*see* Grouper)
for hickory shad (*see* Shad, hickory)
for jack crevalle (*see* Jack crevalle)
for ladyfish (*see* Ladyfish)
for long-running fish, 240, 272, 282, 283–284, 286, 287
northeastern waters, 234–239
for redfish (*see* Channel bass)
for seatrout, 38, 218
for shark (*see* Shark)
for snapper (*see* Snapper)
for snook (*see* Snook)
for striped bass (*see* Striped bass)
tackle for, 8–10, 14, 18, 20, 23, 24, 36–37, 38, 230–231
for tarpon (*see* Tarpon)
types of fish for, 217–219, 232, 280
for white shad (*see* Shad, white)
Salt Water Sportsman Magazine, 217, 336
Saltus bonefish and permit fly, 225
Sands, Hagen, 224, 274
Sandy Mite nymph, 128, 137
Sautso Beat, Norway, 303
Scarlet ibis fly, 124
Schueren, Arnold, 149
Schueren, Eleanore, 149
Scientific Anglers, Inc., of Midland, Michigan, 18
Scientific Anglers Wet Head sinking/floating line, 20, 186, 232, 327
Scotland, 339
Scott, Genio, 217
Scott, Jock, 307, 316
Sculpin minnow, 160, 185
Sea urchin, 362
Sea Wulff billfish fly, 229
Seattle, Washington, 327
Sebago Lake, Maine, 318, 320
Serpentine Lake, Newfoundland, 116
Serpentine River, Newfoundland, 309, 333
Shad, 39, 218, 241–243
flies for, 226–227, 242–243
hickory, 241, 243
white, 241–243
Shark, 38, 234, 268, 280–284, 290
Shellcracker, 344
Shenandoah River, Virginia, 196
Sheperdstown, West Virginia, 56, 195
Shirley Mill Pond, Virginia, 203
Shooting the line, 25, 42, 46–48, 61, 62, 64, 75, 231, 329
Sibun River, British Honduras, 278
Silk, 17
Silver crappie (*see* Crappie, silver)
Silver doctor fly, 297, 301, 334, 341
Silver garland marabou streamer, 159
Silver gray fly, 301, 305
Skating spiders, 93, 118–121
Skeena River Watershed, British Columbia, 327
Skelton, Randy, 139–140
Skipping bug fly, 181–182, 222, 223, 229, 238, 260

Skykomish sunrise fly, 329, 330
Slate Run, Pennsylvania, 132
Slate skating spider, 93, 120
Smallmouth black bass (*see* Bass, smallmouth black)
Snakes, 211, 355–356
Snapper, 38, 233, 254, 257–258
  with chum, 286, 291, 292
  flies for, 220, 254
  mangrove, 38, 257, 260, 292
  with popping bug, 254
Snead, Sammy, 356
Snook, 38, 219, 233, 277–279, 363
  flies for, 220, 222, 224, 277, 279
  tackle for, 36, 38, 232, 234
Snow fly, 82–84
Snyder, Bill, 169
Sofa pillow fly, 90, 125
South Africa, 274
South Island, New Zealand, 337
Southern waters:
  fishing for largemouth bass in, 199–200
  panfish in, 344
  popping bug for, 180
  snakes in, 355–356
Spain, 325, 336
Spawning fish, 241–243, 244–245, 301–302, 325, 333, 336, 346
Special (dry or wet) fly patterns, 92
Special nymph patterns, 138–139
Special wet fly patterns, 127
Speckled trout (*see* Brook trout)
Specs (*see* Crappie, silver)
Spentwing fly patterns, 93
Spider fly patterns, 9, 93, 108, 115, 118–121, 191–192
Spitsbergen, 325
Spotted seatrout, 38
Spring Creek, Montana, 84, 353
Spruce-fly streamer, 160, 171
Spuddler, 160, 171
Spur Magazine, 118
Standard dry fly patterns, 91
Standard wet fly patterns, 126–127
State Game and Fish Commissions, 352
Steelhead trout, 325, 326–331
  flies for, 159, 329–331, 332
  run of, 326
  tackle for, 37, 329
Stingray, 363
Stocked ponds and lakes, 346–347
Stone fly nymph patterns, 136
Strawberry blonde bucktail, 166, 221, 223
Streamer, fishing with:
  for landlocked salmon, 164, 318–319
  in muddy water, 169
  retrieve, 167–168, 194, 318–319
  tackle for, 7, 12, 24, 29, 37, 169–170
  for trout, 158–175
  in West, 170
Streamer flies, 82, 158–175
  for bass, 8, 183–185
  breather, 82, 159, 220, 278
  color of, 165, 184–185, 223
  description of, 158–162
  for largemouth bass, 204–205, 212, 216
  marabou, 82, 159, 171–172, 185
    patterns, *listed,* 165
  multiwing, 162, 164
    patterns, *listed,* 165, 225
  patterns, *listed,* 165
  for salt water, 220–222, 223, 224, 225, 228, 276, 278
  for smallmouth bass, 184, 193–194
  sparsely-tied, 164, 184
  with spinners, 187
  ties, *listed,* 224, 225, 228–229
  tyers of, 157–158
Striped bass:
  fishing for, 3, 39, 217–218, 234–241, 285
  flies for, 162, 220, 227, 235, 239
  rockfish, 235, 344
  tippet strength for, 38, 232
Striped marlin (*see* Marlin)
Stroud, Paul, 72
Stumpknocker, 344
Sun, protection against, in fishing, 363–364
Sunfish, 344
  green, 344
  longear, 344
Sunnies, 6, 37, 199, 344
Supervisor streamer, 165, 318
Sure strike special fly, 89, 92, 125

Susquehanna River, 78, 188, 193, 213, 218, 241, 242
Susquehanna shad fly, 227
Swedish anglers, 337

Tables and diagrams:
fish for fly fishing, 37–38
flies (*see* Flies, *listed*)
knots, 374–381
matched equipment, 22
rod action, 7
tippet strengths, 37–38
Tackle, fly fishing, 5–38 (*see also* Matched equipment)
Tamiami Trail Canal, Florida, 243, 244
Tan May fly nymph, 138
Tan shrimp nymph, pink stripe, 138
Tarpon, 3, 218, 219, 231, 243–248, 252
baby, 38, 222, 223, 243–248, 251, 363
flies for, 220, 222, 224, 225, 228–229
tackle for, 3, 6, 36, 38, 232, 233, 234, 247
Tarpon or Silver King (Pinckney), 218
Taylor herring (*see* Shad, hickory)
Taylor River, Colorado, 31, 100
Teagle bee fly, 92
Ted Williams bonefish fly, 225
Ted Williams tarpon streamer, 225
Teifi River, Wales, 338
Tellico nymph, 136, 138, 139
Ten Thousand Islands, Florida, 277
Terrestrials, 78–79, 144–157
Texas, 199, 200, 209
"Thing, The," popping bug fly, 182, 205
Thompson, L. S., 218
Thor fly, 330
Thunder and lightning fly, 297, 301, 341
Tierra del Fuego, 20–21, 160, 164, 325, 340, 341, 343
Tim-rep bonefish in permit fly, 225
Tippet, 29–38, 71, 113–114, 120–121, 132, 152, 169, 171, 197, 232, 233, 234, 284, 289, 323–324
gut, 31, 32
heavy, 30, 31, 34, 35
light, 30–31, 32, 34–35
nylon, 32, 35, 232, 240, 284
strength of, *table* 37–38
thin (*see* Tippet, light)
wire, 284
Tom Loving's original shad fly, 227
Tomichi River, Colorado, 73
Tournament casters, 25, 59
Traful River, Argentina, 120, 319–321
Traverse Brook seatrout fly, 334
Trout, 106–107, 109, 365
brook (*see* Brook trout)
sea-run (*see* Brook trout, sea-run)
brookies (*see* Brook trout)
brown (*see* Brown trout)
sea-run (*see* Brown trout, sea-run)
bulging, 110, 139, 153, 154
coasters (*see* Brook trout, coasters)
cutthroat (*see* Cuttthroat trout)
dry fly fishing for, 87–121
in lakes, 110–118
feeding position of, 66
fishing for:
with ants and beetles, 145–153
with jassids, 154–156
with nymphs, 134–143
with popping bugs, 175–178
with skating spiders, 118–121
with streamers and bucktails, 158–175
flies for (*see* Flies, for trout)
grayling, 37, 150
habits of, 74–76, 97–100
lake, 110–118
memory of, 101, 351
native (*see* Brook trout)
rainbow (*see* Rainbow trout)
sea-run (*see* Steelhead trout)
red (*see* Brook trout)
rising, 98–110, 132, 134, 140
selective feeding of, 134, 140, 141–42, 166
speckled (*see* Brook trout)
tackle for, 6–7, 14, 18, 21, 24, 29, 30–31, 35, 37, 71

that go to sea, 325–343 (*see also* Trout, sea-run)
vision of, 101–102
wet fly fishing for, 122–134, 334
wilderness (*see* Brook trout)

Trout, sea-run:
blueback (*see* Cutthroat trout, sea-run)
brook (*see* Brook trout, sea-run)
brown (*see* Brown trout, sea-run)
cutthroat (*see* Cutthroat trout, sea-run)
definition of, 325
Eastern brook (*see* Brook trout, sea-run)
fishing for, 325–343
with dry fly, 329, 330–331
with streamer, 341–342
with wet fly, 330, 332, 334
flies, *listed,* 330–331
harvest (*see* Cutthroat trout, sea-run)
in lakes, 116
mud (*see* Brook trout, sea-run)
in Newfoundland, 332–336
in Norway, 337–338
rainbow (*see* Steelhead trout)
speckled (*see* Brook trout, sea-run)
squaretail (*see* Brook trout, sea-run)
steelhead (*see* Steelhead trout)
in Tierra del Fuego, 340, 341–343
winter steelhead, 37

Trowbridge, Dr. George, 218
Trude fly patterns, 89, 90, 92
True wooly bear fly, 127
Tuna, 6, 38, 234
little (*see* False albacore)
Tup's indispensable fly, 91
Turle knot, 373, 378
double Turle, 379
TVA lakes, 209
Twin Bridges, Montana, 74, 105, 175

Umpqua fly, 330
United States, 124, 180, 199, 335, 355
Upper Potomac River, 56, 195

Van Luven fly, 330
Variant fly patterns, 92, 115, 192
Victor, Captain Howard, 290, 293
Virgin Islands, 274
Virginia, 50, 154, 191, 203, 205, 213, 237, 346
Virginia, Pond, Virginia, 347
Vision of fish, 101–102, 183, 278

Wading:
balance in, 360–361
clothing, 361–362, 367, 368–372
in salt water, 362–363
in streams and lakes, 356–362
Wales, 338
Ward, Russ, 144
Warmouth, 344
Washington, state of, 326, 327, 331
Wayne, David, 319
Weakfish, 235
Web Robinson billfish fly, 229
Weber, Walt, 59, 61–62, 192, 194–196, 214
Weberfoot hair bug, 192
Welaka, Florida, 206
Welch, Herb, 51–52
West Coast, 219, 241
West Indies, 274
West Lake, Florida, 244
West Virginia, 56, 70, 154, 195, 196
Western fishermen, 170, 330, 352m, 355
Western streams, 90, 326–330, 368
Wet flies, 122–128
bi-flies, 125
Canadian, 124
favorite, 80, 123, 126
northern (*see* Wet flies, Canadian)
patterns of, *listed,* 126–128
Rocky Mountain, 124, 125
rubber-bodied hair-hackle, 125
for salt water, 242–243
used with spinner, 187–188
western, 125
wooly worm, 124, 125–126
Wet fly, fishing the:
casting, 128–130
retrieve, 124, 130, 134

tackle for, 7–8, 12, 23, 24, 34, 132, 134
for trout, 122–134, 334
Whitcomb fly, 60, 91
White ant, 149
White bucktail, 36, 184, 185, 216, 223, 242, 277, 334
White marabou muddler, 160, 166
White marabou streamer, 82, 165, 171, 173, 335
White miller fly, 91, 126, 346
White muddler minnow bucktail, 166
White perch (*see* Perch, white)
White, Tom, 314
White Wulff fly, 92, 115, 301, 318
Whitecraft fly, 115
Widewater Lake, Montana, 110
Wilderness trout (*see* Brook trout)
Williams, Ted, 225, 283–284
Willow fly, 91, 186
Wilson's special streamer, 165
Wishard, Bob, 168–169
Wood, Arthur, 308–316
Wooly worm fly patterns, 123, 124, 125–126, 144, 148
Wulff hairwing fly patterns, 89, 90, 92, 93
Wulff, Lee, 229
Wyoming, 110, 150, 151
Yellow and barred yellow wings multiwing streamer, 165
Yellow Breeches River, Pennsylvania, 107
Yellow and brown streamer, 168, 172, 193
Yellow bucktail, 185, 216
Yellow fibber fly, 128
Yellow marabou streamer, 165, 335
Yellow May fly nymph, 136, 138
Yellow muddler minnow bucktail, 166
Yellow nymph, 138
Yellow perch (*see* Perch, yellow)
Yellow Sally fly, 127, 158, 169, 187, 346
Yellow and white streamer, 165
Yellow wooly worm fly, 127, 146
Yellowbreast, 344
Yellowstone Park, Wyoming, 83
Yellowstone River, Montana, 31, 43, 51, 62, 82, 136, 146, 148, 171, 174
Yellowtail, 38, 286–287, 288
York's Kennebago streamer, 165
Young, Jim, 333, 334

Zug bug, 135
Zululand, South Africa, 274